D0152302

Jains in the World

Jains in the World

Religious Values and Ideology in India

JOHN E. CORT

OXFORD
UNIVERSITY PRESS

2001

BL
1356
.C67
2001

OXFORD
UNIVERSITY PRESS

Oxford New York
Athens Auckland Bangkok Bogotá Buenos Aires Calcutta
Cape Town Chennai Dar es Salaam Delhi Florence Hong Kong Istanbul
Karachi Kuala Lumpur Madrid Melbourne Mexico City Mumbai
Nairobi Paris São Paulo Shanghai Singapore Taipei Tokyo Toronto Warsaw

and associated companies in
Berlin Ibadan

Copyright © 2001 by John E. Cort

Published by Oxford University Press, Inc.
198 Madison Avenue, New York, New York 10016

Oxford is a registered trademark of Oxford University Press

All rights reserved. No part of this publication may be reproduced, stored in a retrieval system, or transmitted, in any form or by any means, electronic, mechanical, photocopying, recording, or otherwise, without the prior permission of Oxford University Press.

Library of Congress Cataloging-in-Publication Data

Cort, John E.
Jains in the world: religious values and ideology in India/
John E. Cort.
p. cm.
Includes bibliographical references and index.
ISBN 0-19-513234-3
1. Jainism—Doctrines. 2. Religious life—Jainism. I. Title.
BL1356 .C67 2000
294.4—dc21 99-28440

1 3 5 7 9 8 6 4 2

Printed in the United States of America
on acid-free paper

LONGWOOD COLLEGE LIBRARY
FARMVILLE, VIRGINIA 23901

Nokār Mantra

Praise to the Jinas
Praise to the Siddhas
Praise to the Ācāryas
Praise to the Upādhyāyas
Praise to all Sādhus in the world.
This fivefold praise
destroys all bad karma
and of all holies
it is the foremost holy.

Acknowledgments

In any intellectual project, especially a book that is nearly two decades in the researching and writing, an author acquires a good many debts. The original dissertation research on which most of this book is based was funded by a Fulbright-Hays Research Abroad Grant awarded by the U.S. Department of Education through Harvard University. A Charlotte W. Newcombe Doctoral Dissertation Fellowship and a fellowship from the Committee on the Study of Religion of Harvard University provided support for the writing of the dissertation. Subsequent research in India was done in conjunction with other research projects funded in whole or in part by the Center for the Study of World Religions of Harvard University, an Art and Religion Fellowship of the Asian Cultural Council, a Getty Grant Program Senior Research Grant, and a Denison University Research Foundation Grant. Several Denison University Summer Professional Development Grants aided in the writing and revising of the book. In India my research was facilitated by the L. D. Institute of Indology in Ahmedabad. I thank Shrenikbhai Lalbhai, whose vision guides the L. D.; the scholars there who aided me in many ways, especially Naginbhai Shah, Dalsukhbhai Malvania, and Lakshmanbhai Bhojak; and the librarians and support staff. In the course of my fieldwork I interviewed and talked with dozens of Jain mendicants. Three in particular gave expressions of public support to this research that were particularly helpful: Muni Śrī Jambūvijayjī Mahārāj Sāhab, Paṅnyās Śrī Abhaysāgargaṇijī Mahārāj Sāhab, and Ācārya Śrī Padmasāgarsūrijī Mahārāj Sāhab.

Fieldwork was made enjoyable by the warm friendliness with which hundreds of Jains throughout India responded to me and my research. In particular, my wife Cynthia and I were incorporated into several families in Patan and Ahmedabad. To the families of V. T. Shah, Mukund Pandya, Kantibhai Salvi, Chhottobhai Salvi in Patan, Kantibhai Vora and Hakubhai Shah in Ahmedabad, we both express our deepest gratitude.

In the early days of fieldwork in the fall of 1985, I had the good fortune to be able to work with two other American scholars of Jainism. Thomas Zwicker was a graduate student of anthropology from the University of Pennsylvania who had been conducting fieldwork for a year on the everyday moral economy of Jain businessmen. Kendall Folkert, professor of comparative religion from Central Michigan University and author of a dissertation and several articles on Jainism (Folkert 1993), was in the middle of a research project into lay-mendicant interactions and the history of *pratikramaṇ*. For two and a half months we formed an informal research team, conducting fieldwork together, typing joint research notes, and discussing and analyzing our research for hours on end. Ken and Tom died in a road accident on October 29, 1985. Had they lived and our collaboration continued, I am sure that this book would be very different in form and much richer in content. But even that brief period of working with them left a deep imprint on my research, and hence on the book. I thank Ruth Folkert Magnell, Tony Zwicker, and the University of Pennsylvania Museum Archives for permission to reproduce some of their photographs.

I have benefited from the advice and criticism of many friends, teachers, and colleagues. Joe Elder and David Knipe of the University of Wisconsin, and John Carman and Diana Eck of Harvard University have all been invaluable advisors and guides. At Harvard I also had the privilege of working with Loki Madan and Jyotindra Jain, both of whom have influenced this book in multiple ways. Padmanabh Jaini of the University of California has been an unfailing supporter and advocate of my studies of Jainism. Arthur Duff produced the original drawings for several of the maps, which were then prepared for publication by Laurie MacKenzie-Crane. Cynthia Read, Theo Calderara, MaryBeth Branigan, and the rest of the editorial staff at Oxford University Press have done an excellent job turning my manuscript into a book. The following have read all or part of the manuscript in various forms, some of them multiple times, and provided excellent suggestions: Alan Babb, Paul Dundas, Kathleen Erndl, Phyllis Granoff, Brian Hatcher, James Laidlaw, Patrick Olivelle, and Bob Zydenbos. Conversations with many other friends, colleagues, teachers, and students at Wisconsin, Harvard, Columbia, Denison, and academic conferences in North America, England, and India have enriched my understanding of Jainism. All photographs are by either the author or Cynthia Cunningham Cort, unless otherwise noted.

I first went to Gujarat and Patan in 1979 with my wife Cynthia as part of her research on ikat textile production in India. She returned with me in 1985 and participated in many of the events detailed in these pages. She attended festivals and rituals, traveled to distant pilgrimage shrines, took photographs, and asked questions of friends and informants. Most of what I understand of India has been seen and experienced with her. Certainly the thoughts and insights in this book developed in significant part through many conversations with her about the data. She has lived with this research and book for nearly two decades, and has always been my most perceptive reader. When I thought the manuscript was complete, Cynthia made me see that I needed to rearrange the chapters and thus reconceptualize the book in a manner that now seems obvious. I dedicate this book to her.

For any faults of omission or commission in this book, *micchāmi dukkaḍaṃ*.

Contents

Note on Language, Transliteration, and Names

One reason why scholars have shied away from Jain studies is the large number of languages employed by Jains over the centuries. In the research that went into this book I have relied heavily upon sources written in Prakrit, Sanskrit, Gujarati, and Hindi, and unless otherwise noted all translations from these languages are mine. In addition, almost all the fieldwork was conducted in Hindi or Gujarati (often intertwined). The presentation of material from four different languages poses a major problem. Since the focus of this book is upon the contemporary Śvetāmbar Mūrtipūjak Jain laity of Patan, I have chosen to write most terms in their Gujarati form, even technical terms for which most scholars are more familiar with the Sanskrit form. For example, I have used *tap* instead of *tapas*, and *saṅgh* instead of *saṅgha*. In the matter of the medial and final short *a*, which is pronounced in Prakrit and Sanskrit but generally silent in Gujarati and Hindi (except where it follows a consonant cluster), I have followed my own admittedly imperfect ear. Thus, I use Jina instead of Jin, karma instead of karm, Mahāvīr instead of Mahāvīra and *saṅgh* instead of *saṅgha*. I do not italicize titles such as Jina and Tīrthaṅkar, proper names, and words of Indian origin that have found their way into English such as karma and dharma. When my discussion is directly dependent upon a Sanskrit or Prakrit text, I have recognized that language shift by using the Sanskrit or Prakrit form. In accordance with standard Jain practice, and in order to minimize the linguistic complexities, in many cases I have used the Sanskrit form, even if the discussion is based upon a Prakrit source. For example, I use *tapas* instead of *tava*, and *darśana* instead of *daṃsaṇa* or *dassaṇa*. One idiosyncratic spelling is *Nokār Mantra*, to represent the Gujarati pronunciation of this most important of Jain *mantras*; a literal transliteration would be *Navkār Mantra*. In writing place names, I have used the English forms as printed on official maps.

I have employed a fairly standard system of transliterating Indic letters and sounds into the Roman script. The short vowels *a*, *i*, and *u* are pronounced like the vowels in the words b*u*t, f*i*ll, and p*u*t. Pronunciation of the long vowels *ā*, *ī*, and *ū* approximates that of the corresponding vowels in the words f*a*ther, mar*i*ne, and rule. The dipthongs *e*, *ai*, *o*, and *au* are pronounced as in the words prey, time, mow, and cow. Vocalic *ṛ* is pronounced in Gujarati as *ru*, and in Sanskrit as *ri*. C and *ch* are both pronounced like English *ch* as in church, with Indic *ch* being more strongly aspirated. Both *ś* and *ṣ* are pronounced *sh* as in *sh*ow. The difference between dental (*t*, *th*, *d*, *dh*, *n*, *l*) and retroflex (*ṭ*, *ṭh*, *ḍ*, *ḍh*, *ṇ*, *ḷ*) consonants, although crucial in Indic languages, and therefore to advanced scholars of India, need not concern most readers. The aspirated consonants *th* and *ph* are pronounced not as in *th*in and *ph*ial, but as in the consonant clusters in po*th*ole and shep*h*erd. The conjunct *jñ* is pronounced in Gujarati as *gy*; thus the word *jñān* is pronounced *gyān*. The letter *ḥ* indicates an aspiration, not a hard letter. The letter *ṃ* also represents a nasalization, not a hard letter; the nasalization of final vowels is indicated by a tilde.

Many of the authors of books, pamphlets, and articles used in this study are Śvetāmbar Mūrtipūjak Tapā Gacch mendicants. At the time of initiation into the mendicant order, a man receives a new religious name, as well as a title. Part of the name is specific to him, and part indicates which branch of the Tapā Gacch he belongs to. Nowadays there are two branches of the Tapā Gacch, Vijay (Victory) and Sāgar (Ocean). In accordance with Gujarati and Hindi usage, I have listed all mendicants in both the text and the bibliography by their "personal" names, and appended vijay or sāgar directly to their name. For example, one will find references to Bhadraṅkarvijay and to Buddhisāgar. Many Tapā Gacch mendicants change their names when they receive the seniormost initition as *ācārya*; more common (but not universal) is to reverse the branch and personal names. For example, Ānandvijay became Vijayānand. In addition, every *ācārya* receives the additional title of *sūri*, which is appended to his name as a suffix. So the proper full form is Ācārya Vijayānandsūri. In order to simplify citations, I continue to alphabetize him under "a," as Ānandsūri.

There are four ranks of male mendicants: *muni*, *paṅnyās-gaṇi*, *upādhyāy*, and *ācārya-sūri*. In both the text and bibliography I have appended the suffix ranks of *gaṇi* and *sūri* directly to the name, in accordance with Jain practice.

In polite conversation, a mendicant is addressed even more elaborately, by prefacing his name by *śrī*, "blessed," appending the honorific *-jī* to his name, and then giving him the additional titles *mahārāj sāhab*, "Great King and Master." A monk with whom I had many conversations was therefore referred to in conversation as Muni Śrī Jambūvijayjī Mahārāj Sāhab. I have omitted these honorifics to simplify matters for readers who are not specialists in South Asian matters.

No transliteration system is perfect, and the problem is compounded when the number of languages and dialects increases. I hope that in the process of trying to satisfy the conflicting criteria of transmitting local flavor (and thereby being faithful to my Jain audience) and ensuring consistency and clarity (and thereby being faithful to my academic audience) I have not hopelessly confused the reader. I am sure that the perceptive reader will find instances in which I have not followed my own principles.

Hymn to Pañcāsar Pārśvanāth

Supreme Soul! Supreme Lord! Lord of the World!
Jina King! Friend of the World! Sun of the World!
Praising you is a ship
that carries me across the ocean of rebirth.

Savior! You destroy delusion.
You are the support of my virtue and fulfillment.
You are the exceedingly beautiful bride of good fortune.
Marry me to success.

Knowledge and faith are endless,
your feet are boundless.
In gifting and similar deeds one experiences the sentiment of scrubbing off karma.
Your virtues are endlessly endless.

Within one verse
there are thirty-two letters.
You are not to be found in one letter in this world, O Lord,
so how can your generosity be sung?

Who can count your virtues
unless he is enlightened?
You manifest all the virtues,
they just seem to be hidden.

Blessed Pañcāsarā Pās-jī
I have just one request:
make manifest your mercy.
O storehouse of grace, have compassion for me.

Blessed Jina, you are supreme.
I have much hope, O Great King.
Padmavijay says, I desire only this:
remain the imperishable, unshakable king of the city of liberation.

Padmavijay, *Pañcāsarā Pārśvanāthnū Stavan*,
in *Sudhāras Stavan Saṅgrah*, pp. 44–45.

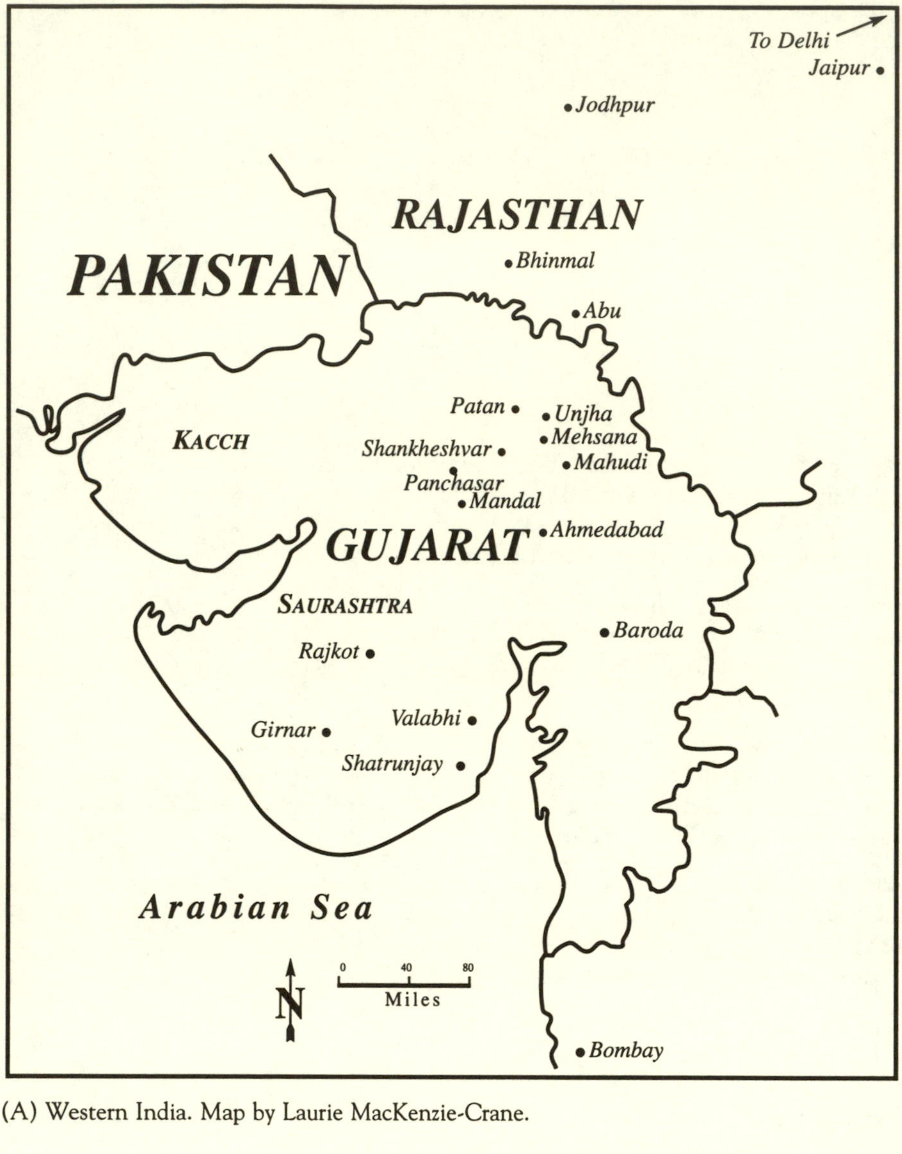

(A) Western India. Map by Laurie MacKenzie-Crane.

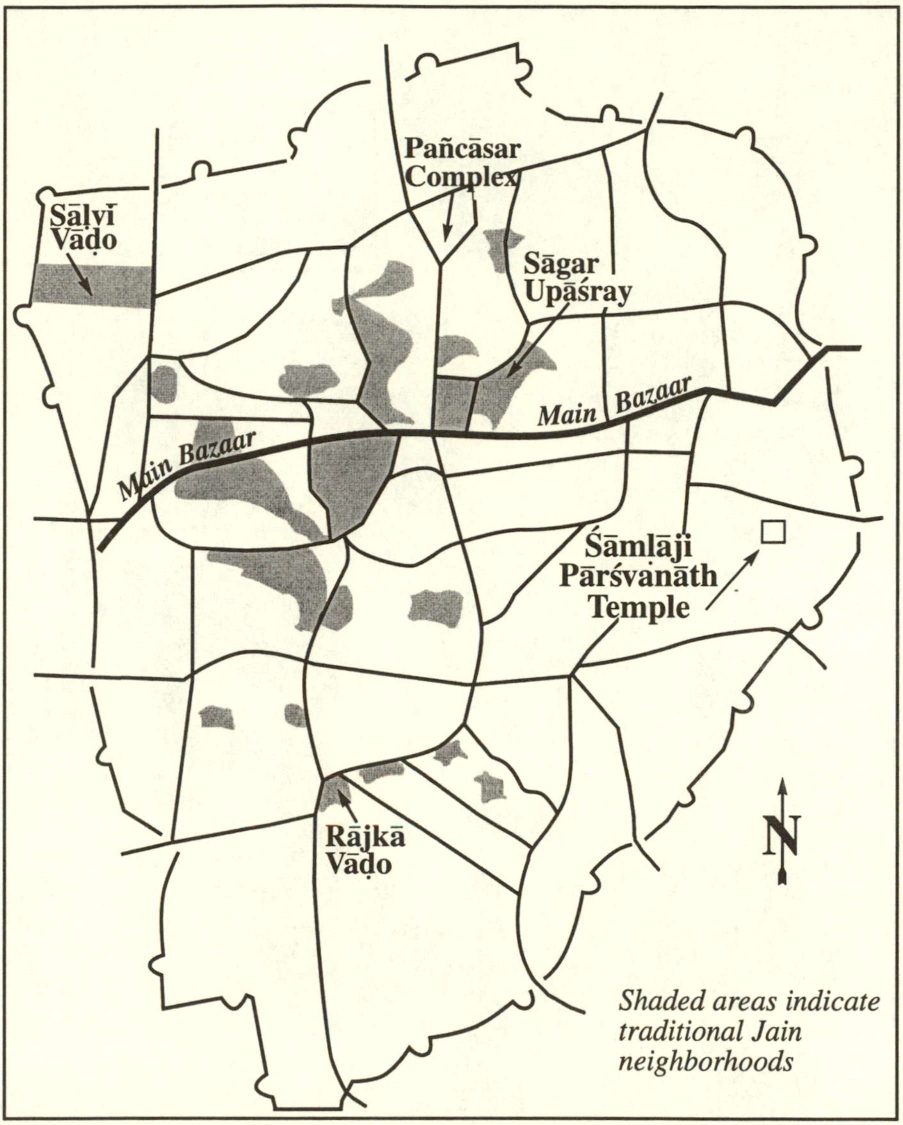

(B) Patan. Map by Laurie MacKenzie-Crane.

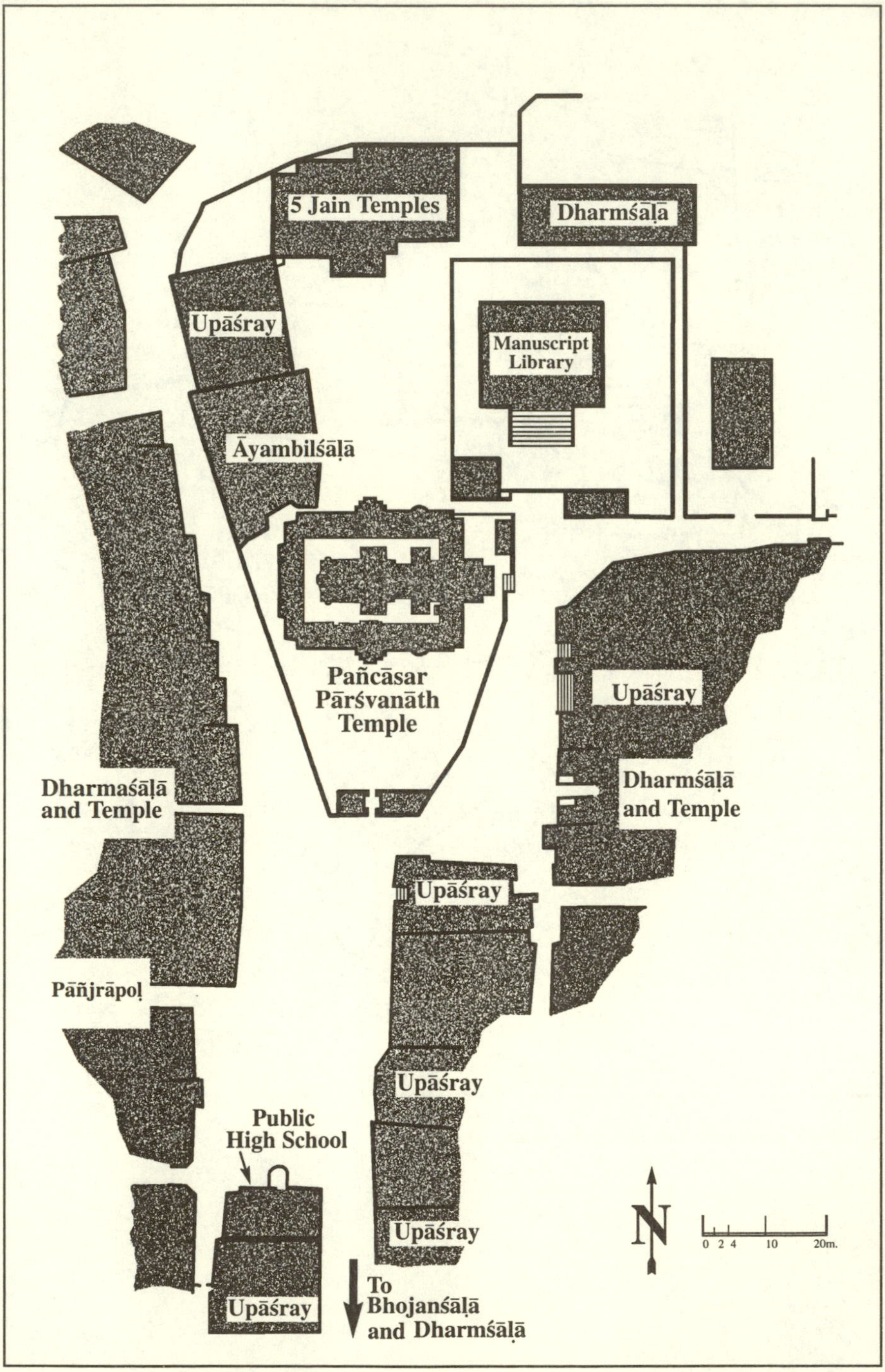

(C) Area around the Pañcāsar Temple. Map by Laurie MacKenzie-Crane, from original plan by Arthur Duff.

Jains in the World

Introduction

On the Occasion of the Blessed Installation of the Lord

I arrived with my wife Cynthia in Ahmedabad on an evening in late August 1985, planning to spend the next two years doing fieldwork in Gujarat for a doctoral dissertation on the Jains. I had done some preliminary fieldwork on the Jains as an undergraduate a decade earlier in Banaras and then briefly in Patan earlier in my graduate career. I had done extensive reading of primary and secondary sources on Jainism. I had a serviceable knowledge of the basics of Jain philosophy and orthopraxy. The first intense immersion in fieldwork in Ahmedabad showed me clearly how little I knew, how problematic what I did know was, and set the stage for questions I am still asking.

Almost immediately upon arrival in Ahmedabad, I met with Thomas Zwicker, an anthropology graduate student from the University of Pennsylvania who had been in Gujarat for the previous nine months, and with whom I had been in correspondence. He said that he was interested in researching the rites surrounding the installation of an image in a new temple, rites collectively known as *pratiṣṭhā*. Since rituals were to be a centerpiece of my research, I was of course interested, and he suggested we work together. A few days later, over lunch with a Jain friend, we mentioned our interest in observing a *pratiṣṭhā*. He recalled seeing an announcement of one in that morning's newspaper. We stopped by the new temple on our way back to the university, and there met several men who gave us the complete program for the nine-day festival, explained to us which events had already occurred, and invited us to return the following morning.

Looking back on my fieldwork notes from the next four days, with the hindsight of having observed three more *pratiṣṭhās* during the subsequent twenty-one months, I am struck by the inchoateness of those notes, but also by the way themes that are central to this book surfaced so readily. The first day we observed four highly complex and colorful rites (*pūjās*) designed to locate this particular temple within the vast cosmos of Jain geography. The first *pūjā* involved the invocation and pacification of the nine planets, so that no negative astrological forces would obstruct the efficacy of the temple. The next involved the invocation and pacification of the ten directional guardians. The third dealt not with deities but with the abstract holy symbols known as the eight *maṅgaḷs*, multivalent signs of all that is good and powerful in Jainism, and for which we have art historical evidence of two thousand years. Each of these *pūjās* involved songs, *mantras* (spells), and costly offerings onto silver trays in the center of the temple. The fourth *pūjā* involved offerings onto a large painted cloth *yantra* (magical diagram) of a *nandyāvart*, another holy symbol.

The second day involved the anointing (*abhiṣek*) of all the images, as well as of the entire temple. In multiple locations, Jains poured sanctified water over the images and the temple spire to purify them of any faults that had accrued during the construction process. These rituals bore a strong similarity in basic structure to those performed at the consecration of a Hindu temple. They were performed by lay members of the congregation, and presided over by a lay Jain ritual specialist.

All of this seemed very far from the Jainism of world renunciation and asceticism that dominated the scholarly literature. It would have been possible to dismiss this activity as merely some lay activity that exhibited the impact of centuries of interaction between Jains and Hindus, if it were not that all of this was supervised and attended by a well-known, charismatic mendicant, Ācārya Padmasāgarsūri, and a dozen of his disciples. The morning before the anointing he delivered a sermon to a large crowd of Jain laity.

Padmasāgarsūri began by talking about purification of the soul, a well-known theme in Jain philosophy with which I was familiar from my previous studies. It is necessary, he said, for a person to exercise self-control, for this is the only way to wear away (*nirjarā*) the karma that imprisons the soul. Here he introduced the first note that jarred with what I had read of Jainism. He said that in addition to self-control one needs confidence, for confidence leads to faith (*śraddhā*), and faith is essential if one is to attain God (Paramātmā). He continued on the theme of God, talking in terms that were very foreign to the picture in most scholarship of the Jains as ascetic atheists. He asked, if one abandons God and runs after the world of rebirth (*saṃsār*), how can one attain that which is holy (*maṅgaḷ*)? But if one hears the sound of the temple bell, he said, pointing in the direction of the partially constructed temple, one will hear the sound of the divine preaching inside one's heart, and through the grace (*kṛpā*) of God no more harmful karma (*pāp*) will be born in one's heart.

He then turned to several stories about a fictional businessman named Mafatlāl from Bombay. Mafatlāl worried about his financial losses year after year, but never about his religious (*dhārmik*) losses. It's bad if a business loses money for one year, worse if it loses money two years in a row, and what business can survive if the losses continue for a third year? But who ever thinks about the effects of continued religious losses? This world renouncer, clad only in a few simple white cotton robes, who walked all over India barefoot, ate only the most uninteresting of foods, and in just a few days would pull out by hand all of his head and facial hair, was at the same time perfectly at ease talking about the affairs of the world. His theme was the need to focus on religious rather than worldly matters, but his smiling, laughing demeanor bespoke a man for whom the religious life was not grim.[1]

He was not finished with the business metaphor. If one worships God (Bhagvān), he said, then one can reap a profit of merit (*puṇya*). One should use one's material wealth to worship God. If one uses one's money on the temple, it's even better than depositing it in the bank. From one's initial investment of material wealth, one accrues spiritual interest of merit, since some of the merit from every act of worship accrues to the temple's patron.

Here he was commoditizing religion in a manner I didn't expect from a world renouncer. But the surprises still weren't through. He told another story, of a man who regularly beat a path between the temple and his office. He bowed once to the feet of the Lord, but then bowed five times to the "poison box" in which he kept his money. As of today, concluded Padmasāgarsūri, only 60% of the funds needed for the construction of the temple have been raised; 40% are still outstanding. And with that, he turned matters over to several of the leading men of the congregation, who proceeded to make a pitch (and a successful one) for more money.

In one sermon, Padmasāgarsūri had presented a litany of themes that would take an entire book to unpack, and many of which we will return to. The sermon was in the context of an expensive, lavish nine-day festival for the consecration of a new temple in a well-to-do suburb. Possessionless, world-renouncing mendicants rubbed shoulders with wealthy, world-affirming businessmen who had multinational interests. Absolute poverty and absolute wealth flowed together. At the center of all the attention was the main image of the temple, a carved marble statue of a Jina seated dispassionately in meditation, but which daily was elaborately ornamented to look like a king (see Figure I.1). The image of the Jina, the lives of the mendicants and the lengthy fasts being undertaken by many of the participants all bespoke a concern for liberation from this world, while the beauty of the temple and image, the warm, friendly faces of the mendicants, and the fancy silk clothes of the laity all bespoke a comfortable acceptance of what this world has to offer.

I am using the term "world" here in the manner that has become standard in the sociology of religion and sociology of knowledge. The best and most extensive introduction to this usage is Peter Berger (1969), who in turn based much of his thinking on the earlier scholarship of Max Scheler (1926, 1930) and Max Weber (1922). In brief, this approach posits "that human knowledge is given in society as an *a priori* to individual experience, providing the latter with its order of meaning. This order, although it is relative to a particular socio-historical situation, appears to the individual as the natural way of looking at the world" (Berger and Luckmann 1967:8, summarizing Scheler 1926). This understanding of "world" has become such an assumed cornerstone of modern studies of religion (see, for example, Bechert and Gombrich 1984, Dumont 1980:267–86, Falk and Gross 1989, Lewis 1976, Tambiah 1976) that its pedigree is rarely even acknowledged. At the same time, this academic use of "world" intersects with a specifically Indian concern, as indicated by the works of Louis Dumont, Patrick Olivelle (1975, 1982), and Stanley Tambiah, among others, on "world renunciation," and T. N. Madan (1987), Olivelle (1993), and others on what Madan, echoing Dumont, calls "the life of the man-in-the-world." As will become evident in this book, the ultimate status of the "world" (*saṃsār, loka*) is highly problematic in the religious traditions of South Asia; in fact, the proper attitude toward the world is open to debate. This book is dedicated, in part, to an investigation of these debates within Jain contexts.

Figure I.1. Image of a Jina, ornamented to look like a king. Image of Pañcāsar Pārśvanāth, August 1996.

This book is an exploration of the practices and beliefs of the Śvetāmbar Mūrtipūjak Jains, the largest of the four divisions of Jains, with a geographical focus on north Gujarat, and more particularly on the small city of Patan. The theme around which this exploration is organized is the interaction between the realm of wellbeing and the ideology of the path to liberation (*mokṣa-mārg*).[2] I intentionally use the somewhat old-fashioned, but still acceptable, spelling of "wellbeing" rather than the more common "well-being" to emphasize that I am using it as an analytical category, the meanings of which will become clear in the course of the book. In these we see two different yet interrelated Jain definitions of the religious life and of the sacred.

The *mokṣa-mārg* is the orthodox ideology of the path to liberation, as symbolized in the temple image of the liberated Jina, who in the past traveled the path to liberation and then taught it to the world, and the living figure of the world-renouncing ascetic mendicant. It consists of correct faith (*samyag-darśan*) in the truth and efficacy of the Jain teachings, correct knowledge and understanding (*samyak-jñān*) of those teachings, and correct conduct (*samyag-cāritra*) which leads one along the path to liberation. These are the three jewels (*ratnatraya*) that make up the Jain religion, to which are often added a fourth jewel of correct asceticism (*samyak-tap*), which emphasizes the central place of ascetic practices in Jain soteriology. Traveling the *mokṣa-mārg* involves increased faith in and knowledge of the true nature of the universe. It also involves conduct designed simultaneously to reduce and ultimately halt the influx of karma and to scrub away the accumulated karma of this and previous lives. Karma is the "problem" according to the *mokṣa-mārg* ideology. According to the Jains, karma is a subtle material substance. Every unenlightened thought, deed, and word causes karma to stick to the soul like invisible glue. This karma both creates ignorance of the true nature of the universe and blocks the inherent perfection of the soul. The soul in its pure, unfettered state is characterized by the four infinitudes (*ananta-catuṣṭay*) of knowledge (*jñān*), perception or intuition (*darśan*), bliss (*sukh*), and power (*vīrya*). When finally freed of its enslaving karma, the enlightened and liberated soul floats to the top of the universe to exist forever as a self-sufficient monad absorbed in the four infinitudes. The *mokṣa-mārg* thus necessitates the increased isolation of the soul, and emphasizes separation of the individual from worldly ties and interactions.

The realm of wellbeing is not ideologically defined, and is therefore somewhat more difficult to delineate. Wellbeing involves what Glenn Yocum (1997:5) has described as "how human beings negotiate and cope with life's quotidian difficulties . . . the mundane, ordinary stuff—aspects of everyday life that are probably shared by almost all human beings." Whereas the *mokṣa-mārg* involves the increasing removal of oneself from all materiality in an effort to realize one's purely spiritual essence, wellbeing is very much a matter of one's material embodiment. It is marked by health, wealth, mental peace, emotional contentment, and satisfaction in one's worldly endeavors. In the Gujarati language, wellbeing is indicated by a family of polyvalent concepts such as *maṅgaḷ*, *śubh*, *kalyāṇ*, *lābh*, *puṇya*, *śreyas*, *śrī*, *lakṣmī*, and *śānti*, which have a range of overlapping English meanings that include holiness, good fortune, prosperity, wealth, good luck, auspiciousness, goodness, welfare, health, gain, benefit, merit, beauty, calmness, quietude, and peace. The "goal" of this realm, to the extent that it is at all goal-oriented, is a state of harmony with and satisfaction in the world, a state in which one's social, moral, and spiritual interactions and responsibilities are properly balanced.

The episode with which I started above indicates that both the *mokṣa-mārg* ideology and the realm of wellbeing are clearly evident in Jain practice and discourse. But they are not evident in the same ways. The ideology is easily and regularly foregrounded by Jains. In response to my questions, people readily pointed me toward the *mokṣa-mārg* ideology, using it as best they could to interpret behavior, and when they felt unable fully to answer my questions they pointed me to ideologues such as mendicants, *paṇḍits* (professional lay intellectuals), and learned orthoprax laity. But these answers often deflected my questions from observed behavior onto an ideological template. It was readily apparent that there was a large body of data that could not be adequately understood through this ideology alone. Previous studies of the Jains had tended to dismiss this entire realm of religious experience as non-Jain, and therefore as unimportant in the study of the Jains.[3] This was a step that I found intellectually unacceptable and was therefore unwilling to take, for it omitted from consideration much of the behavior that constitutes the lived experience of Jains as people. Such an interpretive strategy did violence to much that is unique and distinctive about the Jains, and devalued much of what they value. As indicated in the sermon of Ācārya Padmasāgarsūri, I also discovered that one cannot so neatly distinguish between the mendicant and lay communities. The *mokṣa-mārg* and wellbeing do not correspond to the mendicant and lay communities, and are not specifically mendicant and lay values. Mendicants and laity interact as part of the larger, polycentric Jain community, and expressions of the values of the *mokṣa-mārg* and wellbeing are found among both. After all, no one is born a mendicant, and so the distinction between mendicants and laity is more complex than is commonly supposed.

A second event that emphasized the importance of wellbeing in interaction with the *mokṣa-mārg* occurred soon after my arrival in Patan in early September, just a few weeks after the image installation in Ahmedabad. This was the centrally important annual festival of Paryuṣaṇ, to which I will return in chapter 6. During this nine-day festival, most laity conform their conduct at least in part to that of the mendicants, and strongly emphasize the values of the *mokṣa-mārg*. In the middle of Paryuṣaṇ, however, falls the celebration of the birth of Mahāvīr, the twenty-fourth and final Jina of this era and so an embodiment of the goal of the *mokṣa-mārg*. On this occasion the entire congregation gathered and with great festivity reenacted the seeing of fourteen auspicious dreams by the Jina's mother upon his conception. The various acts involved in displaying these dreams were auctioned off for large amounts, totaling over Rs. 10,000 (almost $850 in 1979) on this one afternoon, with the proceeds going to a congregational fund for the construction and renovation of temples. The occasion culminated in throwing rice and breaking open coconuts, both actions clearly symbolic of values of fertility and prosperity. Furthermore, the mendicants, whose presence was required to read the relevant passage from the *Kalpa Sūtra*, were active, laughing participants in these world-affirming festivities. On the one occasion when a mendicant attempted to introduce a note of the *mokṣa-mārg* ideology into the occasion, he was politely but firmly reminded by the congregation that to do so was inappropriate, and that his role was just to read the text.

Here was an event that clearly could not be adequately explained in light of the *mokṣa-mārg* ideology alone. But neither could it be dismissed as a marginal aberration, since the Jains themselves saw this occasion as one of the two most important events during Paryuṣaṇ, and indeed as one of the highlights of the Jain ritual year. What on other occasions was only an implicit or subordinate realm of value was on this occasion evident for all to see. This book is the record of my subsequent research, in the field and in the library, into understanding the value of wellbeing, the ideology of the *mokṣa-mārg*, and the complex ways in which they interact in the Jain world.

Wealth and Holy Poverty

A constant theme in scholarly studies of the Jains as a religious community (as opposed to studies of Jainism as a metaphysical and soteriological system) has been that of the seeming contradiction between the extreme wealth of the Jain laity and the extreme ascetic poverty of the Jain mendicants. This was the theme of the very first serious sociological treatment of the Jains, Max Weber's 1916 *Die Wirtschaftethik der Weltreligionen, Hinduismus und Buddhismus*, translated into English in 1958 as *The Religion of India.* Weber studied the Jains as part of his global comparative project on the role of religious teachings and practices in the development (or not) of industrial capitalism. His analysis was flawed, perhaps fatally, by the unevenness of his data: reports of British missionaries and civil servants, coupled with a few preliminary epigraphic and textual studies by European Indologists. The many factual inaccuracies and errors in Weber's brief eleven-page discussion have been readily apparent for decades. But beyond this, the major problem was that Weber's sources did not allow him to distinguish clearly between ideological prescriptions for lay life and the actual practices. His reading of lay asceticism and renunciation is simplistic, as his sources led him to assume that Jains live strictly and solely according to the rules set out in the texts. Weber's theme nonetheless remains one of enduring interest in the study of the Jains.

With the exception of another exercise in armchair ethnography (Nevaskar 1971), Weber's study remained the only word on the subject until the 1980s, when the situation began to change significantly. In the past fifteen years, a number of scholars in Europe, the United Kingdom, and North America have undertaken fieldwork studies of the Jains, with the result that the scholarly knowledge of Jain practice and belief has expanded tremendously. Although no one has returned exclusively to Weber's thesis, the broader theme of how extreme wealth and extreme poverty coexist within one relatively small religiously defined community (or, more accurately, family of communities) has been a dominant one in this scholarship. The titles alone of several recent studies should indicate that this distinction between wealth and renunciation has been a motif: "Profit, Salvation and Profitable Saints" (Laidlaw 1985), "Renunciation and Ostentation" (Reynell 1985b), *Délivrance et convivialité* (Mahias 1985), "Giving and Giving Up" (Babb 1988), "Monks and Miracles" (Babb 1993), *Riches and Renunciation* (Laidlaw 1995), and *Absent Lord: Ascetics and Kings in a Jain Ritual Culture* (Babb 1996). On the one hand we have salvation, renunciation, deliverance, giving up, monks, asceticism, and liberation; on the other we have profit, ostentation, donation, miracles, riches, kings, and wellbeing. The range of concepts involved indicates that we are not dealing with a single narrowly defined structural dichotomy in Jainism but rather with a fluid, multivalent range of tensions that find expression in many ways, and collectively serve as a dynamic spring in the creation of the ongoing Jain tradition.

Ideology

I have characterized the *mokṣa-mārg* as an ideology. Given the importance of the term "ideology" in the theoretical framework of this book, let me take a brief look at how other scholars have used it, and in turn how I use it. The literature on ideology has expanded exponentially over the past several decades.[4] Almost all those who write on it begin by stating how difficult, if not impossible, it is to define. Ferruccio Rossi-Landi (1990) begins by giving eleven headings under which we can understand ideology, and Terry Eagleton (1991) outdoes him by presenting sixteen possible meanings. Each laments that this extreme polysemousness threatens to render the concept unuseable—and then proceeds to write a book on the subject.

Much writing on ideology has been frankly hostile. Many authors contrast their own reasoned pragmatism with what they characterize as the unreasoning rigidity of ideology. In an oft-quoted formula of Clifford Geertz (1973:194), the dominant attitude toward ideology is, "I have a social philosophy; you have political opinions; he has an ideology." As a single example of this hostility on the part of one of the leading lights of critical theory, Michel Foucault (1980:118) has said that ideology is not a very useful category because "it always stands in virtual opposition to something else which is supposed to count as truth."

So how am I using ideology? By it I mean a mode of interpreting reality based upon a systematic, idealist quest for order. It is systematic in that it seeks to provide a single perspective from which a wide array of data can be brought together and harmonized within a single intellectual framework. An ideology often posits a number of binary oppositions: "Ideologies like to draw rigid boundaries between what is acceptable and what is not, between self and non-self, truth and falsity, sense and nonsense, reason and madness, central and marginal, surface and depth" (Eagleton 1983:133). The systematic and unitary nature of the formulation means that it is taken as authoritative by its adherents. This authority may be locatable, such as the perfect knowledge of the Jina. It is also presented with a degree of naturalness or matter-of-factness, as simply the way things are, as we will see in the Jain teachings of the *tattvas* or "reals." An ideology claims to be based upon a transcendent reality or truth; to the extent that such a truth is treated as sacred, the ideology takes on a distinctly religious cast.

An ideology is presented as a timeless, universal truth, and so its proponents resist the notion that it can ever change or need to be changed. Changes that do occur are interpreted as simply restatements of earlier formulations or clearer perceptions of the truth.[5]

Within an ideological context, conduct is guided by the ideology. The ongoing life of the ideology depends upon a particular social class of spokespersons for its perpetuation; these are ideologues, who propagate it through actions and through spoken and written words. Those who accept and act upon the ideology form a primary, cohesive group, with varying degrees of tension between themselves and others. An ideology often aims to alienate the individual from the existing order, which it characterizes as ignorant or illusory, in order to reconstruct the individual in light of the ideology.

An ideology is not separate from the society and culture in which its adherents live. It is, in the words of Clifford Geertz, a "cultural system." It is part and parcel of society, even if the adherents attempt to renounce and withdraw from that society. An ideology is expressed in the language, actions, and symbols of the culture in which it is embedded. It shapes that culture, and in turn is shaped by it. For all that an ideology makes empirical claims, and to a large extent consists of literal, nonfigurative statements, it is not simply a rational, consciously understood intellectual framework. An ideology has affective, symbolic, mythic, and experiential elements to it. An ideology may present itself as systematic, unified, and rational, and certainly appears so in contrast to less well articulated (or unarticulated) realms of value. But there are disagreements and inconsistencies within an ideology, even if they are denied or papered over. Paul Ricoeur (1984) has argued that ideology mediates between the interior world of thoughts, imaginations, and emotions and the exterior world of social relations. The mechanisms of that mediation operate as symbols, and so are open to the ambiguities and multiple interpretations that are inherent in symbols.

What this rough characterization of ideology does not address directly is the relationship between ideology and power. For the most part, ideology has been seen either as an apologetic method of legitimating and rationalizing the existing power structure, or as the programmatic agenda of those who are out of power but want to effect a total transformation of the power structure. Some have attempted to develop a more inclusive definition, but still one that ties ideology intimately to power relations, as in David McLellan's (1986:83) conclusion that ideology is best viewed as "an aspect of every system of signs and symbols in so far as they are implicated in an asymmetrical distribution of power and resources." McLellan's rhetorical addition to this statement—"And of which system is this not the case?"—indicates clearly that most scholars of ideology view power as ubiquitous.

By concentrating so exclusively on the relation between ideology and power, scholars have obscured some of the ways in which ideology can operate within culture as a fundamental mode of organizing reality. There is much to be gained by seeing ideology as a drive to impose intellectual order upon the world. This does inherently imply power relationships, but there are instances—and I think the Jain case is one—in which power relationships are muted, as in the authority granted a Jain mendicant on the basis of his or her ascetic, renunciatory lifestyle.

My use of ideology is similar to that of one of the great twentieth-century theorists on Indian culture, Louis Dumont, but differs from his in some key respects. His definition of ideology is relatively straightforward: "The word 'ideology' commonly designates a more or less social set of ideas and values" (Dumont 1980:343). He recognizes that ideology does not make up the whole of Indian society: "ideology is not everything. Any concrete, localized, whole, when actually observed, is found to be decisively oriented by its ideology, and also to extend far beyond it. . . . [I]n every concrete whole we find the formal principle at work, but we also find something else, a raw material which it orders and logically encompasses but which it does not explain, at least not immediately and for us" (37–38; see also 343). He further stresses that the sources to which we go to study ideology and these other principles are not the same: "The distinction between the ideological (or conscious) aspects and the others is required methodologically in virtue of the fact that these are not both known in the same manner" (343).

I differ from Dumont, however, in a key assumption. For Dumont, an ideology is always hierarchically superior to a nonideological realm of value. The ideology "orders and logically encompasses" (37) these other realms. He states this quite clearly:

"Methodologically, the initial postulate is that the ideology is *central* with respect to the social reality as a whole" (343). But in this he mistakes relative ease of perception and interpretation with logical and cultural priority. It is easier to see and interpret an ideology, because the ideologues themselves take great pains to foreground it for us. One has to resist the obviousness of the ideology and be attentive to other voices in order to perceive the role of other values within a culture. There are times when the *mokṣa-mārg* ideology appears clearly at the center of Jain culture, and takes precedence over all other values. But there are also times when it recedes into the background, and wellbeing comes to the fore. There are some surface similarities between my usage of ideology and realm of value, and the recent distinction made by William Sax (1991:9) between "explicit formulations" and "the implicit categories and habitual practices—the world view." But what Sax calls explicit formulations, which he says "may be anything from simple statements to complex metaphysical systems," cover a wider range of articulations than an ideology. Many of these explicit formulations lack the programmatic critique, found in an ideology, of the implicit worldview assumptions, nor do they involve the totalizing, conversion-oriented, and argumentative thrust of an ideology. Further, many of them lack ideologues, which is essential for the very existence of an ideology.

How the Jain *mokṣa-mārg* ideology functions in relation to the Jain culture as a whole should become clearer through the body of this book. But a final word of caution should be voiced. Scholarship on ideology has shown that in many ways it is a universal or near-universal cultural activity. Even though the word was not coined until the very end of the eighteenth century in the context of revolutionary France, and much of its context derives from Marxist and post-Marxist thought, it is possible to speak of ideologies in earlier times and in other places. What is lacking in these other contexts is the concept of ideology itself. We can speak of the Jain ideology and ideologues of the *mokṣa-mārg*. But this is not the same as to speak of an ideology and ideologues in nineteenth- or twentieth-century Europe or North America, for in the Jain case the interpretive category of "ideology," as well as any self-awareness of being an ideologue, are missing (Rossi-Landi 1990:5).

A Note on Method

This book is based on fieldwork study of the Jains of north Gujarat. The bulk of this fieldwork was conducted over a period of twenty-one months in 1985–1987, with subsequent shorter visits in 1989, 1995, 1996, 1997, and 1998. The result in many ways approximates what is known in anthropological circles as an ethnography. Much of my research consisted of observing, participating in, and documenting a wide variety of religious practices, and discussing these practices formally and informally with a wide network of Jains (and some non-Jains). Most of the fieldwork was done in Patan. My fieldwork methodology was largely one of informal discussion and participant observation, with much greater emphasis on observation than on participation. My wife and I lived in a predominantly Jain neighborhood of Patan, and spent much time with several Jain families who effectively adopted us as kin.

With these families, with other Jains of Patan, and on my own, I observed and documented the full range of annual, monthly, and daily rituals. Both before and after any ritual I talked about it with as many people as possible. Instead of using intensive, lengthy interviews, which can easily make the researcher an unwelcome guest, I developed a wide network of lay men and women, male mendicants, and lay religious functionaries whom I frequently visited and talked with for anywhere from five minutes to several hours. When detailed or specialized information was needed, I conducted more formal interviews with mendicants and important lay leaders. In the interests of privacy, I have changed the names of most people. The exceptions to this are the mendicants, who are essentially public figures.

Some of the fieldwork was also conducted in Ahmedabad, and in Bombay, Saurashtra, Kacch, Marwar, Jaipur, and Delhi. The Jains are a highly mobile people: businessmen have migrated and traveled in pursuit of their financial interests; women have married into families who live as near as the next street and as far away as the United States; and Jain mendicants criss-cross India on foot. To study the Jains, the researcher must travel, as well.

I also did research in libraries in India and the United States. Information derived from fieldwork was supplemented by information from books and pamphlets in Gujarati and Hindi. Rather than start with the literature and then move to fieldwork, I let the data as observed determine the areas in which to pursue further research through reading. I followed a rough process of limitation in selecting what printed primary sources to use. There are four main divisions of Jainism; among them, I avoided Digambar, Sthānakvāsī, and Terāpanthī sources except insofar as they provided comparative information or were otherwise directly relevant, and focused on Śvetāmbar Mūrtipūjak sources. The Śvetāmbar Mūrtipūjak Jains are also subdivided into mendicant lineages known as *gacchs*, to which are allied lay congregations. Since the Mūrtipūjak Jains of Patan are now almost exclusively Tapā Gacch, I went first to sources written by Tapā Gacch authors. Finally, I ranked written sources by two further principles of language and geography. In terms of language, Gujarati sources were preferred to those in Hindi or English. In terms of geography, I preferred to use books that I either saw in the homes of Patan Jains, or that were recommended to me in Patan. Most of the books were purchased from booksellers in Ahmedabad who specialize in such literature, or read in Jain libraries in Patan and Ahmedabad. One should remember, however, that the Jains themselves as merchants, migrants, and mendicants are a mobile community, so ideologies and practices spread quickly within the community. Especially in the late twentieth century, with the relative ease of transportation and communication, there is much less regional variation than in previous centuries.

This emphasis on written sources marks a significant departure from the classic model of ethnography, in which the only written references are other scholarly studies. The Jains are (and for many centuries have been) a highly literate community. It is the rare Jain household that does not have a number of dog-eared religious pamphlets and books. To understand the Jains adequately, one must read what they read.

This study makes certain assumptions about the role and influence of texts as bearers and reflectors of ideology within a tradition, and about the creation of texts as an ideology-making process (see also Cort 1990a). It views conscious ideologies as always in a dialectical relation with unconscious (or less conscious) realms of value. It views religion as a dynamic, changing process, rather than as a static, unchanging structure. This book has as its object of study not Jainism as an abstract system of ideas, part of the intellectual history of the high points of human thought, but instead the practices, ideologies, and beliefs of the Jains as people, both today and throughout their long history.

This indicates another way in which this study marks a departure from the standard ethnography. An ethnography is usually a synchronic study, dealing with what is called "the ethnographic present," even when dealing with the issue of social change. But here again the student of the Jains has to take a different tack. Jainism is an ancient religious tradition, and the Jains themselves are deeply aware of the historically constituted nature of their tradition (Cort 1995c). As a result, no investigation of the Jains can ignore history and perceptions of history. One cannot, for example, fully study image worship or asceticism in the Jain tradition on the basis of fieldwork alone, for one has to take into account the fact that the Jains have been thinking and writing about the significance and meaning of these practices for over two thousand years. I have used many Prakrit and Sanskrit sources to attempt to understand better the temporal contingency of the practices and beliefs as I observed them. There is rarely a direct influence on contemporay practice and belief that can be traced from any given Prakrit or Sanskrit text, although one will certainly encounter constant references to these texts in the sermons and writings of the tradition's ideologues. Some of these texts have been read by many mendicants over the centuries in order to gain an ideological understanding of the norms for practice. But the impact of any given text has also been mediated by a number of intervening texts in what is clearly an interwoven textual "cumulative tradition" (Smith 1964). I have been guided in my choice of texts by my fieldwork experience; I read those Prakrit and Sanskrit texts to which I was directed by contemporary Jains. One will find many texts in the bibliography that rarely if ever appear in the bibliographies of Indological studies of Jainism, and by the same token many of the ancient "canonical scriptures" of the Jains that form the basis for most Indological scholarship and translation are absent. My guides in the selection of texts were contemporary Jains, not scholarship on the Jains.

It is here that my work differs in approach from that of Dumont and other structuralists. The structuralist approach assumes that when dealing with a culture, even as complex and multiform a culture as that of South Asia, we are dealing with a single whole. The goal is to find those aspects and concepts within the culture that mediate seemingly conflicting relationships, and so constitute a deeper structural unity beneath the seeming disjunctures. The problem with such structural models is that they tend to be atemporal and ahistorical, as they assume that the essential structures do not change over time. This is precisely why a structuralist can then pull in material from a wide range of times and places to advance an argument. I adopt more of a poststructuralist position. My approach accepts the basic linguistic premise of structuralism—that one is studying the underlying relationships among structures, not merely the surface phenomena—but then insists that one has to bring history into one's study. In this book I investigate the interplay of the *mokṣa-mārg* and the realm of wellbeing in the late twentieth century. I am not saying that this interplay has not existed in the past and, in fact, once one is attuned to the relationship one can see its analogues in some of the very earliest data on Jainism. But this relationship has taken very different forms in the past, and has often been geographically localized. For example, in medieval Gujarat we find an ideology of Jain kingship (Cort 1998c) that has largely disappeared in contemporary Gujarat. But it is not completely absent—and here the advantage of historical study becomes clear, for in looking at medieval Gujarat we see ideologies and values that are largely submerged in contemporary Jain culture. There is not one structure, different parts of which are more or less visible at different times, that makes up the essence of Jainism. The structures themselves and the relationships among them change over time.

My presentation of the Jains of north Gujarat does make certain rhetorical assumptions of holism, because such assumptions are inevitably part of any move toward generalization, and without some degree of generalization all scholarly discussion can only founder. I paper over some crevasses, and decline to provide a battery of contrasting examples to all my data. Anyone who has ever taught about India knows that for every true statement about India there is an opposite, contradictory, yet equally true statement. The holism of north Gujarat Jain life is a heuristic fiction. But it is not untrue. I have chosen for strategic purposes to imagine the Jain culture of north Gujarat as a whole; I could have just as easily chosen to emphasize the ways in which it is not a whole. That would have been another book.[6]

The resulting portrait of the Jains will probably appear to many readers as strikingly different from many text-based studies of the Jains, although it bears reassuring affinities with the fieldwork-based studies of the past two decades. I feel confident that this study is fully responsive to scholarly imperatives, while at the same time the Jains of Patan will recognize themselves.

1

The Ideology of the Path to Liberation

In this chapter I give a synthesized presentation of the Jain ideology of the path to liberation, the *mokṣa-mārg*. This presentation is based on those ancient and medieval Prakrit and Sanskrit texts, combined with their more modern vernacular glosses, that make up the basic curriculum for contemporary Śvetāmbar mendicants and *paṇḍits*, that is, the professional ideologues of the tradition.[1] In line with the way in which the *mokṣa-mārg* is understood by these ideologues, my discussion will present it as an unchanging, timeless, eternally true system. However, a close reading of the texts themselves, along with the vast number of other texts on Jain metaphysics and practice (a reading that has yet to be done adequately, as we lack good histories of intellectual changes in Jainism), shows that, as with all ideological schemas, there is a history to the *mokṣa-mārg*—albeit a history that exhibits greater conceptual conservatism than do most ideologies—and there are multiple, sometimes conflicting voices and viewpoints within the ideology.

This presentation of the *mokṣa-mārg* ideology very closely approximates to the standard academic portrait of Jainism found in earlier generations of scholarship (Cort 1990a). What this scholarship has presented as Jainism has been, I would argue, not so much Jainism as a lived religious tradition as Jainism as a normative ideology. Clifford Geertz (1973:93) some time ago developed a distinction between a "model for" and a "model of": a "model for" is a prescriptive model of what behavior should be, whereas a "model of" is a descriptive model of what behavior is. To use an architectural analogy, a "model for" is an architect's blueprint from which a contractor builds a building, and a "model of" is a drawing of an existing building. Geertz's distinction has some value in allowing us to see more clearly how most Jain scholarship has functioned. Earlier scholarship presented as a model *of* Jainism what more accurately is a model *for* Jainism. Introducing the concept of ideology allows us to see more clearly the interpretive power of this academic model, as well as its location within the Jain tradition itself.

Jain ideologues have defined their tradition as the *mokṣa-mārg*, the path to liberation, for over 2,000 years. The very first verse of the *Tattvārtha Sūtra*, one of the first and most important Jain attempts at a systematic presentation of Jain thought and belief—a text sometimes referred to as a *mokṣa śāstra* or "manual on liberation" that is still widely read and regarded as authoritative by both Śvetāmbars and Digambars—reads, "The path to liberation consists of correct faith, understanding, and conduct."[2] We have here the Jain version of a cosmological ordering principle that Richard Burghart (1983) has observed is common to all the renunciant ascetic traditions of South Asia. The world of everyday concerns and interactions is seen as an endless circle into which one is reborn again and again. In the words of W. Norman Brown (1970), from this perspective "time is a noose." This is expressed by the common Indian concept of *saṃsāra*, or the circle of transmigration, literally "that which flows together." It is also seen in the Buddhist *bhavacakra*, the wheel of rebirth with six realms into which a person can be reborn.[3] In the Jain tradition, this concept is visually symbolized by the *svastika*, in which the four arms are understood to represent the four realms of rebirth: those of humans, celestial beings, hellish beings, and plants and animals. In contrast to this circle of rebirth and delusion is the concept of a straight path, constituted by correct faith, understanding, and conduct, and visually symbolized by the three dots above the running cross of the *svastika*, which leads the individual out of the transient imperfect world to a permanent perfect state of enlightenment and perfection. This perfect state of liberation is symbolized by the crescent and dot at the top of the *svastika* (see Figure 1.1). The soul in this state is characterized as abiding eternally in the four infinitudes of infinite joy, infinite energy, infinite consciousness, and infinite knowledge.

As stated in the verse from the *Tattvārtha Sūtra*, the path to liberation for the Jains consists of the three jewels (*ratnatraya*) of correct faith, correct understanding, and correct conduct.[4] The remainder of the *Tattvārtha Sūtra*, as well as the many voluminous commentaries upon the text, is a detailed exposition upon these three

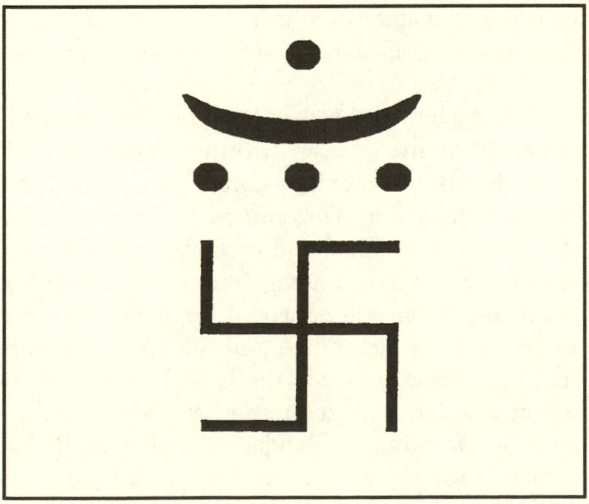

Figure 1.1. Drawing of a Jain *svastika*. The four spokes represent the four possible realms of birth; the three dots represent the three jewels on *mokṣa-mārg*; and the crescent moon and top dot represent liberation.

constituents of the path. Another very early depiction of the *mokṣa-mārg* is found in the *Uttarādhyayana Sūtra*, one of the most important texts of the Śvetāmbar "canon."[5] The text is said by Jains to consist of the final set of lectures given by Mahāvīra before his liberation. The twenty-eighth chapter is entitled "The Course of the Path to Liberation," and consists of a discussion of basic philosophical categories of the Jain worldview and the path to liberation.[6]

The three jewels are seen as intertwined. Verses 29 and 30 of the *Uttarādhyayana* chapter stress, "There is no conduct without faith. . . . Right faith and conduct are conjoined. . . . There is no knowledge without faith. There are no virtues of conduct without knowledge." The Jain who wants to travel the path to liberation must have faith in the Jain worldview, must have knowledge of the details of that worldview, and must act properly in accordance with that worldview.

This worldview is characterized in both the *Tattvārtha Sūtra* (1.2) and the *Uttarādhyayana Sūtra* (28.14) in terms of certain verities (*tattva*).[7] These are enumerated as seven in the *Tattvārtha*, but as nine in the *Uttarādhyayana* and the subsequent tradition, as exemplified in the medieval "Textbook on the Nine Verities" (*Navatattva Prakaraṇa*).[8] The *Tattvārtha*, in fact, focuses on these verities, as its title translates as "Aphorisms on the Meaning of the Verities." These nine are:

1. sentient soul (*jīva*)
2. insentient nonsoul or matter (*ajīva*)
3. influx of karma into contact with the soul (*āsrava*)
4. bondage of the soul by karma (*bandha*)
5. meritorious forms of karma (*puṇya*)
6. demeritorious forms of karma (*pāpa*)[9]
7. blockage of this influx (*saṃvara*)
8. dissociation of the soul from karma (*nirjarā*)
9. liberation (*mokṣa*, *nirvāṇa*)

The *Tattvārtha* includes *puṇya* and *pāpa* under the verity of *āsrava*, so according to the ideologues there is no significant difference between the lists of seven and nine.

According to Jain metaphysics, these nine verities have existed and will exist forever, and therefore define the universe within which the individual lives and strives for liberation. The first two provide a concise Jain definition of the universe as consisting of both soul and matter. The universe is therefore not merely a mental construct, as in some Vedāntin and Buddhist cosmologies, nor is it solely a material world, as in some other Indian and contemporary western cosmologies. Both the spheres of cognitive, sensory soul and noncognitive, nonsensory matter exist.

The verities of bondage, karmic influx, and the types of karma—meritorious and demeritorious, or good and bad—are the basic Jain depiction of the human predicament, the Jain description of the nature and cause of the imperfect and unsatisfying nature of human existence. Bondage according to the Jains is physically real; unlike its nature in some Buddhist and Hindu cosmologies, it is neither a delusion nor solely a matter of ignorance. Jain literature contains extensive discussions of the many categories and subcategories of karma.[10] It is divided into two broad categories. The four *ghātiyā* karmas have a directly negative impact on the soul by impeding the four infinitudes. These are the karmas that bring about bondage. The four *aghātiyā* karmas are not binding in themselves, but are dependent upon the *ghātiyā* karmas. They govern the details of rebirth. The four *ghātiyā* karmas are: (1) those that obscure knowledge (*jñānāvaranīya*); (2) those that obscure perception (*darśanāvaranīya*); (3) those that obstruct energy (*antarāya*); and (4) those that obscure perception and obstruct bliss (*mohanīya*). The four *aghātiyā* karmas are: (1) those that cause pain and pleasure (*vedanīya*); (2) those that determine lifespan (*āyus*); (3) those that determine personality traits (*nāma*); and (4) those that determine family and related factors (*gotra*). Few Jains, however, are knowledgeable of the eight categories and their many subcategories, for they are considered to be the province of specialized study. In everyday conversation, Jains refer to karma more generally as a cause-and-effect mechanism of the straightforward "as you sow, you are like to reap" variety.

The last three verities—the stoppage of karmic influx, the dissociation of the soul from previously accrued karmic influx, and finally the attainment of liberation from all karmic influence—constitute the Jain definition of the solution to the human predicament.

Correct faith consists in accepting and living by the reality of these nine verities. An alternative translation for *samyag-darśana* (also termed *samyaktva*) in this context would be correct worldview, which very accurately states the situation for the Jains. Other translations are correct attitude or correct conviction. These nine verities *are* the world according to Jain metaphysics, and therefore constitute the way a Jain with *samyag-darśana* should see the world.

Correct knowledge is the more detailed knowledge of each of these nine categories that is necessary if one is to advance toward liberation. In the words of the great twelfth-century ideologue Hemacandrasūri (*Yogaśāstra* 1.16), "Correct knowledge is defined by scholars as detailed and extensive knowledge of the nature of the verities." Within this category falls the voluminous Jain literature on philosophy and metaphysics.

Finally, correct conduct is that conduct done in accordance with these verities that will lead one to liberation. Correct faith and correct knowledge are useless without correct action, and the only way that people can judge the correctness of another's faith and knowledge is by the visible evidence of that person's conduct. Similarly, if faith and knowledge do not lead to correct conduct, then that faith and that knowledge are themselves tainted and incorrect.

Understanding the correct Jain worldview also involves understanding both the unique Jain cosmography and universal history.[11] The Jains conceive of the universe as having the shape of a colossal human figure, known as the "cosmic person" (*lokapuruṣa*). This physical universe is uncreated; it has existed since beginningless time and will exist for all eternity.

The earthly plane upon which humanity dwells constitutes the waist of the cosmic person. This middle world also contains the residences of powerful beings such as unliberated gods and goddesses who are sympathetic to Jains and so can assist pious Jains in solving worldly problems.

Much vaster in terms of geographical area, and therefore the residence of vastly more transmigrating souls, is the lower world of seven infernal or hellish regions stratified below the earthly plane. These regions in the pelvic cavity, legs, and feet are occupied by countless souls whose previous bad actions have caused the accrual of karma that results in such a painful rebirth. As one goes lower, each successive hell is darker and gloomier, occupied by souls suffering greater and greater torments in retribution for their previous deeds and thoughts.

Stratified above the human plane, in the chest cavity, shoulders, neck, and head, is the upper world, a number of celestial or heavenly realms in which reside countless souls whose previous good actions have resulted in their positive rebirth. These also occupy a much vaster area than the earthly realm (although smaller than the lower realm), and so are inhabited by many more souls. Each of these realms is ruled over by a king and queen, an Indra and Indrāṇi.

Above the celestial realms, at the very top of the cosmic person, is the realm of all perfected souls (*siddha*), known as the Abode of Perfection (*siddha-loka*), also known as Slightly Bent (*īṣat-prāgbhāra*) because of its unique shape. The perfected souls reside self-sufficiently in the four infinitudes. These three realms are the totality of all possible past, present, and future destinies for all the souls in the universe. Outside this figure are three layers of atmosphere encompassed by endless empty space.

The thin middle region, which constitutes a nearly infinitesimally small percentage of the total height of the cosmic person, is the only region inhabited by human beings. Since liberation is attainable only from a human life, this is also the only realm from which liberation is possible. Although this region is minute on the vertical plane of the cosmic person, on the horizontal plane it is still vast. It consists of an innumerable number of concentric rings of alternating continents and oceans. But most of this region is also uninhabitable by human beings. Only the innermost two and a half continents are humanly inhabitable: the central continent of Jambūdvīpa, the second continent of Dhātakīkhaṇḍa, and the inner half of the third continent, Puṣkaradvīpa. Jambūdvīpa is situated around the central axial mountain, Mount Meru. A series of six parallel mountain ranges running from east to west divides Jambūdvīpa into seven different countries. All seven are inhabited by human beings, but there are only two and a half countries in which a Jina, the teacher and founder of the Jain religion, can be born, and so it is only in these two and a half countries that liberation is possible on Jambūdvīpa. Because these are the countries in which there is sufficient perspective on moral choices that one's karma can be affected, they are known as karma lands (*karma bhūmis*), whereas the other countries, where life is so dominated by sensual enjoyment without concern for the moral status of the soul that liberation is impossible, are known as enjoyment lands (*bhoga bhūmis*). The two and a half karma lands are Bhārata in the south, Airāvata in the north, and half of Mahāvideha in the middle. Bhārata, according to this traditional cosmography, is the realm of India.[12]

In addition to this complex cosmography, a full understanding of the correct worldview also involves understanding the unique Jain biology.[13] As mentioned above, there are four possible states into which souls are born: human, infernal, celestial, and plants-and-animals. Humans, who are born only in the middle region, constitute the demographically smallest of these states. There are many more infernal and celestial beings. By far the largest category is that of plants-and-animals. Jain biology distinguishes bodies inhabited by souls as ranging from those possessing one sense (touch) to those possessing five senses (touch, taste, smell, sight, and hearing). Among the single-sense bodies, which are also called immobile because they do not have the ability to propel themselves, are earth bodies, water bodies, fire bodies, air bodies, and plant bodies. Mobile bodies contain from two to five senses. A further distinction among five-sensed beings is between those that are sentient and those that are not; some animals, all celestial and infernal beings, and most but not all humans fall in the former category.[14]

Third, in addition to cosmology and biology, correct understanding also involves the study of chronology, for liberation is not always possible on either Bhārata or Airāvata. According to the Jains, time does not operate in the same way everywhere in the universe. Time is qualitatively constant in the half of Mahāvideha where liberation is possible. As a result, liberation is always possible there. The Jina Sīmandhar Svāmī is currently living and teaching the Jain tradition in Mahāvideha, and it is possible for the soul of a pious Jain to be reborn in Mahāvideha and attain liberation (Dundas 1992:230–31). But in Bhārata time is not qualitatively constant. Rather, some periods of time are inherently better than others, and the period in which one lives has a profound effect on the type of religious life it is possible to live. In Bhārata, time is seen as a cosmic wheel that is forever turning. It has twelve spokes, which are the twelve periods of each full cycle of time. Each regressive half cycle descends from a very happy period through happy, more happy than unhappy, more unhappy than happy, unhappy, and very unhappy periods. Only in the middle two periods of mixed happiness and unhappiness are the types of moral choices possible that can lead to liberation. In the others, people are either too content with or too oppressed by their lot to have the degree of perspective and initiative needed to make moral choices that will significantly affect their karmic status. In Bhārata, time is presently in the fifth, unhappy period of a regressive half cycle, and so liberation is impossible.

Let us pause to review this potentially mind-numbing array of cosmographical, biological, and chronological schemes. In the Jain worldview, we inhabit a vast but bounded universe that is teeming with life, with an infinite number of souls. Little of this life is human: the vast majority of souls are born into celestial, infernal, or plant-and-animal states. Even within the human realm, most people are born in regions that are sufficiently Elysian that the inhabitants lack any moral perspective on their existence. Only in a small region, of which India is a part, are the cosmographical circumstances conducive to a life in which one experiences and perceives good and bad, and so is able to make choices that will affect one's karmic status. But even here such circumstances are not always possible, for currently we live in a time when such choices are inherently based on inadequate understanding, and so cannot lead to liberation. Since only human beings possess the sort of intelligence that allows for such moral reflection, we see that the chances of a soul being born in a body from which liberation is possible, and in a time and place where liberation is possible, are almost infinitesimally small.

This allows us to discern the pedagogical and ideological thrust behind these vast schemes. The intended audience consists of humans who, although incapable of attaining enlightenment directly, are capable of making moral choices in their lives and so living a Jain life. The cosmographical, biological, and chronological schemes of the *mokṣa-mārg* ideology are designed to draw forth a sense of *saṃvega* from the person who gives them serious consideration. *Saṃvega* is a sense of existential shock at the seemingly hopeless condition of living beings trapped in the noose of time, circling around and around in birth, suffering, and death after birth, suffering, and death. But *saṃvega* is simultaneously a sense of the rare opportunity one has gained to acquire a human birth in a time and place when living a Jain life is possible.[15] The person who is overcome with *saṃvega* will seize the opportunity provided by this birth to renounce a life in the world of rebirth (*saṃsāra*) and set forth upon the path of liberation.

Ernest Gellner (1979:118) has said of ideologies that they "contain contentions which are inherently fear- and hope-inspiring and are meant to be such to anyone, anywhere." An ideology does not consist of hypotheses and questions. It consists of assertions concerning the nature of the world, assertions designed to give offense to people living in that world by violating what common sense tells us about the world. By presenting an alternative vision of reality, these assertions shake the individual's confidence that his or her unexamined understanding of the world as daily lived is in fact adequate. This vision is presented not as a possible theory but as an actual description. The disjunction between the previous naïve understanding and the new ideological understanding is intended to induce in the individual a sense of what the philosopher and theologian Søren Kierkegaard, on whom Gellner bases his discussion, terms "fear and trembling."[16] The individual now sees the world from a new, ideological perspective, and is alienated from his or her prior perspective. But the point of such an ideological exercise is not just to paralyze the individual in a state of existential angst. To shake the individual loose from the prior inadequate perspective on the world is merely the first step. The second step is to induce the individual to accept the new ideological perspective as the only one that provides an answer to the ontological dilemma in which he or she now finds him or herself. An ideology provides hope, because it provides an answer to the individual's perilous condition, and it provides this answer with as much certainty as it presented the problem. The *mokṣa-mārg* ideology with its overwhelming array of continents, life-forms, and temporal cycles is intended to instill in the perceptive individual the realization that the vast majority of life situations are unsatisfactory and marked by acute suffering, and then through this realization to instill a feeling of fear and loathing (*saṃvega*) of the everyday social world. At the same time that the individual is thus encouraged to reject this social world, the ideology makes available a compelling alternative vision of how life can be lived so that eternal peace can be attained. This vision is encapsulated in the history of the enlightened teachers and saviors of Jainism, the Jinas.

Within the two periods of each half cycle of time when moral choice and therefore liberation are possible on Bhārata, twenty-four individuals are born who through their own correct faith, knowledge, and conduct overcome the bonds of karma and become enlightened and, at the end of their bodily lives, attain liberation. These twenty-four, because of special actions in previous lives that generated an exceedingly refined kind of karma, are also teachers and founders of the Jain religious tradition. They are known as Jinas, "Conquerors," because they conquer the bonds of karma. They are also known as Tīrthakaras, because they establish (*kara*) the ford (*tīrtha*) to cross the river of rebirth to liberation, and because they establish the four estates (*tīrtha*) of the Jain community: the male mendicants (*sādhu*), female mendicants (*sādhvī*), laymen (*śrāvaka*), and laywomen (*śrāvikā*). The first Jina in this era was Ṛṣabhanātha, also known as Ādinātha (First Lord).[17] His biography makes of him something of a culture creator (Jaini 1977). Other important Jinas of the Jain universal history were the sixteenth, Śāntinātha (popular as a cultic figure in large part for emblematic reasons because of his name, "Peace Lord"), and the last three, successively Neminātha, Pārśvanātha, and Vardhamāna Mahāvīra. According to the Jains, Neminātha lived in Saurashtra in western India and was a cousin of Kṛṣṇa (Krishna); Pārśvanātha lived in the eighth century B.C.E. in Banaras; and Mahāvīra lived a little over 2,500 years ago in what is today the state of Bihar in northern India.[18] Shortly after the death and liberation of Mahāvīra, the wheel of time rolled into the fifth spoke of time, and so liberation is no longer possible on Bhārata, although we live close enough to the time of Mahāvīra that some moral choice and therefore some religious life is still possible.

The Jain pantheon, the focus of Jain devotion, is divided into two distinctly different types of beings. On the one hand are the Jinas (and all other liberated souls), the exemplars of the religion. According to Jains, liberated souls are *vītarāga* or freed of all desire. This means they have overcome *all* desires, even the desire to act (and all action, reason the Jains, is preceded by a desire to act).[19] As a result the liberated souls do not interact in any way with individuals on earth. The Jinas collectively are the God of the Jains.

Jainism is often characterized by both scholars and non-Jain ideologues as atheistic or nontheistic. This is inaccurate, however, and is strenuously denied by Jains. Jains reject the definition of God as the creator of the universe, found in many Hindu and Abrahamic theologies, but they do not reject the concept of God. They use many of the same terms used by Hindus, such as Bhagavān, Deva, Īśvara, Paramātmā, and Parameśvara. According to Jains, as we have seen above, the universe is eternal; as Jains frequently say, it has existed from beginningless time to endless time. God, therefore, has nothing to do with creation of the universe. Instead, Jains define as God any soul who has become liberated, and in particular those souls who were also the teachers and founders of Jainism, the Jinas or Tīrthaṅkaras.[20] Each of these souls exists in identical perfection, and so is indistinguishable from any other such soul. Due to this identity of perfection, God for the Jains can be understood as singular. Because there are many liberated souls, God can also be understood as plural. We will return to the Jain understanding of God at greater length in chapter 3.

On the other hand, in the Jain pantheon there are various types of powerful but unenlightened and unliberated souls. They are not *vītarāga*, and can act. These souls are not liberated, and so do not possess infinite power; they can respond only in limited ways to prayers and petitions. They cannot grant liberation, but they can grant worldly wellbeing, assist in spiritual pursuits, and protect pious Jains from harmful forces. In this latter category fall various types of male and female deities. Also in this category of unliberated beings are those human beings who have progressed further along the *mokṣa-mārg* than most, that is, the Jain mendicants.

The specifically Jain pantheon is symbolically expressed in the notion of the Five

Supreme Lords (*pañca-parameṣṭhī*) of the Jain tradition, who respresent the hierarchy of the *mokṣa-mārg*. These are: (1) *arhats* or Jinas; (2) *siddhas*, all other enlightened souls; (3) *ācāryas*, mendicant leaders of the Jain community; (4) *upādhyāyas*, mendicant teachers; and (5) *sādhus* (all other mendicants).[21]

The Five Supreme Lords are those who are either already liberated or are advanced in correct conduct. As we have seen, perfect conduct is, ironically, no conduct at all, but instead the enlightened stasis of the Jina and the *siddha*. Correct conduct is that which is aimed at counteracting the Jain definition of the human problem, that is, which is aimed at stopping the influx of new karma into contact with the soul (*saṃvara*) and dissociating the soul from karma that already binds it (*nirjarā*). For the Jain mendicant, correct conduct is encapsulated in the five great vows (*mahāvrata*) that are part of the rite of initiation, and the six obligatory rites (*āvaśyaka*) that constitute the ritual core of mendicant praxis. The great vows have been the subject of extensive theorizing by Jain ideologues. They are:

1. *ahiṃsā*, causing no harm
2. *satya*, speaking only the truth
3. *asteya*, not taking what is not freely given
4. *brahmacarya*, celibacy
5. *aparigraha*, possessing nothing[22]

Correct conduct is further defined as that which conforms to the eight matrices of mendicant doctrine (*pravacana-mātṛkā*). These consist of two key elements of mendicant practice, the five rules of self-control in walking, speaking, accepting alms, picking up and putting down objects, and excretory functions; and the three restraints of mind, body, and speech. The five rules of self-control are designed to ensure that the mendicant is fully mindful of all of his or her activities, and strives to reduce karmic influx at all times. Thus the mendicant walks very carefully, paying attention not to harm any living thing whether from intention or accident, even an invisible insect or a plant. The mendicant says only what is helpful and balanced. The mendicant accepts only food and water that has been carefully inspected to insure that it adheres to the requirements of *ahiṃsā*. The mendicant picks up and puts down all objects with care not to hurt any living thing. The mendicant disposes of all bodily wastes in places devoid of any living thing.

The three restraints entail the progressive controlling of all mental, vocal, and physical activities. Pandit Sukhlal Sanghavi (1974:321–22), in his modern commentary on the *Tattvārtha Sūtra*, has given the following description of them:

1. While receiving or placing anything whatsoever, while sitting, getting up, or walking, in all such acts so to restrict bodily operations that discrimination is maintained between what is to be done and what is not to be done—that is called [restraint] pertaining to body.
2. Whenever there arises an occasion to speak then to restrict speech—if needs be to keep silent altogether—that is called restraint pertaining to speech.
3. To give up volitions that are evil or are a mixture of good and evil, as also to cultivate volitions that are good—that is called [restraint] pertaining to [mind].

Sanghavi further explains that the rules of self-control focus on observing correct conduct, whereas the restraints focus on refraining from improper conduct.

Correct conduct also entails a prescribed set of six daily rituals, known as the obligatory actions (*āvaśyaka*), as follows:

1. *sāmāyika*, a meditative attentiveness that pervades the mendicant's life
2. *caturviṃśati-stava*, a hymn of veneration of the twenty-four Jinas
3. *vandanaka* or *guru-vandana*, a rite of veneration of one's mendicant leader
4. *pratikramaṇa*, a rite by which a person ritually negates the karmic impact of words, actions, and thoughts
5. *kāyotsarga*, a form of standing meditation in which one mentally "abandons the body" in order to focus upon one's spiritual core
6. *pratyākhyāna*, a vow to perform certain karmically efficacious acts

In practice, these six are all intertwined. As part of the rite of mendicant initiation, one vows to perform constant *sāmāyika*. *Kāyotsarga* is not practiced on its own, but rather forms an integral part of the remaining four obligatory actions. *Guru-vandana* is performed both on its own and as part of *pratikramaṇa*. *Caturviṃśati-stava* has been expanded into the lengthier rite of *caitya-vandana* or "veneration of the image," to be performed in the temple, but is also part of *pratikramaṇa*. *Pratikramaṇa* takes five forms: morning and evening, to negate the previous half-day's karmic influx; and fortnightly, every four months, and annually, to negate successively larger karmic buildup. Finally, *pratyākhyāna* can be performed on its own, but is usually integrated into *pratikramaṇa*.[23] Taken together, the obligatory actions aim to produce a life in which one is constantly on guard against the many ways in which one can harm the myriad living creatures that surround one, and thereby reduces the amount of karmic influx that binds the soul. Further, since it is impossible not to commit any harm at all, one is performing frequent acts of asceticism to counteract the effect of previous karmic influx and so gradually release the soul from bondage.

The path to liberation is described as consisting of fourteen rungs (*guṇasthānas*).[24] In each *guṇasthāna* the soul exhibits different virtues (*guṇa*), indicative of increasing independence from karmic bondage (von Glasenapp 1942:68). The fourteen are as follows:

1. wrong faith
2. mixed faith
3. indifference
4. correct faith
5. receiving the vows (*vratas*) of the layman
6. receiving the great vows (*mahāvratas*) of the mendicant
7. overcoming negligence
8. overcoming the subtle passions of joking, liking, fear, and disgust
9. overcoming the subtle passion of greed
10. overcoming subtle veilings of knowledge and perception, as well as the subtle passion of fame
11. suppression of all passions
12. elimination of all passions
13. embodied omniscience
14. a momentary state before final liberation at death

This model in fact covers more than just the mendicant life, as it is broadly enough construed to include in it all of humanity, both Jain and non-Jain. The first rung on the ladder is that of wrong faith, and so includes all those souls who either have never heard the Jain teachings or else have consciously rejected them. The second rung, that of mixed faith, allows for those souls who have some knowledge and appreciation of the Jain teachings, but who still for the most part adhere to another tradition. The third rung, that of indifference, is for those who have no opinion or interest at all; but this rung is higher than that of mixed faith, for it is considered that in the second rung wrong faith will outweigh correct faith. Only at the fourth rung, that of correct faith, do we find true Jains, and the real beginning of the path to liberation. But accepting correct faith does not necessarily entail any great change in the ways one leads one's life; that is accomplished in the fifth rung, when one accepts the formal vows of a Jain layperson.

From the point of view of a Jain mendicant, all five of these rungs are preliminary and inferior to the more important event on the path to liberation, the acceptance of the five great vows of the mendicant on the sixth rung. From here the model of the *guṇasthānas* deals less with obvious outward forms of faith and conduct, and more with the psychological and soteriological details of the Jain analysis of the process of liberation. The seventh rung involves the overcoming of negligence in one's practice. The eighth through tenth rungs involve the sequential overcoming of increasingly subtler passions. At the eleventh rung the mendicant has suppressed all passions, and so it is no longer possible to slip lower down the ladder. But it is possible for the mendicant to remain stuck at this level for some time; further progress is inevitable only at the twelfth rung, when all passions are totally eliminated. The thirteenth rung is the state of embodied omniscience or enlightenment. At this stage the individual is no longer subject to the influx and influence of new karmas; only those subtle karmas accrued in previous lives that determine the feelings, body, length, and environment of this life are still present. The fourteenth rung is a brief moment of unembodied enlightenment; it is instantly followed by total liberation.

There are two distinct phases in the process of liberation within the Jain tradition. Enlightenment (*kaivalya*, *kevala-jñāna*) is omniscience or "knowledge isolated from karmic obstruction" (Jaini 1979:344). The enlightened soul remains embodied until the moment of death, when liberation (*mokṣa*, *nirvāṇa*) occurs. In the latter state the soul is forever freed from the cycle of birth and death. One should not, however, understand enlightenment as a purely epistemological event and liberation as a purely ontological event; each event is simultaneously epistemological and ontological.

According to the *mokṣa-mārg* ideology, a true Jain, that is, a person who has fully understood the world from the Jain perspective, should renounce the world and become a mendicant. But what if one is incapable of taking this drastic step? In that case, one strives to transform one's conduct into that of an ideal layperson (*śrāvak*).[25]

The Jain ideological descriptions of the religious life of the ideal layperson are closely modeled upon the descriptions of the mendicant life given above.[26] The life of the layperson is conceived as also following a path, for, as noted earlier, path models are dominant features in the ideologies of all world-renouncing ascetic traditions in South Asia. The life of even the best layperson is seen in essence as either inferior or preliminary to the career of the mendicant. This *mokṣa-mārg* ideology of the lay life is spelled out in the earliest Śvetāmbar prescription for the lay life, found in the *Upāsakadaśāḥ* (Ten Chapters on Exemplary Laymen).[27] This ideological model was repeated and elaborated by many mendicant authors through the centuries in the genre of literature known as *śrāvakācāra*, "Lay Conduct." The core of the *mokṣa-mārg* ideology of the ideal layperson is a set of twelve vows (*vratas*). In their sermons and writings, contemporary ideologues refer frequently to the twelve vows. More than one mendicant, in response to the information that I was researching lay practice, gave an impromptu discourse on the vows. In the words of a contemporary nun, "The vows are the gateway to liberation" (Hitajñāśrī 1985:19).

The first five of these vows are the *anuvratas* (lesser vows), the sixth through eighth are the *guṇavratas* (reinforcing vows), and the remaining four are the *śikṣāvratas* (vows of spiritual discipline). The five *anuvratas* are modeled directly on the five *mahāvratas* of the mendicant, differing only in the degree to which they are observed. The conduct of the mendicant, composed of the five great vows, is considered to be universally applicable, whereas the practice of the layperson, composed of the twelve vows, is considered to be applicable within specific limitations defined by context. The twelve vows are as follows. The five *anuvratas* are: (1) *ahiṃsā*, causing no harm; (2) *satya*, speaking only the truth; (3) *asteya*, not taking what is not freely given; (4) *brahmacarya*, celibacy; and (5) *aparigraha*, possessing nothing. The three *guṇavratas* are: (6) *dig*, restricting the geographical limits within which one travels; (7) *bhogopabhoga*, restricting what one uses and consumes; and (8) *anartha-daṇḍa*, restricting one's activities, especially one's occupation. The four *śikṣāvratas* are: (9) *sāmāyika*, in this case meditation lasting at least one "hour" of forty-eight minutes; (10) *deśāvakāśika*, a further temporary restriction of the geographical limits to one's activities; (11) *poṣadha*, a vow of temporary mendicancy; and (12) *atithi-saṃvibhāga*, or *dāna*, gifting to mendicants.[28]

As mentioned above, the five *anuvratas* are seen as lesser versions of the five *mahāvratas*. In terms of *ahiṃsā*, for example, mendicants are required to desist from all forms of violence to all six kinds of living organisms (earth beings, water beings, fire beings, wind beings, vegetable beings, and mobile beings), whereas it is recognized that laypersons can observe nonharm only toward some beings. The mendicant is enjoined to avoid both gross and subtle forms of violence, whereas the layperson can avoid only gross violence. A contemporary mendicant ideologue, in writing of the *ahiṃsā anuvrata*, gives the following examples (Kuśalcandravijay 1977:VI.10). A layperson should not desire, intend, or act in such a way as to harm any moving creature, but instead try to protect them. A layperson should not act heedlessly in anger and beat living creatures. A layperson should not needlessly pierce the skin of a living creature. A layperson should not overwork either animals or people. A layperson should not kill beings by beating them. A layperson should not let people and animals in one's care go hungry.

Similarly, the other four *anuvratas* are seen as lesser versions of the *mahāvratas*, working on a less subtle scale. *Satya* for the layperson involves avoiding various types of lies, especially in the business field, and not bearing false witness. *Asteya* involves not stealing, not avoiding taxes, and fair business practices. *Brahmacarya* involves having sex only with one's spouse, as well as the avoidance of ardent gazing or lewd gestures, although most people, both mendicants and laity, would understand *brahmacarya* to mean total chastity. *Aparigraha* involves renouncing attachment to one's wealth, and limiting either the value of various types of possessions or of all one's possessions in total. Contemporary pamphlets written to explain the twelve vows include charts in which one can list the vowed limits to wealth, with separate lines for items such as gold, silver, stock shares, jewels, pearls, clothing, shops, and land (Hitajñāśrī 1985:7–8).

Whereas the five *anuvratas* involve fundamental changes in the very bases of one's conduct and being, the three *guṇavratas* involve restricting one's activities and therefore one's interactions with the world. The importance of the *dig guṇavrata*, the restriction of the geographical limits to one's travels, is seen when one remembers that travel is essential to the livelihood of many Jains, since most of them are merchants. Restricting one's travel, therefore, can result in a significant lessening of one's business contacts and one's general interaction with the world. In a modern context, this vow can also entail restrictions upon long-distance forms of communications such as letters, telegrams, and telephone calls. The *bhogopabhoga guṇavrata* involves the renunciation both of consumables that can be used only once, such as food or perfume, and of more permanent items of repeated usage, such as clothing, jewelry, or houses. Included under this vow are the renunciation of both eating at night and eating twenty-two food items considered to be especially harmful karmically. The *anartha-daṇḍa* (pointless occupation) *guṇavrata* does not necessitate the total renunciation of worldly occupation called for on the part of the mendicant, but rather the avoidance of certain professions that are particularly violent. Listed among such occupations are keeping animals, selling grinding tools, and engaging in violent or nonedifying pastimes such as performing animal sacrifices or, in a modern context, watching television. Principal among these professions, of course, is farming, which involves extensive violence to earth bodies during plowing, to water bodies during irrigation, to vegetable bodies during reaping, and to moving bodies during all agricultural operations.

Finally, there are the four *śikṣāvratas*, vows relating to specific mendicant-like spiritual practices. A central part of the initiation rite of a mendicant is the vow of permanent *sāmāyika*. For the layperson, the *śikṣāvrata* of *sāmāyika* is only temporary. The *deśāvakāśika śikṣāvrata* is an intensified version of the *dig guṇavrata*. Whereas the *dig guṇavrata* usually involves a long time span and a large geographic compass,[29] the former involves much more tightly defined parameters, such as going no further from home than the neighborhood temple for the four months of the rainy season. *Poṣadha* involves the taking of *sāmāyika* for extended periods of four or eight *prahars* (one *prahar* = three hours). Finally, the *atithi-saṃvibhāga* or *dāna śikṣāvrata* governs the proper conduct of the laity toward the mendicants, in terms of what is given, to whom it is given, and the manner in which it is given.[30]

The mendicant-based path ideology of the life and practices of the ideal Jain layperson has been the subject of extensive theorizing by Jain ideologues over the centuries. R. Williams (1963) in his important study of the classical texts of this literature used twenty-nine Sanskrit and Prakrit texts by twenty-two authors from the fifth through the seventeenth centuries, and could have used many more texts.

He intentionally did not employ the large body of similar material in Gujarati and Hindi. Discussions and depictions of the ideal layperson according to the ideology of the *mokṣa-mārg* continue to be the subjects of both books and sermons by mendicants and other *mokṣa-mārg* ideologues today. Books abound with titles that echo the path vocabulary such as "Acquaintance with the Jain Path" (Bhadraṅkarvijaygaṇi 1977), "Twenty Steps on the Path to Liberation" (Padmasāgarsūri 1986), and "The Holy Gate to Liberation" (Hemcandravijay 1977). Many of these books and sermons are directly dependent upon the older sources, especially the *Yogaśāstra* of Hemacandrasūri. More often, though, the ideology is expressed in more general terms, with a stress upon renunciation, asceticism, and devotion. In other words, within the context of the three jewels, the emphasis is more upon correct faith and correct conduct (as well as the unofficial fourth jewel of correct asceticism) than it is upon correct knowledge, which is considered to belong more properly to the specialized intellectual life of the mendicants, *paṇḍits*, and other ideologues.

The *mokṣa-mārg* ideology is not a descriptive model of Jain behavior. There is much in the religious, social, and private lives of Jains that does not fit into the ideology. It is a prescriptive model for Jain behavior. It provides a template of worldview assumptions and behaviors based on those assumptions. The greater one's commitment to the ideology, the more one will use it to shape and inform one's behavior. According to the ideology itself, the logical result of such commitment would be to become a mendicant, but the prescriptions for ideal lay behavior recognize that it is neither likely nor in the end desirable that more than a small minority of Jains take this step. Mendicants are expected to live in conformity with the *mokṣa-mārg* ideology. Accordingly, the Jain laity are exposed to this ideology whenever they encounter mendicants either in person or through written materials. Since the expectations are that lay lives are not as fully informed by the ideology, there is a built-in tolerance of a broader but still bounded range of lay behavior.

It is the rare person, however, who is willing and able to shape his or her life completely by an ideology, and ideology can be interpreted differently. We find a range of behavior even among mendicants and laity who would consider themselves, and be considered by others, to be firm, orthodox adherents of the ideology. The *mokṣa-mārg* ideology is one realm of value among others within the Jain tradition (and within the surrounding South Asian culture), and so in any one life and any one event we can discern multiple values in play. One of these almost inevitably will be the *mokṣa-mārg* ideology. But it will not be the only value, and to use it as the sole frame for the presentation and interpretation of the Jain tradition is scholarly reductionism. Among the other values that can be clearly discerned in conduct and speech is what I term wellbeing.

Wellbeing is not, however, expressed as a conscious ideology in the same way as the *mokṣa-mārg*. There are no wellbeing ideologues. Since wellbeing is not systematically discussed in the same way as the *mokṣa-mārg*—since it is not an ideology in the literal sense of the word—it is not amenable to the same sort of synopsis as I have given for the *mokṣa-mārg*. This is not to say that Jains are unaware of it. Even if it does not have a single name within the tradition—which is why I have had to give it the English name of wellbeing—it is much discussed by all manner of Jains. These references are most strikingly notable when wellbeing is negatively compared to the *mokṣa-mārg* in sermons or writings. But there is ample additional evidence available to the scholar about the realm of wellbeing in writings, spoken discourse, and rituals. To understand wellbeing more fully we need to see it in multiple frameworks. This will be a major task of the remainder of this study. After I have introduced the reader to a wide presentation of wellbeing in context, as well as to a fuller understanding of the ideology of the *mokṣa-mārg* in lived contexts, in the last chapter I will return to a formal discussion of wellbeing and some of the ways in which it interacts with the ideology of the *mokṣa-mārg*. The values of the *mokṣa-mārg* and wellbeing do not exist in a vacuum, however. They are expressed and enacted in the lives of Jains, lives that are significantly shaped by their cultural and social locations. In chapter 2, I will provide the historical and social frameworks for this study.

2

Jains and Jainism in Patan

The people here participate in shining devotion, gifting, morality, and asceticism; the mendicants are firm in upholding the blossom of equanimity; the many Jain temples are blessed with a multitude of images; and even in time of drought the people obtain success in religious actions by means of their merit.

The merchants here have built up a mountain of gold; there are many playful young women with swift feet and side-glancing doe-like eyes; gifting is given as if to a divine tree which will sing their praises; and even those focused on *mokṣa* at once touch that true excellence amidst the pleasures of transmigration.

Jinodayasūri, C.E. 1375[1]

Different Śvetāmbar Mūrtipūjak Jain communities, whether in Bombay, Gujarat, or Marwar, do not exhibit striking dissimilarities in the values and ideologies expressed in and through annual festivals, asceticism, lay-mendicant interaction, and temple ritual. There are important regional differences in the cultural styles through which these values are expressed, and the extent to which different values are emphasized, but the values themselves are largely the same. This is not the case, however, for history and social structures, as these are regionally much more distinctive.[2] The history of Patan is important for the self-identity of the Jains of Patan, in large part because of the central role Jains have played in this history for over a millennium. For many centuries before the establishment of Ahmedabad in 1411, Patan was the capital of the Cāvaḍā, Caulukya, and Vāghelā dynasties, who at their height controlled much of what is today Gujarat and southern Rajasthan. The Jains of Patan were centrally involved in the activities of these dynasties, and in the social, economic, and political history of western India. Patan Jains of today are well aware and proud of the deeds of the great Patan Jains of the past. A full history of the Jains of Patan would require a separate book; but some sense of that history and of Jain perceptions of it is necessary for a fuller understanding of the cultural world in which Patan Jains situate themselves.

The Town of Patan

Patan is a trading and service town seventy-eight miles northwest of Ahmedabad, the principal city of Gujarat. For the traveler, the more relevant fact is that it takes three and a half hours to reach Patan from Ahmedabad by bus. Few people take the train to Patan, since the trip is several hours longer than it is by bus. The railway line to Patan, built during the time when it was part of the northern district of Baroda State, was a meter-gauge branch line. The only passenger service consisted of slow local trains, known popularly as *bāpunī gāḍī*, "grandpa's train." The line dead-ended several miles to the north in the village of Kakoshi, and from the late 1980s ended in Patan itself, before the floods of 1997 washed out several bridges and brought all rail traffic in and out of Patan to a halt.

The city is situated on the banks of the Sarasvati River, which in even the best of times was never more than a seasonal river that dissipated into the desert of the Little Rann of Kacch to the southwest of Patan. It is one of several such rivers known as "virgins," because they never reach the ocean, considered to be the husband of all rivers in India. In recent years, the Sarasvati was dammed upstream and so has ceased to flow at all. Historical references to the Sarasvati and the Sarasvati Mandal (the "circle" comprising the river valley and its watershed) indicate that the river as the center of an eco-social area was formerly of greater significance than it is at present.

The drive from Ahmedabad to Patan is through increasingly dry and brown countryside, with fewer and fewer trees. The landscape becomes even more desertlike to the west of Patan, as one comes closer to the Rann of Kacch. Approaching Patan from the south or east, on either of the two main roads from Ahmedabad, one first passes the large wholesale grain market on the eastern edge of town and crosses under the railroad tracks before coming to the bus station. The bus station on the east side of town is nestled against one of the few remaining stretches of the wall built around Patan by the Marāṭhās in the eighteenth century. Entering the old town from the bus station, one passes close to the remains of one of the eighteenth-century gates, and then comes to the main bazaar street, which bisects Patan on an east-west axis. The names on the signboards in front of the shops in the bazaar indicate that many of them are owned by Jains. Many smaller streets and alleyways run off from the main bazaar in both directions. Pīmpḷāno Śerī, a narrow street running north from the center of the bazaar, takes one to an area dense with Jain temples, including that of Pañcāsar Pārśvanāth, the most important Jain temple in town, and other Jain institutions.

The neighborhoods on all sides of this street are inhabited by Jains. Neighborhoods themselves are clearly defined. There are usually between thirty and fifty narrow, deep, and tall houses in each neighborhood. Many of the houses are expensive structures built in the 1920s and 1930s, when their owners made money in Bombay, Burma, and elsewhere. They all face inward onto a few adjoining narrow alleyways, and these alleys in turn lead to a single gate, which in earlier times was closed every night for security. Nowadays the doors of the gates rarely can be closed. But they are still solid structures, with a small residence situated above the gate for the neighborhood watchman. In some neighborhoods, the temple is located on a central open square, and in others it is located on one of the side streets. Although the fronts of most Patan Jain temples are covered with brightly painted, carved figures dating from the nineteenth and twentieth centuries, the temples are basically large, houselike buildings. Only in the twentieth century have patrons started rebuilding the neighborhood temples in the classical style associated with temples at pilgrimage shrines. Each neighborhood has a small shrine to a protector deity, sometimes a shrine to the snake-god Ghoghā Bāpjī located in a common area, and sometimes a shrine to a male protector deity located inside the Jain temple. If the neighborhood has an open square—and most of them do—it is also likely to contain a raised platform for feeding birds (see Figure 2.1).

Taking either of two narrow streets to the south from the same intersection of the main bazaar with Pīmpḷāno Śerī, one passes more Jain-owned shops and comes to still more Jain neighborhoods. In the southernmost part of town, there is a large Muslim neighborhood.[3] At the western end of the main bazaar, after passing under the Triple Gate and clocktower built several decades ago by a wealthy Bombay-based Hindu industrialist, one comes to the town library, the city hall, and the

Figure 2.1. Jain neighborhood in Patan, showing a bird feeder in central square and a shrine of Ghoghā Bāpjī at the base of the bird feeder. September 1995.

remains of the eighteenth-century Marāṭhā fort, which itself was built on the site of older forts. To the west and south of Patan are extensive Muslim cemeteries. The Hindu and Jain cremation grounds are outside the gate to the north, near the sandy bed of the Sarasvati. To the northwest of town are the important archaeological remains from the Caulukyan era: the Rāṇīnī Vāv stepwell, the Sahasraling tank, and several Muslim tombs and mosques that incorporate parts of Hindu or Jain temples in their structures. Other Caulukyan era remains are found to the west (including, according to local tradition, the ruins of Hemacandra's monastery) and south of town.

The population of Patan according to the 1991 census was 96,109, making it the second largest city in Mehsana district (Varsani 1991:63). It is a major retail and wholesale trading center for the surrounding villages. Because of low annual rainfall, northern Gujarat was formerly largely a single-crop area. Dual cropping has become possible with the increase in the number of tube wells in recent decades. Previously the dominant crops were grains such as millet (Gowda 1944:18), but in the years since independence there has been a shift to cash crops such as cotton, groundnut (peanut), rape, mustard, and castor (Rajyagor 1975:270–71). The resulting increased monetization of the agricultural economy has benefited Patan through the growth of activity in the wholesale grain market on the eastern edge of town, and through the increased purchasing power of farmers who visit Patan's busy retail market areas.

Recent decades have also seen the growth of Patan as a major service center in northern Gujarat. The city has the most extensive medical services in Gujarat north of Ahmedabad. It has long been an educational center, and the establishment in Patan of the headquarters of the new North Gujarat University in 1986 has spurred new growth in this area. Patan also provides other professional services such as legal and accounting services.

Patan was once famous for its various crafts, such as weaving, wood carving, clay toys, and pottery. All of these have seriously declined in recent decades, and no longer make significant contributions to Patan's economy. Due to the lack of adequate electrical power and water, Patan has not developed as an industrial center. Drilling for oil and natural gas in the area by the Oil and Natural Gas Commission since the mid-1980s has made a slight contribution to the city's economy, but finds have not been as significant as in other parts of Gujarat.

As of 1971, Jains made up 5.66% of the total population of Patan.[4] In 1901, they constituted 15.29%,[5] and as recently as 1931 the Jains were 11.12%[6] of the total Patan population. The twentieth century has seen a massive emigration of Jains from Patan to Bombay and elsewhere, which has been offset only in part by an immigration of Jains from villages in northern Mehsana district and Banaskantha district.

Patan in Jain History

The historical origins of the Jain tradition lie far to the northeast of Patan, in the present-day state of Bihar, but within a few centuries of the death of Mahāvīra the

Jains had spread to most parts of India. The earliest archaeological evidence for the presence of Jains in western India comes from a set of twenty rock-cut cells near Junagadh in Saurashtra, dated to the second century C.E. (Shah 1974:89–90). Jain bronze images from the sixth and seventh centuries have been found in Mahudi, in eastern Mehsana district (Sastri 1939:6–10); in Akota near Baroda (Shah 1959); and Valabhi in Saurashtra (Shah 1952:36). Stone images from the fourth century have been found in Dhank in Saurashtra (Sankalia 1938), and from the late sixth or early seventh century in Idar (Shah 1961). Literary evidence also indicates a Jain presence in the area. For example, Vinayavijaya, in his seventeenth-century *Subodhikā Ṭīkā* on the *Kalpa Sūtra* (pp. 15–16), preserves the legend that the *Kalpa Sūtra* was first recited to the Jain laity in 454 or 467 C.E. in the presence of King Dhruvasena in Anandapura, modern Vadnagar in eastern Mehsana district.

Valabhi, an important Gupta center and then capital of the Maitraka dynasty from the fifth to eighth centuries, was the site of two Jain councils held to standardize the recensions of the scriptural "canon." The first was held under Ācārya Nāgasena in the mid-fourth century C.E., and the second one under Devardhigaṇi Kṣamāśramaṇa in either 454 or 467 C.E. (Kapadia 1941:63).[7] Medieval narrative traditions record that the Jain logician Mallavādisūri lived in Valabhi in the mid-fourth century (L. B. Gāndhī 1952). But Valabhi does not appear to have been in any sense a Jain stronghold, and the archaeological evidence points to a more prominent Buddhist presence there (Sankalia 1941:210; Virji 1955:178).

A more important influence on north Gujarat was the kingdom of the Gurjara-Pratihāras, based in Bhinmal (also known as Shrimal), in what is now southern Rajasthan, from the early seventh century, and then in Kanauj on the banks of the Ganga from the early ninth century. Bhinmal was a flourishing capital city, in which, according to both textual and inscriptional evidence, the Jains played a major role.[8] A thirteenth-century tradition, recorded both in an inscription and the *Śrīmālī Purāṇa*, says that Mahāvīra himself visited Bhinmal (K. C. Jain 1972:161). Most of the Jains of Patan and Gujarat trace their ancestry back to Bhinmal and the related nearby town of Osian, and claim to have migrated south over the intervening centuries.

The story of the founding of Patan, itself largely a Jain story, begins some thirty-five miles to the southwest, in the village of Panchasar.[9] In the eighth century, Panchasar was the seat of the Cāpotkaṭās or Cāvaḍās, a local dynasty. In the early years of that century, King Jayaśekhara was killed by a Gurjara-Pratihāra king. According to the *Prabandhacintāmaṇi* of Merutuṅga, the king's pregnant wife Rūpasundarī fled from the town into the surrounding countryside, where she gave birth to a son. Since he was born in the jungle, she named him Vanarāja (Forest King). One day when Rūpasundarī had gone off to gather fuel, the infant was seen by the Jain Ācārya Śīlaguṇasūri, who recognized from the infant's bodily signs that he was destined to further Jainism. The *ācārya* assumed that this meant the boy was to be a great mendicant, and so purchased the boy from his mother, and placed him in the care of the *sādhvī* Vīramati. When the boy was eight years old he was entrusted with the duty of preventing rats from eating the offerings of flowers and fruit in a Jain temple. He employed the distinctly non-Jain expedient of killing the rats, whereupon Śīlaguṇasūri decided that he should prepare the boy's horoscope. He saw that Vanarāja was destined to promote the Jain faith as a king, not a mendicant, and so the boy was given back into the care of his mother, and lived with his maternal uncle Sūrapāla, a local bandit. Vanarāja followed his uncle's profession for many years before he decided to settle down and build a capital. He and his ministers searched on the banks of the Sarasvati, near the town of Lakkharama.[10] There they were given a stretch of land by a herder named Aṇahilla, and so Vanarāja named the new capital Anahillapura. It was also known as Anahilla Pattana (Anahilla town), and from this comes the contemporary shortened name of Patan. The new capital was established in 746 C.E., and Vanarāja had himself enthroned as king. The royal lustration was performed by Śīlaguṇasūri and his disciple Devacandrasūri. Vanarāja was assisted in setting up and ruling his kingdom by a number of Jain laymen. In repayment and recognition of their assistance, Vanarāja arranged for the construction of a Jain temple to Pārśvanāth, and named the main image in the temple Pañcāsar Pārśvanāth, after his home town. This is still the most important temple in Patan, although the image is undoubtedly of a later date, and the temple has been relocated and totally rebuilt several times, most recently in the 1940s and 1950s (Dave 1976:213–14).[11]

The Cāvaḍās never controlled an area greater than the Sarasvati valley. They were supplanted by Mūlarāja, the founder of the Caulukya or Solaṅkī dynasty, in the mid-tenth century. Although Mūlarāja's donations were largely focused on the important Śaivite temple of Somnath on the Saurashtrian coast, he, built a Digambara and a Śvetāmbara temple in Patan (Dhaky 1968:294).[12]

The Caulukya kingdom, and Patan as its capital, reached their political and cultural zenith during the reigns of Jayasiṃha Siddharāja (r. 1094–1143 C.E.) and Kumārapāla (r. 1143–1175 C.E.).[13] The Caulukya rule stretched from Kacch to Malva, and from south Gujarat to Marwar (Sankalia 1941:202). Patan was an important link on the trade routes between the rich cities of north India and the ports of western India (V. K. Jain 1990:115–16). The importance of Patan was always as a trading entrepot, not as a military center, and it lacked any significant fortifications until the fourteenth century (R. N. Mehta 1983). The reigns of Jayasiṃha Siddharāja and Kumārapāla also saw a highwater mark for Jain influence at the political level in Gujarat. Jain laymen were influential both as merchants and as government ministers, and Jain mendicants were influential as spiritual and intellectual advisors.

In the contemporary Gujarati historical imagination, the greatest of the Caulukyas was Jayasiṃha Siddharāja. He and his queens are credited with the construction of massive public projects throughout Gujarat, many of which are either still in existence today or are famous ruins. Jayasiṃha had close contact with many of the Jain mendicants who came to Patan. During his reign, in 1125 C.E., a famous debate occurred in Patan between the Śvetāmbara Devasūri and the Digambara Kumudacandra on the disputed questions of whether or not the enlightened but not yet liberated soul eats while still embodied (Dundas 1985), whether or not a woman can attain liberation (Jaini 1991a), and whether or not a mendicant must wear clothes. It was held in the royal court, with Jayasiṃha himself as judge. Kumudacandra was defeated by Devasūri's eloquence and logic, even though he tried to counter the Śvetāmbara by magically lodging a hair ball in Devasūri's throat. The result was the banishment of all Digambara mendicants from

Patan, and Jain historians credit this event with the virtual disappearance of Digambara Jains from Gujarat (Bühler 1936:14–15).

Devasūri was assisted in the debate by a more famous junior colleague, Ācārya Hemacandrasūri. Hemacandra was born as Caṅgadeva in 1088 in Dhandhuka, southwest of Ahmedabad, in a Jain family. His mother gave him to the mendicant Devacandra (later Devasūri) when he was just five years old, and he was initiated into the mendicant order as Somacandra. After thorough training under several mendicants, he was promoted to the post of *ācārya* in 1109, at the age of only twenty-one, and took the new name Hemacandra. He eventually became the court scholar and annalist of Jayasiṃha.

Jayasiṃha Siddharāja died without a son, and was succeeded by his grand-nephew Kumārapāla. Jain historians portray Hemacandra as being instrumental in Kumārapāla's accession. Kumārapāla was the one king in the Caulukya dynasty who personally became a Jain. Under the guidance of Hemacandra, he took the twelve vows (*vrat*) of a Jain layman. Following this "conversion," Kumārapāla requested his teacher Hemacandra to compose several books on the Jain religion. These were the *Triṣaṣṭiśalākāpuruṣacaritra*, a telling of the Jain universal history; the *Yogaśāstra*, on how to be a proper Jain layperson; and the *Vītarāga Stotra*, a hymn in honor of the Jina, which describes the proper Jain understanding of divinity. Kumārapāla is credited with the establishment of twenty-one libraries (Dalal 1937:33), and with building even more temples.[14]

During the reign of Kumārapāla, the symbolic center of the Śrīmāḷī Vāṇiyās, the most important merchant caste in north Gujarat, shifted from Bhinmal/Shrimal in Marwar to Patan. Jain Vāṇiyās had been migrating from Bhinmal into Gujarat for many centuries, as is evidenced by the ministers who aided Vanarāja Cāvaḍā. This migration accelerated after the mid-ninth century, when the capital of the Gurjara-Pratihāras was shifted north from Bhinmal to Kanauj (Sankalia 1941:210), and after the Rāṣṭrakūṭa invasions of the Gurjara kingdom in 915 and 940 and the sacking of Kanauj by Mahmud of Ghazni in 1018 (Majmudar 1960:219, 221). According to legend, a later impetus was a twenty-five-year drought in Bhinmal, from 1119 to 1144 C.E. (A.P. Śāh 1953:57). According to the *Śrīmāḷī Purāṇa* (Dave 1967:95–96; Parmar 1990:48), the caste *purāṇa* of the Śrīmāḷī Brāhmaṇs and Vāṇiyās, the main image of Mahālakṣmī in Bhinmal was shifted to Patan in 1147 C.E. at the request of a Śrīmāḷī Vāṇiyā named Sunand. Also shifted at this time were the wooden images of Jagatsvāmī Sūrya, caste god of the Śrīmāḷī Brāhmaṇs, and his wife Rāndal Devī. According to local legend, all three of these images are still found in Patan in the Mahālakṣmī temple in Mahālakṣmīno Pāḍo.[15]

In the historical imagination of the Jains of Gujarat, Kumārapāla represents one of the high points of that history. Another came a century later, with the Jain brothers Vastupāla (d. 1240 C.E.) and Tejaḥpāla (d. 1248–1252 C.E.). They were ministers for the Vāghelā feudatory princes Lavaṇaprasāda (d. 1232–1238 C.E.) and his son Vīradhavala (d. 1238 C.E.) of Dhavalakka (modern Dholka); the latter's son Vīsaladeva eventually supplanted the last Caulukya king (Sandesara 1953:26–34). Vastupāla and Tejaḥpāla were simultaneously government ministers, military generals, and merchant princes. In the words of Bhogilal Sandesara (1953:20), "by their valour and statesmanship [they] spread the power of the Vaghelas in the entire region between the rivers Sabarmati and Narmada, and having established peace and order in the whole of Gujarat made the country secure from disruptive forces." The brothers became fabulously wealthy, and used this wealth to further the glory of Jainism. They built spectacular temples at Abu and Girnar, and the poet Arisiṃha, a contemporary of the brothers, gives a description in chapters 4 through 10 of his *Sukṛtasaṃkīrtana* of the vast congregational pilgrimage they led to the holy mountains of Shatrunjay and Girnar in Saurashtra. Arisiṃha also lists forty-three Jain religious endowments throughout Gujarat paid for by Vastupāla, which included the renovation of the temple of Pañcāsar Pārśvanāth in Patan. Other sources (Dalal 1937:33) say that Vastupāla spent 180 million rupees on three libraries in Patan.[16]

The rule of the Vāghelās came to an end with the conquest of Gujarat by the armies of 'Alā' al-Dīn Khaljī in the very last years of the thirteenth century. 'Alā' al-Dīn appointed his brother-in-law Alap Khān to rule as governor of Gujarat from Patan, now a provincial capital of the Tughluq Sultanate. Although there was undoubtedly great destruction of Jain temples as well as other religious and secular buildings during the original plunder of Patan (the Adina mosque built by Alap Khān from Jain and Hindu temples was the largest in Gujarat until the eighteenth century), much of this was probably limited to the royal citadel. The present city of Patan lies slightly to the southeast of the ruins of the Caulukyan capital. The evidence of extensive temple building and image consecration in the early decades of the fourteenth century, as well as the description of the town as "New Patan" by the Jain poet Ambadevasūri in his *Samarārāsu* (5.6) composed in 1315, have been taken by some scholars to indicate the rebuilding of a largely new city after its destruction (Dave 1976:178, Kalyāṇvijaygaṇi 1928:16–19, Sāṇḍesarā 1976a:12). This evidence can also be interpreted as indicating significant continuity in the population of Jain merchants. Certainly Patan continued to be an important city as the provincial capital of the Tughluq Sultanate. S. C. Misra (1982:68–70) notes that Alap Khān went to great lengths to ensure cordial relations with the Jain merchants, whose continued prosperity was vital to the new rulers. Alap Khān not only allowed a wealthy Jain of Patan, Samaru Śāh, to undertake the renovation of the temples of Shatrunjay in 1315 but also made a personal contribution to the project. A letter from Jinodayasūri in Patan to Lokahitācārya in 1375, quoted at the beginning of this chapter, indicates that the Jain population of the city was then flourishing. Jinodayasūri spent the rainy season of 1375 in Patan with his nine mendicant disciples at the request of a Jain layman named Vira, after Vira had led a congregational pilgrimage to Shatrunjay, Girnar, and Somnath. Vira is called a *mantri*, "government minister," and may well have had an official position in the city or state administration, although this was probably merely a matter of elegant language on the part of the author, as Jinodayasūri calls many other laymen *mantri*.

The historical event with the most profound impact on the Jains of Patan was Ahmed Śāh's shift of the capital of Gujarat from Patan to his newly founded city of Ahmedabad in 1411 C.E. Patan went into a gradual economic decline from which it has never fully recovered. Its condition since the seventeenth century has been further aggravated by increasing soil dessication, which has had a negative long-term impact on trade in agricultural goods (R. N. Mehta 1995:85). This has only recently been counteracted by the digging of tube wells and the shift to cash crops.

The fortunes of Patan and Ahmedabad have been tied to each other in an inverse relationship since the fifteenth century. In the decades in the eighteenth century of political turmoil and economic instability in Gujarat due to frequent Marāṭhā incursions, raids, and invasions, Ahmedabad went into a decline, while Patan again revived. In the first half of the eighteenth century, when Ahmedabad was held by successive Muslim and Marāṭhā leaders, Patan was the capital of a local Muslim ruler, Javān Mard Khān Bābī. In 1763, the Marāṭhā Dāmājīrāv Gāykvāḍ [Gaekwad] captured Patan, and in 1766 shifted his capital from Songadh in south Gujarat to Patan. Under Marāṭhā rule, the present wall was built around Patan, the bottom half using stones from the ruins of old Patan, and the top half being built of brick (Tod 1839:229). The Marāṭhās also leveled the great Adina Mosque. Dāmājīrāv died in Patan in 1768 (allegedly from an unsuccessful alchemical experiment), and the victor of the ensuing succession struggle was Sāyājīrāv, whose base at Baroda then became the capital of the state. Patan was again reduced to a small town, this time in the northern district of Baroda State.

The shift of the center of political and economic power from Patan to Ahmedabad in the fifteenth century also had the result that the Ahmedabad Jain *saṅgh* (congregation) replaced that of Patan as the preeminent *saṅgh* in Gujarat. Whereas the entire Śvetāmbar community was convened in Patan in 1248 to discuss issues of mendicant practice (Shah 1955a), in later times councils were more likely be held in Ahmedabad, as have been several in the twentieth century (Cort 1995b). The important pilgrimage site of Shatrunjay, the symbolic center of Gujarati Jaindom, was under the overlordship of the Patan Jains from the time of Jayasiṃha Siddharāja and Kumārapāla, but in the sixteenth century came under the control of the Ahmedabad Jains (R. D. Desāī 1983:50–55).

The establishment of British rule over Gujarat in the late eighteenth and early nineteenth centuries led to a final great change in the fortunes of Patan and its Jain population. The British took over Ahmedabad in 1817, and gradually restored its position as the economic capital of Gujarat. By the middle of the nineteenth century, Ahmedabad had so recovered that in 1848 the Jain merchant Haṭhīsiṅg Keśrīsiṅg could spend one million rupees on the construction of a large temple near his bungalow outside the northern gate of the city (Gillion 1968:56).

Patan, on the other hand, was by then a relatively unimportant town within the dominions of the Gaekwads of Baroda. Many of the Jains in Patan were shopkeepers, moneylenders, pawnbrokers, and landlords of agricultural land in surrounding villages. Desai and Clarke (1923:330) report that the wealthier businessmen focused their business on insurance for long-distance trade and on the growing opium trade based in southern Rajasthan and northern Gujarat. The need for insurance was eliminated by the peace and stability of British rule, combined with the development of the railroad system. Opportunities in the opium trade were sharply curtailed in 1878, when its manufacture and sale were made a state monopoly (1923:388).

As a result of the restricted possibilities for commerce in Patan, many Patan Jains joined Jains (and others) in the massive migration from all over western India to Bombay in the late nineteenth century. They did not move to Ahmedabad, which at the time was seeing a boom in the textile manufacture industry, because the economy there was already closely controlled by Ahmedabad families, and presumably also because of the long-standing rivalry between Patan and Ahmedabad Jains. Bombay, on the other hand, was an economic frontier city, with great possibilities for immigrants. Some of the first to come were jewelers to princely families. The Jain family of Amīcand Pannālāl, who was the personal jeweler to the Nizam of Hyderabad, contributed most of the money to the Ādīśvar Jain temple in Valkeshvar. Built in 1904, this is one of the oldest and most important Jain temples in Bombay. The trust that manages this temple, the Amīcand Pannālāl Ādīśvar Temple Trust, continues to be a major contributor to temple renovations in Patan. Other Patan Jains went into the hardware, machinery, chemical, and pharmaceutical businesses. There was thus a major shift among Jains from moneylending and small-scale (often retail) commerce to manufacturing and wholesale commerce. As Patan Jains became successful in Bombay, more and more followed. Writing for the 1911 census, G. H. Desai (1911:58) noted that between 1901 and 1911 there had been a 14% decrease in the Jain population of the northern province of Baroda state, in which Patan was located, due principally to migration to Bombay. There was a temporary lull in the migration during the depression of the 1930s and the Second World War, when many Jains moved back to Patan. But the migration accelerated in the years following independence, and now the vast majority of Patan Jains reside in Bombay. Significant colonies of Jains from Patan are also found in Kobe, Japan, where they are involved in the pearl business, and in Rajkot. A 1982 residence list of the Pāṭaṇ Jain Maṇḍaḷ, the Bombay-based circle of Mūrtipūjak Jains whose native place is Patan, gives the total population of Patan Jains as 11,596. Of these, 8,861 (76%) resided in Bombay, 1,746 (15%) in other places such as Ahmedabad, Rajkot, Japan, and the United States, and only 989 (9%) still resided in Patan (Pāṭaṇ Jain Maṇḍaḷ 1982:5).[17] The economic niche formerly occupied by the Jains who have migrated to Bombay has been filled in part by other castes, such as Paṭels, but also by Jains who have migrated to Patan from villages and small towns in Mehsana and Banaskantha districts. As of the 1971 census, there were 3,648 Jains resident in Patan (Doctor 1975:224).[18] No more than 25% of these are natives of Patan; the rest are recent immigrants. The control of the various Jain institutions in Patan, however, remains almost exclusively in the hands of Patan Jains who live in Bombay.

Mendicant Lineages

The close interaction between the laity and the mendicants in terms of both organization and practice is a feature that distinguishes the Jains from many if not most Hindu traditions. The details of social organization are also central to the ways in which the Jains understand their own tradition. Ideas and doctrines do not exist in a social vacuum. They exist only as they are studied, taught, and practiced in the lives of people both individually and collectively, and the continuity of those doctrines is dependent upon the continuity of the social institutions that value and preserve those doctrines. Social structures are inextricably interwoven with ideologies and practices in any religious tradition. Changes in ideology or practice are mirrored by changes in social structure, and vice versa. The profound changes in Śvetāmbar Mūrtipūjak mendicant organization and conduct over the past hundred years are in large part the result of an ideologically driven reform movement.

The basic units into which the mendicant community is subdivided, in order of size and inclusiveness, are the *gacch*, *samudāy*, *parivār*, and *saṅghaḍā*.[19] The history of the Śvetāmbar Mūrtipūjak mendicants is the history of these subdivisions. As Kendall Folkert (1993:153–66) has stressed, the history of the Jains will be understood only partially until more research is done on these subdivisions.[20] These units, and the nature of Śvetāmbar Mūrtipūjak mendicancy as a whole, have not been static over time. The mendicant community has undergone dramatic changes in the past century. In the mid-nineteenth century, full-fledged "liberation-seeking" mendicants (*saṃvegī sādhus*) were rare, and most mendicants were *yatis*, who resided in one place, handled money, and followed other practices perceived as "lax" (*śithil*) by ideologues. In the course of the past century, the *yati* institution has almost totally disappeared, whereas the number of *sādhus* has increased tremendously. There is no single, clear-cut answer as to why these changes have occurred, but their importance for the constitution of contemporary Śvetāmbar Mūrtipūjak society cannot be overestimated. These changes are indicative of some of the ways in which ideological agendas can directly shape social practice.

The most important division within Jain society through the centuries has been that between the Śvetāmbars and the Digambars. The difference between these two sects is in large part that of mendicant praxis, as indicated by their names, which refer to the dispute concerning whether the true *sādhu* should shun all clothing and be clad only by the directions (*dig-ambara*), or else should wear simple white robes (*śveta-ambara*).[21] This major sectarian difference also partially overlaps a geographical one: Śvetāmbars have lived mostly in Gujarat, Rajasthan, and the Panjab, whereas Digambars have lived in urban north and central India, southern Maharashtra, and Karnataka. In the twentieth century, these patterns have broken down, as Jains from all parts of India have moved to the major metropolitan centers in pursuit of economic opportunities.

The Śvetāmbar Jains have undergone further division. The Sthānakvāsī sect gradually separated from the other Śvetāmbars between the mid-fifteenth and early seventeenth centuries C.E.[22] The origins of the Sthānakvāsīs lie in a movement initiated in the mid-fifteenth century by the layman Loṅkā (or Lumpakā) Śāh in Ahmedabad, partly in response to perceived laxity in contemporary mendicant practice, and partly in opposition to worshiping images of the Jinas. Although Loṅkā Śāh rejected image worship, his successors, who formed the Loṅkā Gacch, accepted it once again. In the mid-seventeenth century, the mendicants Lavjī Ṛṣi, Dharmsiṃhjī, and Dharmdāsjī, along with their followers, broke away from the *yatis* of the Loṅkā Gacch and their perceived lax behavior. This new movement eventually became the Sthānakvāsīs, those who reside in halls (*sthānak*) in contrast to the temple-dwelling *yatis*. Lavjī was also responsible for two of the most immediately noticeable facets of Sthānakvāsī practice: The mendicants always wear a *muhpattī*, a cloth over the mouth, and image worship is rejected. The Terāpanthīs split off from the Sthānakvāsīs under the mendicant Bhīkhanjī in 1760, over issues of authority, perceived lax practices, and Bhīkhanjī's doctrine that giving assistance to living beings other than mendicants is futile from a religious perspective.[23] The remaining, numerically dominant section of the Śvetāmbars came to be called the Mūrtipūjaks, "image worshipers," in contrast to the iconoclastic Sthānakvāsīs and Terāpanthīs. In Rajasthan they are often known also as Mandirmārgīs, "temple goers." Mūrtipūjaks and Sthānakvāsīs are found throughout the areas inhabited by Śvetāmbars, whereas the Terāpanthīs are found primarily in Rajasthan in Marwar and Shekhavati, and areas inhabited by migrants from there. Mūrtipūjak mendicants can be distinguished from Sthānakvāsī and Terāpanthī mendicants in that they carry their mouth-cloths in their hands, whereas the latter always wear them tied in front of their mouths.

The basic subdivision within the Śvetāmbar Mūrtipūjak mendicant community is the *gacch*, which can be translated as "those who travel together." The *gacchs* as organizational units gradually supplanted four *kulas* (lineages) in the first several centuries of the second millennium C.E., although Paul Dundas (1993:252) notes that as late as the mid-thirteenth century, referring to the four *kulas* was a convenient shorthand way of indicating the totality of the Śvetāmbar mendicant community. According to Jain tradition, the *kulas* (Candra, Nirvṛti, Vidyādhara, and Nāgendra) had been established by Vajrasenasūri in the first century C.E. during a time of drought, when it was necessary to disperse the mendicant community.[24]

A large number of *gacchs* existed in medieval times, with the number eighty-four often given as a convenient shorthand.[25] There are currently five Mūrtipūjak *gacchs*: the Tapā, Añcal, Khartar, Paican (Pārśvacandra), and Tristuti. The vast majority of contemporary Mūrtipūjak mendicants belong to the Tapā Gacch. It has been dominant in Patan and much of Gujarat for most of the past century, if not longer. It currently comprises about 90% of the Mūrtipūjak *sādhus* and 85–90% of the total Mūrtipūjak mendicant community.[26] The Tapā Gacch was established in Chitor by Jagaccandrasūri in the early thirteenth century, in reaction to the lax discipline of the existing mendicants.[27] Because of Jagaccandra's own fierce austerities (*tapas*) over a twelve-year period, and his emphasis on ascetic practices by his followers, the *gacch* established by him became known as Tapā.

The other *gacchs* are much smaller, and have not had a presence in Patan for decades. For much of the medieval period, the Khartar Gacch was just as important in Patan as the Tapā Gacch. The foundational event of the Khartar Gacch was a public debate before King Durlabha in the royal court in Patan in 1024 C.E. Jineśvarasūri defeated the domesticated mendicants known as *caityavāsīs*, who argued that it was acceptable for Jain mendicants to live in temples and own property. He established that the proper mendicant conduct necessitated homelessness. He was given the title Kharatara, "formidable [in debate]," by the king, and the name was applied to his followers (Klatt 1882:248). Histories of the Khartar Gacch indicate that its leaders frequently came to Patan, both while it was the imperial capital and later.[28] There is still significant material evidence of the former presence of Khartar Gacch mendicants in Patan. The Hemacandra Jñān Mandir, the Jain library in Patan, contains an important collection of Advaita Vedānta philosophical texts copied in 1429 at the behest of Jinabhadrasūri of the Khartar Gacch. The temple of Vāḍī Pārśvanāth, the largest Jain temple in Patan for several decades after its complete renovation between 1908 and 1918, contains an important inscription from the time of the temple's first consecration in 1596, which gives the entire Khartar Gacch lineage (Cort 1994a, Sandesara 1976b, Singh 1987). A memorial temple (*thup*, from Sanskrit *stūpa*) to deceased Khartar Gacch mendicants contains seven inscriptions from the early seventeenth century.

Within the past century, the Khartar Gacch has all but disappeared from Patan, and survives only in Rajasthan (as well as Bombay, where all strands of Jainism are well represented). It is rare for any but Tapā Gacch mendicants to come to Patan. The temple of Vāḍī Pārśvanāth, for example, became the center for the *yatis* of the Vaḍī Pośāl branch of the Tapā Gacch. The other Khartar Gacch temple, the memorial temple dedicated to seven Khartar Gacch *sādhus* who are memorialized by marble footprints, is in a run-down condition.[29] Most of the time it is locked with the key in the care of a Hindu watchman. It is located in a field outside the town wall to the south, and its presence in the lives of Patan Jains is so minimal that I never learned of its existence in the twenty-one months I lived in Patan. Only after returning to the United States did I discover a printed reference to it (Jośī 1963), and I was able to visit it in 1990. An annual fair is held there in the month of Bhādarvo, which was described to me as more of an occasion for a family outing in the countryside than a religious celebration.

The Añcal Gacch for many centuries had a significant presence in Patan, but is now found largely to the southwest of Patan in Kacch and Saurashtra. A number of image inscriptions indicate that Añcal Gacch *ācāryas* were active in three adjoining neighborhoods in western Patan from the mid-fifteenth to the early-sixteenth centuries (Pārśva 1964). There is also a reference to an Añcal Gacch *upāśray* (hall where mendicants stay) in Patan in the late nineteenth century (Dharmsāgar 1929:410), and in the early twentieth century over 400 Patan Jains had some degree of affiliation with the *gacch* (Conference 1909:45).

Yatis: Domesticated Monks

In the mid-nineteenth century, the state of the mendicant community was very different from what it is today. Most Mūrtipūjak mendicants were not full-fledged *saṃvegī sādhus* who had taken and observed the five great vows (*mahāvrats*), but rather were *yatis*.[30] *Yatis*, commonly known in Gujarat as *gorjīs*, were mendicants who took lesser vows. Most of them took only the vow of celibacy in its *mahāvrat* form, and the other four in lesser forms that approximated to the *anuvrats* (Ḍuggaḍ 1979:341–42). The conflicts between *saṃvegī sādhus* and *yatis* were a continuation of those between *vanavāsī* ("forest dwelling," that is, itinerant) and *caityavāsī* (temple dwelling, that is, domesticated) mendicants that were a major feature in the rise of many of the *gacchs* (Premī 1956:478–95, Cort 1991b).

Each *gacch*, however, fell victim to what Michael Carrithers (1989) has called "domestication." This is the tendency for mendicants to settle in one place, abandon the observance of the full letter of mendicant praxis, and instead adopt what ideologues term "lax conduct." Oscillation between the domesticated conduct of *yatis* and the reformed conduct of *saṃvegī sādhus* has been a constant theme in Tapā Gacch history. Jagaccandrasūri established the *gacch* in the thirteenth century as a reform of the lax conduct of the Vaṭa or Bṛhad Gacch. In the very next generation there was a split between the lax Vāḍī Pośāl Tapā Gacch under Vijaycandrasūri and the *saṃvegī* Lodhī Pośāl Tapā Gacch under Devendrasūri, and the latter became the ancestor of the current *gacch*. However, the Lodhī Pośāl branch also became lax. It saw subsequent reforms under Ācārya Ānandvimalsūri in 1526 and under Paṅnyās Satyavijaygaṇi in 1653.[31] Most of the contemporary *saṃvegī sādhus* trace their pupilic descent back to Satyavijaygaṇi. A *saṃvegī sādhu* should maintain a peripatetic lifestyle, owning nothing and always walking barefoot on his journeys.

A *yati* sat on a *gādī* (throne), possessed property, resided in one place, and, in more recent times, traveled by mechanized conveyance such as trains and ships.[32] All of these are examples of lax behavior, according to the ideologues. *Yatis* also followed much less strict regimens of daily asceticism. Ideologues aver that *yatis* were concerned chiefly with magic (*mantra-yantra*), astrology, and medicine, rather than practices directed toward liberation. In Marwar, many also served as caste genealogists. Since the *yatis* were permanently resident in the major cities and towns, they played a much more important role in the daily religious life of the laity than did *saṃvegī sādhus*.[33]

The leader of a lineage of *yatis* was a *śrīpūjya*. In former times he traveled in a palanquin, was shaded by a parasol in public, and exhibited other signs of ascribed royal status. In medieval times, *śrīpūjyas* often lived in great splendor, and exercized great influence as wizards (*mantravādins*) and royal preceptors.[34]

There was no significant difference in dress between a *saṃvegī sādhu* and a *yati*. Both wore unstitched white upper and lower garments. Many *yatis* also wore elaborate shawls (Cort 1996a:628–30), and the donation of a shawl by a wealthy layman was a central part in the installation ceremony of a *śrīpūjya* (Ḍuggaḍ 1979:343–45). In the late nineteenth century, the *saṃvegī* Buddhivijay (better known as Buṭerāyjī) had his followers don yellow robes to distinguish themselves from the *yatis*.[35] A major visual distinction between the two comes from the expectation that *saṃvegī sādhus* will pull out all their head and facial hair on a regular basis, often twice a year. As a result, they tend to have a rather scraggly appearance. *Yatis* were exempt from this practice, and so often had a full head of hair and luxuriant mustaches, both signs of sensuality in India. This visual distinction between *saṃvegī sādhus* and *yatis* is clearly marked in paintings (Cort 1996a:628–30).

Several English-language descriptions of *yatis* from the middle of the nineteenth century give us a vivid portrait of the nature of Mūrtipūjak mendicancy at that time.[36] The few *saṃvegī sādhus* tended to be born Jains, although some were born in non-Jain families, and took mendicant initiation out of religious conviction. Most *yatis* were purchased as infants from the families of poor Paṭels, Brāhmaṇs, and Hindu or Jain Vāṇiyās. Some were first-born sons who had been dedicated to mendicancy in fulfillment of a vow. Others were said to be the illegitimate sons of Brāhmaṇ widows. The children were taught the basics of the Jain religion, trained to minister to the Jain laity, and initiated as *yatis*.

A further indication of the organizational structure of the *yatis* of the Tapā Gacch is seen in a letter of instruction issued in 1867 by Ācārya Vijay Dharaṇendrasūri, *śrīpūjya* of the major domesticated branch of the *gacch*, in which he told each *yati* where to spend the four-month rainy season retreat (Sandesara 1974). His letter listed over one hundred cities, towns, and villages (including Patan) throughout Gujarat. The geographical limits of Dharaṇendrasūri's authority are seen in that all of Marwar was listed as the responsibility of just a single *yati* and his immediate followers. The letter concluded by warning that any *yati* who exchanged or sold the rights to his assigned location was to be strictly censured.[37]

One of the major thrusts of the nineteenth- and twentieth-century reform movement was the gradual elimination of the *yati* institution, so that *yatis* are rarely found today in the main centers of Jain population in Gujarat.[38] This was accomplished largely by *saṃvegī sādhus* and lay leaders, who urged *saṅghs* to withdraw their patronage of the *yatis*, and more importantly to cease arranging for the social reproduction of the institution by not purchasing boys to succeed the *yatis*. The *yatis*' property was then appropriated by the lay Jains.

In the nineteenth century, there were seats of at least four or five *yatis* in Patan. Each seat included an *upāśray* (monastery) and sometimes a temple or other property of which the *yati* had legal possession, and which he bequeathed to his successor. Now there remains only one seat of a *yati*, in Ḍhanḍher Vāḍo. This was formerly the seat of a branch of the Puṇimā (also Pūṇamīyā, Pūrṇamīya and Pūṇamīo) Gacch.[39] After a series of lawsuits between the last two *yatis* and the lay Jain *saṅgh*, and at least one quarrel concerning the succession to the post (Dalal 1937:38), the last distinctly Jain *yati* had no formal successor. When he died, his cook, an illiterate Paṭel, successfully claimed to be his successor, and he in turn was succeeded by his Brāhmaṇ advisor, who now holds legal and spiritual rights to the seat, but does not claim to be a *yati*. His clientele is largely middle and low-caste Hindu. He gives advice on a wide range of spiritual, social, and emotional matters, and prescribes *mantras* and gives protective strings (to be tied around the right wrist) to counter spiritual obstacles. Similarly, the married descendant of the Puṇimā Gacch *yati* in nearby Chanasma, whose family name is Gorjī, has drifted to the margins of the Jain fold. He claims that he himself is a Jain, but he is not respected by any of the other Jains of the town, nor does he fulfill any of the Jain ritual functions formerly associated with *yatis*.[40] He serves primarily as the attendant of a shrine to the goddess Ambājī located in his house, and performs rituals to her for Hindu, Muslim, and Jain clients.

Thomas Zwicker's (11/25/84.1) description of the Tapā Gacch *yati* in the small village of Ved on the edge of the Little Rann of Kacch gives a good view both of the *yati* institution and of its demise. The parents of Premcandvijay, the last *yati*, were low-caste herders who had come from Marwar in the great famine of 1899–1902. They sold their one-year-old son, along with papers that claimed he was a Brāhmaṇ, to the Jain *saṅgh* of Ved for eighteen rupees. The *saṅgh* gave the boy to the contemporary *yati* to raise as his successor. Since Premcandvijay did not know even common *mantras* very well, the Jains of Ved turned to other sources for their magical needs. He was not replaced after his death in the mid-1970s. The lands that had been in Premcandvijay's possession were divided between the Jain *saṅgh* and a family of Brāhmaṇs who had come from Marwar some twenty-five years earlier and claimed to be related distantly to Premcandvijay.

There is no accurate information concerning the number of *saṃvegī sādhus* in the mid-nineteenth century, but various people have estimated the number to have been no more than several dozen.[41] In the mid-nineteenth century, several activist *sādhus* reinvigorated the institution of the *saṃvegī sādhus*. Over two-thirds of the more than 1,000 *sādhus* in the Tapā Gacch today trace their lineage back to Paṅnyās Maṇivijaygaṇi (1796–1879), known as Dādā (paternal grandfather).[42] One of his three disciples was Muni Buddhivijay (1807–1882), a former Sthānakvāsī *sādhu* who had been reinitiated as a Mūrtipūjak, but was still commonly known by his Sthānakvāsī name of Buṭerāyjī. He was very active in the Panjab among both mendicants and laity, convincing Sthānakvāsīs of the correctness of the Mūrtipūjak teachings. Among Buddhivijay's four disciples was another former Sthānakvāsī, the charismatic Ātmārāmjī (1837–1896). In 1876 in Ahmedabad, Ātmārāmjī was reinitiated as the Mūrtipūjak *saṃvegī sādhu* Ānandvijay, along with eighteen other Sthānakvāsī *sādhus*. Eleven years later in 1887, he was promoted to *ācārya* at Palitana in a ceremony sponsored by the lay leaders of the Mūrtipūjak *saṅgh*.[43] Since the *saṃvegī sādhus* had previously consisted of only lower-level mendicants at the levels of *muni* (monk) and *gaṇi* (group leader), and all the *ācāryas* were domesticated *śrīpūjyas*, this was an important event in the reform of mendicant practice to *mokṣa-mārg* ideals. Under the leadership of Ātmārāmjī and other similar-minded *sādhus*, and later under the umbrella of the Śvetāmbar Mūrtipūjak Conference founded in 1902, a wide-ranging campaign was waged to reform both mendicant and lay practices (Cort 1995b). As a result of this reform, the institution of the *yati* has virtually disappeared from Mūrtipūjak society in Gujarat. Furthermore, under the leadership of these charismatic *sādhus*, the Tapā Gacch became the dominant *gacch* of Mūrtipūjak mendicants.

Samudāys, *Parivārs*, *Saṅghaḍās*

In the course of a century, the number of *sādhus* within the Tapā Gacch has increased from several dozen to over 1,200. Much of this growth has occurred in the years since the Second World War. As the Tapā Gacch has grown, it has subdivided into about eighteen *samudāys* (literally "those with the same origin," that is, pupilic descendants of the same *sādhu*). The boundaries of a *samudāy* tend to be much fuzzier than the boundaries of a *gacch*, for there are subtle liturgical differences between *gacchs* but not between *samudāys*. Some *samudāys* have very coherent self-identities, and the authority of their leaders is fairly extensive. Others are looser structures, and there is a sense of kinship between *samudāys* that are closely related in terms of pupilic descent. In these *samudāys*, the attitude toward the nominal leaders is more one of respect for seniority than submission to authority (Cort 1999a).

Within a *samudāy*, the mendicants (usually no more than two or three dozen *sādhus* and perhaps twice as many *sādhvīs*) who follow one particular *ācārya* are usually known as a *parivār* (family). The *parivār* is an informal grouping, capable of great fluidity. If upon the death of the leader there is no successor who inherits his charisma, the *parivār* will simply dissolve into the larger *samudāy* of which it was a part.

A large *parivār* rarely travels or meets together, unless it is involved in a group pilgrimage or has some urgent business to discuss. Because such a large gathering of *sādhus* constitutes a heavy burden on the host lay *saṅgh*, and because the leader of the *parivār* will want to disperse his *sādhus* among his lay devotees to minister to their needs, a *parivār* of thirty *sādhus* is usually broken down into six or seven smaller groupings, usually called *saṅghaḍās*. These temporary groupings are even more informal and fluid than *parivārs*; the *sādhu* who is seniormost in terms of length of time since initiation is in charge of any *saṅghaḍā*.

Sādhvīs

There are many more *sādhvīs* than *sādhus* among the Śvetāmbars. In 1994, there were 4,233 *sādhvīs* in the Tapā Gacch, compared to only 1,205 *sādhus* (B. Jain 1994). The large number of female mendicants is one of the distinguishing features of the Jains in contrast to both the Hindu and Buddhist traditions. The preponderance of female mendicants is also of long standing; according to the *Kalpa Sūtra*, the mendicant congregation founded by Ṛṣabhanātha consisted of 84,000 *sādhus* and 300,000 *sādhvīs*; that of Neminātha had 18,000 *sādhus* and 44,000 *sādhvīs*; that of Pārśvanātha had 16,000 *sādhus* and 38,000 *sādhvīs*; and that of Mahāvīra had 14,000 *sādhus* and 36,000 *sādhvīs*. The present 3.5:1 ratio of *sādhvīs* to *sādhus*, therefore, is not a recent phenomenon, and *sādhvīs* have possibly always constituted a significant portion of the total mendicant population. Sources for a history of this important women's socio-religious institution, however, are nearly nonexistent. N. Shântâ (1985) gives some scattered references, and research in manuscript collections and temple inscriptions would add further information, but it is unlikely that it will ever be possible to reconstruct a fully adequate history of women's mendicancy in Jainism.

The demographics of the *sādhvī* population have also undergone a dramatic shift in the past century. Earlier, Jain women were married in their early teens, and often became widows before ever having children. Many of these widows became *sādhvīs*, and the majority of the *sādhvī* population consisted of widows. This has changed in the decades since Independence, due to the rise in the age of marriage and the improvement in health standards. Most Jain women are now married when they are in their early or mid-twenties, and so even if they become widows they are likely to have children. The need to raise the children means that becoming a *sādhvī* is less of a realistic option for a widow. Changing social attitudes toward widows also makes it less likely that a Jain widow feels that she has little choice but to become a *sādhvī*. Similarly, in the past a certain number of women became *sādhvīs* in reaction to an unsatisfactory marriage; nowadays, although divorce is still rare, it is increasingly possible for a woman to leave her husband and either return to her natal family or live on her own. Today the vast majority of *sādhvīs* have never been married, and becoming a *sādhvī* is now seen as an alternative vocation to that of housewife.[44]

Within the Tapā Gacch, *sādhvīs* occupy a somewhat marginal position vis-à-vis both *sādhus* and laity. As a matter of custom, *sādhvīs* do not preach.[45] In those *samudāys* that view themselves as the most orthodox in terms of the *mokṣa-mārg* ideology, *sādhvīs* are not permitted to study the most important texts on praxis;

they are expected to restrict their reading to devotional and inspirational texts in the vernacular. Nor are they allowed to perform any of the many image-related ritual functions that account for much of the *sādhus*' interaction with the laity. As part of mendicant praxis, *sādhus* and *sādhvīs* should not touch a member of the other gender; to do so, even accidentally, requires an expiation, usually a dietary restriction for one or more days. *Sādhus* command a degree of social respect, and as a result have a social presence, such that they rarely have to worry about accidentally touching a woman. But such is not the case with most *sādhvīs*, who as a result develop the skill in public of constantly sensing and avoiding the presence of men. *Sādhvīs* are frequently seen, in fact seen much more often than *sādhus*; but their presence seems to be symbolized by their practice of skirting crowds and avoiding contact. The many comments I heard, mostly from men but surprisingly often from women as well, concerning the relative ritual inutility and burdensomeness of having *sādhvīs* staying in a neighborhood indicates that this perception is not restricted to foreign male researchers.[46]

Temples, Upāśrays, and Saṅghs

The basic unit of lay organization is the *saṅgh*. This term has three different connotations within Jain society. As the *caturvidh* (fourfold) or *sakaḷ* (complete) *saṅgh*, it refers to the congregation of *sādhus*, *sādhvīs*, *śrāvaks*, and *śrāvikās*, that is, the totality of Jain society consisting of male and female mendicants and male and female laity. As the *sādhu saṅgh* or *sādhu-sādhvī saṅgh*, it refers to the totality of the mendicant community. Third, it refers to neighborhood or city-wide lay congregations.[47] Although such lay congregations are often affiliated with one particular mendicant *gacch* or *samudāy*, they function largely as autonomous units. Under the religious charities laws of contemporary India, most neighborhood *saṅghs* are legally constituted bodies with a board of trustees.

Two basic elements of lay Mūrtipūjak Jain religious behavior are worship of the Jinas through rituals directed toward images in a temple (chapter 3), and interaction with *sādhus* through either listening to sermons or participation in *sādhu*-like rituals that are not directed at images (chapters 4 and 5). Corresponding to these two forms of religious activity are two different religious buildings, the *derāsar* (temple) and the *upāśray*.[48]

An *upāśray* is a largely empty building, sometimes of two stories, with a central open hall used for sermons and large collective rituals, and several smaller side rooms where mendicants can study and eat in privacy (see Figure 2.2). Mendicants stay in an *upāśray* whenever possible, and the laity go there to take temporary mendicant vows and perform mendicant-like rituals.

Many Jains perform the rituals of *pūjā* and *darśan* at the temple every day, and so there is usually at least one temple in every neighborhood in which Jains live. This temple is built and maintained by the neighborhood *saṅgh*. In the case of a large neighborhood, where the large population causes congestion at the morning *pūjā*, the *saṅgh* might build a second temple. More often, the second (or third, etc.) temple in a neighborhood is built by a wealthy member of the neighborhood who

Figure 2.2. Modern *upāśray*, with decorations for *comāsu*. A *sādhu* sits on the raised dais to deliver sermons. Ahmedabad, October 1995.

wants to enhance his prestige and social renown by building a temple. Ideologues have promoted such construction, by stating that one gains great karmic merit from constructing a temple, since some of the merit generated by all those who henceforth worship in the temple accrues to the patron. Many of these were built as household temples, and then later opened to the entire *saṅgh*. In addition, in new suburban areas of Bombay, if a housing developer wants to attract Jains to his development, he will contribute to the construction of a temple in or near the development.

Few Jains perform rituals that require an *upāśray* on a daily basis. Most such rituals are performed communally on a periodic, calendrical basis. As a result, there is a need for fewer *upāśray*s than temples. *Upāśray*s are generally located so that one *upāśray* can serve several neighborhoods. It is the temple that is more likely to be the primary defining structure of a neighborhood *saṅgh*'s identity. An *upāśray* is not a necessary part of that self-definition; but if in addition to the temple the neighborhood *saṅgh* also possesses an *upāśray*, there is no need for residents to leave the neighborhood for any ritual functions, and the overlapping definitions of neighborhood and *saṅgh* are reinforced.

Saṅghs and Gacchs

Formerly, when different *gacchs* were active in Patan, and many of the mendicants were *yatis* who legally owned temples, most temples and neighborhood *saṅghs* were affiliated with one or another of the *gacchs*. Nowadays the organizational units of the mendicant *gacch* and the lay *saṅgh* overlap most clearly in the institution of the *upāśray*, and much less so in the temple. This is underscored by the ritual functions of these institutions. The *upāśray* and the mendicant-like rituals performed therein orient the laity toward the mendicants. Since image worship is largely a lay activity, the temple orients the laity more toward the Jina, although the connection between mendicants and temples is never totally severed. The temple, however, does not require the ongoing involvement of mendicants, but in the absence of mendicants, an *upāśray* is just an empty building. In some neighborhoods, the same building serves the two functions of *upāśray* and *vāḍī*, an eating hall used for caste, neighborhood, or *saṅgh* meals.

Overriding the neighborhood *saṅghs* is the sense that all of the Patan Jains constitute one single *saṅgh*, the "complete *saṅgh*" (*sakaḷ saṅgh*). This sense is especially strong in a city like Patan, where almost everyone is affiliated with the same *gacch*; but the notion of *sakaḷ saṅgh* also exists in cities where the *saṅgh* is subdivided into different *gacchs*. For example, in the town of Mandal, south of Patan on the route to Saurashtra, the Jain community is divided among the Tapā, Añcal, and Paican Gacchs. Each *saṅgh* has its own temple. In recent years, the *sakaḷ saṅgh* of Mandal has built a fourth temple that belongs to the *sakaḷ saṅgh* rather than to any one *gacch* (Zwicker 1984–1985:11/12/84.20).

The *sakaḷ saṅgh* in Patan exists much more on the level of ideology than actual practice or organization. There is no single legal entity that could be said to represent the *sakaḷ saṅgh*, although previously, when the municipal administration of Patan was in the hands of a Jain *nagarśeṭh*, he could speak with the authority of the *sakaḷ saṅgh* in many religious matters. The *nagarśeṭh* was an inherited post loosely equivalent to a mayor; the Patan Nagarśeṭh family was given this title and the accompanying rights and responsibilities, as well as the revenue from two nearby villages, by the Gaekwads in the eighteenth century. But even the *nagarśeṭh*'s authority was probably circumscribed by religio-political realities, that is, he could speak with full confidence in his authority only on noncontroversial matters, and did not have the authority single-handedly to resolve religious disputes. Today the *sakaḷ saṅgh* is the final authority within the Jain community, with authority over even the heads of the *samudāys*; but as long as there is no regularized and commonly recognized means for invoking a meeting of the *sakaḷ saṅgh*, and thereby invoking its authority, this authority remains largely on the level of abstract ideology, and cannot be directly translated onto the level of practice.[49]

At a more practical level, the Jains of Patan can be said to be divided into two *saṅghs*, those centered on the two citywide *upāśrays* of Sāgar and Maṇḍap. I must stress that although all Jains of Patan recognize the division between these two *saṅghs* in practice, in conversation they also deny that the division has any real importance. Jains resist allowing the practical realities of human divisions to insert themselves into the ideological concept of the unity of all Jains. These two citywide *saṅghs* are both based on their respective *upāśrays*; neither has any direct affiliation with a temple, although on occasions when an image is required, such as a chariot procession, nearby temples provide the mobile images. This division has developed over the past forty years, as the Tapā Gacch has loosely divided over issues of strictness of interpretation of proper mendicant conduct and concessions to the technological and social changes of the twentieth century.[50] Those who adhere to a stricter interpretation, brooking less compromise with modernity, gravitate toward Maṇḍap; those who are not quite as concerned with absolute strictness gravitate toward Sāgar.[51] This difference does not correspond to the informal division of the Tapā Gacch into Sāgar *samudāys* and Vijay *samudāys*, so distinguished by the lineage names of Sāgar or Vijay adopted by all Tapā Gacch *sādhus*. Sāgar Upāśray is considered to be the logical place for Sāgar *sādhus* to stay in Patan, but Vijay *sādhus* can and have stayed there, as well. The difference between the two *saṅghs* might appear slight to the outside observer, but issues of orthopraxy have always been much more divisive in India than issues of orthodoxy, and *mokṣa-mārg* ideologues tend to be very concerned with the details of praxis. Two examples will suffice to indicate the nature of the division. The great scholar Muni Puṇyavijay stayed in Patan for over ten years to organize the manuscript collection at the Hemacandra Jñān Mandir. During that time he stayed at Sāgar Upāśray, because the laity and *sādhus* associated with Maṇḍap objected to Puṇyavijay's use of an electric light to work at night. They considered this a violation of strictly interpreted mendicant praxis. Similarly, Ācārya Vijay Vallabhsūri also stayed at Sāgar, since the people associated with Maṇḍap objected to his involvement in issues of broader social reform, such as wearing *sādhu* robes made of *khādī*, the cloth made of homespun and handwoven cotton associated closely with the Gandhian movement. Neither camp, however, brooks mendicant practice that even remotely approximates that of *yatis*, and clearly the memory of the recent dominance of *yatis* underlies the emphasis on strictness. A further story told of Puṇyavijay underscores this. Another *sādhu*, seeing that Puṇyavijay was using an electric light, also began to use one, but in his case to read magazines and novels. When criticized by the laity for this, he pointed to Puṇyavijay's example, whereupon Puṇyavijay turned off his light and stopped working at night, lest he be the cause and excuse of another's laxity. The other *sādhu* was mortified that he had caused the great scholar to curtail his work. He asked Puṇyavijay to resume using a light a night, and promised never to use one himself. In general, laity treat all mendicants with respect and reverence, but there have been occasions when a particular *sādhu* has been criticized for staying too long at one *upāśray*, or otherwise seeming to become too closely involved in the affairs of a particular *saṅgh* or temple.

Sāgar Upāśray was formerly the residence of a *yati* (as were most of the *upāśrays* a century ago), and the seat of one Dayāsāgarjī Mahārāj is cemented into the floor in a central location. The present building was built in 1888, but that was a rebuilding of an older structure. Maṇḍap Upāśray (its actual name is Nagīnbhāī Poṣadhśāḷā, since the original construction was paid for by one Nagīndās Karamcand Saṅghvī) was built in 1925, at the request of two leaders of the *saṃvegī* revival, Ācāryas Kamalsūri and Nemisūri, and extensively renovated in 1964. Because the older *upāśrays* were the private property of *yatis*, the reformist *saṃvegī sādhus* often had to ask their lay followers to build new *upāśrays* for them to stay in. Maṇḍap is close to the pilgrimage temple of Pañcāsar Pārśvanāth, which also has an *upāśray*. But this was the residence of Patan's principal Tapā Gacch *yati* (whose wooden seat is still in the now dilapidated building), and so Maṇḍap was built to accommodate the *saṃvegī* reformers. To some extent, Maṇḍap attracts those Jains who have migrated to Patan from small villages in the past thirty years, whereas Sāgar attracts those Jains whose families have been in Patan for centuries.

A further, informal subdivision of the Patan *saṅgh* emerges when one looks at the *samudāy* affiliations of different *upāśrays*. Many neighborhood *upāśrays* do not have any specific affiliation. For example, the *upāśray* in Saṅghvīno Pāḍo was formerly the seat of a *yati* of the Lodhī Pośāl branch of the Tapā Gacch. With the disappearance of the Lodhī Pośāl lineage in the early twentieth century, this *upāśray* has not developed an affiliation with any *saṃvegī samuday*, and in fact has fallen into disuse. Other neighborhood *upāśrays* do have specific affiliations. The *upāśray* in Khetarvasī was built in 1929 under the influence of Paṅnyās Dharmvijay of the Ḍehḷāvāḷā Samudāy, and continues to be the *upāśray* where *sādhus* of this *samudāy* stay when they are in Patan. Similarly, the *upāśray* in Bhābhāno Pāḍo is affiliated with the Vimal Gacch (a branch of the Tapā Gacch), although none of its *sādhus* has been to Patan for many years due the diminution and near disappearance of the Vimal Gacch. The trust that manages both the neighborhood temple and the *upāśray* is known as the Bhābhā Pārśvanāth Jain Derāsar and Vimal Gacch Ārādhak [worshipers] Trust. The Jains of Rājkā Vāḍo, in the southern section of Patan, have always had a strong neighborhood identity, and the residents of the eleven Jain neighborhoods in the area have joined together to form a larger entity. The Jains of Rājkā Vāḍo tend to act as a unified whole, and consider themselves loosely affiliated with the Sāgar *samudāys*, and therefore also with Sāgar Upāśray. The Rājkā Vāḍo Jain Sabhā also has several small trusts to manage such undertakings as a Jain reading room, a religious school, a social welfare fund, and a fund for daily feeding of dogs and birds. Finally, the several new suburban *saṅghs* established since the 1960s have distinct identities. They have both temples and *upāśrays*, and the majority of the houses in these new suburbs are occupied, unlike most of the houses in the older, crowded downtown neighborhoods, which are largely unoccupied since their owners migrated to Bombay. This population density alone enhances community identity.

The situation was clearly very different as recently as the early twentieth century, before emigration to Bombay depopulated the Jain neighborhoods, and before the *saṃvegī* revival drastically changed the structures of the Mūrtipūjak *saṅgh*. When most of the mendicants were *yatis*, there was often fierce competition among them to have laity listed as members of their office (*daftar*), for the *yatis* could then demand financial and other support from those laity.[52] The 1909 *Jain Śvetāmbar Directory*, prepared in Bombay by the Jain Śvetāmbar Conference, listed six *gacch* affiliations among the fourteen *upāśrays* and *poṣadhśāḷās*[53] in Patan (see Table 2.1).

A separate list gives the *gacch* affiliation for the Jain population of Patan (see Table 2.2). Thus, ninety years ago the Patan Mūrtipūjak Jains were much more clearly divided in their affiliation.[54] Although the notion of the *sakaḷ saṅgh* presumably prevailed, at the operational level the Jains were divided among several different *gacchs*, and different laity owed allegiance to different *yatis*. Today, almost all Patan Mūrtipūjak Jains are affiliated with the Tapā Gacch, and allegiance to the different *samudāys* within the Tapā Gacch has not replaced the former allegiance to *yatis* of different *gacchs* in terms of exclusivity. As we will see in chapter 4, many

Table 2.1 *Gacch* Affiliations of *Upāśrays* and *Poṣadhśāḷās*, Patan 1909

Tapā Gacch	3
Sāgar Gacch*	1
Vimal Gacch*	1
Vaḍī Pośāl Gacch*	1
Khartar Gacch	1
Doḷiyā (?) Gacch	1

Source: Conference 1909:73

* part of Tapā Gacch

Table 2.2 *Gacch* Affiliation for Jain Population, Patan 1909

Tapā	2,749
Sāgar*	116
Devsūr*	7
Lodhī Pośāl*	51
Khartar	146
Sājī	3
Pūṇamīo	403
Raysūr	7
Loṅkā	18
Añcal	415
Gorakṣ†	16

Source: Conference 1909:45.

* part of Tapā Gacch

† The Gorakṣ or Goyarakṣa Gacch was a branch of the Añcal Gacch, established in the early sixteenth century (Klatt 1894:179 and Miles 1835:366).

individuals are devotees of *sādhus* belonging to different *samudāys*, but this allegiance does not translate onto the level of the neighborhood *saṅghs*.

The identity of the neighborhood *saṅgh* is reaffirmed in the ritual of the *varṣgāṇṭh* of the temple, the annual ritual on the anniversary of the day when the temple's main image was formally installed. In addition to the ritual of replacing the red-and-white striped flag atop the temple, on this day all members of the *saṅgh*, defined as those who reside in the neighborhood and pay a nominal annual membership fee (usually twenty-five or thirty rupees), gather for a communal meal. In cases where the vast majority of a *saṅgh*'s members reside in Bombay, many of the *saṅgh* members may return to Patan for the annual festival. This is especially the case if the festival falls during the popular May-June vacation period, when many people return to their native towns. This vacation period overlaps with the months of Cait, Vaiśākh, and Jyeṣṭh, when there are many astrologically auspicious days for consecrating and installing images, so many annual festivals fall during this period. Members of some *saṅghs* whose members mostly reside in Bombay gather there instead for a special meal on this day.

The network of the eighty neighborhood temples provides one element of self-definition for the Mūrtipūjak Jains of Patan.[55] Another element is provided by the two citywide temples that belong to no neighborhood *saṅgh*, but rather function as *tīrths*, shrines that serve as unifiers for the Patan Mūrtipūjak Jains and tie Patan into the nationwide network of other pilgrimage temples. The most important of these is Pañcāsar Pārśvanāth, the main image of which is intimately connected with the foundational history of Patan, and which was renovated (that is, totally rebuilt) at great expense between 1942 and 1960. The other *tīrth* is Śāmḷājī Pārśvanāth. Although this temple is not known to Jains outside of Patan, it is highly revered by almost all Patan Mūrtipūjak Jains, and the predawn *darśan* (viewing) at Śāmḷājī on New Year's morning is one of the few events attended by all Patan Mūrtipūjak Jains. This temple has also been expensively renovated from the ground up in a process starting in 1987 and continuing as of 2000. It is now the largest temple in Patan. The money for this renovation came almost exclusively from wealthy Jains now resident in Bombay.

Other Institutions

A number of other Jain institutions that are independent of *gacch* and *samudāy* affiliation further define the Mūrtipūjak Jains of Patan, and together make up a distinctive Jain culture. Most of these were built in this century, as Jains who had made money in Bombay (and elsewhere) contributed to the development of their native town. Many of them are located in the heart of Patan surrounding the temple of Pañcāsar Pārśvanāth. The number and variety of institutions in this neighborhood is found only in cities with a significant Jain population, and indicates what makes up a full-fledged Jain urban culture.

For the convenience of pilgrims who come to Patan, as well as Jains who come to Patan for other purposes such as business or studies, several *dharmśāḷās* (pilgrim resthouses) have been built downtown near Pañcāsar. The two oldest extant *dharmśāḷās* were built in the early years of the century, and are rarely used nowadays. In the 1970s, two new *dharmśāḷās* were built, one by the Bombay-based Pāṭan Jain Maṇḍaḷ and the other by the Pañcāsar Trust. These more closely resemble modern Indian businessmen's hotels, and are much more popular; the *dharmśāḷā* managed by the Pāṭan Jain Maṇḍaḷ has over 6,000 visitors per year.

For the dietary requirements of visiting Jains (and also mendicants), there is a *bhojanśāḷā* (eating house) downtown. It was started in an old house in 1899, and as it became more popular a new dining hall was constructed in 1983. Many businessmen and students purchase monthly passes, and some 250–300 people eat there daily. For those performing the specialized fast of *āyambil* (see chapter 5), an *āyambilśāḷā* was constructed in the Pañcāsar compound in 1943.

Jains have long emphasized the importance of the written word, and therefore of handwritten manuscripts and printed books. The traditional institutional expression of this is found in the manuscript libraries or *bhaṇḍārs* (Cort 1995d). Before the coming of printed books, these were frequently consulted both by mendicants and by learned laymen, although in recent years their importance has decreased for all but a handful of scholars. According to tradition, Kumārapāla established twenty-one *bhaṇḍārs* in Patan, and Vastupāla established three *bhaṇḍārs* at a cost of 180 million rupees (Dalal 1937:33). None of these medieval *bhaṇḍārs* has survived, and few manuscripts from that time are extant. There are over 25,000 manuscripts in Patan, distributed among three *bhaṇḍārs*. The earliest manuscript dates from the thirteenth century, and most date from the fifteenth century onward. Formerly the collections were kept either in cabinets or storerooms of *upāśrays*, or in specially built basements of temples. In the early twentieth century, the manuscripts were scattered among at least fourteen different collections, some in the possession of *yatis*, some in the possession of individual laymen, and some under the supervision of lay *saṅghs*. For much of the first half of this century, the renowned mendicant scholars Pravartak Kāntivijay, Muni Cāturvijay, and Muni Puṇyavijay studied, organized, and catalogued the collections, a process finished only recently by Muni Jambūvijay. Under external pressure from the government of Baroda state, and at the instruction of Kāntivijay and Ācārya Vijay Vallabhsūri, most of these *bhaṇḍārs* have been consolidated into one collection, for the housing of which the Hemacandra Jñān Mandir was built in the 1930s. This large building stands on a raised plinth (for protection from flooding) in downtown Patan near the temple of Pañcāsar Pārśvanāth. The manuscripts are kept in specially built airtight and white-ant-proof wooden boxes. The boxes are kept in locked metal cabinets, and the cabinets are inside three rooms, each of which has a heavy metal door similar to that found on a bank vault.

One of the oldest Jain institutions in Patan is the *pāñjrāpoḷ*, or animal shelter. The Pāṭan Mahājan Pāñjrāpoḷ was started in the 1850s, and is the largest and oldest *pāñjrāpoḷ* in Mehsana district. It has a small operation in downtown Patan, consisting of offices, a small cow barn, and a bird house, but most of its activities are in nearby Khalipur village, on land given to it for that purpose by the Baroda government. As with other *pāñjrāpoḷs* in Gujarat, this is not strictly a Jain institution, as the Mahājan or Merchants Association traditionally consisted of both Jain and Hindu merchants. But in Patan, Jains make up the largest percentage of the Mahājan, and so the major support for the *pāñjrāpoḷ* is from the Jain community.[56]

As the Jains of Patan migrated to Bombay, contacts among the networks of Patan Jains already in Bombay were central to the immigrants' success. In 1912, the Pāṭaṇ Jain Maṇḍaḷ was established in Bombay, to help Jains move from Patan to Bombay, and to improve the lot of Jains in Patan. The first undertaking of the Maṇḍaḷ was the establishment of a school (known as Jain Boarding) in Patan in 1914; the opening ceremony was presided over by the German Jainologist Hermann Jacobi.[57] A fund to provide assistance to fellow Patan Jains in Bombay was established in 1915. In subsequent years, the efforts of the Maṇḍaḷ have been divided between Patan and Bombay. In Patan, the Maṇḍaḷ has built a public dispensary, schools, technical institutes, a public swimming pool, and college hostels. In Bombay, the Maṇḍaḷ has established a reading room, cooperative stores, hostels, scholarships, a cooperative bank, and loan funds. A major undertaking was the construction of three large apartment buildings for Patan Jains on Marine Drive in Bombay in the 1930s, and later four smaller apartment buildings in Borivali. New buildings have more recently been constructed in Bhayandar. Under the Bombay Charities Act, the Maṇḍaḷ itself cannot be used as a mechanism for overtly religious donations, so it runs the Marine Drive Jain Ārādhak Trust, which has contributed to most of the temple renovations in Patan in recent years.

With the extensive migration of Jains to Bombay, the Jains of many neighborhoods in which there are several temples have found it increasingly difficult to maintain them. Eight such temples are managed by a citywide trust, the Dharamcand Abhecand Peḍhī. This trust also has a small shop in the Jain-dominated Dośīvat Bazaar downtown, which sells all the materials needed for image worship. Another institution, the Bhuvancandra Jñān Mandir, sells the paraphernalia needed by mendicants. These items are purchased by laity for gifting to mendicants. This institution also runs religious classes for children, as do several other *pāṭhśāḷās* (schools). The Hemacandra Jain Sabhā, established in 1904, runs a Jain reading room and library of printed books. For several years the Bhogīlāl Lahercand Institute of Indology, founded in 1980 by a wealthy Bombay-based Patan Jain, was located in Patan. Due to the difficulty of getting competent scholars to resettle in Patan, the research activities of the institute were moved to a site outside of Delhi in 1984, and the Patan staff has been reduced to a *paṇḍit*, a lay teacher who instructs *sādhvīs* in Sanskrit and Prakrit. Finally, Jains have donated money for a large number of public institutions in Patan, including high schools, hospitals and clinics, and the local arts and sciences college; in the 1980s the college became the core of the new North Gujarat University, the seed money for which was given by a wealthy Bombay-based Hindu businessman from Patan.

Pujārīs

Each temple employs one or more *pujārīs*. In a Hindu temple, the *pujārī* functions as the principal ritual practitioner, and only the *pujārī* can actually enter the innermost shrine and touch the image. But Mūrtipūjak Jain laity themselves perform all the aspects of worship, and the *pujārī* is not needed as an intermediary between the worshiper and the image. In a Mūrtipūjak temple, the function of the *pujārī* is essentially that of a low-paid menial: he keeps the temple clean, prepares the ingredients needed for worship, occasionally decorates the image, and will perform the daily worship in places where there is no resident Jain population.[58] Part of the *pujārī*'s compensation comes in the form of the food (mostly uncooked rice) offered before the Jina in the temple. To consume this food, which after it has been offered is considered to be *dev dravya* (God's goods), is considered a moral fault by Jains, and so almost by definition *pujārīs* are non-Jain.[59] In Patan, most of the *pujārīs* in Jain temples formerly were Bhojaks (see below); nowadays, one also finds other "clean" (that is, not Untouchable) castes such as Kumbhārs (potters), Ramīs (gardeners), and Audīc Brāhmaṇs.[60]

Jains and Caste in Patan

Many Jain scholars (for example, Jaini 1979:286–91 and Sangave 1980:67) have discussed caste as a "Hindu" feature borrowed by the Jains. But references to caste are found at the earliest levels of evidence of Jainism, and it is unlikely that the Jains have ever been less caste-organized than the surrounding population. In Indian culture, caste is perceived as a "natural" category, not a "cultural" one. Asking another person's caste is as basic a part of social interaction as asking where someone was born. The American response that one is of no caste leaves many Indians as puzzled as if one had responded that one is of no race or no gender. According to the Indian cultural logic, in this lifetime one cannot change the caste into which one has been born, any more than according to Western cultural logic one can change one's race or gender (at least before the wonders of modern surgery). Jains have never denied the existence of caste. But, in contrast to the Brāhmaṇical insistence on the centrality of caste to eligibility for many religious practices, Jains for the most part have insisted that caste is not the sole determinant of spiritual propensities or of eligibility to pursue the *mokṣa-mārg*. Nonetheless, most Jains assume that the caste into which one is born is a direct result of one's karma, and therefore highness or lowness of caste is assumed to be a good indicator of one's innate spiritual propensities.

The Jains of Patan exhibit a richer diversity of castes (*jñātī*) than most Jain communities, in large part due to the sheer size of the Patan Jain community.[61] But caste differences have not been reflected in *saṅgh* differences. In this the Jains of Patan differ from other Jain communities, such as Jamnagar and Jaipur, where caste and *saṅgh* identities reinforce each other, and many *saṅghs* are known by caste names.

At the core of the Patan Jain community are the six Vāṇiyā castes of the Vīśā Śrīmāḷīs, Daśā Śrīmāḷīs, Vīśā Porvāḷs, Daśā Porvāḷs, Vīśā Osvāḷs, and Daśā Osvāḷs.[62] *Vīśā* means "twenty" and *daśā* means "ten." There are elaborate stories to explain the differentiation of these castes into the seemingly hierarchically ranked twenty and ten divisions (as well as a putative third stratum of *pañcās*, or fives). The stories usually involve a form of "lower" practices, especially those that revolve around marriage customs, which results in one group being labeled "ten" in distinction to the purer, more orthoprax, and more prestigious group, which is known as "twenty." People use twenty and ten in conversation as generalized indicators of social status, but there is no operational hierarchy between the actual twenty and ten castes.[63] Traditionally, these six were endogomous, ranked as equivalent in terms of ritual purity measured by food and marriage transactions, but the two Śrīmāḷī castes were ranked slightly higher in terms of social status because of their perceived greater wealth. T. B. Naik (1974:232) has rightly observed that social status in Gujarat is a matter of wealth: "if you want to achieve status . . . you must have money and more money." Among the same Vāṇiyā castes in Ahmedabad, the Osvāḷs are considered to be superior to the Śrīmāḷīs and Porvāḷs precisely because of their wealth, and there is some evidence that during the rule of the Cāvaḍā and Caulukya dynasties, the Porvāḷs were the most prestigious. Each of the Patan castes had hypergamous marriage relations with the same castes of the villages and smaller towns surrounding Patan, with brides going from the villages to Patan. Within this century, the bounded nature of these castes has broken down, and intermarriage among them is now frequent. These castes contain both Jains and Puṣṭimārg Vaiṣṇavs (followers of the Kṛṣṇa devotional sect established by Vallabhācārya five hundred years ago), with the Jains far outnumbering the Vaiṣṇavs. Religion was traditionally no barrier to intermarriage, although in this century reformist pressures have resulted in a preference for intra-Jain marriages.

These six castes lived mixed together in the same neighborhoods, so there did not develop in Patan the close identification between caste and *saṅgh* that one finds elsewhere. The six Vāṇiyā castes are lumped together by non-Jains into one perceived caste, called either Jain or Śāh, after the predominate surname.[64]

Slightly lower than the six Vāṇiyā castes are two castes unique to Patan, the Sāḷvīs and Sāṇḍesarās. These castes also contain both Jains and Vaiṣṇavs (although not necessarily Puṣṭimārg), with the majority being Jain: 70% in the case of the Sāḷvīs (Bühler and Fischer 1979:I.258), 75% in the case of the Sāṇḍesarās (Sandesara 1987b). The Sāḷvīs were traditionally weavers, primarily of the famous double-ikat *paṭoḷā*, but also of other cloth. The Sāṇḍesarās were traditionally landlords and, at the lower end of the economic scale, farmers (Sandesara 1987a). The two castes have intermarried with each other, and have had hypergamous relations with Paṭels, the dominant agricultural caste throughout Gujarat (see Pocock 1972), of some neighboring villages; the brides go from the Paṭels to the Sāḷvīs and Sāṇḍesarās. Marriage relations with the Paṭels now go in both directions, as the social and caste status of the Paṭels has risen dramatically in the past 150 years. Although interdining between these two castes and the Vāṇiyā castes poses no problem, intermarriage is still rare, occurring only at the highest socio-economic levels in Bombay and Ahmedabad. They traditionally tended to imitate the Vāṇiyās in dress, names, and behavior.

The Sāḷvīs are the one Jain caste in Patan to inhabit their own area, a cluster of five neighborhoods in the northwestern corner of town known collectively as Sāḷvī Vāḍo. Because the weavers needed suitable space to lay out their warps, Sāḷvī Vāḍo is distinctive for its long straight alleyways, in contrast to the twisting alleyways of the other neighborhoods. The Sāṇḍesarās live in the neighborhoods of Rājkā Vāḍo, near their original home village of Sanderpati, just to the southwest of Patan.

One also finds scattered members of other castes, such as Ghāñcīs (oil-pressers) and Paṭels who worship at Jain temples and might consider themselves to be Jain. Evidence from inscriptions tells us that in the past an even wider array of communities participated in Jain ritual life, including Vāṇiyā castes such as Moḍh and Vāyaḍ that have subsequently become totally Vaiṣṇav, and other high castes such as Nāgars and Gūrjars (Buddhisāgarsūri 1917:39–66).

The Bhojaks and the Nāyaks are two castes that have been vital to Jain ritual life in Patan, but are not themselves fully practicing Jains. Traditionally, Nāyaks have been performers of *bhavāīs* (religious dramas), whereas Bhojaks have been *pujārīs* and in other ways religious menial functionaries for the Jains. The two groups interdine and intermarry. They are subunits of the broader Targalā (also known as Bhavaiyā) caste who claim to be "fallen" Brāhmaṇs.

Written sources give two accounts of their origin. According to one account, they are descended from Brāhmaṇs of Vayar village near Disa in north Gujarat, who lived among Jains. They had no land, and due to their dependence on the Jains grew to be like them. With the passage of time they started to share food with the landlords, as well as with the Jains. Because of this they came to be called Bhojaks, "eaters," and were viewed as ritual servants of the Jains (Tripuṭī Mahārāj 1952:603). According to another account, they are descended from an Audīc Brāhmaṇ who was the family priest of a family of Paṭels from Unjha. In order to rescue the Paṭel's daughter from the importuning of a Muslim official, the priest impersonated and interdined with Paṭels. He was famous for composing *bhavais*, dramatic performances for the goddess, and his descendants followed this profession (Rajyagor 1975:191). In Marwar, the Bhojaks claim to be descended from sun-worshiping Mag Brāhmaṇs who migrated to India from the mythical continent of Śākadvīp (Singh 1895:320–26, von Stietencron 1966). I met only one Bhojak *pujārī* in Patan who recounted this story.

Bhojak *paṇḍits* from Patan told me two other accounts. According to one, King Kumārapāla built a temple every day, and needed *pujārīs* to serve in them. He brought some Brāhmaṇs from the village Phulera near Jaipur. A *śrīpūjya* consecrated them as Jain *pujārīs* by sprinkling them with *vāskep* powder (chapter 4). They started to accept food from the local Jain Vāṇiyās, for which they were outcast by other Brāhmaṇs and called by the derogatory name Bhojak. As a result, the Bhojaks could not find brides from other castes and so started intermarrying with Gujarati Nāyaks. The two castes have been basically one for three or four hundred years.

According to the other *paṇḍit*, King Jayasiṃha Siddharāja brought Mag Brāhmaṇs from Mandal, south of Patan near Saurashtra. They had been in royal service there, but upon coming to Patan they began to function as Jain *pujārīs*. Because they accepted the food offered in the Jain temples, they became known as Bhojaks. This new group was too small a caste to maintain proper marriage patterns (the bride and groom should have no common ancestor for seven generations), so they began to intermarry with the Nāyaks, who were also a "Brāhmaṇ-like" caste. Before living in Mandal, the Mag Brāhmaṇs had lived in Marwar, where they were *pujārīs* in Sūrya temples.

These stories give two explanations for the name Bhojak: accepting food from non-Brāhmaṇs, and eating the edible offerings in Jain temples, offerings that cannot be eaten by any orthoprax Jain.[65] They traditionally served as *pujārīs*, performers of other elaborate image-related rituals, singers, and manuscript copyists. In many of these activities they worked closely with *yatis*. In recent years, some Bhojaks have become Jain *paṇḍits* and clerks in Jain trusts.[66] I met only one Nāyak who served as a Jain *pujārī*; it may have been in the past that when a Nāyak accepted a hereditary post as Jain *pujārī* he became by ascription a Bhojak. There are over one hundred families of Bhojaks in Patan, and many still serve as low-paid temple *pujārīs*. Their own religious status is ambiguous; some call themselves Jain, others Hindu, often within the same family. Their involvement in Jain religious life has been almost exclusively in terms of temple worship, and not in the forms of asceticism discussed in chapter 5. The donation list in the old Śāmḷājī Pārśvanāth temple showed several donations from Bhojak families. Jogī Vāḍo, where the temple is located, is inhabited by Paṭels and Bhojaks but not Vāṇiyās. Because they have traditionally consumed the offerings to the Jinas, other Jains do not accept a Bhojak as a Jain, even if he does not function as *pujārī* and eat the offerings.

Sthānakvāsīs and Terāpanthīs

The distinctions among castes are important for social identity, but do not necessarily denote religious differences. There is a proclaimed unity within the Mūrtipūjak *saṅgh*, in contrast to Hindus and Muslims, but also in contrast to Sthānakvāsīs and Terāpanthīs. Although the Mūrtipūjaks are the focus of this study, it is worth noting that there are small communities of both Sthānakvāsīs and Terāpanthīs in Patan.

There are forty to forty-five families of Sthānakvāsīs. Some of them are Vāṇiyās, but the majority are of the Bhāvsār caste, with a few of the Ramī caste.[67] Bhāvsārs were traditionally dyers,[68] and Ramīs traditionally gardeners. Because of the predominance of Bhāvsārs in the Patan Sthānakvāsī *saṅgh*, Mūrtipūjak Vāṇiyās tend to forget that there are also Sthānakvāsī Vāṇiyās, and instead to see all Sthānakvāsīs as being Bhāvsārs, and therefore socially lower than themselves. Because they are Sthānakvāsī, they are ritually other than Mūrtipūjaks. The Vāṇiyā-Bhāvsār and Mūrtipūjak-Sthānakvāsī differences overlap to create a greater combined sense of otherness.

The sense of separation from the Terāpanthīs in Patan is not as great, in large part because the Terāpanthīs are all Vāṇiyā. There are fifteen houses of Vīśā Osvāḷ Terāpanthīs who have migrated to Patan from Kacch over the past fifty years; they are all descended from the same man. There is also one family of Marwari Vīśā Osvāḷ Terāpanthīs. The Terāpanthīs have their own Terāpanth Bhavan built in 1983, but they go to the Sthānakvāsī *upāśray* if a Sthānakvāsī mendicant is giving sermons. When Ācārya Tulsī (1914–1997), the charismatic leader of the Terāpanth, came to Patan to open the Terāpanth Bhavan, at least one respected Mūrtipūjak Jain was on the welcoming committee, and many Mūrtipūjak Jains turned out to greet and hear him. To have ignored the visit of Tulsī would have been a matter of the greatest disrespect, and Tulsī was a renowned Jain within the broader self-definition of the Patan Jains as "Jains" rather than "Hindus"; but on the level of daily interaction, the Terāpanthīs and the Sthānakvāsīs are both "other" in terms of the Patan Mūrtipūjak Jain self-definition.

In this chapter, I have presented in brief the historical and social location of this study. There is much here that is similar to Mūrtipūjak Jain communities elsewhere in western India, although the richness of the historical record and the completeness of the social structures are found in few Jain communities. The values of wellbeing and *mokṣa-mārg* that form the focus of this study do not exist in a vacuum; they are available for us to study only as they are discussed, enacted, and lived by Jains. The remainder of this book will present a detailed study of the values of *mokṣa-mārg* and well-being as expressed in the thoughts, actions, and speech (to use the classical tripartite Indian categorization of experience) of the Jains of Patan.

3

Going to the Temple

How to Worship God

The performance of *sāmāyik*, *pratikramaṇ*, and other rites is considered to be an instrumental cause of liberation. In other words, they are like a road to liberation. But the rite of viewing God (*dev-darśan*) is the king's highway itself, because in it contemplation of the innate essence of God's divinity is conjoined with ritual performance

(M. D. Deśāī 1989:6).

O Master of Shankheshvar, Lord who is the inner controller of the world!
We venerate you, Master of the pleasure of liberation.
My only resolution, O Master, is to become your slave.
I will recite your name with my every breath.
O Master who erases the afflictions of suffering, grant my desires!
Take away my bad karma and give the pleasure of liberation![1]

In the next three chapters I will explore three realms of Jain activity. The first two involve interaction with "sacred others" in order to change one's ontological and moral position in the cosmos. These sacred others are deities, especially the Jinas (chapter 3), and mendicants (chapter 4). Then in chapter 5 I will look at action that involves working directly upon oneself by using the technologies of asceticism to change one's karmic condition. Asceticism can also be expressed as an interaction with a sacred other, in that the *mokṣa-mārg* goal of asceticism is to deconstruct karmic formations of the social self in order to bring to the fore the pure soul that is buried within (Cort 1998b:10–12). To a significant extent, all three of these interactions—with deities, mendicants, and the self—are structural variants of the same basic interaction, for in the Jain worldview soul constitutes all that is alive and holy in the universe, from the layperson through the mendicants to the Jinas themselves. The order of this discussion—God (*deva*), guru, and asceticism—reflects a traditional ordering of the ideological presentations of this material, as seen, for example, in the order of Devendrasūri's thirteenth-century *Bhāṣyatraya*, three commentaries on basic mendicant liturgical texts.

In this chapter, I investigate some of the ways in which Mūrtipūjak Jains interact with God through ritual and devotion. The complex of rites and practices to be discussed in chapter 5 under the broad rubric of asceticism is, with important differences of style and emphasis, common to all three Śvetāmbar sects. Similarly, we find in each of the three an emphasis on the importance of lay-mendicant interaction, as will be discussed in chapter 4. What most sharply sets the sects apart is the practice and doctrine of *mūrtipūjā*, the worship of *mūrtis* or images of the Jinas as a major facet of devotion to and worship of God.[2] The major sect of the Śvetāmbars, in fact, defines itself as the congregation of Jains who perform *mūrtipūjā* : the Śvetāmbar Mūrtipūjak Saṅgh. This self-definition sharply distinguishes it from the smaller Sthānakvāsī and Terāpanthī sects, which reject the cult of temples and *mūrtis*. *Mūrtipūjā* is also the basis for the thousands of temples that are the Jains' most visible representation of themselves to the non-Jain world. The capital investment in Jain temples in India is immense, and as Jain communities in East Africa, England, Japan, and North America accept the permanency of their emigration and begin to put down roots, one of the first things they do is erect a temple. Similarly, pilgrimage is a major activity of many Mūrtipūjak Jains, whether large congregational pilgrimages to major shrines hundreds of miles away, or individual and family outings to nearby towns or villages. In every case, the pilgrimage is to a temple, or, more precisely, to the *mūrti* enshrined in that temple.

I first became aware of the centrality of *mūrtipūjā* to contemporary Śvetāmbar Jain self-identity in reading a biography (Vallabhsūri 1957) of the great nineteenth-century reformer Ācārya Vijayānandsūri (Ātmārāmjī), and discussing his life with several contemporary mendicants. Ātmārāmjī (1837–1896), as discussed in chapter 2, was a Sthānakvāsī *sādhu* who, in Ahmedabad in 1876, took a second initiation as a Mūrtipūjak *sādhu* along with eighteen other Sthānakvāsī *sādhus*. Their initiation was at the hands of Muni Buddhivijay (Buṭerāyjī) (1807–1882), also a former Sthānakvāsī *sādhu*, who was active in propagating the correctness of the Mūrtipūjak position among Sthānakvāsī mendicants and laity. Ātmārāmjī continued this mission of his guru, converted many Sthānakvāsīs in the Panjab to the Mūrtipūjak position, and was responsible for the building and renovation of many temples.

When I started my research, I had assumed, in line with most scholarship on the Jains (such as Jaini 1979:191–96), that *mūrtipūjā* was primarily a lay practice that was of little concern to the mendicants. A corollary of this assumption has been that if the mendicants and their emphasis on asceticism and renunciation comprise the core of the Jain tradition, *mūrtipūjā* has therefore been a marginal Jain activity. I knew that mendicants are not allowed to perform external worship with physical offerings (*dravya pūjā*), and should only perform internal meditative worship (*bhāv pūjā*). I therefore expected that the mendicants would take a quasi-Sthānakvāsī position on the correctness of *mūrtipūjā*, dismissing *dravya pūjā* and emphasizing that laity should perform only *bhāv pūjā*. One does in fact find such opinions in the writings and sermons of many *mokṣa-mārg* ideologues. But, as indicated in the introduction, I quickly learned how central *sādhus* are to the institution and propagation of the cult of *mūrtipūjā*. Not only is their active participation required in the rites of consecrating and installing a *mūrti*, but many mendicants actively urge the laity to build more and grander temples. Furthermore, in the case of Ātmārāmjī, here was a dynamic and charismatic Sthānakvāsī *sādhu* who had converted to the Mūrtipūjak fold, having been convinced from his study of the texts that the Sthānakvāsī position was incorrect.

In addition to converting Sthānakvāsīs to the Mūrtipūjak position, Ātmārāmjī and other turn-of-the-century reformers were concerned to ensure that *mūrtipūjā* was performed correctly, that is, in accordance with the principles of the *mokṣa-mārg* ideology. The passage by M. D. Deśāī at the head of this chapter comes from a 1910 book by one such ideologue. There was and remains a widespread perception that many Hindu Vaiṣṇav practices have crept into Jain ritual, especially from the Puṣṭimārg Vaiṣṇav tradition. Jain and Puṣṭimārg families have intermarried for many centuries. In most cases, the wife is expected to recognize her husband's tradition as the family norm, but is allowed to retain some elements of her natal tradition as a minor theme in the family's ritual life. Since as a mother the woman is the principal transmitter of ritual within the family, there has naturally been much interaction between what Lawrence Babb (1996) has termed Jain and Vaiṣṇav "ritual cultures." Many Jains also aver that Vaiṣṇav practices crept into the Jain ritual culture through the non-Jain *pujārīs*. By means of sermons and books, the reformers instructed laity on the correct Jain way to do *mūrtipūjā*, and the correct way to understand both the *mūrti* as symbol and God as symbolized. They also issued vigorous defenses of the practice of *mūrtipūjā*, in terms of its authentic antiquity and its spiritual necessity, against Sthānakvāsī iconoclastic polemics.

These concerns continue to the present day. *Sādhus* frequently preach to the laity concerning the proper spirit in which to perform *mūrtipūjā*, and the proper soteriological perspective in which to understand it. J. A. B. van Buitenen (1966:30) perceptively remarked that in India there is much greater concern for orthopraxy than for orthodoxy: external behavior is more important than internal belief. But this generalization does not hold true in the case of Jain *mūrtipūjā*. The spokespersons (both mendicants and laity) for the *mokṣa-mārg* ideology are very much concerned with what the worshiper intends and believes, as well as how the worshiper performs the rituals. Statements such as the following are frequently encountered:

> Our distinctiveness is lost in the form of *pūjā* that occurs today. In Jain *pūjā*, it is necessary to meditate strongly on dispassion. *Pūjā* done with passion is not permitted in the Jain scriptures. The form of water *pūjā* that was done in former times was important. [Correct] conduct was built upon it. Today the water *pūjā* has become deformed. This is not right. Water is a symbol of purity. The person who performs *pūjā* needs to find the inspiration for purity. . . . If we want to return to our distinctiveness, then first of all we need to add [correct] conduct to our *pūjā*, and we need to reform the whole *pūjā* rite, so that we are inspired to attain the sentiment of dispassion. The materials used are not all that important; the important thing is that at the moment of *pūjā* the person create a spiritual personality. Having recognized this, we need to begin to perform *pūjā* which is full of correct faith. *Pūjā* of the Jina *mūrti* is a task that is beneficial to both the soul and the world, and so we need to perform it with discipline and the proper rites. (Abhaysāgargaṇi 1985:128)

Jain ideologues have written about image worship for well over a millennium. As is typical of the *mokṣa-mārg* ideology, they have developed a variety of typological lists for worship: twelve *adhikāras* or objects of worship, five *daṇḍakas* or chants, five *abhigamas* or preparatory features, and ten *trikas* or typological triads. *Pūjā* has been defined as being of three kinds: *aṅga pūjā* in which offerings are made directly onto the *mūrti*, *agra pūjā* in which offerings are placed in front of the *mūrti*, and *bhāv pūjā*, in which material offerings are omitted in favor of recitations and gestures. *Pūjā* has been further characterized according to the number of offerings as eightfold, seventeenfold, or twenty-one-fold (Williams 1963:187–98, 216–24). At its simplest, worship is discussed by ideologues in terms of two dominant paradigms, a pattern that I employ in the following discussion: *caitya-vandan* (image veneration),[3] and *aṣṭaprakārī pūjā* (the rite of eightfold worship). These paradigms are not prescriptive models for ritual from which individuals pick and choose to construct their own personal forms of worship. Rather, in the concepts of *caitya-vandan* and eightfold *pūjā* we see attempts to frame a complex range of actions and intentions within a single ideology. Framing here expresses a concern with boundedness, with keeping the activity within a framework of *mokṣa-mārg* ideology. The perceived need for repeated ideological definitions of worship, and the multiple interpretive schemas employed, point to the limits of the ability of ideology to shape experience.

Framing is done within and outside the tradition, as both Jain ideologues and scholars frame the actions. But there are different motivations for the framings. The framing by Mūrtipūjak ideologues is a prescriptive framing, for the purpose of trying to keep the activity, intentions, and understandings within the *mokṣa-mārg* ideology. The external framing is a descriptive, interpretive framing employed by scholars in an attempt to control the number of variables, so that the interpretation of Jain worship remains manageable.

A further categorization of *mūrtipūjā* employs a division into *dravya pūjā* and *bhāv pūjā*. The former is the "external" worship of the *mūrti* with physical offerings, especially the eightfold *pūjā*. *Bhāv pūjā* refers to the *caitya-vandan*, but can also include simpler rites such as *darśan* (viewing of the *mūrti*), repetition of a *mantra*, and singing of praise hymns. The daily *pūjā* of most Jains, as we shall see below, involves a combination of all these. In this chapter I will present the ideological prescriptions for the rites of *caitya-vandan*, *aṣṭaprakārī pūjā*, and *darśan*, and then show how elements of these are used as the building blocks for distinctive personal styles of worship, before concluding with a discussion of understandings of divinity and intention in Jain worship.[4]

Prescription 1: *Caitya-vandan*

The concept of *vandan* can be found at the earliest levels of the Jain tradition, and is an important but hitherto unstudied and unacknowledged source for the later concept of bhakti in both the Jain and Hindu traditions (Cort forthcoming-a). *Vandan* is the veneration of any superior being. In the contemporary Jain tradition, there are *vandans* of the twenty-four Jinas (*dev-vandan*), the image of the Jina (*caitya-vandan*), and the living mendicant (*guru-vandan*).

The rite of *caitya-vandan* is an expansion of the obligatory action (*āvaśyak*) of *caturviṃśati-stava*, the homage to the twenty-four Jinas. Since it is derived from the obligatory actions, it consists of a fixed order of actions and recitations, performed in the same manner by both mendicants and laity. Unlike the *pūjā*, it is not open to extensive individual modification. To learn the rite requires a commitment of study and practice. Those who do not know it, or are unsure about the performance, follow the printed instructions in many books and pamphlets, copies of which are always found in temples. At the same time, there are small variations found in the prescriptions for the rite, and those Jains who have memorized one form are quick to notice these differences. Many Jains have memorized the rite, and perform it daily. The discussion here is summarized from several texts and books, as well as my observations of it many times.[5]

The Rite of *Caitya-vandan*

The worshiper enters the temple wearing pure clothes. Using the end of the upper-body cloth, s/he carefully sweeps the floor immediately in front of her/himself three times in order to remove any living creatures. S/he then performs an act known as *khamāsamaṇ* (five-limbed prostration), after the second word recited in the liturgy. In this s/he stands facing the Jina *mūrti*, and recites the following Prakrit phrase: "I wish, O forbearing mendicant, to praise with strong concentration and with renunciation." S/he does a five-limbed prostration, kneeling with hands folded before the chest, and then touching the floor with two hands, two knees, and forehead, while saying in Prakrit, "I praise with my forehead" (see Figure 3.1).

S/he then stands, and with hands folded in front recites a long Prakrit passage, as follows:

> Instruct me, O Lord, according to my desire. Should I do *pratikramaṇ* for faults committed while walking? It is desired. I desire to do *pratikramaṇ*.[6] For injury committed in walking, going and coming, treading on living things, treading on seeds, treading on green plants, treading on dew, insects, mold, mud, clay, spiders, and cobwebs;

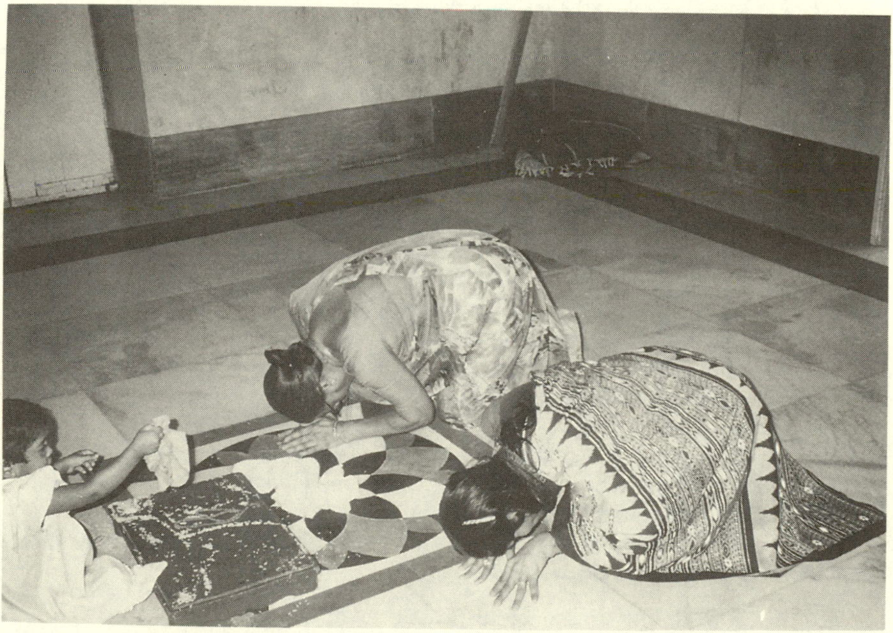

Figure 3.1. Laywomen prostrating before a Jina image as part of *caitya-vandan*. Patan, April 1987.

whatever living beings have been injured by me, one-sensed, two-sensed, three-sensed, four-sensed, five-sensed, have been hurt, knocked down, squashed, struck, collided with, oppressed, fatigued, frightened, displaced from one spot to another, or deprived of life—for all those, may the wrong action be of no karmic consequence.

I stand in *kāüssagg* as an additional effort, as penance, as purification, in order to be free of the thorns of harmful karmas, for the destruction of harmful karmas, resulting from those wrong actions.[7]

May my *kāüssagg* be unbroken and unhindered except for inhaling, exhaling, coughing, sneezing, yawning, hiccuping, passing wind, dizziness, fainting, very slight movements of the limbs, very slight movements of mucus, very slight movements of the eyes, and other such faults.

S/he then stands in the *kāüssagg* posture, with feet slightly apart, arms hanging down and slightly away from the body, palms turned inward, and eyes fixed in a meditative gaze, for the time it takes to repeat silently either the *Nokār Mantra* four times or the *Logass* once (see Figure 3.2). The *Nokār Mantra* is the most sacred and widespread of all Jain praises.

Praise to the Arhats [Jinas]
Praise to the Siddhas
Praise to the Ācāryas
Praise to the Upādhyāyas
Praise to all Sādhus in the world.
This fivefold praise
destroys all bad karma
and of all holies
it is the foremost holy.

The *Logass* is the ancient *caturviṃśati-stava* or Hymn to the Twenty-four Jinas. It is better known after its first word, Prakrit *logassa*.

I will glorify the Illuminators of the world, the Creators of the ford of dharma, the Jinas, the Arhats, the twenty-four Omniscient Ones.

I venerate Ṛṣabha and Ajita, Sambhava and Abhinanda and Sumati, I venerate Padmaprabha, Supārśva Jina, and Candraprabha.

Suvidhi Pupadanta, Śītala, Śreyāṃsa, and Vāsupūjya, I venerate Vimala and Ananta, the Jina Dharma, and Śānti.

I venerate Kunthu, Ara, and Malli, Munisuvrata, and the Jina Nami, I venerate Ariṣṭanemi, and Pārśva, and Vardhamāna.

Thus I have praised those who are freed from the dirt of karma, and who have destroyed illness and death. May the twenty-four excellent Jinas, the Tīrthaṅkaras, be gracious to me.

Thus glorified, venerated, and honored, supreme in the world, the Perfected Ones, may they grant the benefits of health [= liberation] and knowledge, and the best, highest enlightenment.

Purer than the moon, much more radiant than the sun, deeper than the ocean, may those Perfected Ones give me perfection.

S/he then repeats the Prakrit *Logass*, this time aloud.

S/he performs three more *khamāsamaṇs*, the five-limbed prostration.

S/he sits in the yoga posture, right leg tucked under the right buttock, left knee raised, and hands folded together before the mouth, and says in Prakrit, "Instruct

Figure 3.2. Laywomen performing *kāüssagg* as part of *caitya-vandan*. Patan, April 1987.

me, O Lord, at my wish, to do praise. Should I perform *caitya-vandan*? It is wished" (see Figure 3.3).

While still seated in the yoga posture, s/he recites several hymns. The first is a verse in Sanskrit, as follows:

> Like a vine of all that is good, like a blue-lotus cloud;
> like the sun that drives away darkness, like the wish-granting tree;
> like a raft on the ocean of rebirth, the cause of all success;
> may he be forever beneficent to us, Śāntinātha.[8]

This is followed by a vernacular hymn. The choice of the hymn is up to the individual. It may be one appropriate for a festival day, one appropriate to the main *mūrti* of the temple, or a personal favorite. Most prescriptions give the following Gujarati hymn as an example:

Hail wish-fulfilling Pārśvanāth! Hail Lord of the three worlds!
Victor over the eight karma enemies, attainer of liberation.
The root of joy is found in the name of the Lord, so obtain happiness and success.
Fear of rebirth is removed by the name of the Lord, so burn off all sins.
Recite the *mantra* "oṃ hrīṃ," repeat the name of Pārśva.
Poison is transformed into nectar, and so attain liberation.

This is followed by the following Prakrit verse:

In whatever is called a shrine in the celestial, infernal, or human realms,
however many Jina *mūrtis* there are, I venerate them all.

This is followed by the *Śakra Stava*, or "Indra's Hymn," so called because Jains say that this is the hymn recited by Indra (also known as Śakra), king of a celestial realm, at the moment of a Jina's conception.

Praise to the Arhats, the Lords, who cause beginnings, the Tīrthaṅkaras, who by themselves have attained enlightenment, the best of men, lions among men, excellent lotuses among men, excellent perfumed elephants among men, the best in the world, lords of the world, benefactors of the world, lights of the world, illuminators of the world, givers of freedom from fear, givers of insight, givers of the path, givers of refuge, givers of enlightenment, givers of dharma, expounders of dharma, leaders of dharma, guides of dharma, the best world emperors of dharma, possessors of the irrefutable best knowledge and insight, freed from bondage, victors, conquerors, who have crossed over, who bring others across, wise, enlightened, liberated, who liberate others, omniscient, all-seeing, who have attained the place called Abode of Perfection which is beneficent, firm, inviolable, eternal, imperishable, undisturbed, and from which

Figure 3.3. Laywomen performing yoga posture as part of *caitya-vandan*. Patan, April 1987.

there is no return; praise to the Jinas who have conquered fear. In this threefold manner I praise all the Perfected Ones, those who have been, those who will be in the future, and those who are in the present.

S/he then recites another Prakrit verse: "As many Jina images there are in the upper, lower, and middle worlds, I residing here venerate them all residing there."

S/he performs another *khamāsamaṇ*.

S/he returns to the yoga posture, and recites the Prakrit verse: "As many mendicants there are in Bhārata, Airāvata, and Mahāvideha[9] who maintain the three discplines of mind, speech, and body—I bow down to them all."

This is followed by a Sanskrit mantra: "Praise to the Arhats, Siddhas, Ācāryas, Upādhyāyas, and all Sādhus."

S/he then sings another vernacular hymn. If none comes to mind, the individual is recommended to sing the Prakrit *Uvasaggaharaṃ Stotra* or "Obstacle Remover Hymn," attributed to the ancient Bhadrabāhu Svāmī, as follows:

I praise Pārśva the obstacle remover, Pārśva who is freed from clinging karma,
destroyer of the venom of the poisonous serpent, abode of holiness and goodness.
The man who always holds in his throat this serpent-slayer *mantra*
is freed from evil planets, disease, pestilence, troubles, and senility.
Should this *mantra* remain out of reach, just bowing to You gives great rewards.
Souls in men and even animals are saved from sorrow and bad rebirth.
Attaining correct faith in you, greater than a wish-granting gem or a wish-granting tree,
souls easily attain that state free from old age and death.
Singing this hymn, O Greatly Glorious, with my heart full of devotion,
O God! Grant me wisdom in birth after birth, O Pārśva Jinacandra!

S/he then sings a final four-verse Prakrit hymn, the "Hymn to the Dispassionate One" (*Jayavīyarāya*), to which is appended a popular Sanskrit verse. While reciting this, s/he is seated in the pearl oyster posture, which is identical to the yoga posture except that the folded hands are held in front of the forehead instead of the chest.

[Prakrit] Victory to the Dispassionate One, Guru of the world; through your splendor
may these be mine, O Lord:
detachment from the world, following the path, attainment of desired results,
renunciation of what is censured in the world, worship of gurus and parents,
practice of aid to others,
finding a good guru, service of his words, in full in this world.
Even though I have renounced and stopped pursuing worldly aims, O Dispassionate
One, according to your teachings,
nonetheless I want to serve your feet in birth after birth.
May suffering be destroyed, may karma be destroyed, may death in meditation and the
reward of enlightenment be granted to me, O Lord, by my bowing to you.
[Sanskrit] The holiness of all holies, the cause of all beneficence,
the chief of all dharmas: the Jain teaching is victorious.

S/he then stands in the *kāüssagg* posture and recites the following Prakrit phrases, which repeat in part the liturgy from the beginning of the *caitya-vandan*:

I do *kāüssagg* to the *caityas* of the Arhats. I stand in *kāüssagg* with faith, intelligence, steadfastness, and increasing absorption for the sake of venerating, worshiping, gifting, honoring, and the reward of enlightenment.

> May my *kāüssagg* be unbroken and unhindered except for inhaling, exhaling, coughing, sneezing, yawning, hiccuping, passing wind, dizziness, fainting, very slight movements of the limbs, very slight movements of mucus, very slight movements of the eyes, and other such faults.
>
> I shall do *kāüssagg* in this place, in silence, in meditation, as long as I have not completed the homage to the blessed Arhats.

S/he then performs *kāüssagg* for the duration of one silent recitation of the *Nokār Mantra*, following which s/he says aloud the Prakrit mantra, "Praise to the Arhats."

S/he sings a final vernacular hymn. Most authors give the following Gujarati hymn as an example:

> Worship Śaṅkheśvar Pāsjī,[10] take the benefit of your human birth!
> Hail the most beautiful human-born, the wishing tree of all your heart's desires.

S/he concludes by doing a final *khamāsamaṇ*.

Much of this rite is recited in the ancient liturgical language of Prakrit, and so is not directly intelligible to any but a small minority of learned mendicants and laity. An English translation is therefore misleading, for it presents the rite with greater clarity than it is usually understood by lay participants themselves. But those Jains who perform *caitya-vandan* are not mindlessly uttering what to them are nonsense syllables. Many Jains have a general sense of the meaning of what they are saying, and the similarities between Prakrit and Gujarati word forms can also be of some help. The level of comprehension of the meaning of the *caitya-vandan* for many Jains is analagous to the understanding of the Latin liturgy on the part of many pre-Vatican II Catholics. Comprehension is augmented by the inclusion of vernacular hymns. Further, many of the written descriptions of the rite provide vernacular summaries of each section. The detailed texts studied by more pious Jains go further, and parse the Prakrit into a word-by-word vernacular translation.

These detailed expositions express an ideological concern for proper understanding of the meaning of the rite. We see that the rite itself is linked with other obligatory actions, in particular *pratikramaṇ* and *kāüssagg*, to which we will return in chapter 5. In the portions that overlap, we see the individual stating that his or her intention in performing the rite is "as penance, as purification, in order to be free of the thorns of harmful karmas, for the destruction of harmful karmas, resulting from wrong actions." These parts of the rite are seen to be efficacious as they are forms of renunciation and equanimity, which allow the person to act directly upon his or her karmic status.

But the efficacy of *caitya-vandan* more significantly comes through the positive karmic effects of praising the virtues of the Jinas. This is a theme repeated by the ideologues in their discussions of *caitya-vandan*. Explanations such as the following are frequently encountered: "The person who begins to praise the virtues of the virtuous lays the foundation for the development of his own soul. The Tīrthaṅkar Gods are the most virtuous beings in the world, for they have conquered passion and hatred and so attained to a state of dispassion. By praising their virtues one quickly develops these virtues in one's soul" (Nirvāṇa Sāgara 1986:7).

Such statements are by no means limited to mendicant ideologues. In conversation, one layman said the following as to why he worshiped daily in the temple: "We attribute certain virtues to God. He is liberated from passion and hatred. He looks upon us all equally. Whether we do *pūjā* to him, or do him some harm, he looks upon us the same. We try to attain those virtues. One becomes as one meditates. If we spend one hour every day before the picture of someone, we will attain some of his virtues."

The virtues that the man wanted to attain are clearly spelled out in the hymns of the *caitya-vandan*. In the *Logass*, a hymn known by many Jains, and the meaning of which I found many to be quite clear about, one sings of the Jinas that they are "freed from the dirt of karma, and have destroyed illness and death." One of the Gujarati hymns describes the Jina as "victor over the eight karma enemies, attainer of liberation." In the *Uvasaggaharaṃ Stotra*, the person sings of "Pārśva who is freed from clinging karma, destroyer of the venom of the poisonous serpent, abode of holiness and goodness." Several of the hymns, especially the well-known *Śakra Stava*, are little more than litanies of epithets, listing the virtues of the Jina in a string of metaphors.

Not all those who perform *caitya-vandan*, however, are conversant with the detailed meanings of the Prakrit liturgy. Even in the cases of those who are conversant, we cannot assume a direct correlation between the person's intentions and understandings and those expressed in the hymns. I will return to the subject of the worshiper's intentions later in this chapter. But before doing so, let me introduce the other paradigm for the daily temple ritual, the eightfold *pūjā*.

Prescription 2: *Aṣṭaprakārī Pūjā*

Almost all Jains know how to perform *mūrtipūjā*, and many perform it daily. Many learn it as young children. The following prescription is based on a number of contemporary books and pamphlets, most written by mendicants.[11] In addition to giving instructions for the performance of the *aṣṭaprakārī pūjā*, and verses to sing to accompany the various acts, these sources usually address two related concerns. One is that the worshiper avoid committing any expiable moral fault (*āśātnā*) in the performance of the rite. This closely overlaps with the concerns to maintain purity (*pavitratā*, *śuddhatā*) in Hindu temple discourse. T. N. Madan (1987:60–61) has noted that one distinguishing feature of impurity for Hindus is that there are prescribed and readily available procedures for the removal of impurity. Similarly, for the Jains an *āśātnā* can be corrected and atoned for by specific expiations. The Jain notion of *āśātnā*, however, covers a broader compass than the Hindu notion of impurity, for it also involves a detailed concern that the ritual actions involve a minimum of harm (*hiṃsā*). In the interest of focusing this discussion upon the intentionality and theology involved in *pūjā*, in the following description I have avoided the many points at which the writers address ritual purity and propriety. The second concern is for the underlying inner spiritual meaning (*bhāv*) of the ritual. The authors take care to explain the meaning of each action according to the *mokṣa-mārg* ideology, so that the worshiper can perform the rite in a properly religious frame of mind. I have included some of these *mokṣa-mārg* interpretations of the rite in my discussion; other understandings will be discussed later, when I turn to devotion and intention.

Most people who perform *pūjā* do so in the morning, before going to work in the case of men, or between the morning and noon meals in the case of women. Many men perform *pūjā* only on Sunday, their day off from work. Its performance is a central activity in pilgrimage to the many important Mūrtipūjak shrines (*tīrth*) throughout western India. The full rite is performed by more women than men. Women are banned from performing *pūjā* during the three days of pollution during menstruation. In some families, this is followed by a further prohibition of four days against entering the central shrine; during this time, a woman can only take *darśan* or perform *bhāv pūjā*. Likewise, neither the men nor women of a family in which there has been a birth can enter the temple for ten days due to pollution.[12]

Before leaving home, the worshiper should bathe and don clean, unstitched clothes. S/he utters the Prakrit word "nisīhi" (it is abandoned) and enters into the temple. Standing in front of the Jina, with hands held in front of the chest, s/he bows from the waist and says, "namo jiṇāṇaṃ" (homage to the Jinas). If there is a circumambulatory around the central shrine, then s/he thrice circumambulates it clockwise. One interpretation is that the first circumambulation is for the victory of one's own soul, the second for the protection of the temple, and the third to symbolize the way in which all souls revolve in the world of rebirth. Alternately, the three circumambulations can symbolize the three stages of life (birth, old age, and death) or the three gems (correct faith, correct knowledge, and correct conduct). There are various verses available for each rite in the *pūjā*. Ideologues recommend these verses, as they help reinforce the *mokṣa-mārg* understanding of the acts. Yet, as we see, there are multiple ideological interpretations of the acts, demonstrating both the ideological concern that there should be a single meaning and at the same time the fact that the actions cannot be so reduced to a single meaning. If the person does not know any such verses, then it is recommended that s/he recite the *Nokār Mantra*. Among the possible verses for recitation during circumambulating are the following:

> From beginningless time, there is no end to wandering in lives;
> for release from that wandering, I offer three circumambulations.
>
> I circumambulate in the circumambulatory to drive away the obstacles in life;
> I offer three circumambulations in the form of faith, knowledge, and conduct.
>
> Caught in fear of birth, death, etc., I see the work of suffering;
> attaining and speaking the three gems, grant me faith, O Jina King.
>
> There is much knowledge in this world, and knowledge is the cause of happiness;
> but the world subsists without knowledge, desiring not even a hint of reality.
>
> They acquire a hoard of karma, although this anxiety is meaningless;
> having erected my conduct, I praise your virtues.
>
> Faith, knowledge, and conduct: these three gems are the gateway to liberation.
> Therefore I thrice circumambulate, to destroy the suffering of rebirth.

S/he stands in front of the central shrine, with hands folded in front of the chest, bows slightly from the waist, and takes *darśan* or sacred vision of the image, while reciting a hymn such as the following:

> *Darśan* of the God of gods, *darśan* which destroys sin;
> *darśan* which is the stairway to heaven, *darśan* which is the means to liberation.

The worshiper then makes a small round mark upon her/his own forehead with sandalwood paste. This signifies that the worshiper bears the instruction of the Lord upon the head, that the *pūjā* will be performed not from any desire on the part of the worshiper but at the instruction of the Jina, and that the worshiper now has the right to do the *pūjā*. The worshiper should also be careful not to make this mark in the line of sight of the Jina *mūrti*, as to do so would be a sign of disrespect, in essence a statement that one considered oneself equal to the Jina.

S/he ties a cloth, known as a *muhpattī*, over her or his mouth, so that "the bad smell from the mouth doesn't touch the Lord, and so that [the offerings] don't become spoiled" (Cāraṇvijaygaṇi 1950:20), and so that s/he will not commit subtle violence through exhaling against either insects or the *mūrti* while in the central shrine. After again saying, "nisīhi," s/he enters the central shrine. Using a peacock feather or other fine instrument, s/he removes from the *mūrti* any flowers and other offerings and decorations from the earlier *pūjās* of other people, and carefully wipes clean the *mūrti* with a damp cloth. S/he is now ready to begin the *aṣṭaprakārī pūjā* proper.

The *pūjā* is conceptually divided into two parts. The first are the three *aṅg* (limb) *pūjās*, so called because in these the offerings are made onto the limbs of the Jina *mūrti*: water,[13] sandalwood paste (more commonly called "saffron," since a small amount of saffron is usually mixed into the paste),[14] and flowers. The remaining five are the *agra* (facing) *pūjās*, because in these the offerings are made not onto but in front of the Jina *mūrti*: incense, lamp, rice, food, and fruit.

For the water *pūjā*, the worshiper fills a small pot with pure water (many temples have special water tanks or wells to provide such water), and sometimes also the five "nectars" of milk, curds, sugar, ghee, and flowers (or sandalwood). This anointing is in imitation and remembrance of the anointing of each Jina performed at the time of his or her birth by Indra and the assembled gods atop Mount Meru. One ideologue says of this *pūjā*, "As the anointing water is poured over the Supreme Soul, a layer of karma is washed away. . . . The blade of the anointing water cuts away a little at the wall of the palace of the world" (Oṃkārsūri 1984:147).

While performing the water *pūjā*, the worshiper can recite one or more of the following verses:

> Skillfully do the water *pūjā* to destroy beginningless dirt;
> I ask of Lord Pās, may I gain the reward of the water *pūjā*.
>
> On Mount Meru the king of the gods did the bath, on Mount Meru he did the bath,
> at the birth of the Best of Jinas
> who had the five kinds of knowledge; the king of the gods on Mount Meru did the bath.
>
> The soul is the knowledge-pot which is full, full of the juice of equanimity;
> karma is eradicated by bathing the Blessed Best of Jinas.

Following the water *pūjā*, the worshiper again carefully cleans and dries the *mūrti*. S/he now performs the sandalwood *pūjā*, also known as the "nine-limbed" *pūjā* because the sandalwood is applied to nine places on the *mūrti*. Khokhar (1986) recommends that one avoid using too much saffron, as it tends to give the *mūrti* a reddish hue, and red is associated with heat and passion. Because sandalwood paste is considered to be cooling and therefore beneficial in the subduing of passions and the destruction of karma, while performing this *pūjā* one should generate the meditational sentiment (*bhāvnā*), "may I attain a coolness like that of sandalwood"

(Manojitāśrī n.d.:6). Before performing the *pūjā* to the nine limbs, the worshiper first recites the following:

> In whom resides the quality of coolness—the color of the Lord's mouth is coolness.
> I speak to make the soul cool, and do *pūjā* to the Jina's limbs.

The worshiper gently applies the sandalwood paste to the following nine places on the body of the *mūrti*, using only the ring finger of the right hand: 1. the two big toes; 2. the two knees; 3. the two wrists; 4. the two shoulders; 5. the top of the head; 6. the forehead; 7. the throat; 8. the chest or heart; and 9. the navel (see Figures 3.4 and 3.5). Hemratnavijay (1983:69) admonishes the worshiper to apply the

Figure 3.4. Places on the body of a Jina *mūrti* for nine-limbed sandalwood *pūjā*. Drawing by Laurie MacKenzie-Crane.

Figure 3.5. Laywomen performing nine-limbed *pūjā*. Patan, April 1987.

sandalwood slowly and carefully, "not like someone striking a typewriter." Many *mūrtis* have silver knobs at the thirteen places where the paste is applied, to prevent damage to the *mūrti* itself. Stone, especially marble, is surprisingly soft, and many images show signs of wear within a very few years of consecration. The ideologues detail the intentions that should lie behind the rite as follows:

1. Toes. At the time of the initial anointing, Indra worried that the water might harm the Jina, so the Jina pushed down on Mount Meru with his toe to show that he was in no danger.
2. Knees. They carried the Jina on his travels, and standing upon them he attained enlightenment.
3. Wrists. Before renouncing the world, the Jina spent a year giving away his wealth with his own hands; thus the worshiper can remove attachment to wealth.
4. Shoulders. By their strength, the Jina overcame karma and took himself across the ocean of rebirth; by doing this *pūjā*, the worshiper aims to attain such strength.
5. Head. When the Jina pulled out his own hair in five handsful, he attained direct perception of the thoughts of others. The Jina presently reigns in the land of the perfected at the top of the universe; the top of the *mūrti*'s head reminds us of that realm.
6. Forehead. The Jina is the forehead mark of the triple universe.
7. Throat. Before he attained liberation, Mahāvīr preached for forty-eight hours. Similarly, Ṛṣabhnāth gave a sermon lasting centuries. By doing *pūjā* to the throat, the worshiper aims to attain such beneficial wisdom.
8. Heart. Passion and hatred are destroyed by the pacifying strength of the Jina's heart-lotus. The worshiper seeks to attain the nectar of pacification in his or her own heart.

9. Navel. The Jina was conceived in a true mine of gems. Through the *pūjā* to his navel-gem, one attains the three gems of faith, knowledge, and conduct that lead to the pleasure of liberation.

The verses that the worshiper can recite while performing these nine *pūjās* reflect these symbolisms and intentions. One author (Muktiprabhvijay n.d.:53) admonishes the worshiper to be silent during these *pūjās*, so as not to disturb other worshipers in the central shrine. Another (Manojitāśrī n.d.:8) says that the worshiper should perform the entire *aṣṭaprakārī pūjā* in silence, and sing aloud only the hymns of the *caitya-vandan*, "in a sweet voice."

Toes
The water fills the concave surfaces, I do *pūjā* to them both,
on the big toes of the Ṛṣabh's feet, who grants an end to the ocean of rebirth.

Knees
By the strength of those knees standing in *kāüssagg*, he traveled in lands near and far,
and stood in the enjoyment of enlightenment. The king does *pūjā* to those knees.

Wrists
When the *laukāntik*[15] gods made their request you gifted your wealth for a year;
worship that which is to be honored by doing *pūjā* to the wrists of the Lord.

Shoulders
Pride was broken in half from the mere sight of your endless might;
do *pūjā* to that greatly persevering one, by the strength of whose shoulders we are carried across the ocean of rebirth.

Head
The virtues shine in the realm of the perfect, for the Lord is at the top of the world;
his residence there is the cause, so do *pūjā* to the tuft on the head.

Forehead
Beings in the three worlds serve him because of the merit of His Tīrthaṅkar status;
the Lord is like the forehead-mark of the triple world, so hail to his forehead-mark.

Throat
The Lord preached for forty-eight hours from the round cavity of his throat;
men and gods heard that honeylike sound, so I make a mark on that unequaled throat.

Heart
The pacifying strength of His heart-lotus overpowers passion and hatred
just as ice does a burning forest fire, so may marking his heart give me contentment.

Navel
The virtues of the three gems shine in that abode of all good virtues;
by doing *pūjā* to the navel lotus, may I attain the unshakable abode of liberation.

The sandalwood *pūjā* can also include a further rubbing of the *mūrti* with camphor paste.[16] A final part of the sandalwood *pūjā* can be applying gold or silver leaf to the *mūrti*, but only if no one else is going to perform *pūjā* to that particular *mūrti* on that day.

The third and final of the *aṅg pūjās* is the flower *pūjā*. The worshiper is admonished to use only whole, unbroken flowers. They are placed on the lap, knees, shoulders, and head of the *mūrti*. While offering them, the worshiper can recite the following:

I take this fragrant unbroken flower, for doing *pūjā* with it drives away sorrow;
right-minded faithful people do this, for it is the mark of right faith.

For the first two of the *agra pūjās*, the worshiper remains in the central shrine.[17] To perform the incense *pūjā*, the worshiper takes up a small pot of burning frankincense in her or his right hand, and waves it before the *mūrti*, while reciting the following verse:

Meditation illuminates the dense darkness, just as I offer the incense before the beautiful eyes of the Jina;
driving away the bad smell of wrong faith, the innate nature of the soul is illuminated.

The second *agra pūjā* is that of the lamp. The worshiper takes a small brass lamp of ghee, into which is inserted a piece of camphor. Using both hands, s/he waves the lamp before the *mūrti*, with care taken that the lamp travel neither below the navel of the worshiper nor above the eyes of the *mūrti*. S/he recites the following:

Sorrow is rendered useless from the true discrimination of this physical lamp;
when the spiritual lamp shines forth the entire universe is illuminated.

The worshiper now exits the central shrine and sits in the main pavilion of the temple, facing the *mūrti*. S/he places a small table in front of her/himself. The final three *pūjās* are done on this table as an integrated set of offerings. Using unbroken grains of rice, s/he makes the mark of the Jain *svastik* (Gujarati *sāthiyā*) (see Figure 1.1). Some people instead use the rice grains to draw a *nandyāvart*; this is an extended *svastik* (von Hinüber 1974 and Srivastava 1991) (see Figure 3.6). Kuśalcandravijay

Figure 3.6. Marble inlay *nandyāvart* in a temple at Shatrunjay. January 1986.

(1983:V.17) explains the symbolism of the white rice as follows: being white, it symbolizes purity and peace; being dehusked, and therefore incapable of sprouting, it symbolizes the desire to attain liberation from the cycle of rebirth; and being unbroken, it symbolizes the unbreakable happiness of liberation. While drawing the *svastik*, the worshiper can recite the following:

> May I be successful by doing the rice *pūjā*, O Incarnation;
> I desire success and so offer this before you; save, save, save me.
>
> I sing to attain that unbreakable state, this is the essence of the rice *pūjā*;
> the *sāthiyā* pulverizes the four realms of rebirth; save, save, save me.
>
> I make a large *nandyāvart* of pure unbroken rice.
> When finished I face the Lord who removes all worldly troubles.
>
> I am wandering in the world of repeated births, the worldly troubles of birth and death;
> I seek the essence of success, liberation from the eight karmas.

The remaining two *pūjās*, of food and fruit, are made onto the rice diagram. For the food *pūjā*, items that are relatively free from spoilage such as sweets are used. Whereas the *mokṣa-mārg* symbolism of all the other *pūjās* is fairly straightforward, the interpretation of this offering involves a reverse symbolism. One of the definitions of liberation is *anāhārī pad*, "the state of not consuming," since by definition perfected souls do not need food. Food is necessary to maintain the physical body which is both an obstacle to liberation and a symbol of bondage. The food is offered, therefore, to symbolize the worshiper's aspiration to attain the nonconsuming state of liberation. To emphasize further this symbolism, the food is placed atop the center of the *svastik*, as food is part of the physical fuel that drives the round of rebirth.

The ideological interpretation that the Jina does not consume the food offerings is especially striking in light of the dominant non-Jain South Asian ritual paradigm of the deity consuming food offerings, which are then returned to the worshiper as *prasād*, the tangible and digestible sign of the deity's grace.[18] Sharing food is a powerful statement of social and even ontological interaction and intermingling in many religious traditions. By explicitly denying this paradigm, Jain ideologues are making a clear statement concerning both the Jain definition of God (see below) and the Jain religious path as one that is largely a matter of individual effort, independent of any divine aid. God for the Jains is the goal, not a merciful and active being.

The fruit offering (which can also be a nut) is placed atop the crescent. Since liberation is the fruit of *pūjā*, and the crescent symbolizes the realm of liberation, placing the fruit atop the crescent expresses the desire of the worshiper for liberation. Most people also offer a small coin atop the *svastik*, as another aspect of the physical world that must be given up if one is to attain liberation. While doing these *pūjās*, the worshiper can recite the following verses:

Food

> You have attained that state of not consuming which is forever beyond the body;
> remove my troubles and grant that liberation and goodness which are not consuming.

Fruit

> Indra and the other gods say the *pūjā* as they offer fruit in their passion;
> I do *pūjā* to the supreme person, for I seek liberation, the fruit of renunciation.

The *aṣṭaprakārī pūjā* proper ends here, but three other *pūjās* have been added to this basic structure. Since these are not found in the traditional lists, the order is not set. These are the bell, fan, and mirror *pūjās*. The bell *pūjā* consists simply of the worshiper ringing the temple bell. For the fan *pūjā*, the worshiper takes up the yak-tail fan (which in most temples hangs either on or next to the door into the central shrine) and gently waves it back and forth while doing a slight hopping dance step. The fan *pūjā* is done "to show our love, respect, and devotion to our Lord" (Kuśalcandravijay 1983:V.18). While doing this *pūjā*, the worshiper can recite this verse:

> The devotee[19] waves the whisk with a gay mind, he waves it with vigor;
> he lowers the whisk over the head of the Lord and merit rises up.

For the mirror *pūjā*, the devotee stands in the main pavilion of the temple and holds a mirror so that s/he is looking at the *mūrti* in it. S/he then dabs sandalwood paste onto the forehead of the reflected image. Kuśalcandravijay (1983:V.18) explains this *pūjā* as follows: "Having seen the face of the Lord in the mirror, and meeting his innately dispassionate qualities, we look into the mirror so that we may also become free of passion and hatred." While performing this *pūjā*, the worshiper can recite this verse:

> See with true perception one's true form in the mirror;
> the mirror is the gift of experience from the Lord of mendicants who delights in correct knowledge.

After the last of these *pūjās*, the worshiper for a third time says, "nisīhi," to indicate that s/he is now abandoning entirely the external worship with physical matter (*dravya pūjā*) and commencing the internal spiritual worship (*bhāv pūjā*), in the form of *caitya-vandan* or other such performance. After the *bhāv pūjā*, the worshiper exits the temple, taking care not to show his or her buttocks to the *mūrti*, and returns home, "with a sad heart due to the separation from the Lord" (Hemratnavijay 1983:107).

We see in this prescription for the daily eightfold *pūjā* two related processes: a gradual spatial narrowing into the center of the temple, accompanied by a gradual renunciation of worldly and then physical concerns. Entering the temple, the worshiper utters "nisīhi," to denote a sharp break between the profane realm of *saṃsār* outside the temple and the sacred realm of the *mokṣa-mārg* inside. S/he takes *darśan* of the Jina, thrice circumambulates the central shrine, and takes a further *darśan* before finally entering the central shrine. Here s/he again says "nisīhi," to denote the renunciation of all thoughts and actions inappropriate for one in the presence of the Jina. There, in the center of the temple, in physical proximity to the Jina, the stone representation of the Jain religious ideal, the worshiper performs the three *aṅg pūjās* onto the *mūrti* itself. Then s/he commences a gradual retreat from the world of matter to a more spiritual plane. The first two *agra pūjās*, of incense and the lamp, which involve the shift from offering onto the image to offering in front of the image, are performed while s/he is still inside the central shrine. For the last three *agra pūjās*, the worshiper further distances herself or himself from the Jina, offering the rice, sweets, and fruit from outside the central shrine.

The *bhāv pūjā* is also performed while in the main pavilion of the temple, outside the central shrine. Before commencing the *bhāv pūjā*, s/he utters the third "nisīhi," to indicate the renunciation of all physical material. If the worship has been performed according to the *mokṣa-mārg* prescription, the worshiper should now be on a plane of pure spirituality, devoid of any attachment to obstructing and clinging matter—a state approximating to that of the liberated soul.

Worship in Practice

The *aṣṭaprakārī pūjā* is rarely performed in exactly the manner described here. There is much room in the rite for the worshiper to develop a personal style of devotion. Most people combine the *aṣṭaprakārī pūjā* with some form of *bhāv pūjā* in their daily ritual. The colloquial terms most commonly used by laity to describe their own daily ritual are *dev pūjā*, "the worship of God," and *sevā pūjā*, "worship through service."[20] To indicate some of the range of possible individual styles found in the daily worship, I will give five examples, one in full detail, and the other four in more abbreviated fashion.

Dev Pūjā 1: Kīrtilāl M. *Śāh* Kīrtilāl is a sixty-four-year-old independent businessman. He performs *pūjā* every morning before going to work in his office in the main bazaar.[21]

After taking his morning bath, he puts on his *pūjā* clothes. These consist of a lower wrapped cloth known as a *dhotī*, and an unstitched upper wrap. Many strict Jains also do not wear stitched underwear while performing *pūjā*, but Kīrtibhāī does.[22] He walks barefoot to the temple, which is less than one hundred yards from his house. He carries with him fresh flowers from his garden, a small metal tray, and a bag containing the various implements he will need. He stops at the door of the temple, and thrice says, "nisīhi": "This means that I leave behind all things of the world. I shall think of nothing but God."

He enters the temple, and places the plate in the corner. He goes to the door into the central shrine, and takes *darśan* for five to ten seconds with his hands folded before him, while he silently repeats a hymn. The central shrine in this temple has a circumambulatory around it, so he thrice circumambulates it, with his hands folded, while he recites a hymn to Shatrunjay, the holy shrine in Saurashtra. "This is for release from the rounds of *saṃsār*." At the conclusion of the circumambulations, he stands again at the doorway into the central shrine. He briefly bows to the Jina, and recites another hymn. Even though the main *mūrti* of this temple is Pārśvanāth, this prayer he usually addresses to Ādināth, usually in Sanskrit, such as a verse from the *Mahādeva Stotra* of Hemacandra or the *Bhaktāmara Stotra* of Mānatuṅga.

Returning to where he placed the tray, he prepares for the sandalwood *pūjā* by mixing some sandalwood and water in a small metal bowl. He ties on his *muhpattī*. Some men use a separate cloth or handkerchief; most men, including Kīrtibhāī, tie the end of their upper wrap over their mouths.

Standing in the center of the main room of the temple, he holds a mirror so that he can see the main *mūrti* reflected in it. He sings a hymn while he dabs sandalwood paste on the forehead of the reflected image, "so I can close my eyes and see

You in my heart." He puts down the mirror and makes a sandalwood mark on his own forehead. "This is in order to obey God's command," and is done "with the emotion of surrender."

Kīrtībhāī now enters the central shrine, grasps the knees of the main *mūrti* in his hands, and bows his forehead onto its feet. Since the water *pūjā* is performed only by the first people to do *pūjā* to the *mūrti* on any given day, he starts with the sandalwood *pūjā* . He uses the ring finger of his right hand to dab sandalwood paste onto the nine limbs of the main *mūrti*, thirteen places in all. While performing this *pūjā*, he recites the *Nokār Mantra*. He repeats the sandalwood *pūjā* to the main *mūrti*, and performs flower *pūjā* by placing several flowers in it. He then performs nine-limbed sandalwood *pūjā* to the other Jina *mūrtis*, followed by sandalwood *pūjā* to the *mūrtis* of Padmāvatī and Dharaṇendra (the attendant *yakṣī* and *yakṣ* of Pārśvanāth) in their recesses in the shrine doorway, and finally to the *mūrti* of Śāntidevī in the base of the altar.[23] He takes care not to perform the full nine-limbed sandalwood *pūjā* to the latter three *mūrtis*, saying that to do so would be a mark of disrespect to the Jina's teachings by treating an unenlightened and unliberated deity with the respect due only to the enlightened and liberated Jina.[24] He dabs sandalwood on four places on the *mūrtis* of Padmāvatī and Dharaṇendra: each of the three snake hoods above them, and the forehead. After the sandalwood *pūjā*, he bows his head to the feet of the other Jina *mūrtis*.

He performs the incense *pūjā* by standing in front of each Jina *mūrti* in turn while holding the pot of smoking incense. He recites the following Gujarati verses:[25]

> Let us do this incense *pūjā*, O honorable delighter of my mind.
> As followers of the Lord we wave the incense pot, O honorable delighter of my mind.
> Lord, there is none to match you, O honorable delighter of my mind.
> In the end you are the final refuge, O honorable delighter of my mind.

Similarly, he performs the lamp *pūjā* by standing before each *mūrti* in turn, while holding the metal ghee lamp and reciting one or more verses from the standard *āratī* hymn (see below).

Kīrtibhāī now exits from the central shrine, and removes his *muhpattī*. He sits in the center of the main pavilion, facing the central shrine, with a small table in front of him. From the small bag he brought with him from home, he takes out a handful of white rice, and two coins of small denomination. With the rice he draws a *svastik* on the table. He places one coin on the center of the *svastik*, and the other on the dot at its top. "The four arms show that one must abandon the four realms of rebirth. Then one meets the three gems of faith, knowledge, and conduct. With their assistance, one can become a perfected soul and go to liberation."

He now performs *caitya-vandan*, essentially as described above. Following this, he sweeps the coins and rice from the table into the store-chest in the middle of the temple. These items, having been offered before the Jina, are now *dev-dravya*, "God's goods," and cannot be consumed by any Jain. The rice will be given to the temple *pujārī* as part of his payment, and the coins will go into the *dev-dravya* account of the temple trust. This account can only be used for construction and maintenance of this or another temple.[26]

Kīrtibhāī again stands in front of the central shrine, where with folded hands he recites a final hymn, and stands in silence for a moment. He takes the yak-tail fan from a hook on the door of the central shrine, and waves it in front of the *mūrtis*, while reciting a verse. Leaving the central shrine, he stands silently with folded hands before the painting of Shatrunjay on the temple wall. As he exits from the temple, he briefly gestures one final time to the Jina, bringing his hands to his chest.

Dev Pūjā 2: Śreyāben K. Śāh Śreyāben is the twenty-seven-year-old married daughter of Kīrtilāl Shah, who at the time was visiting Patan from her home in Bombay. For *pūjā* she wears her red wedding sari. She walks to the temple barefoot, and rinses her feet before entering. She goes to the back corner of the main room of the temple, where the necessary implements and supplies for *pūjā* have been laid out earlier by the temple *pujārī*, and makes a sandalwood dot on her forehead. She prepares some sandalwood paste in a brass dish. After tying a scarf over her mouth as a *muhpattī*, she goes to the central shrine. Before entering, she stands with her hands folded and says a brief hymn. She enters the central shrine, and makes sure that the lamp and the incense are both lit. She puts her hands on the knees of the main *mūrti*, and bows her head to its feet. She quickly performs the nine-limbed sandalwood *pūjā* to the main *mūrti* and the other stone Jina *mūrtis*. She places flowers on the *mūrtis* in the same order. She then places a single sandalwood dot on the forehead of each of the metal Jina *mūrtis*, on each of the seven snake heads above the main *mūrti* of Pārśvanāth, and on the forehead of the *mūrti* of Śāntidevī in the altar. She picks up the yak-tail fan, briefly waves it before each Jina *mūrti*, and then exits the main shrine. She makes a sandalwood dot on the forehead of the *mūrtis* of Padmāvatī and Dharaṇendra, then places a flower on each. All the while, there are other women performing their own *pūjās*, around whom Śreyāben must work.

Śreyāben then takes off her *muhpattī*, and sits on the floor in the center temple pavilion, facing the central shrine. She places a small table in front of her, and on it makes a *svastik* of rice, placing one almond each on the center of the *svastik* and the dot at its top. She sings several hymns, and performs three *khamāsamaṇs*. She performs *caitya-vandan* (but a slightly shorter version than her father), and then uses a twenty-seven-bead rosary to recite one round of the *Nokār Mantra* (see Figure 3.7). She circumambulates the central shrine three times, rings the bell once, and takes a final *darśan* of the Jina. She sweeps the rice and nuts from the table into the store-chest, puts a few small-denomination coins in it, and exits the temple.

Dev Pūjā 3: Śāntilāl N. Śāh Śāntilāl is a sixty-four-year-old doctor. He enters the temple for his morning *pūjā* and proceeds directly to the central shrine, where he holds his hands in front of his chest and bows to the Jina. Without donning a *muhpattī*, he picks up the incense stand and waves it before the *mūrtis*, first of the Jinas, then of Padmāvatī and Dharaṇendra, and finally before two *guru murtis* in niches in the main room of the temple.[27] He rings the temple bell once. Still carrying the incense stand, he circumambulates the central shrine three times, stopping on each round to wave the incense stand before the *mūrtis* inside. After the third circuit, he replaces the incense stand in the shrine and ties a kerchief over his mouth for a *muhpattī*. He quickly does sandalwood *pūjā* to each of the Jina *mūrtis*. He exits the central shrine, takes off the *muhpattī*, bares his torso, and sits

Figure 3.7. Laywoman using a rosary to recite a *mantra*. Patan, April 1986.

in the center of the temple pavilion facing the shrine. He sits silently for a minute, then recites aloud five of the nine remembrances (*Navasmaraṇ*).[28] This recitation takes about half an hour. He then redons his upper wrap, and approaches the central shrine. He takes up the yak-tail fan and waves it before the *mūrtis*, while reciting a Sanskrit *mantra* to the main *mūrti*, "oṃ hrīṃ śrīṃ śaṅkheśvara-pārśvanāthāya namaḥ" (*oṃ hrīṃ śrīṃ* [these are untranslatable Tantric syllables that invoke power] praise to Śaṅkheśvara Pārśvanātha). He folds his hands in front of his chest, and bows once to the main *mūrti*. He then bows to Padmāvatī and recites a verse to her. He stands before the painting of Shatrunjay, and recites another verse. He goes to the rear right corner of the temple, where the *pūjā* implements and supplies are kept, and dabs his right hand in the pot of water from the morning water *pūjā*. He explains that he puts this water on his eyes for good health.[29] He bows again briefly to the main *mūrti*. He now stands before the painting of Sammet Shikhar, the mountain in Bihar where twenty of the Jinas of this age attained liberation, and says another verse. He again faces the shrine with folded hands, repeats the *mantra* to the main *mūrti*, and exits from the temple.

Dev Pūjā 4: Vijay R. Coksī Vijay is a forty-four-year-old wholesale grain dealer. He enters the temple, makes a sandalwood dot on his forehead, and ties the end of his upper wrap over his mouth as a *muhpattī*. He picks up the incense stand and waves it before the Jina *mūrtis*. Still holding the incense stand, he circumambulates the central shrine once, waving the incense stand before the two *guru mūrtis* and the two paintings of the shrines of Shatrunjay and Sammet Shikhar as he passes them. He reenters the central shrine, and bows his head to the feet of the main *mūrti*. He performs the nine-limbed sandalwood *pūjā* to it, and then flower *pūjā*, using auspicious green *āsopalav* leaves he brought from home. He then performs these two *pūjās* to the other Jina *mūrtis*. He puts a sandalwood dot on the foreheads of the *mūrtis* of Śāntidevī, Padmāvatī, and Dharaṇendra, and places green leaves on the latter two. He takes off his *muhpattī*, bows once with folded hands to the Jina, and sits on the floor in the temple pavilion. Using a 108-bead rosary, he recites one round of the *Nokār Mantra*, followed by one round of a *mantra* to the main *mūrti*. The recitation takes a total of five minutes, after which he reties his *muhpattī* and reenters the central shrine, bowing his head to the feet of the main *mūrti*. He bows to the other *mūrtis*, exits the shrine, and takes off the *muhpattī*. On his way out of the temple he stops at the pot with water from the morning water *pūjā* to dab some on his eyes.

Dev Pūjā 5: Hemlatā V. Coksī Hemlatā is the thirty-eight-year-old wife of Vijay Coksī. She comes to the temple for her morning *pūjā* after he has returned home from the temple and left for his office in the grain market. She approaches the central shrine, and stands outside it with folded hands for five minutes, silently repeating a hymn. She then sits on the floor of the temple, and uses a 108-bead rosary to recite a *mantra* to the main *mūrti*. After five minutes of recitation, she stands, bows to the Jina, and exits from the temple.

As can be seen from these descriptions, there is great variety and flexibility in the *pūjā* performed by different people. This variety is based on family tradition (most Jains learn how to perform *pūjā* from their parents, usually their mothers), personal preference, physical constraints of the temple such as smallness or absence of a circumambulatory, available time, and the occasion. Just as an Indian musician improvises within the constraints of the given notes of a *rāga*, so the Jain worshiper improvises his or her daily *pūjā* within the constraints of the available rites of *aṣṭaprakārī pūjā* and *bhāv pūjā*. There are certain boundaries that should not be crossed, such as singing so loudly that others are disturbed, making inappropriate offerings, or any action that is classified as an *āśātnā*.[30] But as long as the ritual proprieties are observed, most Jains will stress that what is important in an individual's *pūjā* is not the precise form of the rite but rather the spirit and intention (*bhāv*) with which it is performed.

Before discussing the intentionality and theology of Jain temple worship, there are two other rites that need to be briefly discussed. The first of these is *darśan*, "holy viewing." This rite has been discussed in its broader Indic context by Diana Eck (1980), Lawrence Babb (1981), and Michael Meister (1995). The majority of Jains, including many who never or rarely perform *pūjā*, frequently go to a temple for *darśan*, especially on the occasion of a festival, when the main *mūrti* is elaborately ornamented (Cort 1996b). To facilitate this viewing, glass eyes are prominently applied to almost all Śvetāmbar *mūrtis*. This is perhaps the most immediately noticable difference between Śvetāmbar and Digambar *mūrtis*, for the Digambar Jains do not apply such eyes (Cort 1996b). Śvetāmbar Jains argue that these added eyes enhance the efficacy of the rite of *darśan*; the worshiper feels vividly that s/he is having a direct vision of the absolute reality embodied in the Jina (see Figure I.1). In the words of one anonymous writer, "one should do *darśan* with the complete emotion (*bhāv*) that the Tīrthaṅkar God himself is present" (*Sādharmik Bhakti* n.d.: 5). The eyes are placed upon the *mūrti* precisely to enhance this emotion.

The second rite is the offering of lamps (*ārati*), performed in every temple in the evening. This offering has two parts: the *ārati* proper, in which a five-wick lamp is offered by waving it in a circle, and the *maṅgaḷ dīvo*, the "holy lamp," in which a single-wick lamp is offered. On occasion of special festivals, or at the end of a large *pūjā*, a 108-wick lamp is offered.

Prescription 3: *Darśan*

Darśan as described by contemporary ideologues is similar to *agra pūjā*, or the physical offerings made in front of, but not onto, the *mūrti* of the Jina. The following is the rite for *darśan* as given by contemporary mendicant authors.[31]

The worshiper leaves home and walks to the temple, thinking, "I am going to the best power in this world" (Bhadraguptvijaygaṇi 1983:2), and thinking about the qualities of the Jina's life, message, and helpful actions. Upon seeing the tower and flagpole of the temple, the worshiper folds her or his hands in front of the chest, bows the head, and says "namo jiṇāṇaṃ" (Praise to the Jina). At the door of the temple the worshiper removes her or his shoes, and three times says, "nisīhi," to symbolize the total abandonment of all worldly matters with mind, speech, and body. Upon entering the temple, the worshiper makes a mark on her or his forehead with the sandalwood-saffron paste to indicate obedience to the Jina's teachings. Again s/he does bows to the *mūrti* and says "namo jiṇāṇaṃ." S/he circumambulates the central shrine three times, symbolizing the three gems of correct faith, knowledge, and conduct, and also "to destroy endless rebirth, and to become mentally absorbed in the one whom he is circumambulating" (Bhadraguptvijaygaṇi 1983:2). While circumambulating, s/he should sing in a sweet manner, preferably singing verses from the Sanskrit hymns *Ratnākara Paccīsī* or *Bhaktāmara Stotra.* S/he bows each time s/he passes in front of the central *mūrti.* After the third circumambulation, s/he stands in front of the central shrine (men should stand to the *mūrti*'s right side and women to the left), with hands folded, bows from the waist three times, each time saying again, "nisīhi." Still standing outside the shrine, s/he sings a hymn of her or his choice (or performs *caitya-vandan*), and then offers in front of the Jina the incense pot, the lamp, the yak-tail fan. On a small table in the center of the temple s/he makes a *svastik* of rice, on which s/he also places food and fruit. S/he rings the bell once. S/he then stands in front of the *mūrti*, with mind fixedly single-pointed, and gazes into the two eyes of the Jina. S/he sings another hymn, "to establish an inner relationship with God" (Bhadraguptvijaygaṇi 1983:2). The worshiper's mind and body are spiritually elevated by singing the hymns. For a third time s/he says three times, "nisīhi," and exits the temple.

Darśan in Practice

Kīrtibhāī M. Śāh, whose daily *pūjā* was desrcibed above, usually goes for *darśan* every evening to the temple of Śāmḷājī Pārśvanāth. On special occasions, he will also go to Pañcāsar Pārśvanāth, and perhaps another temple if there is a festival there. He enters the temple, and approaches the central shrine. He stands with his hands folded, and gazes into the eyes of the Jina *mūrti*. He sings the following two verses every evening:[32]

> I have come to you for shelter, O Best of Jinas, so fulfill my hopes.
> If I don't come, I'll die without you at the end of life; who in the world has a medicine for death?
> Today I joyfully sing to the Jina king, who creates an excess of supreme bliss.
> Wandering in birth after birth is destroyed by *darśan* of you, O Lord of us all.
>
> See the lamp which burns brightly in its pot.
> He is the illuminator of life: keep it burning every day.
> My breath flies higher and higher in the world just like a bird.
> I recognize you as the faultless Lord; come and give your *darśan*.

He then does three *khamāsamaṇs*, puts a few small coins in the temple store-chest, and exits.

Āratī

This encompasses two sequential offerings: a five-wick lamp of ghee (*āratī*), and a single-wick ghee lamp into which a small quantity of camphor is placed to create a pleasing odor (*maṅgaḷ dīvo*). There is no specific rite for performing *āratī* according to the *mokṣa-mārg* ideology. Ratnasenvijay (1983:II.27–28), for example, merely says that *āratī* and *maṅgaḷ dīvo* are performed at the conclusion of the *aṣṭaprakārī pūjā*, "in order to attain a holy sentiment (*bhāv-maṅgal*)." Each lamp is waved before the Jina, starting at the worshiper's upper right and going toward her/his lower left. While the *āratī* and *maṅgaḷ dīvo* are offered, the temple bell is rung, "to purify the atmosphere and to demonstrate devotion (bhakti)" (Kamalratnavijay 1986:58). All those present clap their hands and sing (see Figure 3.8). The hymns are as follows:[33]

Āratī

> Hail hail the lamp, Ādi Jiṇandā, O joy of King Nābhi and Marudevī.[34]
> Do the first lamp *pūjā*, take advantage of this human birth.
> The second lamp, O tender-hearted, cleanses the world in the pure temple pavilion.
> Indra, king of the gods, offers the third lamp in service of you, O Lord of the triple world.
> The fourth lamp destroys the four realms of rebirth, so we attain the mind-pleasing city of the bliss of release.
> The fifth lamp is the means for merit. Mūḷcand thus sings the virtues of Ṛṣabh.

Maṅgaḷ dīvo

> Lamp O lamp, holy lamp, we attain long life from offering the *āratī*.
> Our children are dressed up and play in our decorated home on the Dīvāḷī festival.
> Illuminate the family by singing the lamp, and so remove obstacles by one's *bhāv*.
> We sing the lamp in this Kali era, just as King Kumārpāl offered the lamp.[35]
> Our house is holy, your house is holy, may the fourfold congregation be holy.

In larger temples, the rights to offer the *āratī* and *maṅgaḷ dīvo* are auctioned. In smaller temples, the lamps are prepared by the *pujārī*, and then offered by anyone who happens to be present; on more than one occasion, the visiting scholar was

Figure 3.8. Congregation performing *ārati*. Ahmedabad, August 1985.

the only other person present, and so he offered it. If no one comes, the rite is performed by the *pujārī* alone. The evening *ārati* is usually performed about 8:00 P.M. The two lamps are left burning on a metal tray, and people coming to the temple for *darśan* will pick up the tray to offer the lamps, run their right hands over the flames and then touch their eyes and the tops of their heads, for health and protection. Most temples are locked up for the night between 9:00 and 10:00 P.M.

Worship, Devotion, and Intentionality

From the perspective of the *mokṣa-mārg* ideology, *mūrtipūjā* is a means whereby the worshiper through praise (*vandan*) of the virtues (*guṇ*) embodied in the Jina reduces his or her own karma, and thereby advances upon the path toward liberation. "The *caitya-vandan* includes hymns describing the true virtues of God. By singing the virtues of the Lord there is elimination (*nirjarā*) of the karma binding the soul," writes one contemporary ideologue (Ratnasenvijay 1990:7). This is an old formula; a number of authors quote the following Sanskrit verse, found in the eighth-century *Lalitavistarā* (p. 2) of Haribhadra Yākinīmahattarasūnu, who quotes it from an unknown earlier source:

> A good sentiment (*bhāva*) arises from correctly done *caitya-vandana*.
> From this there is complete destruction of karma and the attainment of a good condition (*kalyāṇa*).

Mendicant ideologues view *pūjā* as an extension of their own meditative and self-reflexive praxis, but performed by the laity with physical objects. Due to their vow of nonpossession (*aparigraha*), mendicants own nothing, and therefore have nothing to give. They can do only *bhāv pūjā*, not *dravya pūjā*. When they address the issue of *pūjā*, they tend to speak of it in terms of *bhāv pūjā* and *vandan*. They stress that most people, especially laity who are daily involved with the physicality of the world, need some physical representation of the ideal of liberation, as embodied in the Jina. They have developed a symbolic interpretation of *pūjā*, wherein *pūjā* is understood to be directed not to the *mūrti* but to what it symbolizes. A commonly heard equation is that *pūjā* is not of the *mūrti* but of the *mūrtimān*, that which the *mūrti* embodies or symbolizes: "When people praise the Dispassionate Lord who is projected onto the *mūrti*, and say 'O transcendent one! O formless one! O unattached one! O desireless one!' . . . through these virtues they are praising the virtuous Lord" (Bhadraṅkarvijaygaṇi n.d.:95). In semiotic vocabulary, *pūjā* is of the signified, not of the signifier. Another way to express this is that by praising the virtues (*guṇ*) of the virtuous (*guṇvān*) Jinas, one can actualize those virtues in one's own soul. This has been succinctly stated by the Khartar Gacch *sādhvī* Maṇiprabhāśrī: "The aim of *pūjā* is to acquire virtues. It is definitely necessary to do *vandan* of virtues to acquire them. *Vandan* of the virtues is essential. The fulfillment of all virtues is God, the Dispassionate Perfect Lord. To do *vandan* of the Dispassionate, a person needs a material support through the medium of which he can incline toward the virtues" (1985:54).

A key concept from Jain karma theory that underlines this understanding is *anumodan*. Although much karma theory is known only by specialists, *anumodan* is a common term in all Jain discourse. There are three ways to acquire meritorious karma (*puṇya*) and to remove demeritorious karma (*pāp*), or to remove all karma: by performing a rite oneself, by having another perform the rite, and by assent and approval of the performance of the rite by another person (*anumodan*). The logic of this is straightforward. As several people explained to me, if by approving of a harmful, demeritorious deed a person accrues a negative karmic result, then it is only logical that by approving of a good, meritorious deed the person must accrue a positive karmic result. There are two loci classici for this formulation. One is in the lifelong vow of *sāmāyika* taken by a mendicant as part of the rite of initiation (*Daśavaikālika Sūtra* 4.11): "As long as I live, I [renounce] in three ways the three modes of harm: in thought, speech, and action, I will not do, nor cause others to do, nor approve of others doing harm." The other is a description of what a Jain should believe, found at the beginning of the canonical *Ācārāṅga Sūtra* (1.1.1.5): "He affirms that the soul is real, he affirms that the world is real, he affirms that karma is real, he affirms that actions are efficacious, he acknowledges that karmic harm results in the world in all these ways, 'I have done it, I have caused another to do it, and I approved of others' actions,' and he renounces them."

This concept has been extended to apply to all actions, as in the following passage from Hemacandra's *Vītarāga Stotra* (17.1–4):

> Censuring my own bad deeds and approving of good deeds,
> O Lord, I go to your feet, the shelter of the shelterless.
> May karmically harmful actions done, commissioned, and approved in mind, speech, and body be of no result, nor repeated.
> I approve of all of that has been done which is good
> in accordance with the three gems, for that is how to follow the path.
> Whatever virtues of *arhat*ness, etc., there are in all the *arhats*, etc.:
> I praise all of those [virtues] of those Great Souls.

A contemporary mendicant expands on this, saying that the censure of bad deeds severs one from bad karma, whereas *anumodan* of good deeds leads to correct faith, an increase in meritorious karma, and a good rebirth (Hemcandravijay 1977:12–14, 71–79).

Laity and mendicants who perform extended fasts or other praiseworthy deeds are usually felicitated at the conclusion. These public felicitations, which often include a special congregational *pūjā*, provide an opportunity for all Jains to benefit karmically from the meritorious actions of one Jain. The person who performed the deed earns merit and destroys bad karma through his or her own action; the others also earn merit and destroy bad karma through *anumodan*. Congregational *pūjās* last for several hours. They are based upon the *aṣṭaprakārī pūjā*, although usually performed to a portable metal festival image placed on a bathing stand in front of the central shrine, not to the stone main image permanently installed in the main shrine. These *pūjās* include much devotional singing, both on the part of professional singers and on the part of the assembled congregation. The *anumodan* is expressed in large part through the devotion generated by the singing.

Although any good deed is an occasion for *anumodan*, *mūrtipūjā* provides a daily opportunity for laity to earn merit and destroy bad karma. But *mūrtipūjā* has not been without its critics. The Sthānakvāsīs insist that through *mūrtipūjā* the worshiper becomes attached to what is merely a piece of stone (or metal), thereby showing disrespect for the disembodied Jina by equating inanimate stone with the Jina. An oft-heard Mūrtipūjak response is that the *mūrti* is merely a material support for the active meditation in *pūjā* of praising the virtues of the Jina. One *sādhu* in conversation said that without the *mūrti* of the Jina, there is no arising in the worshiper of the proper sentiment (*bhāv*) that leads to the destruction of karma. He said that the *mūrti* is the cause and the sentiment is the effect, and that without the cause there can be no effect. Bhadraṅkarvijaygaṇi (1980:155) makes a similar claim when he says, "the physical matter (*dravya*, here meaning *mūrti*) is the cause, and the sentiment (*bhāv*) is the effect." The early-twentieth-century Ācārya Buddhisāgarsūri (1978:18) makes a similar point, using the *sākār/nirākār* ("with form"/"without form") vocabulary also found in Hindu bhakti theology. He writes:

> Devotion and the material support of the image with form are necessary for meditation. One can't just suddenly meditate on the formless Lord. And no one can love the formless Lord. Devotion begins with the image with form of the Lord and with the Lord with form. When one sees the established form[36] of the Lord Jina, one can remember the virtues of the Lord, and from that attain those virtues by which one's soul becomes zealous. . . . The Lord is not actually visible in the Jain scriptures, nor in the images of the Lord. But by means of the Lord's image, the Lord's devotee can cause the Lord to be seen in his own heart.

According to Jain theology, the Jina cannot respond to the actions and entreaties of the worshiper.[37] The Jina is *vītrāg*, "one who has conquered all passions." To respond in any way to the worshiper, even compassionately, would be a sign of attachment. The results of *pūjā* are therefore reflexive: the worshiper causes the virtues of the Jina to arise in himself or herself by praising them in word, thought, and deed. This is clearly stated by Ācārya Jayantsensūri of the Tristuti Gacch: "All that we do in *pūjā*, such as the requests and prayers we do before the Lord, are simply means for awakening ourselves, nothing else. . . . We are not requesting anything of Him, but that we have awakened our own lost creativity and are fulfilling or awakening our own consciousness. . . . True *pūjā* is just . . . arousing one's life to follow His word" (1985:107).[38]

Mokṣa-mārg ideologues consistently maintain this view of *pūjā* as a reflexive, meditative act. They frequently admonish the worshiper not to sing hymns that contain requests such as one might make of another person, or in other ways make requests of the Jina. One *sādhu* in conversation said that performing *pūjā* to the Jina for worldly gains would lead to bad karma (*pāp*); one should do *pūjā* solely to be reborn as a *sādhu* in a place where liberation is possible. Another *sādhu* stressed that one should not perform *pūjā* even to acquire merit (*puṇya*), for although merit is necessary for worldly ends, it is still a hindrance on the path to liberation. *Pāp* and *puṇya* are both forms of karma according to Jain karma theory, and therefore are ultimately to be discarded in order to attain liberation. This is seen in a formula repeated in several places (such as Kalāpūrṇsūri 1985:43, Kalyāṇsāgarsūri 1985:128) that the goal of *pūjā* is to progress from the realm of inauspicious and harmful karma (*aśubh*) to the realm of auspicious and positive karma (*śubh*), and thence to the realm of pure liberation (*śuddh*).[39]

But not all Jains who are performing their daily *pūjā* in the temple, or taking *darśan*, are thinking exclusively of liberation. The fact that the *mokṣa-mārg* ideologues—both mendicants and laity—feel it necessary to preach and write frequently concerning the proper spirit in which to perform *pūjā*, and to admonish people not to perform *pūjā* for worldly ends, is clear evidence that many people do indeed perform *pūjā* for precisely these ends. Jains recognize in discussion among themselves (and in interviews) that many people perform *pūjā* for worldly ends, and attribute their worldly success to their daily *pūjā*. They all know the *mokṣa-mārg* response to this, and so upon a moment's reflection usually criticize such motivations. But the ubiquity of such worldly motivations is freely recognized.

In further recognition that most laity are motivated primarily by worldly ends, not by the goal of liberation, some *sādhus* have promoted cults specifically designed to respond to the laity's worldly needs. The orthodox support for the development of Jain goddess traditions is in significant part connected with the efforts to meet the worldly needs of the Jains within the context of the Jain tradition (Cort 1987). The goddess Padmāvatī continues to be popular for these reasons; many people travel to Shankheshvar to worship her as much as to worship the miracle-working *mūrti* of Pārśvanāth there. Similarly, the cults of male protector deities such as Māṇibhadra Vīr and Nākoḍā Bhairav have been propagated by ideologues to try to prevent lay Jains from worshiping non-Jain deities to meet their worldly needs.[40] This is clearly seen in the twentieth-century history of Ghaṇṭākarṇ Mahāvīr.

The cult of Ghaṇṭākarṇ Mahāvīr is closely linked with the career of Ācārya Buddhisāgarsūri (1874–1925) and his successor *samudāy*.[41] Buddhisāgarsūri was concerned that Jains in the area of his native Vijapur (in eastern Mehsana district) were resorting to the shrine of a Muslim *pīr* (deceased saint) for help in problems of childlessness, spirit possession, and other misfortunes. They made offerings to the *pīr* and ate the *prasād*. Since the offerings included goats, the *prasād* included meat. Buddhisāgarsūri undertook a lengthy fast at the Jain temple at Mahudi, near Vijapur. On the final day, he had a direct vision of the Jain protector deity Ghaṇṭākarṇ Mahāvīr, who instructed Buddhisāgarsūri to install an image of himself (that is, Ghaṇṭākarṇ) and to institute his cult. In the past several decades, the cult of Ghaṇṭākarṇ has become enormously popular among Mūrtipūjak Jains, and the temple at Mahudi is now one of the wealthiest Jain temples in India. In discussing this cult, Buddhisāgarsūri has written: "It is not a fault to believe in and do *pūjā* to the passionate Vīr as a fellow Jain.[42] He is a devotee of Lord Mahāvīr. Whoever desires the assistance of their fellow Jain Ghaṇṭākarṇ Mahāvīr should worship him by *pūjā* and other means. The fellow Jain Vīr has correct faith. His assistance in fulfilling desires is preferable to the assistance of gods and goddesses who possess incorrect faith" (1983–1984:55).

Nonetheless, many Jains do worship the Jina for worldly ends. The question of how and why *pūjā* "works," that is, how the individual attains worldly benefits as a result of his or her *pūjā* to the Jina, is complex and open to multiple interpretations. It is an important area of Jain practice for which there is no single ideological theory, and so reminds us that no ideology ever speaks with a single hegemonic voice. Before addressing this question, it is necessary to look at Jain theology in greater detail to understand more fully the varying Jain theories of how *pūjā* works, for the two issues are intertwined.

Jain Theology

Western authors such as Auguste Barth (1882:146) and Margaret Stevenson (1915:292–94) have frequently characterized the Jains as atheists or non-theists.[43] Western scholarship was following the Brāhmaṇical characterization of the Jains as *nāstikas*, although this more accurately refers to the Jain rejection of the authority of the Vedas, not the Jain rejection of the concept of God. *Dev-tattva* or the verity of God is one of the three fundamental categories of Jain philosophy, according to one oft-cited formula. Jain ideologues have long been concerned to refute the characterization of Jainism as atheist. For example, Ātmārāmjī gave the following explanation in his 1884 *Jain Tattvādarś*, "The Ideals of the Jain Tenets," an explanation that closely followed arguments found in many texts from the previous millennium:

> Question: We have heard that Jains do not believe in God (Īśvar). Their tradition is atheist. But in the first chapter [of your book] in many places you have written "Lord God Arhat" (Arhant Bhagvant Parame Śvar), and the first chapter gives a complete description of the Lord. How is this possible?
>
> Answer: O faithful one! Whoever says that Jains do not believe in God is mistaken. They have never read or heard the scriptures of the Jain tradition, nor have they ever met an educated Jain. Those who have read or heard the Jain scriptures never say that the Jains don't believe in God. . . . [He then supports his argument by quoting and discussing verses 24 and 25 of the *Bhaktāmara Stotra*.] If people say that Jains don't believe in God, then to whom are these hymns addressed? Therefore, those who say that Jains do not believe in God speak falsely.
>
> Question: You have removed that doubt from my mind very effectively. But I still have one doubt. You believe in God, but is it believed in the Jain tradition that God created the world or not?
>
> Answer: O faithful one! If it could be proven that God created the world, then why wouldn't Jains believe it? But there is no proof that God created the world. (Ānandśūri 1936:I.80–85)[44]

As is seen in this passage, Jains strenuously affirm their belief in God. Their definition of God, however, differs from other theistic traditions such as the various Vaiṣṇava schools and the three Abrahamic monotheistic traditions of Judaism, Christianity, and Islam, especially on the question of whether or not God is the creator who existed before time and the world. This defense is not a recent phenomenon. The canonical *Bhagavatī Sūtra* (12.9; see Deleu 1970:190–91), for example, contains a discussion of the five kinds of beings to whom the word god (*deva*) can appropriately be applied: beings who will be reborn as gods, kings, mendicants, Jinas, and heaven-dwelling unliberated deities. Creating the universe and effecting salvation have no place in this list. As Paul Dundas (1985:185) has written in commenting on these verses, "divinity in these terms signifies status alone and does not entail any ability or desire to influence human events and destinies."

Another definition is found in the following list of twenty-five synonyms for god (*deva*) given by Hemacandra in his *Abhidhānacintāmaṇi* (II.24–25):

> Worthy; victor; gone beyond; knower of the past, present, and future; with the eight karmas worn away; supreme one; foremost lord; benevolent; self-born; lord; world lord; ford-maker; congregation-maker; victor lord;
>
> speaker of the doctrine of maybe; giver of fearlessness; universal; omniscient; all-seeing; enlightened; god of gods; giver of wisdom; supreme person; with desires conquered; trustworthy.[45]

Again, neither creating the universe nor actively saving souls is involved here. God, according to the Jains, is any soul who has attained liberation. Some of the terms, such as ford-maker and congregation-maker, indicate that while still embodied the Jinas created the Jain religion, and so showed the path to liberation. But they did not create the universe, nor do they grant liberation. This is clearly seen in the following definition of God given by Hemacandra (*Yogaśāstra* 2.4–7); the first two verses describe the dispassionate Jain god, in contrast to the description of the passionate Hindu gods Viṣṇu and Śiva in the last two verses:

> Omniscient, with desires and other faults conquered, honored by the triple world,
> and explaining the true meaning: He is God, Arhat, the Supreme Lord.
>
> He is to be meditated upon, He is to be worshiped, He is to be gone to for refuge, and
> His teaching is to be obeyed with one's will.
>
> Those who are soiled by women, weapons, rosaries, and the like, and by the marks of
> desire, etc.,
> who are subjugated [in rebirth] and grant boons to others—
> such gods are not liberated.
>
> Confused by the inundation of dancing, gaiety, singing, etc.,
> how can such beings attain liberation?

Hemacandra in his autocommentary (pp. 166–68) explains that there are four superior qualities found in the godness of God: knowledge of the nine verities (*tattva*) discussed in chapter 1; destruction of that which is to be destroyed, that is, the passions of desire and aversion that stain the soul; the fact that he is honored and worshiped in all manner of ways in all places by all beings; and his explanation of things as they really are. Hemacandra is here describing the positive defining characteristics of God. Because according to Jain cosmography the universe is eternal and uncreated, there is no need to mention that God did not create the universe.

The Jain definition of God, however, does create a problem for Jain theologians. The Jina as liberated soul resides at the top of the universe in a state aptly defined by Padmanabh Jaini (1979:352) as "freed from all activities whatsoever." For our purposes, what is important is that the Jina does not, and in fact cannot, act. The Jina could act if it wanted to, for the perfected soul is endowed with the four infinitudes of perception, knowledge, capability, and bliss. But according to the Jains, any action is dependent upon a desire to perform that action; and since another defining characteristic of the Jina is that it has conquered all desires (*vīt-rāg*), by definition the Jina cannot have the desire to act and therefore cannot act. Thus Hemacandra, in the verses above, gave as part of his description of the incorrect Hindu definition of God that the being in question grants boons to those who request them. A boon-granting deity, argue the Jains, cannot himself (or herself) be liberated, but can only be an unliberated being, albeit more powerful in some ways than humans. The question still remains: If God does not act, then how does worship bear fruit? Different answers to this question are found in the Jain tradition, based on different understandings of the precise nature of God's absence from this world. Let us now turn to these Jain answers.

How Does *Pūjā* Work?

The question of how *pūjā* works is rarely asked. The average Jain, whether a layperson or mendicant, is no more of a systematic theologian than the average

Christian. Many laypeople when asked how *pūjā* works indicated that they could not explain it, and that I should instead talk to a knowledgeable ideologue. But many insisted that they strongly felt God's presence in *pūjā* and other acts of devotion. A favorite Jain hymn in Gujarati has as its refrain, "You are in my mind, you are in my heart," a sentiment expressed and felt by many Jains.[46]

Many Jains also deny that God does not interact with the worshiper and cannot grant requests. Many explicitly said that their financial and professional success was directly due to God's grace. As discussed above, the fact that Jains frequently accuse other Jains of making requests of God indicates that such practices, and belief in their efficacy, are widespread. An important thing to note about such beliefs, however, is that although they are presumably widely held, there is an equally widespread opinion that they run counter to the ideology of the *mokṣa-mārg*.

Most Jains distinguish between worldly benefits and advancement upon the *mokṣa-mārg*. Granting of the former is clearly within the domain of a vast array of unliberated gods and goddesses such as Ghaṇṭākarṇ Mahāvīr and Padmāvatī. The forms of worship of these deities are clearly demarcated from the form appropriate for the Jinas. According to ideologues, nine-limbed *pūjā* should be done only to the Jinas, never to other deities. Similarly, offering a garland of coconuts, as indication that a request has been granted, is appropriate only to unliberated deities. Large signs remind the devotees at Shankheshvar, for example, to offer coconut garlands only to Padmāvatī, not to Pārśvanāth.

The worldly success resulting from worship of Śaṅkheśvar Pārśvanāth and other popular *mūrtis* indicates another theory of how worship is efficacious. In many contexts, Jains distinguish between the Jina and the Jina *mūrti*. Jains talk of miracle-working (*camatkārī*) *mūrtis*, of which Śaṅkheśvar Pārśvanāth is one of the most famous in Gujarat. Although the Jina cannot respond to a worshiper's request, the *mūrti* itself can. I received various answers as to how *mūrtis* become miracle-working. Several mendicants said that these powers are the result of centuries of proper worship by devoted and faithful Jains. Others said that the powers of a *mūrti* derive from the rite by which it is initially consecrated by a mendicant. Several mendicants simply denied the possibility of miracles. There are no *mūrtis* in Patan that display such miraculous powers as Śaṅkheśvar Pārśvanāth. One layman said that Pañcāsar Pārśvanāth used to be *camatkārī*, but that there had been no displays of miracles for many centuries. He was unable to explain how such a deficiency resulted. Nonetheless, even less powerful *mūrtis* in Patan still have a definite presence. For several years, the Patan laity had wanted to rebuild the temple of Śāmḷājī Pārśvanāth. Various methods of prognostication indicated that the main image did not want to be moved. Finally it was decided to move all the other *mūrtis*, erect a temporary shelter around the main image, and then undertake the reconstruction of the temple. Later, after the old temple had been leveled, the architects said that it would not be possible to build the grand temple envisioned by the donors without moving the image. This time the prognostication was favorable, and the image moved.

These miraculous powers can also reside in a temple, as in Ranakpur in Mewar, or in an entire pilgrimage site, as in Shatrunjay in Saurashtra. Some people talk of the *yakṣ* and *yakṣī*, the god and goddess responsible for the protection of the teachings of each Jina responding to the requests of worshipers (Cort 1987:240–43). A popular Sanskrit *mantra* of Śaṅkheśvar Pārśvanāth is "*oṃ* praise to blessed Śaṅkheśvara Pārśvanātha who is worshiped by Dharaṇendra and Padmāvatī."[47] Padmāvatī is included in the *mantra* as a worshiper of Śaṅkheśvar Pārśvanāth, and her power and efficacy derive in large part from her correct faith. In a statement that recalls the concept of the truth act (see below), one worshiper said that even though it is improper to request anything from the Jina, the request of a true Jain cannot be ignored, and so the *yakṣ* and *yakṣī* must respond. In the case of specific *mūrtis* such as Śaṅkheśvar Pārśvanāth, another deity who is often described as responding to the worshiper is the *adhiṣṭhāyak dev*, or "location god." At Shankheshvar, the *adhiṣṭhāyak dev* is said to be the reincarnated soul of the thirteenth-century Ācārya Vardhmānsūri, who was responsible for one of the renovations of the temple. Jains say that his affection for the *mūrti* and the temple was so great that it continued after his death and led to his next birth as the *adhiṣṭhāyak dev*.

No Jain would argue that because God cannot respond to the petitions of the worshiper, worship therefore cannot bear fruit. As mentioned above, the *mokṣa-mārg* ideology views *pūjā*, *vandan*, and other forms of worship as self-reflexive actions. Bhadraṅkarvijaygaṇi (1986:49–50) has answered precisely this question as to how *pūjā* bears fruit according to the *mokṣa-mārg* ideology as follows:[48]

> Question: If the Lord Jina receives no gain from *pūjā*, then isn't it meaningless?
>
> Answer: There is no benefit to the Lord Jina from *pūjā*, but there is certainly gain for the worshiper. By remembering a *mantra*, tending a fire, or studying a science, there isn't any benefit to the *mantra*, fire, or science. But from the remembrance of a *mantra*, poison is destroyed; from tending a fire, cold is destroyed; and from the study of science, knowledge is certainly increased. In the same way, the good resolutions of the worshiper grow by *pūjā*, and from that there definitely result the destruction (*nirjarā*) of karma and the attainment of merit (*puṇya*).

Elsewhere in the same set of questions and answers he spells out the process more clearly (47).

> Question: What is the basis for the fruitfulness of *darśan* of the Lord?
>
> Answer: From *darśan* of the Lord, a good sentiment (*bhāv*) is born in the soul. At the time of *darśan* of the Lord, the worshiper becomes humble. He praises God, by which he demonstrates his sentiment of gratitude. From this gratitude, there is the destruction of karma such as that which obscures knowledge, and the soul progresses on the path to liberation.

A similar description of the process by which *mūrtipūjā* (here, as with many accounts given by mendicants, described in terms of *darśan* as a form of *bhāv pūjā*) is fruitful is given by Kalāpūrṇsūri as follows:

> No matter how troubled one's mind is, it will at once become peaceful from *darśan* of the pure, unmodifying, and peaceful form of God, and one will be attracted by those unworldly virtues. From this attraction one's inner affection for God will increase. Not only that, but when a true guru explains to the worshiper that just such a secret form is also present in one's soul, delight in the innate form of God will develop from the unbroken respect, honor, faith, devotion, and pure observance of his highest and

> purest teaching, and through consideration, thinking upon, and meditation on his pure soul-form and his boundless virtues. Then the *mūrti* of God will beguile the worshiper with its beguiling power. This beguiling destroys the great delusion, and we become absorbed in the undeluded Lord. (1985:136)

We see in these two accounts a progression whereby *darśan* of the virtues of the Jina as embodied in the *mūrti* creates a spirit of inner peace in the worshiper. This inner peace then provides the occasion for the arising of correct knowledge, and through this knowledge the binding karma is destroyed.

A question arises that I asked several mendicants: If the *mūrti* is merely a convenient sign, why must it be installed with elaborate rites of consecration, and then guarded from all manner of worldly pollution and faults? One *ācārya* stated that although the stone is ontologically altered through these rites, the rites are not really necessary. Even if these rites have not been done to the *mūrti*, the suitable sentiment (*bhāv*) will still arise in the worshiper if *pūjā* and *vandan* are done properly. The consecration rites, he stressed, are done so that the common people will believe in the *mūrti*, and thereby the proper *bhāv* will arise in their hearts as they worship it. We see here the central importance of *bhāv* in understandings of *pūjā*. On the one hand, *bhāv* refers to the devotional sentiment that arises from correctly done worship. But *bhāv* also refers to the intention with which the person approaches worship.[49]

Another way of looking at the *mokṣa-mārg* position on the efficacy of *pūjā* and *vandan* is through the concept of the truth act (*satyakriyā*), although this was not mentioned by any Jains with whom I spoke. The role of the truth act in the Hindu, especially Vedic, tradition has been thoroughly discussed by E. W. Burlingame (1917) and W. Norman Brown (1940, 1963, 1968, and 1972), and in the Jain tradition by Paul Dundas (forthcoming). In brief, the basis for the truth act is the belief that if a person performs an action perfectly, in proper accordance with time, place, and participants, then the fruits of that action as declared by the person must of necessity come true. In brief, the formula runs something like this: "If x be true, then may y occur." Several such truth acts are found in Hemacandra's telling of the biography of Mahāvīra in his *Triṣaṣṭiśalākāpuruṣacaritra*, when Mahāvīra's troublesome disciple Gośāla gained his own ends through calling upon the truth inherent in Mahāvīra. The following is one example:[50]

> The Master [Mahāvīra] went to a village of Brāhmans. It had two divisions and their chiefs were two brothers, Nanda and Upananda. To break a fast of two days, the master entered Nanda's division and Nanda gave him curds and old boiled rice. Gośāla entered the other division and seeing Upananda's lofty house, went there, zealous, for alms. At Upananda's order, a slave-girl gave him old boiled rice. As he did not wish that, Gośāla maliciously cursed Upananda, who said, "If he does not take the food, throw it on his head at once," and she did so. Angered, Gośāla said: "If my guru has power from penance or a psychic fire may that man's house burn down at once. May the curse from not receiving holy men not be fruitless." The Vyantaras [a class of deity] who were present burned the house like a bundle of straw.

In the context of Jain *pūjā* and *vandan*, the notion of the truth act can help us see one understanding of how *pūjā* "works." If a true Jain—that is, a person who has correct faith in the Jina's teachings—performs *pūjā* in the proper manner, then there must be a result from this action. It is not necessary that there be a response, only a result. This argument is self-confirming, in that if there is no benefit from the worship then one can assume that there was some unknown mistake or that the person's *bhāv* was inadequate. The active agency of the Jina is not required for the worshiper to benefit from *pūjā*. In the words of the ideologue Dalsukh Malvaṇia, citing the eighteenth-century *Ṛṣabhajinastotra* of Devacandra on how liberation is attained, "soul itself is the doer and the [Jinas] are the instrumental cause" (1986:87–88).

Another explanation of how *pūjā* "works" is that acts of worship performed in the present are efficacious because of the prior actions of the Jinas themselves. Here it is important to remember the two meanings of another name for the Jinas: Tīrthaṅkar, "*tīrth*-maker." On the one hand, this refers to *tīrth* in the pan-Indian sense of a place where one can cross over from the realm of rebirth to liberation (Eck 1981). More specifically, however, it refers to the four *tīrth*s of the Jain congregation: *sādhus*, *sādhvīs*, *śrāvaks*, and *śrāvikās*. In writing of the relationship between the Jina and spiritual gain through the *tīrth* established by the Jina, one contemporary mendicant has written: "The Blessed God Jinas who show the path to liberation in the Jain religion are considered to be unparalleled aids, and the chief aim of their aid is to establish the *tīrth* that ferries faithful souls across rebirth" (Jinendravijaygaṇi 1980:ii). The existing Jain community is the living result of the Jina's saving actions. The Jina does not save the Jain worshiper by carrying the worshiper across to liberation himself, but rather by establishing the means by which the worshiper can him= or herself attain liberation even after the Jina is no longer bodily present.

A related concept that is important here is *kalyāṇ*, "welfare." In the life of every Jina there are five *kalyāṇaks*, or events that generate welfare: conception, birth, world renunciation, enlightenment, and liberation. As long as the Jain congregation and tradition continue, Jains are living within the sphere of influence of those welfare-generating events, and so in some way can tap into the spiritual energy generated by the Jinas. An image for this is that we are living within the shadow of the *kalyāṇ* generated by the Jinas. A contemporary lay *paṇḍit* has written of the fruits of devotion to the Jina in a similar manner: "This path of devotion to the Jina is holy, so those who follow it will not be without any gain. Those who stand beneath a thick tree will surely receive the shade which is its nature, and likewise those who apply the color of devotion to the Jina to their inner being will surely receive great gain" (D. Śāh 1983:12).

In discussion with mendicants on how and why worship is efficacious, another perspective that emerged is based on the fact that all "soul-substance" (*ātma-dravya*) is essentially the same, and merely resides in different contexts. There is no ontological difference between the soul-substance embodied in the single-sensed earth-bodies in a *mūrti* and the liberated soul-substance of a Jina. In the words of Bhadraṅkarvijaygaṇi (1980:152), "The *mūrti* of the Lord is the innate form of pure soul-substance (*śuddh ātma-dravya*). The *mūrti* is a form. Soul-substance is God Himself. . . . In the Lord's *mūrti* is soul-substance just like that in God. . . . The *mūrti* is the best support for faithful souls to gain interior *darśan* of [their own] pure soul-substance, which is identical to the Lord's." Souls are entrapped in different forms of physical matter, and even stained by different karmas, and thus take on different shades (*leśya*), but soul itself is inviolable and so identical.

From this perspective, the *mūrti* is not inanimate stone. It contains a number of single-sensed souls. Centuries of worship by Jains motivated by correct faith can alter the very nature of the soul-substance embodied in the stone. In a similar fashion, through the power gained from his ascetic life, the *sādhu* who installs the *mūrti* can alter the ontological condition of the stone, so that it becomes refined. This transformation can last a long time, and the length of time the *mūrti* remains thus empowered can be directly related to the moral and ascetic qualities of the *sādhu*. Ṭhakkura Pheru in his 1316 *Vāstusāra*, a manual for Jain architecture, says, "If a *mūrti* was installed more than one hundred years ago by a virtuous person then it remains worthy of worship even if it is broken. The *mūrti* does not become fruitless."[51]

Thus, one *sādhu* said that a "supreme power" (*śakti*) comes into the *mūrti* during the performance of the consecration rite—and although the installation of a *mūrti* can be done by a layperson, the consecration can only be done by a *sādhu*, preferably an *ācārya*. He differentiated between the "supreme power" that comes into a Jina *mūrti* and the lesser powers that come into *mūrti*s of unliberated deities such as the goddess Padmāvatī. He further talked in terms of the grace (he used *kṛpā* and *kalyāṇ* interchangeably) of God. He agreed that since the Jina is dispassionate (*vītrāg*), he cannot act in the world. Nonetheless, his grace is still active in the world, and this grace showers down upon the world. Grace exists independently of the person who is the cause of its arising. This *sādhu* also distinguished between desire (*rāg*) and affection (*anurāg*), saying that although the Jina is not subject to desire, one can still speak in terms of God's affection for people. "God doesn't think to himself, 'may all be happy.' But the pure *cetanā* (will) is still there which wishes all beings to be happy."

When I continued to press him on this subject, he finally said that the workings of grace and the related efficacy of *pūjā* are all very mysterious. He said that even though he might not be able to explain the workings of grace, he had experienced them. "Religion is not bound up with history. Religion is bound up with practice, with faith, with experience, and with feeling." In other words, he privileged experience over theory. A similar perspective is expressed by Kalāpūrṇsūri (one of the mendicants with whom I discussed this issue) when he writes: "From doing daily devotion of the Lord, the wandering of the mind is overcome, and the mind becomes fixed in meditation with God as its object. Gradually in place of the *mūrti* God himself becomes present to us—and from experiencing this the mind becomes endlessly joyous and blissful. Continuing still further, the unbroken meditation becomes successful and one realizes, 'That God is me.' Then the meditator, the meditation, and the meditative object become one, and there is final liberation" (1985:138).

There are thus a number of different interpretations of Jain theology, all based on certain basic presuppositions, with important ramifications for how the efficacy of *pūjā* is understood. Jains may not have been able to explain to me this efficacy in a systematic manner, but no one denied the efficacy.[52] The ritual culture of the Mūrtipūjak Jains is founded on the assumption that *pūjā* works. Had they known the work of Ralph Waldo Emerson, I am sure that some of the people with whom I persistently discussed this issue would have reminded me of the "foolish consistency" that is "the hobgoblin of little minds" (1929:57). There are some issues in the Jain worldview that have been the subject of immense effort to attain a single, consistent interpretation. The connection between theology and the efficacy of *pūjā* is not one of them.

4

Gifting and Grace

Patterns of Lay-Mendicant Interaction

A common ideological formula for describing Jainism, which dates back to early comparative compendia of the various philosophical schools, is in terms of three fundamental categories (*tattva*): teachings (*dharma*), divinity (*deva*), and teachers (*guru*) (Folkert 1993:III). For Jains, the true teachings are the *mokṣa-mārg* ideology, as discussed in chapter 1; the true divinity is the Jina, as discussed in chapter 3; and the true teachers are the Jain mendicants, the subject of this chapter. These can then be contrasted with the false teachings, divinities, and teachers of other philosophical and religious schools. In the words of a contemporary mendicant, "The *guru-tattva* is important in Jainism in the same way as the *dev-* and *dharm-tattvas*, for it is the guru who explains to us about *dev* and *dharm*. . . . Among these three *tattvas*, the *guru-tattva* is in many ways the most important, for when we are traveling on the wrong path he grabs our hand and turns us onto the right path. The *guru* questions the forgetful person so that he doesn't turn aside. He saves us when we are drowning in the ocean of *saṃsār*" (Muktiprabhvijay n.d.:33–34).[1]

At any given time during my two years of fieldwork, as well as during subsequent visits, there was a significant population of mendicants in Patan. Almost invariably, at least one group of *sādhus* was in town, and sometimes three or four. There was always a large population of *sādhvīs* in Patan, usually numbering between fifty and one hundred. Although Jains in many remote villages may go for years without seeing a mendicant, frequent if not daily interaction with mendicants was the norm for Patan Jains. In this chapter I discuss the dynamics of this interaction under the three rubrics of ritual gifting (*dān*), veneration and worship (*vandan* and *pūjan*), and devotion (*bhakti*).[2]

The Daily Routine of a Mūrtipūjak Mendicant

The life of the mendicant in both theory and practice is structured by rituals whose aim is to advance him or her along the *mokṣa-mārg*. Since karma is the cause of bondage, these rituals should result in the avoidance of the influx of further karma (*karma-saṃvara*) and the elimination of existing karma (*karma-nirjarā*), the two processes that together form the ideological underpinning of the mendicant's actions and intentions.[3] The daily ritual routine of the mendicant is broadly structured by three ideological formulations, the five great restraining vows (*mahāvrata*), the eight matrices of doctrine (*pravacana-mātṛkā*), and the six obligatory actions (*āvaśyaka*). The first two are negatively framed restrictions on the mendicant's conduct, which specify what the mendicant should not do, whereas the third is positively framed in terms of what the mendicant is enjoined to do daily. As we saw in chapter 1, in adopting the great vows as part of the rite of initiation, the mendicant pledges to refrain from harm (*ahiṃsā*), untruthful speech (*satya*), taking what is not freely offered (*asteya*), sexual conduct (*brahmacarya*), and possessing anything (*aparigraha*). The eight matrices of doctrine are subdivided into the threefold restraint (*gupti*) of mind, body, and speech, and the fivefold care (*samiti*) in walking, speaking, accepting alms, picking up and putting down objects, and excretory functions. The six obligatory actions are intertwined rites that together inform key parts of the mendicant's practice: *sāmāyika*, *caturviṃśati-stava* or *caitya-vandana*, *guru-vandana*, *pratikramaṇa*, *pratyākhyāna* (usually known by the Prakrit form *paccakkhāṇa*, pronounced in Gujarati *pacckkhāṇ*), and *kāyotsarga* (again, usually better known by its Prakrit form *kāüssagga*, pronounced in Gujarati *kāüssagg*). It is this elaborate pattern of obligatory daily rituals that most significantly distinguishes a *saṃvegī sādhu* from a *yati*, who performs fewer if any of them. It is for this reason that the rite whereby a *yati* becomes a *saṃvegī sādhu* is known as *kriyoddhāra*, "reform of rites."

Let us now see how these ideological doctrines are translated into lived experience. The daily routine as I present it is a generalized description derived from observation of a number of mendicants, and from interviews with mendicants concerning their praxis. With an understanding of the daily rhythms of mendicant life, we will be able to see more clearly the ways in which the lives of the mendicants are intertwined and interdependent with the lives of the laity.

The mendicants rise before dawn, most around 5:00 A.M., but some as early as 2:00 A.M., and perform their lavatorial functions. In observance of *utsarg-samiti*, or care in performing these actions, defecation is done in the open, in a place where the feces will cause no harm to living creatures, whereas urination is done into a shallow pan, and the urine then discarded onto a dry patch of ground.[4] Until sunrise, each mendicant engages in personal practice according to his or her own interest. Some recite hymns, some study, some meditate. After sunrise they recite the morning *pratikramaṇ* (chapter 5), the rite of confession for any karmically harmful actions committed during the night. This can be done either collectively or individually. *Pratikramaṇ* is followed by *paḍilehaṇ* (Sanskrit *pratilekhana*), in which the mendicant inspects his or her robes for insects and other minute organisms. The mendicants then perform *guru-vandan* (see below), the formulae of obeisance to the elders. Junior mendicants in a group perform it to senior ones, and the seniormost performs it to a *sthāpanācārya*.

This ritual prop, literally the "established *ācārya*," is a symbolic representation of the mendicant hierarchy. It consists of four sticks of wood bound together and splayed out above and below in the shape of an hourglass (see Figures 4.1, 4.2). When performing *guru-vandan* or *pratikramaṇ* alone, or when giving a sermon, a mendicant opens the *sthāpanācārya* to reveal five conch shells in a folded cloth.[5] The shells represent the five "supreme lords" (*pañca parameṣṭhin*) to whom homage is paid in the *Nokār Mantra*: the Jinas, the *siddhas* or other liberated souls, the *ācāryas* or mendicant leaders, the *upādhyāyas* or mendicant preceptors, and all *sādhus*. The *sthāpanācārya* physically signals that no mendicant is ever on his or her own, but is always in the presence of the entire Jain spiritual hierarchy.

Directly following *guru-vandan*, and performatively indistinguishable from it, they recite the *pacckkhāṇ* (chapter 5). This is a ritualized statement of intention to perform no karmically harmful actions and instead to perform certain specified actions (usually dietary restrictions) aimed at the avoidance and elimination of karma.

Each mendicant is expected to go to a temple once a day if at all possible. Many choose to go after *guru-vandan* and *pacckkhāṇ*. In the temple, each recites the *caturviṃśati-stava*, the hymn of veneration to the twenty-four Jinas as contained in the rite of *caitya-vandan*. If it is raining all day, and therefore the mendicant would violate the great vow of *ahiṃsā* by inevitably tredding on invisible organisms on the wet ground while walking to the temple, or if the mendicant is on his or her travels and staying in a village without a Jain temple, *caitya-vandan* is performed in the *upāśray* in the presence of the *sthāpanācārya*.

Also following *guru-vandan* and *pacckkhāṇ*, some of the mendicants go to the nearby homes of Jain laity to collect food and water in their wooden bowls, a ritualized action known as *gocarī*. If no Jains live in the town or village, the mendicants can collect food from the homes of upper-caste vegetarian Hindus.

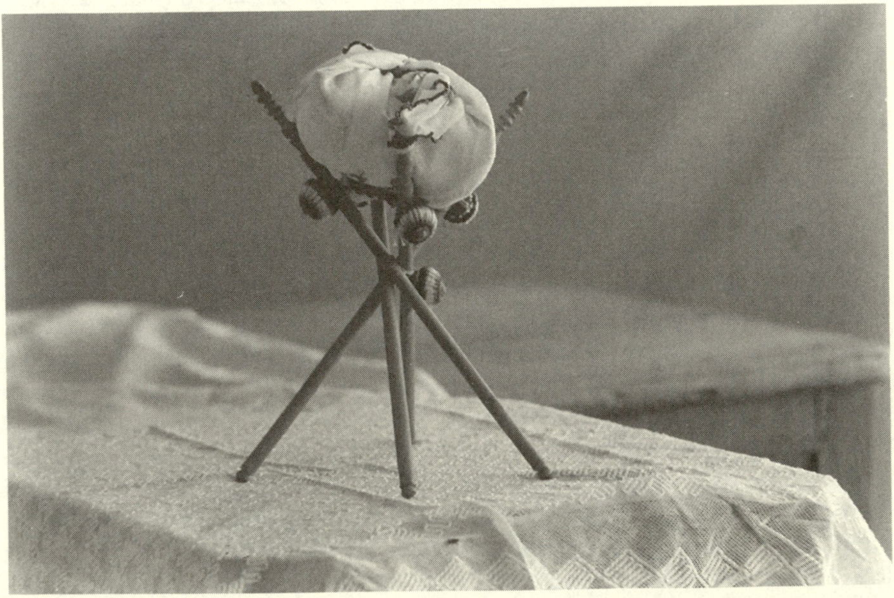

Figure 4.1. *Sthāpanācārya*. Patan, November 1985.

Figure 4.2. *Sthāpanācārya* in front of an *ācārya*. Koba, February 1987.

They bring back the food to the *upāśray*, and, after first confessing and atoning for any karmic faults committed during the food-gathering round, distribute it to all the mendicants. Senior mendicants rarely collect the food themselves, and some ideologues are of the opinion that it is a ritual fault for an *ācārya* to perform *gocarī*.[6] The food is consumed in private; as a matter of custom, laity should not observe a mendicant eating or drinking. This is in sharp contrast to the extremely public manner in which a Digambar mendicant eats and drinks, as described below.

If there is a public sermon, it is given in the mid-morning for an hour or two. Otherwise, the mendicants engage in study, recitation, meditation, or some other personalized practice. This is also a time when many laity visit mendicants for private instruction, pastoral advice, or simply the edifying experience of being in the mendicants' presence. The mendicants inspect their clothes again in mid-morning. Late morning is time for another food-gathering round.[7]

The afternoon is even more unstructured; some rest or nap, some instruct the laity, some pursue their personal practices. In mid-afternoon is the "complete *paḍilehaṇ*." In addition to inspecting their robes, the mendicants also sweep the *upāśray*, taking care not to harm any insects or other minute organisms. Late afternoon is the time for the final food-gathering round and meal, eaten before sunset. Many mendicants again visit the temple at the time of the evening *darśan*, when laity come to view and sing hymns to the ornamented Jina images. After sunset, the mendicants perform the evening *pratikramaṇ*. Unlike the morning performance, this one must be done collectively. The remaining hours of the evening are again devoted to personal practice. Before going to sleep, usually around 11:00

P.M., each mendicant recites the *santhāra porisi*, a formula of renunciation of the body in case he or she should die while asleep.

Sermons

With the exception of their dependence upon the laity for food, water, and shelter, the mendicants' daily routine as outlined above is largely independent of the laity. But in actual practice, there is frequent interaction between the mendicants and lay people in both the private and public spheres.

During the four-month rainy-season period, when the mendicants must stay in one place, the chief *sādhu* of every group gives a daily sermon (*pravacan*, *vyākhyān*), attended mostly by women and older, retired men, but on special days by most of the lay congregation. During their eight months of travel, the *sādhus* give sermons whenever requested, most often when they come to a new village or town in their travels[8] (see Figure 4.3).

A sermon lasts for at least one, and usually two, periods of forty-eight minutes. This is the minimum period for which a layperson can take the vow of temporary *sāmāyik*, in which he or she remains seated on a cloth, mendicant's broom in hand, and performs meditation or some other form of religious practice such as repetition of a *mantra* or listening to a sermon.

At the commencement of the sermon, the senior *sādhu* performs *guru-vandan* to the *sthāpanācārya*, and the other mendicants and the laity perform *guru-vandan* to

Figure 4.3. *Sādhu* delivering a sermon. Photograph by Kendall W. Folkert, 1985.

the senior *sādhu*. Laity who arrive in the middle of the sermon also perform *guru-vandan*, which takes about thirty seconds. The *sādhu* begins the sermon by reciting several holy verses to establish a proper atmosphere of spiritual purity. The sermon itself is tailored to the needs of the occasion. During the four-month residence in the rainy season, sermons tend to be extended commentaries on one or two texts. The rainy-season sermons in many ways resemble a college course, and nowadays this similarity is even more marked, as sometimes there are examinations at the end of the process for school-age Jains. On other occasions, the *sādhu* speaks on the subject at hand, such as image worship if it is during an image-installation ceremony, or renunciation if it is in the context of someone renouncing the world and becoming a mendicant. At the end of the sermon, after any business of the congregation has been concluded, the *sādhu* recites the *pacckkhaṇ* for any laity intending to perform a fast that day. He concludes by reciting several holy verses, usually the following two Sanskrit verses:

> Holy is Lord Vīr [Mahāvīr], holy is Gautam Svāmī,
> holy are Sthūlabhadra and the others; may the Jain religion be holy.
>
> The holiness of all holies, the cause of all goodness,
> the foremost of all religions, victory to the Jain teachings.[9]

Gifting

The *sādhus*' travel is in significant part determined by lay requests that they be present at a variety of special events. These include the special rites of consecration and installation of temple images, large congregational temple rituals in celebration of noteworthy acts such as the completion of a long fast or the anniversary of a mendicant's initiation, or the month-long retreat for the *updhān tap* (chapter 5). The presence of a *sādhu* is requested, and in certain cases required, both to increase the efficacy of the rite and to provide the opportunity for the laity to earn merit from the *sādhu*'s presence.

In the rite of initiation, the Jain mendicant takes a vow of complete nonpossession (*aparigrah*). As a result, the mendicant is dependent upon the laity for food and all the other necessities of life. The laity provide (and legally own) the *upāśray* where the mendicant stays, the food the mendicant eats, the robes the mendicant wears, the books the mendicant reads, medicine for the mendicant, and any ritual paraphernalia required by the mendicant. The general term for such service to the mendicants is *veyāvacc*.[10]

In his twelfth-century *Yogaśāstra* (3.119), Hemacandra describes seven fields (*kṣetra*) in which wealth can be given. In order of precedence they are: images, temples, texts, *sādhus*, *sādhvīs*, laymen, and laywomen.[11] Hemacandra distinguishes between wealth spent in the seven fields, which is done out of a spirit of devotion (bhakti), and giving to the non-Jain needy, which is done out of a spirit of compassion (*dayā*). Whereas the latter is a laudable expense, only the former constitutes gifting (*dān*) in the ritual sense.[12] The benefits to the donor of such gifting are manifold. In an article on the seven fields, based on a sermon delivered to lay Jains, the twentieth-century Ācārya Vijay Suśīlsūri wrote, "Those who use their wealth properly in the seven fields attain great merit. They gain a reputation for having wealth, and so are successful in their human life" (1974:285). He underscored that benefits accrue in terms of both advancing the donor toward the transcendent goal of liberation and improving his or her worldly wellbeing by quoting from the late-twelfth-century Sanskrit *Sindūraprakara* (verse 80) of Somaprabhasūri:

> For the man who himself sows plentifully the seeds of wealth in the seven fields,
> pleasure abides with him, fame is his servant, and wealth yearns for him.
>
> Wisdom is affectionate, and he becomes familiar with the wealth of a world emperor.
> He holds in his hands the rewards of heaven and his desire for liberation is successful.

The various implements required by a mendicant, such as cotton robes, shawl, staff, wooden food and water bowls, and a mat to sit on, are formally gifted to the mendicant for his or her use at the time of initiation. Laity who are special devotees of mendicants replace these items annually. Gifting these items is not a liturgically ritualized act, although when it is done, the layperson usually performs *guru-vandan* and otherwise obtains the mendicant's blessings.

Since a mendicant is in theory both possessionless and striving to attain a state of indifference to material objects, he or she should not specifically ask for anything. Many laity, therefore, when visiting a mendicant to perform *guru-vandan* or otherwise meet with the mendicant, ask if anything is needed, being careful to ask specifically about a large number of basic items. Nonetheless, when mendicants need some other object, such as medicine, writing implements, or a book, spontaneous requests are often made, of visiting scholars as well as of Jain laity.

Gifting of Food to a Śvetāmbar Mendicant

The routine by which mendicants procure their food is relatively straightforward among the Śvetāmbar Mūrtipūjaks.[13] The mendicant comes to the door of the house, and announces his or her presence with the benediction, "dharm lābh" ("blessings of the religion"). If it is proper for the mendicant to accept food,[14] the layperson (usually the housewife) invites the mendicant to enter by saying, "padārche," a Gujarati verbal request which can be translated as, "please grace us with your presence." If the mendicant is observing a particular dietary restriction, he or she accepts only food that meets the requirement. Since a mendicant should not request that a specific type of food be prepared, the laity ask mendicants what dietary restrictions they are observing when they first come to a neighborhood *upāśray*, and incorporate those foods into their daily diet for the duration of the mendicants' presence.

The technical term for the food-gathering round, *gocarī*, literally means "traveling like a cow." This refers to the ideal by which the mendicant goes spontaneously and without any preconceived desire to whatever layperson's house he or she happens to come to first. To express any preference in the matter of collecting food would be a violation of the vow of *aparigrah* (nonpossession). James Laidlaw (1995:306) observes that the *gocarī* paradigm also prevents the mendicant from being, even unwittingly, the occasion of the layperson's accruing negative karma through the violence involved in preparing food. Nonetheless, laity usually are expecting the mendicants, and have prepared any special foods required by their dietary restrictions.

Jains are very explicit that the Jain mendicant does not beg (*bhīkh māgvū*) for food. Rather, in theory the laity request that the mendicant take food to maintain the body while on the path to liberation. There is often a certain amount of back-and-forth activity between the mendicant and the householder, as the mendicant rejects certain foods, or asks for fewer pieces of bread, for example. How much the mendicant takes depends upon the number of mendicants for whom he or she is collecting food.

Gifting of Food to a Digambar Mendicant

The Mūrtipūjak procedure of *gocarī* contrasts sharply with the much more formally ritualized practice of *āhār-dān* or gifting of food among the Digambar Jains, as reported by Mahias (1985:249–51), Shântâ (1985:506–8), Carrithers (1989:227–28), and Zydenbos (1999).[15] In this case, each mendicant, no matter how senior, performs his or her own food-gathering round. The mendicant usually makes a silent resolution to eat only where he or she finds a certain requirement fulfilled, such as a tree in front of the door.[16] The mendicant walks in total silence and in an attitude which indicates that he or she will eat: the tips of the right fingers rest on the right shoulder, a water pot and peacock-feather fan held in the left hand. When the mendicant arrives at a suitable house, the laity address the mendicant in mixed Sanskrit and vernacular as follows: "Hail, hail, hail. Stay, stay, stay. [My] mind is pure, [my] speech is pure, [my] action is pure, this food and water are pure. Please enter into the eating house."[17] The laity thrice circumambulate the mendicant, and then conduct him or her inside the house, and indicate a raised seat or platform where the mendicant is to crouch. The feet of the mendicant are washed with cold water, which is saved. According to Shântâ, the laity perform eightfold *pūjā* to the mendicant, a rite normally performed only in worshiping Jina images in the temple, by making offerings onto a small table. To eat, the mendicant stands on the platform and holds his or her right hand in front with the palm up, cupped in the left hand. Each food item is placed in the right hand, and is carefully inspected by the mendicant before being eaten. The presence of a hair or other sign of impurity in the food is called an *antarāy*, whereupon the mendicant stops eating.[18] The mendicant eats no more than thirty-two such handfuls of food. When the mendicant is finished eating, his or her hands are washed with water. Before departing, the mendicant may retire to a different part of the house for a brief conversation with household members and neighbors. Carrithers notes that in one case of *āhār-dān* he observed, neighbor women took advantage of this opportunity to worship the mendicant by placing bananas and coconuts at his feet. After the mendicant has departed, the family then eats its own meal, considered now as *prasād*, or consecrated leftovers from the mendicant's meal.

Whereas the Śvetāmbar *gocarī* is a relatively simple, unaccented transaction, whereby the laity provide the mendicants with needed food, the Digambar *āhār-dān* is strikingly similar to both Jain and especially Hindu forms of temple worship.

This equation is seen most clearly in Shântâ's description of the eightfold *pūjā* performed to the mendicant. As we will see below, this would be considered a ritual fault (*āśātnā*) among the Śvetāmbars, for it ritually equates the unliberated mendicant with the liberated Jina. The Śvetāmbar rites of *caitya-vandan* addressed to the Jinas and *guru-vandan* addressed to the mendicant have extensive liturgical overlap, but at key places the distinction between the two is maintained by, for example, bowing thrice to the Jina, but only twice to the mendicant.

The Digambar mendicant is fed in a manner that provides the laity with several valuable, spiritually charged leftovers: the water from bathing both the feet and the hands, and the meal itself. Whereas the Śvetāmbar mendicant is treated like a guest with special requirements, the Digambar mendicant is treated like a god. The Digambar ritual interaction conforms to Hindu ritual paradigms that have been discussed by several authors (such as Babb 1975, Fuller 1992, Wadley 1975). In Hindu temple worship, offerings of food, flowers, incense, light, and other pleasing substances are made to the deity in its image form. The edible offerings are "eaten" and absorbed by the deity, and then returned to the worshiper in the form of *prasād*, a term literally meaning "grace" that can also be more broadly translated as "God's leftovers." Through consumption of this valorized food, the worshiper absorbs some of the deity's grace, and becomes in some small manner more godlike him or herself. The acceptance of the leftover food also serves to emphasize the worshiper's lower status in relation to the deity. There is seemingly little difference between Hindu worship of a temple image of a deity and Digambar worship of the deitylike mendicant. Both are quite different from the Śvetāmbar and Digambar rites of worshiping the Jina image. In sharp contrast to Hindu worship—and this contrast is evident to most Jains—the food offerings placed in front of the Jina image are considered to be given up by the worshiper, and after the rite cannot be returned to the worshiper, but must instead be given to a non-Jain recipient.[19]

Gifting, Merit, and Sin

Gloria Raheja (1988), Jonathan Parry (1980, 1986, 1994), and Peter van der Veer (1989:189–211) have discussed the ways in which in Hindu and Brāhmaṇical conceptions of *dān*, the recipient of the gift also accepts and so ingests the *pāp* (sins)[20] or inauspiciousness (*aśubh*, *kuśubh*, *naśubh*) of the donor.[21] The argument has been summarized by Raheja (1988:36) as follows: "inauspiciousness and *pāp*, 'evil,' are thought to be generated not only at death but in most life processes. Birth, marriage, death, harvests, the building of a house, and very many occasions during the calendrical cycles of the week, the lunar month, and the year are thought to generate inauspiciousness (but not necessarily 'impurity') that must be removed and given away in *dān* if well-being and auspiciousness are to be achieved and maintained."

Different forms of inauspiciousness require different recipients for their proper and safe removal: women, untouchables, priests, and poor relatives are all appropriate receptacles in various contexts. Parry has vividly described the anxiety of Mahābrāhmaṇ funeral priests of Banaras concerning the *dān* they receive in the context of funeral rites. According to Parry (1994:124), they feel that if they are incapable of adequately digesting the *pāp* they receive in *dān* through various forms of expiation, they are "liable to contract leprosy and rot; to die a premature and painful death vomiting excrement, and to suffer the most terrible torments thereafter." The inauspicious and dangerous *dān* received by these lower-caste Mahābrāhmaṇs is carefully distinguished from the auspicious *dakṣiṇā* received by higher-caste Karmakāṇḍī Brāhmaṇs who preside over the death rites of more well-to-do patrons who want a more learned officiant.[22] Raheja in her detailed ethnography of a north Indian village shows that such notions of *pāp* and inauspiciousness are ubiquitous in a wide range of Hindu ritual transactions.

The Śvetāmbar Jain understanding of *dān* is different in certain key respects, perhaps in reaction to this Hindu paradigm.[23] The mendicant is not considered to "eat" (*jamvũ*) the food he or she receives, but rather to "use" (*vapārvũ*) it, for the mendicant has no "taste" (*svād*) for food. The mendicant takes the food not out of desire or pleasure, but to sustain the body as the vehicle temporarily inhabited by the soul on its path to liberation. To enforce this understanding, many mendicants mix together all the foods collected in *gocarī* into an unpalatable mush.[24] If the mendicant were to ask for a specific type of food to be prepared, then he or she would accrue bad karma or *pāp*. But in theory the mendicant does not ask for food to be prepared, and takes no interest in the food preparation other than to ensure that it has not violated either of the great vows of nonharm or nonpossession. The mendicant thereby avoids the accrual of karma and *pāp*, either through explicit commissioning or implicit approval (*anumodan*) of the food preparation and its accompanying violence.[25] In this Jain model of gifting, the *pāp* is not passed along with the gift. Lay Jains are not so much concerned with the removal of *pāp* through *dān* as they are with the generation of *puṇya* through *dān*. The layperson accrues *pāp* through the preparation of food for the mendicant, but this *pāp* is more than offset by the *puṇya* accrued through the act of *dān* of the food to the mendicant. Since *pāp* and *puṇya* are mirror opposites (that is, *pāp* is negative *puṇya*), then the end result for the donor is the same in the Jain and Hindu situations—the giver's karmic status has improved. But the end position for the recipient is different, for the Jain mendicant does not have the added *pāp* to contend with. The mendicant accrues no *pāp*, however, only if due to his or her conduct he or she is a proper recipient for *dān*.[26]

Ensuring that mendicants observe proper mendicant conduct, and therefore remain proper recipients for *dān*, has been a long-standing concern in the Jain community. In the twelfth century, Hemacandra defined a proper *sādhu* as one who "through following the teachings of the Jina observes right conduct, makes fruitful this rarely attained human birth, crosses over [to liberation] himself, and causes others to cross over."[27] One of the aims of the late-nineteenth and early-twentieth-century reform movement among the Mūrtipūjak Jains was to remove the institution of domesticated *sādhus* known as *yatis* by convincing the Jain laity that *yatis* were unsuitable as recipients of *dān*, in which case the donor would receive less *puṇya*.[28]

A diagram of the Hindu and Jain transactions can clarify the differences between the two ritual systems (see Table 4.1). An interesting aspect of these transactions is that in the Jain case this same diagram is accurate regardless of whether the

Table 4.1 Hindu and Jain Transactions

Hindu			
	donor	——— (*dān*) ———→	recipient
	(*pāp* –)		(*pāp* +)
Jain			
	donor	——— (*dān*) ———→	recipient
	(*pāp* +)		(no change)
	(*puṇya* ++)		

recipient is a Śvetāmbar mendicant, a Digambar mendicant, or an image of a Jina in a temple. In none of these Jain transactions does the *pāp* associated with the *dān* stick to the recipient. In the case of the Jina, as discussed in chapter 3, this is because the latter is theologically nonresponsive, and the transaction as a result is largely self-reflexive on the part of the donor. As part of their initiation, mendicants have taken vows of *aparigrah*, the universal and lifelong renunciation of all physical and mental notions of ownership. As long as the mendicant is firm in his or her observance of the vow, and as a result is a suitable recipient, the donation has no moral or ontological effect upon the recipient. We see here the importance of the Jain insistence that Jain mendicants in theory do not ask for food, and that they oftentimes must be cajoled by the laity into accepting food in order to sustain their meritorious presence.[29] At the same time, many Jains refuse to give alms to Hindu renouncers (except out of cautious respect and fear for the renouncers' reputed worldly magico-spiritual powers), and refer to Hindu renouncers contemptuously as "beggars," precisely because from a Jain perspective they are not suitable recipients.[30]

What is not explained by this model is what happens to the *pāp* in the Jain instance. Raheja indicates that for north Indian village Hindus, the economy of auspiciousness and inauspiciousness is a closed, zero-sum system: inauspiciousness can be removed only if some other recipient takes it on. Auspiciousness is really only a lack of inauspiciousness. The Jains seem to operate in a different transactional universe, where the ascetic and renunciatory powers of the mendicant to wear away karma (*karma-nirjarā*) allow for the generation of auspicious karma by the layperson's actions. This would seem to hold regardless of whether the food is returned to the donor as *prasād* or is retained solely for consumption by the recipient.[31] The powers of the mendicant result in a network wherein new auspiciousness can be created and inauspiciousness can be destroyed, not just transferred. This seems to be an inherent property of the Jain religion. In the auspicious verses recited at the end of every sermon, the Jain religion is described as "the cause of all goodness" (*kalyāṇ*).[32] The five goodness-creating events (*kalyāṇak*) of conception, birth, initiation, enlightenment, and liberation in the life of every Jina set in motion a process by which within the context of the Jain religion there is a constant supply of new auspicuousness, which is available to devout and faithful Jains. This is one reason the five *kalyāṇaks* are the focus of much of the lay Jain ritual life.

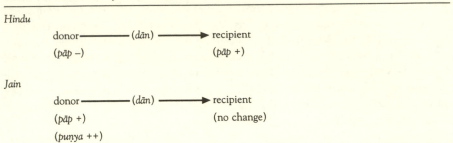

Both Parry and Raheja focus on transactions within the realm of *saṃsār*, in which the recipients are either lower-caste humans or passionate, potentially harmful deities. If these authors had paid attention to devotional forms of religious practice, they might have found that Hindu bhakti also allows for systems in which unlimited auspiciousness is available to the devotee. Vasudha Narayanan (1985) and D. F. Pocock (1973) have shown that God (Viṣṇu and Kṛṣṇa) in the Śrīvaiṣṇava and Puṣṭimārg traditions is the source of worldly auspiciousness for devotees in ways very similar to that by which the Jain tradition itself is a source for auspiciousness. Lawrence Babb's work on contemporary urban Hindu guru-based movements in north India demonstrates a similar understanding, in which "an offering to the guru would appear to be, among other things, a possible vehicle through which the offerer can deliver up impurities, his or her 'sins,' which are taken by the guru into or onto himself" (Babb 1986:66). The Jain ideology of interaction is analogous in many ways to the ideologies found in Hindu bhakti traditions (although there are fundamental differences in the understandings of the transactional ontology involved), and quite different in terms of its having a source of boundless goodness from the zero-sum nondevotional Hindu systems of prestations.[33]

Veneration and Worship

The invocation of Hindu devotion to gurus brings us to similar attitudes within Jain practice, of lay veneration (*vandan*), worship (*pūjā*), and devotion (*bhakti*) of mendicants. We have seen in chapter 1 that at the heart of the Jain pantheon are the five supreme lords, the Jina, *siddha*, *ācārya*, *upādhyāya*, and *sādhu*. The Jinas and *siddhas* embody the perfected virtues of the soul. They reside at the top of the universe in nonresponsive and noninteractive perfection, and so are what Lawrence Babb (1996) has aptly termed an "absent lord." Due to this absence, the living presence of the mendicants takes on a special role in the lives of Jains. In the words of a mendicant, "In the absence of God, the proximate benefactors are the Lord gurus. They have renounced the world themselves, preach to us with no self-interest about the true path, and themselves travel on that path. The monks give peace to those oppressed by suffering, and comfort us with their assurances. By worshiping and praising them we obtain their blessings. By associating with these saints we attain lofty thoughts, and are inspired to travel the true path" (Kuśal-candravijay 1983:I.6).

He then goes on to detail the benefits of devotion to mendicants (10): "From contact with *sādhus*, the sentiments (*bhāvnā*) of affection, bhakti, and praising are born in us. By doing bhakti, we attain knowledge, by which we remove the *pāp* and oppressions of this world." One English-educated layman expressed this same attitude when he said, "the guru is the messenger of God."

Guru-Vandan

Vandan refers to several types of ritualized obeisance and praise from an inferior to a superior. *Caitya-vandan* is usually performed in a temple, and addressed to the Jina enthroned in that particular temple. *Dev-vandan* is an extended *caitya-vandan*, usually performed in an *upāśray*, addressed to all twenty-four of the Jinas of the current time cycle as well as several of the Jinas presently living in other parts of the universe. *Guru-vandan* is performed by laity to any mendicant, and by mendicants to their elders, with a slight difference in the performance.

At the beginning of a sermon, all the laity perform *guru-vandan* to the *sādhu* delivering the sermon, while he performs *guru-vandan* to the *sthāpanācārya* set up in front of him. Devout Jains go to a nearby *upāśray* daily to perform *guru-vandan* to a mendicant. Many times when I was engaged in discussions with mendicants, a steady stream of laity came up, bowing and reciting the *guru-vandan* to the mendicant, who often totally ignored them. This is not a personalized ritual, in which the specific personality of either worshiper or worshiped has any significance. It is a formalized, depersonalized rite of interaction between people who occupy the ritual positions of worshiping layperson and worshiped mendicant.

The prescription for performing *guru-vandan* is found in many lay manuals, and is known and practiced by a great many Jains.[34] The layperson twice bows his or her forehead to the ground, reciting each time the following Prakrit phrase: "I wish, O forebearing mendicant, to praise [you] with concentration and renunciation. So be it. I praise."[35] The layperson then, with hands folded in front of his or her chest, recites the following in mixed Prakrit and vernacular: "[Prakrit:] What is needed? Is it a good morning [or evening]? [Gujarati:] Is the asceticism good? Is the body trouble-free? Is the journey good and in equanimity, sir? Master! Is there contentment, sir? Give [to us] the benefit of [gifting to you] food and water, sir."

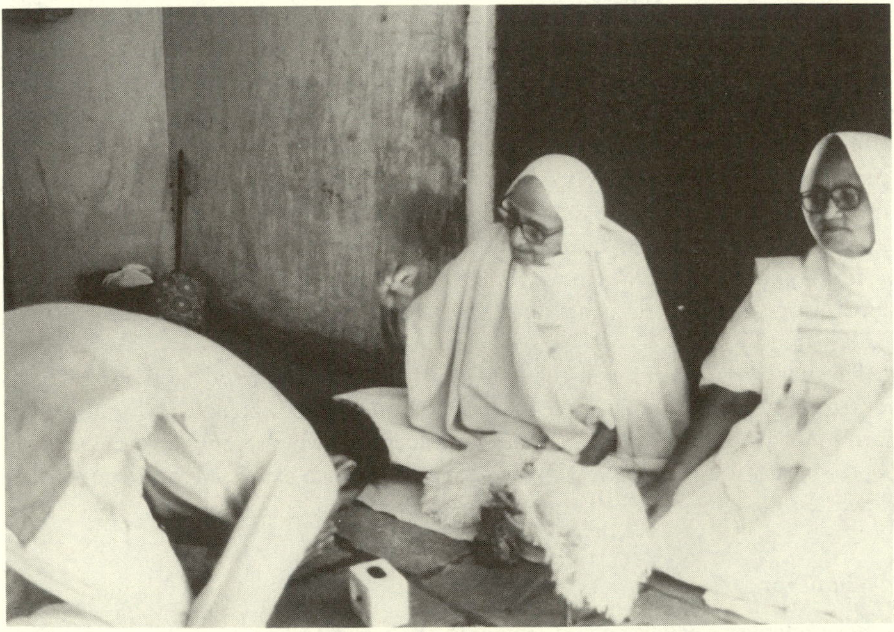

Figure 4.4. Layman bowing to *sādhvī* as sign of devotion; in return, she sprinkles *vāskep* on his head. Photograph by Kendall W. Folkert, 1985.

If the mendicant holds a title above the rank of *muni*, such as *ācārya*, *upādhyāya*, or *gaṇi*, the layperson bows and repeats the initial phrase again. While still standing, the layperson recites the following Prakrit phrases: "Standing here, may I be pardoned for internal daily transgressions, O Lord? As is wished. I ask pardon for daily transgressions. For anything unfriendly or excessively unfriendly in eating, drinking, conduct, transaction, speech, conversation, sitting higher [than the guru], sitting at the same level, interrupting in speech, speaking louder—whatever fault against conduct, great or small, which you know but I do not know, may that have no result." The person then concludes by again bowing and reciting the first phrase (see Figure 4.4).

Guru-vandan is also performed in the ritual context of laity greeting a mendicant (usually an important *sādhu*) on his or her travels, such as entering a city or changing residence (chapter 6). In my fieldwork, I saw this performed only by women, although I know of no prescription to this effect. Women either individually or collectively prepare a rice *svastik*, *nandyāvart*, or other holy design on a small low offering table, and place on the design a coconut, piece of candy, a small coin, or other offering. When the mendicant approaches, the women place the table before him, and then perform *guru-vandan*. The mendicant does not say anything in return (and in many cases that I observed appeared to be distinctly uninterested in the proceedings). At the conclusion of *guru-vandan*, the mendicant may or may not reciprocate with a blessing, the laypeople move out of the mendicant's way, and he or she proceeds (see Figure 4.5).

Figure 4.5. Laywomen performing *guru-vandan* to a *sādhu*. Patan, April 1987.

Guru-Pūjā

An alternate form to *guru-vandan* is *guru-pūjā*, which ideologues try to ensure is bounded by carefully enunciated guidelines of propriety. The correct form of *guru-pūjā* is for the layperson to sprinkle a small amount of *vāskep* (see below) on the right big toe of the mendicant; in return, the mendicant holds his or her right hand aloft in a gesture of protection and blessing, and mutters a *mantra* or else the catch-all mendicant greeting of "dharm lābh" ("blessings of the religion [upon you]"). Usually the layperson also makes an offering of money into a metal tray in front of the mendicant; this money is then put in the local *saṅgh*'s "knowledge account," from which it can be spent only for the purpose of spreading knowledge about Jainism by publishing books and similar activities. The mendicant usually reciprocates by sprinkling a small amount of *vāskep* on the layperson's head; if the layperson is of the same gender, and therefore the mendicant can touch him or her without violating mendicant codes of purity, the mendicant often will reinforce the blessing by patting the layperson on the head or back.

In 1986 a bitter controversy arose within the Tapā Gacch when several laymen proposed performing *guru-pūjā* to Ācārya Vijay Rāmcandrasūri in the "nine-limbed" form done to Jina images. His many detractors within the Tapā Gacch accused him of setting himself up as the twenty-fifth Jina.[36] A fierce debate raged in the newspapers and within Jain circles concerning the textual authority for this ritual. In the end, the followers of Rāmcandrasūri compromised by performing the nine-limbed *guru-pūjā* to Rāmcandrasūri, but while doing so drew a curtain in front of the Jina image in the temple. This way they did not worship the *ācārya* by a ritual normally reserved for the worship of the Jina in the visual presence of the Jina.[37] One layman I talked with accused the followers of Rāmcandrasūri of performing a Vaiṣṇav ritual. He said they were blurring the distinction between the Jinas and the living mendicants, in the same manner that Vaiṣṇavs oftentimes conflate Viṣṇu-Kṛṣṇa and their living gurus.[38] "We do *vandan* to the *sādhu* as our Lord," he said, "but it is not the same as we do in the temple to the Tīrthaṅkars; there is a difference." This line, however, is frequently crossed by the majority of Jain laity. Before the cremation procession of one well-known *sādhu* in November 1986, thousands of people performed *guru-pūjā* to his corpse in the *upāśray*; a large sign reminded people to perform *guru-pūjā* only to the right big toe, and the laymen looking after the body constantly had to remind zealous laity not to sprinkle *vāskep* on the corpse's head.

Devotion and Grace

A layperson who has developed a special relationship of devotion with a particular mendicant is called a *bhakt*, or a *khās* (special) *bhakt* if the relationship is particularly strong. Such a relationship cuts across any traditional allegiances to *samudāy* or *gacch* based on family or neighborhood; in this way it parallels the Hindu phenomena of devotion to a chosen deity (*iṣṭa-devatā*) and devotion to a personal guru. This relationship, however, is not formalized through any rite, and therefore the mendicant's instructions are binding upon the layperson only to the extent that the layperson accepts the mendicant's authority. A *bhakt* knows at all times where his or her guru is on his journeys, and frequently travels some distance to be with him. The *bhakt* counts on the guru for advice in a wide range of religious, family, and economic matters. In return, the *bhakt* is solicitous after the guru's welfare. Whereas laity always use elevated, polite language when addressing a mendicant,[39] a *bhakt* inquires after the health and physical needs of the guru just as one would look after a small child or a spouse. Yet while treating the guru as a dependent on the social sphere, the layperson at the same time considers him or herself to be the spiritual dependent of the guru. One layman described this relationship as like that of father and son: "Guru Mahārāj feels for me just like a father does for a son. If I haven't seen Guru Mahārāj recently, then I will see him in my dreams, and I know it is time to visit him."[40] Another layman commented upon the death of his guru by saying that he felt as much sorrow as when his own father had died. In addition to advice, the guru often makes special demands of the *bhakt*, or does special favors for the *bhakt*. A guru might suggest that the *bhakt* take a temporarily binding vow (*niyam*, *bādhā*), such as strictly observing the ban on eating after dark (chapter 5), or restricting the time spent watching television for several weeks. In one case, a guru told a *bhakt* of his to give up his job as an engineer in the United States and return to Bombay to look after his elderly parents, which he did. In return, many gurus give their *bhakts* special mantras to recite daily, or perhaps a protective string to tie around the right wrist.

Most *bhakts* describe the blessings they receive from their guru in terms of grace or mercy (*āśīrvād*, *maherbāṇī*, *kṛpā*). Several laymen ascribed the beginning of their worldly financial success to the day they met their gurus. The physical form of this mercy is *vāskep* (Sanskrit *vāsakṣepa*, "thrown scented powder"), a mixture of sandalwood, saffron, and camphor powder used in a wide variety of ritual contexts.[41] One author says of *vāskep*: "It is believed that Mahavir himself blessed it and used it. He sprinkled it on the head of Gautam, his first disciple. It has come down passing through the hands of the Munis of the Jain hierarchy, each of them adding to the original store. The faithful attribute miraculous virtues to the powder" (Baakza 1962:57–58).

When a layperson does *guru-pūjā* to a mendicant, he or she sprinkles *vāskep* on the mendicant's right big toe. When a mendicant gives a blessing to a layperson, the layperson bows before the mendicant with folded hands, and the mendicant sprinkles *vāskep* on the crown of the layperson's head. Such powder has usually been previously empowered by the mendicant speaking a *mantra* over it. Most *bhakts* keep a small supply of *vāskep* that has been blessed and given to them by their guru. One couple sprinkled a small amount on their own heads every day before leaving the house. Another man received a packet of *vāskep* from his guru in the mail every year. Many Jains believe that if one keeps *vāskep* in one's safe, one's money will increase.

The palanquin in which the body of a deceased mendicant is taken from the *upāśray* to the cremation site is also believed to possess such beneficent powers. On the occasion of the above-mentioned procession and cremation in November 1986, many members of the crowd tussled to obtain small pieces of the cloth canopy from the palanquin. One young man who obtained a piece told me that he planned to put it in his safe along with a five-paise coin, to ensure his future prosperity. The efficacy of such relics is directly dependent upon the fame and conduct of the deceased mendicant.

The funeral of a mendicant is an occasion for both great rejoicing and great earning of beneficial merit among the laity.[42] The various rites performed to the body, from bearing the palanquin to lighting the fire, are auctioned off, with the merit of the rites going to the donors. The rites in November 1986, in the town of Unjha, were auctioned off for a total of over Rs. 450,000, with the right to light the pyre going for Rs. 100,111.[43] During the procession from the *upāśray* to the cremation site,[44] the people throw auspicious red powder over one another, and shout, "Jay jay nandā, jay jay bhadda" ("Hail hail joy, hail hail goodness"). As one layman explained, "We say 'jay jay nandā' because we have had the opportunity to meet such a superior man. It is a holy death. He lived not for his body, but for his soul, and for the souls of everyone. Therefore we feel much joy (*ānand*) because of his pure life. He has been released from his body, and he cannot go to a bad birth. Therefore everyone is happy."

The final act in the relationship between a *sādhu* and his devotees is the *guṇānuvād sabhā* (assembly to translate his virtues), held wherever there is a significant number of his devotees. In the above instance, they were held in Unjha, Patan, Ahmedabad, and Bombay. At this gathering, various mendicants and laymen stand to remember publicly various good deeds and qualities of the deceased *sādhu*, so that by publicly praising these qualities they may translate the qualities into their own person. The Khartar Gacch carries the *sādhu*-devotee relationship even further, with the cult of the four Dādāgurus (grandfather-gurus).[45] These are four leaders of the Khartar Gacch who lived between the twelfth and seventeenth centuries, and who are worshiped for a variety of worldly purposes. Whereas deceased Tapā Gacch mendicants are viewed primarily as departed saints, the Khartar Gacch Dādāgurus are viewed much more as present deities.

The relationship between *bhakt* and guru among the Śvetāmbar Mūrtipūjak Jains resembles in many ways those in the guru-bhakti cults that are becoming a dominant form of contemporary urban Hinduism, as recently studied by Lawrence Babb (1986). A major difference, however, is that the Śvetāmbar Mūrtipūjak guru remains a human being, albeit a special, powerful human being, whereas among Hindu guru cults the guru tends to assume the status of a deity.

Concluding Observations

In this chapter, we have seen that interaction with mendicants, especially as gurus, is a significant element in the life of lay Jains. This interaction takes place through the rites of gifting, praise, and worship, and through the relationship of devotion. On the ideological level, the mendicant is a model of renunciation for the layperson. The mendicant's status is superior to that of the layperson precisely because he has advanced further along the *mokṣa-mārg*. In the language of the *guṇasthāns*, the fourteen-rung ladder to liberation, the mendicant by virtue of the five great vows is on at least the sixth rung, whereas the layperson is at best on the fourth rung (unless he or she has taken the twelve vows of a layperson, in which case he or she is on the fifth rung).

At the same time, the mendicant is a living source of wellbeing for the layperson. The layperson obtains wellbeing by establishing a personal relationship with the mendicant, a relationship that is actualized through gifting, praise, worship, and devotion. This results in a paradoxical situation for the mendicant. In the pursuit of liberation, the mendicant strives to reduce all transactions and interactions, for it is precisely these which lead to the influx of new binding karma. But in this pursuit of liberation, the mendicant is dependent upon the laity for physical requirements such as food, shelter, and clothing. In pursuit of less interaction, the mendicant must establish an interactive relationship with the laity, especially since the mendicant is required to minister to the spiritual needs of the laity and show them the path. These spiritual needs, however, are met not through providing a remote, abstract ideal but rather through close, personal interactions and transactions with the laity. The mendicants may define themselves as striving for liberation, but in the eyes of the laity it is precisely this striving for liberation that generates the meritorious karma that the laity can tap into for their own wellbeing by transacting with the mendicant.

5

Holy Asceticism

An emphasis upon asceticism (*tap*, Sanskrit *tapas*), used here to encompass a wide range of both restrictions on behavior and techniques of working upon one's inner spiritual condition, has occupied an important place in the Jain tradition from its inception.[1] Energetic striving for perfection through asceticism has been a hallmark of Jain ideology and practice. As Padmanabh Jaini (1993:340) has noted, whereas the Buddhists traditionally shunned extreme asceticism in favor of a balance between world affirmation and world renunciation, the Jains have "found this so called Middle Path of the Buddha as nothing but faintheartedness, a weakness of the spirit unworthy of a true follower of a Jina." Similarly, whereas the various Vaiṣṇav traditions with which the Jains have closely interacted and intermarried over the past five hundred years (especially the Puṣṭimārg Vaiṣṇav tradition) have emphasized the exaltation of sensory experience in dedication to Kṛṣṇa, the Jains have criticized such sensory and aesthetic pursuits, saying that they only tie one more firmly to the rounds of rebirth (*saṃsār*).

The core of the Jain tradition is often defined by the *mokṣa-mārg* ideology as the three jewels of correct faith (*samyag-darśana*), understanding (*samyag-jñāna*), and conduct (*samyak-cāritra*). As noted in chapter 1, the very first verse of the *Tattvārtha Sūtra*, one of the most important systematic statements of the *mokṣa-mārg*, reads, "The path to liberation consists of correct faith, understanding, and conduct." But from an early date, this formulation was felt to be insufficient, and so we find alternative definitions that include correct asceticism (*samyag-tapas*) as equal to the three jewels. For example, the *Uttarādhyayana Sūtra* (28.2–3), in another, even earlier, formulation of the *mokṣa-mārg*, states the following:

> Understanding and faith and conduct and asceticism:
> this is the path taught by the Jinas who have perfect knowledge.
> Understanding and faith and conduct and asceticism:
> those souls who follow this path go to liberation.

The assumption that asceticism is equally important as faith, understanding, and conduct is also seen in the *yantra* of the *siddhcakra* or *navpad* (see Figure 5.1). This diagram, the object of much Jain devotional activity, bears in its center the figure

Figure 5.1. Metal tray depicting *siddhcakra* or *navpad*. Photograph by Thomas A. Zwicker, © 1989 The University of Pennsylvania Museum Archives.

of the Jina; in eight petals surrounding the Arhat are the other four Supreme Beings—the *siddha*, *ācārya*, *upādhyāya*, and *sādhu*, and alternating with them praises to the three jewels and correct asceticism.

Passages in praise of the glory and efficacy of asceticism abound in Jain literature, from the earliest canonical texts to the most recent homiletic pamphlets. The first verse of the *Daśavaikālika Sūtra*, an important ideological text for mendicant praxis that is memorized as one of the first acts of a mendicant's career, reads, "The highest holy is dharma, which consists of non-harm, equanimity, and asceticism. Even the gods revere a mind that is ever fixed on dharma." From a more recent text, one finds the following verses, in the seventeenth-century *Navpad Pūjā* of Mahopādhyāy Yaśovijay, a well-known devotional text for an oft-performed congregational ritual composed by this important ideologue:

Praise praise to fierce asceticism
which uproots karma like an elephant uproots a tree.

It removes the karmas and passions of the past, present, and future,
bound in which one burns.
Asceticism is said to be of two kinds, outer and inner;
joined with renunciation of ill intentions it cuts aimless bad meditation.

Attainments and perfections are gained from its splendor and glory.
From lack of desire comes the purity that stops karma.
Asceticism is the cause of great joy;
like an auspicious woman it is the sign of success.[2]

Both of these passages, composed nearly two millennia apart (and Yaśovijay certainly knew the earlier passage by heart), explicitly use the language of wellbeing to describe asceticism. The authors contrast what they perceive as an unenlightened understanding of wellbeing in worldly terms with an ideological understanding of the true wellbeing that is liberation. The *Daśavaikālika* passage says that asceticism is a defining part of the "highest holy." The term being translated here as "holy" is *maṅgala*, one of the central terms within the wellbeing realm of value. When the author says that the *maṅgala* which is characterized by asceticism is the highest *maṅgala*, he implicitly assumes that there are alternative interpretations of *maṅgala*. His statement is designed to shake the listener (or, since this text is recited by mendicants, the speaker) into the realization that a true, accurate understanding of *maṅgala* rejects the wellbeing understanding in favor of the *mokṣa-mārg* understanding. Similarly, Yaśovijay employs a standard trope of wellbeing, an auspicious woman (*sīmantinī*) wearing red powder in the part of her hair and whose husband is therefore alive, which in the wellbeing perspective is viewed as an obvious sign of worldly success (*siddhi*) that leads to great joy (*mahānand*). But he also uses this symbolism as half of a binary opposition, contrasting the lesser joy, success, and holiness of wellbeing with the greater and truer infinite bliss that is one of the four characteristics of true holiness, the perfection of the liberated soul (*siddha*).

The Ideology of Asceticism

Yaśovijay also succinctly enumerates many of the basic aspects of the ideological formulation of asceticism. As with almost everything else in the *mokṣa-mārg* ideology, the discussion of asceticism is characterized by a mind-numbing succession of lists. One of the earliest formulations, found in such central texts as the *Tattvārtha Sūtra* (9.19–27) and *Uttarādhyayana Sūtra* (30.8–30) and repeated in countless later sources such as Yaśovijay's hymn, divides asceticism into six outer or external practices and six inner or internal practices. As given in the *Uttarādhyayana*, the six outer practices are: complete fasting; eating limited amounts; eating only restricted items; abstaining from tasty foods; mortification of the flesh; and guarding the limbs, that is, avoiding anything that can cause temptation. The six inner practices are: confession and expiation; respecting mendicants; assisting mendicants; study; meditation; and abandoning the body by ignoring bodily wants.

External asceticism focuses on the body. It is called external because the austerities all involve restricting one's dependence on external objects, and so the austerities themselves can be perceived by others. Internal asceticism focuses on attitudes, thoughts, and emotions. It is called internal because the austerities are less tied to interaction with external objects, and cannot easily be perceived by others (Sanghavi 1974:339). All twelve of the outer and inner practices play important roles in contemporary practice. But most lay Jains identify asceticism primarily with the six external forms of asceticism, which, as Williams (1963:238–39) has noted, are "virtually synonymous with fasting." Williams goes on to note that Jain asceticism "lies first and foremost in depriving oneself of food." Josephine Reynell (1985b:22) has similarly said that among the Khartar Gacch Jains of Jaipur, "more emphasis is given to the external behaviour than internal states for it is believed popularly that a person's external actions mirror their internal being." In this chapter, I will accordingly discuss primarily the external forms of asceticism. Instead of dividing my discussion into inner and outer practices, a more useful distinction is between ordinary, everyday ascetic practices that go far toward defining the Jains in the larger South Asian social sphere (where the truism "you are what you eat" has far-reaching social ramifications), and extraordinary, occasional ascetic practices that in many ways serve to mark the "staunch" (*cust*) Jain from most Jains. Although these exceptional practices are often undertaken by Jains who are more consciously involved in the *mokṣa-mārg* ideology, expressions of both the wellbeing realm of values and the *mokṣa-mārg* ideology are found in both ordinary and extraordinary asceticism, as I will discuss in the conclusion of the chapter.

The Ideal of Asceticism: Mahāvīr

For many Jains, the ideal of asceticism is encapsulated in the biography of Mahāvīr. His life is often described as "composed of asceticism." Medieval hagiographies of Mahāvīr detail the many fasts and austerities he practiced during his life as a mendicant. His fasts during the twelve years and six and one half months between renunciation and enlightenment are summarized in one contemporary popular pamphlet as follows (Kuśalcandravijay 1983:IX):[3]

One six-month fast	180 days
One 175-day fast	175 days
Nine four-month fasts	1,080 days
Two three-month fasts	180 days
Two seventy-five-day fasts	150 days
Two forty-five-day fasts	90 days
Twelve one-month fasts	360 days
Twelve fifteen-day fasts	180 days
Thirty-six three-day fasts	108 days
229 two-day fasts	458 days
One *bhadra pratimā*	75 days
One *mahābhadra pratimā*	196 days
One *sarvatobhadra pratimā*[4]	392 days
Total	3,624 days

Of the remaining 915 days, on 349 he took food only once, and he never slept for more than forty-eight minutes at a time. Nobody expects such fierce asceticism in the present age, since an aspect of the decline of time is that such exemplary asceticism is impossible, but it is still remembered as an ideal. This ideal is especially embodied in the lives of mendicants through their frequent fasting, and the charisma of many mendicants is directly related to their career of fasting. In particular, many mendicants observe long fasts, such as the fourteen-plus year *vardhmān āyambil oḷī*, which are considered by all Jains to be beyond the powers of the laity.

Vows and Duties

The ideological model for the layperson, as described in chapter 1, is based upon the notion of ever-stricter reduction of one's activities in order to reduce the intake of new karma and to scrub off accumulated old karma. This ideal is encapsulated in twelve binding *vrats*, or vows.[5] Padmanabh Jaini (1979:170) translates *vrat* from the root *vṛ*, "to fence in," as "restraint"; the *vrats* in his words "provide the means whereby karmic influx can be placed within certain limits, thereby assuring that the worldly activities do not lead to passions which deepen his involvement in saṃsāra." As we saw in chapter 1, there are twelve lay vows, the first five modeled directly on the great vows of the mendicant; the other seven consist of more precisely defined "fences" around one's involvement with the world. The ideal layperson is expected to engage in behavior that closely approximates to that of the mendicant, differing not in kind but only in level of observance. As a result, the ideal lay life is also structured around the practice of the six obligatory actions (*āvaśyak*). Although the *vrats* serve largely as a rhetorical ideal, the *āvaśyaks* do play an important role in the ritual life of many lay Jains, and so we need to look at them in some detail.[6] The six are:

1. *sāmāyik*, a form of meditative equanimity
2. *caturviṃśati-stava*, the hymn of veneration of the twenty-four Jinas which forms the core of *caitya-vandan*
3. *guru-vandan*, the rite of veneration of mendicants
4. *pratikramaṇ*, the rite by which the individual ritually negates the karmic impact of actions and thoughts
5. *käüssagg*, a form of standing meditation in which one mentally "abandons the body" and recites certain liturgies
6. *pacckkhāṇ*, a vow to perform certain karmically efficacious acts[7]

Sāmāyik is a form of meditative mental tranquility. Hemacandra defines it as equanimity or indifference to hatred and passion.[8] A contemporary mendicant has given this extensive definition: "*Sam* means equanimity, a lack of disturbance. *Sāmāyik* is to be absorbed in the essence of oneself and thus quiet various disturbing states. *Sam* means a feeling of sympathy, friendliness, and brotherhood toward all living things. *Sāmāyik* is to treat all others like oneself. *Sam* means a state free of attachment and aversion and all notions of likes and dislikes. *Sāmāyik* is the determination not to cause suffering to others, and the human aim of developing brotherhood with others" (Kuśalcandravijay 1983:VIII.3).

A major part of the initiation rite for Śvetāmbar mendicants is to take the vow of *sāmāyik* for life (Shântâ 1985:243); in other words, a mendicant by definition is in a perpetual state of heightened meditative awareness. Lay people take the vow of *sāmāyik* for shorter periods, of one or at most two *muhūrts* (one *muhūrt* = forty-eight minutes). As one layman described it, *sāmāyik* is forty-eight minutes of initiation, and conversely to take initiation is to undertake lifelong *sāmāyik* (see also Kalāpūrṇsūri 1987:16). During *sāmāyik*, the person meditates, repeats a *mantra*, studies a sacred text, or listens to a sermon by a mendicant. She or he should avoid any thoughts concerning worldly affairs. Many lay people perform *sāmāyik* during a *sādhu*'s sermon, simultaneously listening to the sermon and reciting a *mantra*. Because so many people perform one or two periods of *sāmāyik* during sermons, they tend to be at least either forty-eight or ninety-six minutes long. Other laity, primarily older retired people, develop a routine of practicing *sāmāyik* once or twice daily, often in the household shrine room. One is essentially a mendicant while performing *sāmāyik*, and so is expected to take extreme care when sitting down that no insect or other minute life be harmed, and if one stands one must take the mendicant's broom in hand. Some mendicants organize special sessions of group *sāmāyik* that last for two *muhūrts*; over 500 people attended one such group *sāmāyik* held in a town near Patan during the rainy season retreat in August 1986. The benefits of *sāmāyik* are succinctly described from the *mokṣa-mārg* perspective as follows: "By doing full *sāmāyik* for forty-eight minutes, even an incompetent layman is freed from bad karma and can effect the dissociation (*nirjarā*) of previous karma" (Kalāpūrṇsūri 1987:16).

Similar to *sāmāyik* is *poṣadh* or *pauṣadh* (also *posah*), one of the twelve lay vows. This is essentially an extended observance of *sāmāyik*, which usually lasts either four or eight *prahars* (one *prahar* equals three hours). One layman described *poṣadh* as twelve or twenty-four hours of *sāmāyik* and twelve or twenty-four hours of mendicant initiation. He further said that if a person dies while observing *poṣadh*, in theory the body should be treated like that of a mendicant in terms of the cremation rites. To observe *poṣadh*, the layperson usually resides in an *upāśray*, and observes a fast such as *āyambil* or *ekāsan* (see below). Although *poṣadh* is observed by some very pious laity during the year—on Sundays in the case of some working people, or on five or ten *parvs* (see chapter 6) in the month by people with sufficient time—the main time in the year when people observe *poṣadh* is during Paryuṣaṇ (chapter 6). At Maṇḍap Upāśray in 1986, some four dozen men observed *poṣadh* for all eight days of Paryuṣaṇ, and some forty women observed it in the nearby *upāśrays* of the *sādhvīs*. Most of these were elderly, retired people, and a few were students who might have been considering the mendicant life.

The second obligatory action is the rite of veneration to the twenty-four Jinas, *caturviṃśati-stava* or *caitya-vandan*, and the third is the veneration of mendicants, *guru-vandan*, discussed in chapters 3 and 4.

The fourth obligatory action is *pratikramaṇ*, defined by a contemporary mendicant as "the rite which returns a person into his soul from the external attacks [of karma]" (Nirvāṇa Sāgara 1986:6).[9] The following is an analysis of the function of *pratikramaṇ* in the life of a Jain:

> The root essence of the soul is correct faith, understanding, and conduct. The soul remains in its own home when it enjoys the virtues of correct faith, knowledge, and

conduct. But when it leaves its own home and starts wandering in nonessential states due to the arising of delusion-karma, then it is inclined toward all sorts of harmful karma (*pāp*).[10] In this negligent state the soul performs all sorts of karmically harmful actions based on ignorance, such as violence, lying, theft, sex, possessiveness, anger, pride, delusion, greed, attachment and aversion, strife, false accusation, backbiting, copulation, arguing, and misleading speech.

When one forgets and abandons the main path, one keeps traveling on lesser paths. When one remembers the true path, then one's mind is filled with remorse. While traveling on the lesser path, one's efforts are worthless and one's time is wasted. Even the careful soul when under the spell of delusion becomes careless and engages in improper behavior. When the power of that delusion comes to an end, the soul remembers its own essence. One feels shame at one's improper endeavors. The true meaning of *pratikramaṇ* is to abandon fully and feel remorse for karmically harmful activities and so to return to one's essence. (Ratnasenvijay 1984:29–30)

The core of the *pratikramaṇ* ritual is the recitation of formulae of atonement for faults committed since the last recitation of *pratikramaṇ*. It is thus frequently characterized as a form of penance for karmically harmful actions. Also included in the *pratikramaṇ* recitation are a number of devotional hymns, and the performance of *kāüssagg*. There are five kinds of *pratikramaṇ*: performed in the evening, to atone for the day's transgressions; performed first thing in the morning, to atone for the night's transgressions; performed every fortnight; performed every four months; and performed annually, the *saṃvatsarī pratikramaṇ* performed on the last day of Paryuṣaṇ. There are slight differences in the texts recited for each one. The recitation and performance of the accompanying rituals take between one and two and a half hours. The performance of all five *pratikramaṇ*s is a major element in the life of a mendicant, but they are performed with less frequency by laity (see Figure 5.2). Performance of *saṃvatsarī pratikramaṇ* is the most nearly universal of the five. Many laity perform the evening *pratikramaṇ* daily during Paryuṣaṇ, and sporadically during the four-month rainy-season period, and as James Laidlaw notes for Jaipur, there are occasional informal groups of mostly elderly men or women who gather to perform evening *pratikramaṇ*. Few lay Jains have memorized the entire lengthy Prakrit and Sanskrit liturgy, and so although many Jains know at least part of it (especially some of the hymns), there are many manuals containing the texts recited in *pratikramaṇ* for use in its performance.[11] Nearly every Jain household contains at least one such manual, and every *upāśray* will have multiple copies on hand.

The fifth obligatory action is *kāüssagg*. Its literal meaning is "to abandon the body." Its fuller sense is as follows: "[*Kāüssagg*] is to abandon attachment to the body. As long as one is concerned about the body there is no concern for the soul. The majority of one's life is spent in maintenance and nourishment of the body. Thus there is no time for remembering the soul. One forgets that no matter how much concern one spends on the body, nevertheless one day it will perish. If one is concerned about the soul then it is necessary to forget the body; this pure rite is called [*kāüssagg*]" (Nirvāṇa Sāgara 1986:9–10).

Kāüssagg is not, however, an independent practice. It is part of other rites such as *caitya-vandan* and *pratikramaṇ*. At certain set times in these rites, the participant is called upon to perform *kāüssagg*. The person stands erect, with feet slightly apart, the arms hanging down parallel to and slightly away from the body,

Figure 5.2. Layman performing *pratikramaṇ*; here he inspects his mouth-cloth for living organisms. Photograph by Kendall W. Folkert, 1985.

and the palms facing inward. This is the same pose as that of many standing Jina images. While in the *kāüssagg* posture, the person recites, depending on the context, either the *Nokār Mantra*, or the longer *Logass* hymn in praise of the twenty-four Jinas (chapter 3). In its original form, *kāüssagg* was observed for a certain set number of exhalations and inhalations; the recitation of these hymns is designed to equal the required breathing cycles. At the conclusion of the recitation, each person says, "namo arihantāṇaṃ" ("Praise to the Jinas"), to indicate that he or she has finished (see Figure 3.2).

The sixth and final obligatory action is *pacckkhāṇ*. The benefits from its performance are described as follows:

> [*Pacckkhāṇ*] means to abandon things that are not beneficial for the soul and to accept things that are beneficial. Use and reuse of objects, and attachments to those objects, is worthless and not beneficial to the soul. Every bit of abandonment of those things is advantageous to the soul. As long as the soul remains attached to some object, it is in karmic bondage. As long as the attachment is not removed, the person cannot attain spiritual freedom. The rite for removing the attachment from the soul is [*pacckkhāṇ*]. The pure rite of [*pacckkhāṇ*] works like a medicine, curing the illness of the soul's bondage so it can attain freedom. (Nirvāṇa Sāgara 1986:10)

In practice, *pacckkhāṇ* is the public statement of the intention to perform a religious action, in particular some sort of fast. When a lay person has decided to perform a fast, on that morning he or she should recite the formula of *pacckkhāṇ* for that fast (see Williams 1963:209–12; Nirvāṇa Sāgara 1986:197–205). If a mendicant is in town, it should be recited in front of him or her; otherwise, it can be recited in front of a Jina image. At the end of a sermon, a *sādhu* will always announce, "*Pacckkhāṇ*!" One by one he will rapidly recite the formulae giving permission to do different fasts; as he recites each formula, those who have decided to perform that particular fast rise, face him, fold their hands in front of them, and recite the formula along with him. In effect, the *sādhu* is both giving permission for the layperson to perform the fast and witnessing the intention to perform the fast.

Pacckkhāṇ is similar to the *saṅkalp*, or statement of intention, at the commencement of a Hindu lay vow, but they are not seen as identical. One *sādhu* somewhat judgmentally described the difference as follows: "*Pacckkhāṇ* is a binding force. It is not the same as a *saṅkalp*. We can break a *saṅkalp*, but we cannot break a *pacckkhāṇ*. A *saṅkalp* is merely a mental decision." He further explained that the importance of *pacckkhāṇ* is to prevent one from becoming slack and not finishing the ritual. *Pacckkhāṇ* is also essential for the ritual to be maximally efficacious, either by wearing away karma or earning merit (*puṇya*). One derives less merit if one decides to perform a fast but does it without performing *pacckkhāṇ*. One mendicant quotes the following Sanskrit maxim on the subject, using an analogy easily understood by the mercantile Jains: "If one fasts without having first performed *pacckkhāṇ*, one still accrues the faults of eating; just as one will not receive any interest on a deposit if one hasn't first determined the interest" (Bhuvanvijay 1981b:285). If one merely performs the fast by chance—for example, not eating for a day not out of choice but merely because one is traveling and doesn't have a chance to eat—then one derives no merit at all. In the words of a mendicant, "If you haven't abandoned anything, then you don't get any *puṇya*."

The six obligatory actions are included in a list of seventy-three spiritual practices and states discussed in chapter 29 of the *Uttarādhyayana Sūtra* on the *mokṣa-mārg*. This text briefly gives the results of the practice of the six obligatory actions as follows (29.8–13):

> By *sāmāyik* avoidance of karmically harmful activity is born.
>
> By *caturviṃśati-stava* purity of faith is born.
>
> By *guru-vandan* the karma leading to low birth is destroyed, and karma leading to high birth is acquired. He is popular, his orders are followed and not obstructed, and he creates goodwill.
>
> By *pratikramaṇ* he avoids breaking the vows. By avoiding breaking the vows the influx of karma into the soul is blocked, his conduct is faultless, he observes the eight matrices of doctrine [chapter 4], he travels mindfully and carefully.
>
> By *kāüssagg* he is purified of actions in the past and present which require expiation. By being purified through the expiation, his soul is like a porter freed of his burden. He travels happily, engaged in praiseworthy meditation.
>
> By *pacckkhāṇ* the doors of karmic influx are shut. By *pacckkhāṇ* one stops desires. By stopping desires in his soul, thirst for all objects is destroyed, and he travels coolly.

The six obligatory actions are here described in terms of their karmic effects in the *mokṣa-mārg* ideology. *Sāmāyik*, *caturviṃśati-stava*, and *guru-vandan* ensure that the practitioner avoids and destroys harmful karma, obstructs the influx of karma, and that whatever karma is accrued is only good karma. In the other three even these latter, helpful karmas are renounced, and the practitioner strives for total freedom from the entire realm of karma.

To summarize, the ideological prescription for the lay life involves ever-increasing restrictions upon the layperson's conduct and interactions, with the goal of increasing spiritual purity by both decreasing the previously accumulated store of karma and stopping the influx of new karma. It is based closely upon the prescription for the mendicant life. The bases of the mendicant's conduct are the five *mahāvrats*, the lifelong binding vows, and the six obligatory actions. The bases of the layperson's conduct according to the *mokṣa-mārg* ideology, therefore, are the twelve *vrats* or lay vows, which entail lifelong binding behavior on the part of the layperson,[12] and the six obligatory actions, which are presented as though they were obligatory for laity, as well.

In practice, the twelve vows are rarely taken in the formal *mokṣa-mārg* sense. For example, if a layperson decides to adopt celibacy for the rest of his or her life, as some people do at the end of the wife's child-bearing years, the usual procedure is not to take the formal *anuvrat* of *brahmacarya*, but rather to pledge before a mendicant (or occasionally a Jina image) to observe celibacy. I never met anyone who had taken the twelve lay vows, nor who practiced all the six obligatory actions in the manner prescribed by the *mokṣa-mārg* ideologues. But many Jains insisted that such pious laypeople have and do exist, and could point to laypeople they knew who embodied in their lives much of the *mokṣa-mārg* ideology, and often were self-consciously *mokṣa-mārg* ideologues. Similarly, although most laity know and occasionally perform the obligatory actions, they remain occasional, voluntary practices in lay life. Lay asceticism in practice consists not of obligatory behavior governed by binding, lifelong vows, but rather the voluntary adoption of recommended behavior governed by vows that are binding but of limited duration. Let us now turn to the actual forms of ascetic behavior from which an individual constructs his or her ascetic practice.

Ordinary Asceticism

Four concepts are key in lay ascetic practice. The first is *kriyā*, the most general term for ritual action. It can refer to fasting, to performance of any of the *āvaśyak* rituals such as *pratikramaṇ* or *sāmāyik*, and also to image worship. It is generally contrasted with *jñān*, knowledge, especially in the context of polemics on the part of Jain intellectuals (both mendicant and lay) against a seeming undue focus on the outer form of rituals at the expense of their inner meaning.[13]

The second and third terms are *niyam* and *bādhā*. They are used interchangeably to refer to a pledge. In many ways they are similar to the Hindu *vrat*. A *bādhā* or *niyam* is a voluntary pledge to restrict in some manner one's nonreligious activity, to be extra diligent in some regular religious activity, or to practice some additional religious activity, usually some form of asceticism. Such a pledge is for a limited duration of time. It can be taken privately or in the presence of a mendicant. Often mendicants will direct their lay disciples to undertake such pledges. As with *pacckkhāṇ*, the formal statement of a *niyam* or *bādhā* is considered necessary for the intended action to have its full effect upon one's karmic state. Examples of two such pledges, lasting three months, undertaken simultaneously by one layman at the behest of his guru, were to observe strictly the prohibition on eating after sunset (see below) and to avoid watching any television. Television is considered to be a frivolous activity that stirrs up desires and emotions, and is therefore counter to a proper religious spirit.

The fourth term is *upvās*, meaning any kind of fast. The derivation of the word from Sanskrit *upa* + *vāsa*, meaning "to dwell near," is employed by ideologues in their discourses on fasting, as in the following example: "*Upvās* means to live near yourself. Daily you live near food. This day you are to live near the soul, near the qualities of the soul" (Oṃkārsūri 1984:102).

The dietary restrictions of the Jains constitute one of the hallmarks of the tradition for most Indians.[14] In Gujarat, Jains probably have more of a reputation for being choosy eaters than do Brāhmans. Each will accept food in public only in very carefully controlled circumstances. The cultural logic underlying the Jain food restrictions is quite simple: *ahiṃsā*. The killing and harming of the myriad visible and invisible living creatures that surround one is considered to be a chief cause of the influx of new binding karma, which in turn keeps one tied to the causal round of rebirth in *saṃsār*. All Jains recognize that only a mendicant can practice *ahiṃsā* to the fullest. But the lay Jain is still expected to maintain extreme diligence in terms of diet, and the dietary rules for the laity are designed to minimize violence and killing in the preparation and consumption of food and drink. Although some of the dietary rules are based on easily observable principles, such as not eating meat, others, such as not eating root crops, are based on principles specific to Jain biology.

At the core of the Jain dietary ideology is the concept that certain foods are *abhakṣya*, "not to be eaten." A standard list of twenty-two items dates from at least as early as the eleventh-century *Pravacanasāroddhāra* of Nemicandra (Williams 1963:110n2).[15] This list is an ideological, prescriptive framework. Most Jains know the concept of *abhakṣya* and some of the foods found on the standard list. But very few, except for the ideologues, know all twenty-two items, which include such obvious foods as meat, honey, and alcohol, common foods such as butter, eggplant, and vegetables and fruits with many seeds, and unlikely foods such as snow, poison, hailstones, and clay. Actual Jain dietary practice varies widely from individual to individual and from household to household, and overlaps only in part with the *abhakṣyas*. The list of *abhakṣyas* serves as an ideological frame for mendicant discourse on Jain foodways, but does not serve as a useful prescription for actual dietary practice. In this it differs to some extent from lists of prohibited foods found in the Jewish and Muslim traditions.

Many popular books and pamphlets explain why these foods should not be eaten, and the *abhakṣyas* are frequently the subject of mendicant sermons. Meat and honey are forbidden because of the obvious killing involved. Some items are proscribed because, as Williams (1963:52) notes, they are foods offered to the ancestors in the Brāhmaṇical tradition, and conscious rejection of Brāhmaṇical ancestor worship has long been a feature of Jain ideology. Most of the foods are forbidden because they contain innumerable tiny and invisible organisms. Thus, snow and hailstones contain innumerable single-sensed water bodies; mud contains innumerable single-sensed earth bodies, as well as being the source for five-sensed beings such as frogs; pickles breed innumerable organisms after three days, or if they have not been properly dried in the sun; and both alcohol and butter contain innumerable organisms. This is most obviously the case with eggplants and other foods with many seeds (*bahu-bīj*), as each seed is considered to contain a soul.

A special class of food substances included among the *abhakṣyas* are known as *anant-kāys* (infinite bodies). According to Jain biology, plant life is of two kinds: individual (*pratyek*) and aggregate (*sādhāran*). Individual plants contain only one soul, but aggregate plants contain innumerable souls. A list of thirty-two *anant-kāys* is given by many authors (see Williams 1963:114–15); although there are some vines and sprouts, most of them are tubers and bulbs such as turmeric, ginger, garlic, radish, carrots, and potatoes. From the perspective of Western biology, these are plants in which the edible portion contains the possibility of regenerating a new plant. From the Jain perspective, eating a carrot, for example, results in the accrual of much more harmful karma than eating an apple because one has killed many more living beings. In the words of one mendicant, "When a man eats a root crop, he destroys infinite souls. The bad karma (*pāp*) that he eats is such that he suffers in his next life. O! So many souls are sacrificed when one eats such food!" (Guṇratnavijay n.d.:82).

The prohibition on eating *anant-kāys* is translated into general practice through the concept of *khaṇḍ mūḷ bandh*, "not eating root crops." In practical terms, this prohibition means that the Jain diet tends to be devoid of onions, potatoes, and garlic, and thus is very distinctive in the broader cuisine of northern and western India. As with many dietary practices, this prohibition is observed most closely by women and more orthodox men, and therefore in the home. Many Jain men who do not eat root crops at home, because their wives will not cook them, will eat them outside the home, in restaurants or non-Jain households.

On one occasion, I went on a two-day pilgrimage to Shatrunjay with a Jain family. While in the town of Palitana at the base of Shatrunjay, the husband scrupulously observed all the Jain dietary restrictions. Since we were eating in a Jain *bhojanśāḷā*, this was easily done. On the way back to Ahmedabad we stopped for a snack. He ordered a dish containing potatoes and onions, and ate raw onions as an appetizer. I knew he ate such foods in Ahmedabad, but had expected that he would observe the orthodox diet for the duration of the pilgrimage. When I expressed surprise at his eating the potatoes and onions, he replied, "But we've already left Palitana." In other words, for many people the circumstances under which one observes full dietary orthodoxy are quite narrowly circumscribed.

Also found on the list of the *abhakṣyas* is *rātri-bhojan bandh* (not eating after sunset). The basic logic behind this prohibition is, again, fairly straightforward: in the dim light of pre-electric India, one could not adequately see what one was eating, and therefore was quite likely to eat insects that landed on the food. Given the attraction of night-flying insects for lights of any kind, the chances of insects landing on the food was much greater at night than in daylight. Authors also elaborate the many harmful side-effects both from eating such insects and from eating at night in general, a theme that dates back to at least Hemacandra (Williams

1963:108–9). A contemporary mendicant gives the following reasons not to eat after sunset: "After sunset many subtle and minute living beings are bred. They are invisible even in electric light, and so are killed when they are eaten. Eating at night causes indigestion and harms our health. We feel indolent, and do not feel like rising in the morning. It causes disease. . . . By eating at night, we may die from eating poisonous creatures which come into the food. One reads many reports of such deaths in the newspapers" (Kuśalcandravijay 1983:III.12–4). He continues to list a number of harmful results from eating at night, such as cancer, dropsy, vomiting, leucoderma, fever, and death.

In practice, only the most orthoprax lay Jains observe the prohibition on *rātri-bhojan*. Again, these tend to be mostly women and some retired men. Many Jains observe the prohibition only during Paryuṣaṇ, or perhaps during the whole of the four-month rainy season. In her study of Digambar Jains in Delhi, Marie-Claude Mahias (1985:108–9) observes that the prohibition on *rātri-bhojan* is especially problematic for the families of businessmen and shopkeepers who return home after sunset. Indian custom calls for the women to eat after the men. But if the men, as is usually the case, return home and take their evening meal after sunset, then the general Indian custom comes into conflict with the women's desire to observe the prohibition on *rātri-bhojan* (and women, as bearers of primary responsibility for a family's moral status, are expected to observe such restrictions more closely than men). This typifies what Mahias identifies as the central opposition in the Jain culinary system, between the religious rules based on renunciation of food and the social rules based on consumption of food. In my experience, Jain women solved this dilemma in one of three ways: at the wife's urging, all or most of the family members observed the prohibition on *rātri-bhojan* on limited occasions such as Paryuṣaṇ or other holidays; on many occasions, the wife followed the husband's example, and ate after sunset; and on some occasions, the wife opted not to eat anything in the evening (perhaps having taken a late-afternoon snack) in order both to observe the prohibition on *rātri-bhojan* and not to eat before her husband.

In general, the *abhakṣyas* can be divided into three broad categories when compared with actual diet. First are those items such as snow, hailstones, and clay, which few people are likely to consume in any event. Next comes meat; vegetarianism is almost a sine qua non for being a Jain, and can serve as a defining limit for who is and is not a Jain. As Kendall Folkert once remarked in conversation, "When a Jain asks you if you are a vegetarian, he is not asking a question, he is making an accusation." More than any other facet of the Jain tradition, vegetarianism sees a nearly complete convergence between ideology and practice. Many Jains exhibit an ideological fervor when expressing the vegetarian imperative, and for many living in Europe and North America vegetarianism has become the core of their religious identity. Last come those foodstuffs that many, but not all, Jains do not consume, and which almost all Jains would recognize as *abhakṣyas*; here I would list alcohol, honey, eggplant, *anant-kāys*, *bahu-bījs*, ice, butter, pickles, and eating at night. Within this last group there is great variety in terms of how well known it is that an item is an *abhakṣya*, and how rigorously most Jains observe the prohibition.

Closely related to the ideology of the *abhakṣyas*, but not specifically given in the textual lists, is the concept of *līlu śākh bandh* (not eating green vegetables). Green, leafy vegetables are problematic for orthodox Jains because of the high likelihood that many tiny insects will be hidden in the leaves and therefore accidentally eaten. When preparing foods such as cabbage and cauliflower, extreme care is taken to ensure that no insects are accidentally cooked with the food. What exactly constitutes a green vegetable is a matter of some interpretation. Mendicants tend to be the strictest in their definition. One orthodox family with whom I ate served tomatoes on a no-green day; when questioned, they admitted that mendicants and many strictly orthodox Jains do not eat tomatoes at all, because they have too many seeds, but that they themselves considered tomatoes as fruits and therefore acceptable. Some families will eat pickled green chillies on a no-green day, so long as they were pickled on an earlier day. Similarly, many people will not eat fresh peas but will eat foods prepared with dried peas.

Almost all Jains avoid green vegetables on certain days (*tithi*) of the lunar month.[16] Most observe five *tithis* (see chapter 6): bright fifth, both eighths, and both fourteenths. A few laity observe ten *tithis*: both seconds, both fifths, both eighths, both elevenths, and both fourteenths. Most mendicants observe twelve *tithis* by also observing the new and full moon days. Although there is no single logical principle underlying the different patterns of *tithis*, in general the concept is tied to the Jain theory that the volatility of karma varies in accordance with astrological patterns, and therefore stricter patterns of dietary (and other) practice are called for on those days.

Another category related to the ideology of the *abhakṣyas* but not explicitly found on the list is *garam pāṇī* (boiled water). Concern with the purity and acceptability of water is a major concern for most Jains. According to Jain biology, by boiling water one prevents the birth of infinite invisible organisms, and therefore actually prevents much *hiṃsā*. The small amount of *hiṃsā* that one causes from boiling water is much less than that which results from drinking unboiled water with all its microorganisms. Mendicants can drink only water that has been recently boiled and so is still warm. Since mendicants cannot handle fire (which, obviously, causes much *hiṃsā*), they rely on laity to prepare the boiled water for them. Few laity drink only boiled water all the time, but most Jains drink only boiled water while on a pilgrimage, in part because of a concern for greater orthopraxy but also in recognition of the health risks of unboiled water, especially in smaller towns and villages.

Even if they do not drink boiled water exclusively, almost all Jains are very careful about drinking and cooking water. Clay pots and stainless steel containers used for storing drinking and cooking water in the kitchen are emptied daily, to prevent the growth of mold and microorganisms. Water spouts and pots are covered with cloth filters, to prevent the consumption of any small organisms residing in the water. Milk, whether purchased directly from a milkman or in plastic containers from a store, is also filtered. One of the major complaints Jain ideologues have against restaurants is that the water is not filtered, and is stored for many days, so that inevitably one is performing *hiṃsā* by drinking restaurant water. Filtering could easily be used as a basic metaphor for the Jain attitude toward diet and the entire biological world.

A practice that is an extension of the emphasis on boiled and filtered water is *palī dhoīne pivī* (drinking the rinse water). At the end of a meal, especially during the rainy season or Paryuṣaṇ, some Jains pour water onto the metal plate on which the meal is eaten, rinse all the food particles into one corner of the tilted plate, and drink this rinse water. Again, the basis for this practice lies in Jain biology. If one leaves the food particles on the plate, all these particles will be washed into the gutter, where they will result in the breeding of innumerable organisms. These organisms will quickly live and die, and the person who left the food particles on his or her plate is held karmically responsible for their death. An anonymous pamphlet explained the practice as follows:

> It is necessary to learn how to wash and drink down one's plate every day. From this one gets the benefit of one *āyambil* [see below] fast. From correctly wiping one's plate, one is saved from giving offence to countless souls which would have spontaneously generated there. . . .
>
> After eating, if the utensils remain dirty for two hours, then innumerable spontaneously generating five-sensed souls will arise. These souls then die, so one should not just put aside the dirty utensils. In your little laziness you get the bad karma (*pāp*) of great *hiṃsā*. So don't just put aside dirty utensils. (*Sādharmik Bhakti* 3, 8)

The extent and variety of the dietary restrictions listed above should make it obvious that an orthoprax Jain layperson never eats in a public restaurant. Because of this concern for food, there are special Jain dining halls (*bhojanśāḷās*) in all important Jain pilgrimage places. *Sādhus* in their sermons often harp upon the sin accrued through eating in restaurants. One ideologue in a tirade against eating in restaurants points out that even if a restaurant says that it serves food cooked by Brāhmaṇs, this is still unacceptable for Jains (P. M. Śā 1942:134–36). Similarly, orthoprax Jains avoid the consumption of ready-made foods that can be purchased in stores in most cities and larger towns, and are increasingly advertised on television and in print media as a marker of a modern, Westernized lifestyle. In Ahmedabad, where restaurant dining is becoming a more acceptable form of entertainment (and is also perceived as a marker of modernity), some restaurants have special sections on their menus for "Jain vegetables." In the newer suburbs of Ahmedabad inhabited by many upwardly mobile Jains, one can also find stores which sell "Jain snacks." These are prepared by Jain women's cooperatives and therefore acceptable to many Jains. Because of the general perception that the only acceptable food is that which has been prepared in a carefully controlled, Jain environment, many orthoprax Jains when traveling will make a virtue out of necessity and fast. Because of these dietary restrictions, there are also special Jain hostels attached to some universities. The kitchens attached to these hostels observe the prohibitions on both eating at night and eating root crops.

Some scrupulous, orthoprax Jains can be almost overwhelmed by the profusion of uncontrollable biological processes that surround them, and for which they feel a degree of unavoidable karmic responsibility. This was brought home to me vividly one day in Jodhpur in 1998. An elderly Jain man with whom I was walking down a narrow alley suddenly stopped and looked down. At first I thought he was in pain, for one of his knees was crippled by arthritis. But then I followed his gaze down to the ground, and saw that he was looking at the open sewer. Looking more closely, I realized that the waste water was teeming with hundreds of maggots. My friend, who had strictly followed Jain dietary principles for over thirty years, to the extent that he wouldn't accept even a glass of water anywhere but in a Jain household or institution, was contemplating with a look of horror on his face a world in which countless organisms are born and die every instant, a world the karmic consequences of which he struggled to keep at bay every day of his life.

The Daily Routine of a Jain Household

To help make sense out of the mass of details presented above, let us look at the daily routine of a Jain household in Patan. We see that the many concepts found in Jain ascetic practice do not comprise an abstract, formal list from which people pick and choose. These are all embedded in the very foundation of Jain life, and are observed by Jains as effortlessly and unconsciously as are many other aspects of their lives. The day I describe did not happen, but it is closely patterned on a number of days that I did observe and participate in. The family consists of Kīrtilāl M. Śāh, a sixty-four-year-old businessman whose daily *pūjā* was described in chapter 3, his fifty-eight-year-old wife Maṇiben, his sons Candrakānt (aged twenty-four) and Sunīl (aged nineteen), both of whom are unmarried and living at home, and his daughter Śreyā (aged twenty-seven), who is visiting from Bombay, where her husband works.

The family rises around sunrise, between 6:00 and 6:30 A.M. After going to the lavatory, Kīrtibhāī and Maṇiben[17] walk the two minutes to the neighborhood temple for a quick *darśan*, and then return home.[18] If it is during Paryuṣaṇ, or is a special festival, the family observes *navkārsī* (see below), which means that they will wait until at least forty-eight minutes after sunrise before eating or drinking, or even brushing the teeth. Otherwise everyone brushes his or her teeth upon arising, and when Kīrtibhāī and Maṇiben return home everyone eats breakfast. Kīrtibhāī bathes before the others, changes into his *pūjā* clothes, and goes to the temple for his morning worship. After breakfast, Maṇiben and Śreyāben start to prepare the noontime meal, while the two sons take their baths. Kīrtibhāī returns home, changes into his regular clothes, and leaves for his office in the bazaar around 9:30 A.M. with Candrakānt. Maṇiben and then Śreyāben bathe, and in mid-morning don their *pūjā* clothes and go to the temple to worship, making sure that one of them remains at home while the other is out. Sunīl eats an early meal and leaves for college at 10:45; his schedule is arranged so that he does not have to eat at the college dining hall. Kīrtibhāī and Candrakānt return home at midday to eat. If it is one of the five no-green *tithi*s of the month, the meal contains a dish such as *kaḍhī* (made from chickpea flour and buttermilk) or mung beans in place of vegetables. After Kīrtibhāī and Candrakānt have eaten, Maṇiben and Śreyāben eat. Unless there is a lot of work to do, Kīrtibhāī stays home for the afternoon, and Candrakānt returns to the office alone. The women clean the dishes, do some other household chores, and in mid-afternoon Maṇiben takes a nap while Śreyāben visits friends. Everyone returns home in time for tea and a snack around 4:30. If it is during Paryuṣaṇ, or is a special festival, the family eats the evening meal before sunset; otherwise they might eat as late as 7:30. (This is after sunset, but still earlier than most non-Jains in South Asia eat.) After dinner, Candrakānt takes Kīrtibhāī on the motor scooter to the temple of Śāmḷājī Pārśvanāth for *darśan*; on special days they might also go to Pañcāsar Pārśvanāth, in which case they are joined by Maṇiben and go by ricksha. In the evening, the family gathers in the front room to watch television. Some evenings, rather than watch television, Kīrtibhāī sits on a mat on the floor before his small household shrine in the back room and performs *sāmāyik* for an hour. He repeats a *mantra* addressed to Śaṅkheśvar Pārśvanāth that he was given by his *sādhu-guru*, using a rosary to count the cycles. On some days, he also performs *sāmāyik* in the morning, either before or after worshiping in the temple. At the end of the day, after everyone has gone to bed, if she is not too tired Maṇiben might sit on the front porch for ten to fifteen minutes and also repeat a *mantra*; only on rare evenings does she do *sāmāyik*.

We see from this description that although the family might not appear to be preoccupied with religious concerns, the rhythms and emphases of the day are determined by their being Jain. This is seen most obviously in their doing *pūjā* and *darśan* at the Jain temple and in their diet. The specifically Jain nature of their diet would be more apparent on a no-green *tithi* or a festival, but the perceptive outsider would quickly spot that the food was Jain due to the lack of root crops, in particular potatoes, onions, and garlic. The men also carefully avoid eating outside the home. In other Jain households, there might be more religiously oriented activity, such as a special fast, a visit to a mendicant, or the performance of evening *pratikramaṇ*. In most Jain households, however, these are not ordinary activities. Nonetheless, in even an average household such as I have portrayed above, the daily routine is gently informed by domestic, ordinary asceticism.

Extraordinary Asceticism

The practices described above are part of the everyday ethos of lay Jains, and help to define them within the larger Indian society. Not all Jains observe all of these practices; the degree of observance is determined by personal preference as well as family and regional tradition. Nonetheless, they are practices with which all Jains are familiar. In addition to these ordinary dietary observances, there are a number of extraordinary fasts performed only by those Jains with a stronger personal commitment to their practice.

The basic word for any kind of fast in the Jain tradition is *upvās*. Jains do not use the Hindu term *vrat* for fasts; this term is ideologically marked and so restricted to its more technical sense of the five mendicant *mahāvrats* and the twelve lay *vrats*. On the one hand, *upvās* is used to refer to a day of fasting. On the other, it is used as a cover term for a wide variety of longer fasts, distinguished by the length of time between meals and the severity of dietary restrictions. Standard durations for an *upvās* are one and a half, two, two and a half, eight, fifteen, thirty, and forty-five days, with the longer fasts increasingly difficult and rarer. Laity tend to perform such longer fasts only during the autumnal festival of Paryuṣaṇ. In particular, they try to time eight-, fifteen-, and thirty-day fasts so that they conclude on Saṃvatsarī, the last day of Paryuṣaṇ.

One of the most common of these fasts is the *aṭhṭham tap* or three-day fast. The name means "eighth," so one fasts for eight meals. In north Gujarat, many Jains perform this fast at Shankheshvar (Bhadraguptvijaygaṇi 1981, Cort 1988). According to the Jain universal history, Kṛṣṇa, the cousin of Nemināth, the twenty-second Jina of this time period, fought an epic battle with the demon king Jarāsandha at Shankheshvar. Jarāsandha cast a magic spell that paralyzed Kṛṣṇa's army. Kṛṣṇa performed an *aṭhṭham tap* to counter it. The principal attraction of the site is the charismatic, wonder-working (*camatkārī*) image of Śaṅkheśvar Pārśvanāth in the temple. This eternal, uncreated image was revealed to Kṛṣṇa by the *yakṣ* Dharaṇendra and the *yakṣī* Padmāvatī (the god and goddess who preside over Pārśvanāth's teachings) at the conclusion of his *aṭhṭham tap*, so devotion to the image of Śaṅkheśvar Pārśvanāth and performance of *aṭhṭham tap* are closely intertwined. Kṛṣṇa took the water that had been used to bathe the image and sprinkled it over the troops of his army to break Jarāsandha's spell. He then defeated Jarāsandha. The performance of an *aṭhṭham tap* at Shankhesvar is believed to be even more efficacious if performed at the time of Poṣ Tenth (chapter 6). Pilgrims express the belief that it is relatively easy to fast at Shankheshvar due to the grace of the image itself and the grace of the goddess Padmāvatī, who is closely associated with the shrine. This sentiment is clearly expressed in a pilgrim pamphlet: "Men and women who have never fasted once in their lives can easily perform *aṭhṭham tap* at this shrine due to the auspicious grace of Lord Śaṅkheśvar Pārśvanāth" (Bhadraguptvijaygaṇi 1981:34).

Fasts can be performed in either of two fashions. If the fast is a *caūvihār*, it involves total abstinence from both food and water. A *tivihār* fast involves abstinence from only food; the person can drink boiled water, but only between *navkārsī* and sunset. Every Jain almanac gives at least three times for every day of the year: sunrise, *navkārsī*, and sunset. *Navkārsī* falls forty-eight minutes after sunrise. Those who are observing *navkārsī* wait until this time before eating or drinking, or even cleaning their teeth. Although all mendicants observe *navkārsī* every day, only a minority of laity do so. Most fasts that are longer than two and a half days tend to be *tivihār*, for the simple reason that a long *caūvihār* can quite easily prove fatal. Longer fasts can also be *ekāsan* (one sitting) or *beāsan* (two sittings), referring to the number of times one eats in a given day. Fasting is considered to be difficult. Many people complain that they are physically incapable of doing anything more than an *ekāsan*.[19]

Two more strictly defined fasts are *āyambil* (or *āmbil*; Sanskrit *ācāmāmla*) and *nīvi*. *Āyambil* is defined as food dominated by what Indians consider to be the sour taste, such as unspiced boiled rice, gruel, and barley meal. When performing an *āyambil*, one performs an *ekāsan*. Patan and many other larger Jain centers have *āyambilśāḷās*, where special food is prepared for laity and mendicants performing *āyambil*. Since many mendicants observe *āyambil* throughout their life, such establishments free the laity from having to prepare *āyambil* food especially for the mendicants. A few people perform *āyambil* on the five or ten *tithi*s every month; others perform it once or twice a month, as convenient. Hundreds of people perform nine days of *āyambil* during the twice-annual festival of Oḷī (chapter 6). If one decides to perform *āyambil*, one should go to the *āyambilśāḷā* in the morning to put one's name on the list for that day; but since there is inevitably extra food prepared, one can usually also go at the noon eating time. *Āyambil* food tends to be both dry (items cannot be fried in oil) and bland (few spices are allowed). It is precisely due to this blandness that it is considered to be particularly efficacious in the protection of mental equanimity (R. C. Śāh 1985:125). There can still be a great variety of food items. The Patan *āyambilśālā* regularly serves at least twenty-four different items, and during Oḷī this number increases to thirty-five or forty. One layman complained that such variety is against the spirit of *āyambil*, and so chose to observe it at home, asking his wife to prepare just two or three items for him.

Nīvi (Sanskrit *nirvikṛtika*) is closely related to *āyambil*, but is performed very rarely by laity. In a *nīvi* fast, one must avoid food containing any of the ten *vikṛtis*, foods that have undergone some modification and that tend to give one a bad disposition (Schubring 1962:277). These ten are: milk, curds, butter, ghee, oil, hardened molasses, alcohol, meat, honey, and food cooked in oil that has been used more than three times (Shântâ 1985:399n68; Williams 1963:39–40). Alcohol, meat, and honey are prohibited for all Jains anyway, and the absence of the other seven results in a dry, bland diet, similar to that in an *āyambil*. The logic behind a *nīvi* is that one should avoid foods that, because they have undergone an unwholesome modification in their preparation, cause similarly unwholesome modifications in the individual. *Nīvi* is performed by laity almost exclusively in the context of the *updhān tap* (see below).

In addition to the observance of the five or ten no-green *tithi*s every month, and the occasional *upvās* of one, three, eight, or more days usually observed during Paryuṣaṇ, there are longer, more complicated fasts, known simply as *tap*s. They have a long history within the tradition, and some performed today are first mentioned in the canonical *Antakṛddaśāḥ*. One such ancient *tap* mentioned in chapter 8 of the *Antakṛddaśāḥ* is the *āyambil vardhmān tap* (increasing *āyambil* fast), which is popular among Tapā Gacch mendicants. The one who is fasting performs one *āyambil*, then one *upvās* (here meaning one day of fasting), two *āyambil*s, one *upvās*, three *āyambil*s, and so on in a progression up to a hundred *āyambil*s. Each *āyambil-upvās* cycle is called a "line" (*oḷī*). The total *tap* of 100 lines takes fourteen years, three months, and twenty days to complete.[20] It is believed to be so powerful that it can result in one attaining *tīrthaṅkar-nām-karma*, the special karma that results in being born as a Jina (Jinendravijaygaṇi 1982:94). Some mendicants perform this *tap* throughout their mendicant life. Nityānandvijay (1976:100–1) lists seventeen *sādhus* in one Tapā Gacch *samudāy* who as of 1976 had completed the full cycle (one had died in the hundredth line, and another was in the ninety-fifth line of his second cycle), and seven others who had done more than ninety lines. The charismatic fame of several *sādhus* who came to Patan was due largely to their having completed several cycles. Although other Śvetāmbar mendicants perform *āyambil*, this extensive performance may well be a specialty of the Tapā Gacch; it certainly has an important historical connection, since Jagaccandrasūri, the thirteenth-century "founder" of the *gacch*, earned the title Tapā for his followers twelve years after he took a lifelong vow to eat only *āyambil* food.[21]

*Tap*s are performed primarily by mendicants, but also by some dedicated laity. Laypeople usually perform such a *tap* under the direction of a mendicant, often in the context of a special camp where people gather to perform the *tap* together. The community spirit, accompanied by elaborate congregational temple rituals, sermons, and singing devotional songs in the evening, helps maintain morale among the fasters. As one author puts it, "The best way to observe these rites is collectively" (Vivekcandravijay 1984:2).[22] Collective observance also leads to a competitive spirit, which further pushes people to complete long, rigorous fasts.

A group *tap* that has become popular in recent years is the *updhān tap*. This is also an ancient *tap*, decribed in the seventh-century *Mahāniśītha Sūtra* (III.3.15–III.36.1). Its precise performance was the source of ideological disagreement in the sixteenth century (Dundas 1999), so presumably it has been performed by some laity for many centuries. There is no special time for its performance, but if possible people generally start it on Āso Bright 10 (Ānandsāgarsūri 1979:15). It consists of an integrated program of fasting and the study of specific texts: the *Nokār Mantra* and several sections of the *pratikramaṇ sūtras*. One *sādhu* explains the name as follows: "*Up* means 'near' and *dhān* means 'holding,' so *updhān* is the ritually correct holding of the *sūtras* near the *guru*" (Oṃkārsūri 1957:7). The participants read and recite the texts, and have the opportunity to learn the deeper spiritual significance of the texts from the presiding *sādhu*. Such deeper study requires concurrent asceticism. The participants take the vow of *poṣadh* for the duration of the *tap*, and the daily program consists of extensive mendicant-like rites: twice-daily *pratikramaṇ*, several *caitya-vandans* and *dev-vandans* (extended *caitya-vandans*), not eating until midday, and recitation of the relevant texts. During the program, one also performs *upvās*es, *āyambils* or *nīvis*, and *ekāsans*. At the conclusion of the program, each lay faster takes a garland of flowers used in temple worship and puts it over the head of the mendicant leader. The sponsors and participants usually send out printed invitations to attend the garlanding, a procession is taken out, and the temple and *upāśray* are decorated. As part of the garlanding, the mendicant asks each faster for some form of *guru-dakṣiṇā* (payment to the teacher). Since the mendicant cannot accept any object, this payment usually consists of some sort of vow, as determined by the individual. For some it will be worshiping in the temple additional times every day, for others it will be not watching television, for still others it will be some form of dietary restriction. These vows need not be lifelong, and rarely are. At least two *updhān taps* have been held in Patan in recent years in the suburb Āśīṣ Society, where the large, rarely used *upāśray* provided enough space for the participants, and the quiet of this suburban setting provided a suitable environment. Because of the duration of the *tap*—forty-seven or thirty-five days—most participants are women. Men can rarely take so much time away from their work. In an *updhān* held in a suburb of Ahmedabad in early 1987, there were 13 men and 118 women, and another at Koba (between Ahmedabad and Gandhinagar) in the fall of 1995 had 212 participants.[23]

Another commonly observed *tap* is the *varṣī* (year-long) *tap*. It imitates the *tap* performed by the Jina Ṛṣabhnāth. Since he was the first mendicant of this time period, no one knew the proper etiquette for offering food to him. He traveled for thirteen and a half months without either drinking or eating. He came to Hastinapur, where he met Prince Śreyāṅs. Due to his memory from a former life, the prince knew the proper way to give food to a mendicant, and gave Ṛṣabhnāth some sugarcane juice.

The *varṣī tap* begins on Fāgan Dark 8 (chapter 6), the anniversary of Ṛṣabhnāth's renunciation. It commences with a two-day fast. Then one performs *tivihār upvas* on alternate days, and *beāsan* on the nonfasting days. One observes *tivihār upvās* on the eighth and fourteenth of each fortnight. Every day the person also performs morning and evening *pratikraman̩*, twelve *kāüssaggs* of *Logass* (chapter 3), twelve *khamāsamaṇs* (chapter 3), makes twelve Jain *svastiks* with rice in the temple, and recites twenty rounds on a 108-bead rosary of a *mantra* to Ṛṣabhnāth. For the duration of the *tap*, one drinks only boiled water, and observes the prohibition on eating after sunset. The *varṣī tap* concludes after thirteen and a half months, on Immortal Third (Vaiśākh Bright 3) of the following year, with a special first feeding. The faster is fed sugar-cane juice, ideally by her or his brother.[24]

In recent years other *taps* have become increasingly popular. The *siddhi tap* is performed by groups of 100 to 400 laity under mendicant direction. This forty-three-day *tap* is timed to end on Saṃvatsarī. It consists of one *upvās* followed by one *beāsan*, then two *upvās*es followed by another *beāsan*, and so forth up to eight *upvās*es. The *tap* is designed to dissolve the eight types of karma, so during the eight lines, the fasters also recite *mantras* in praise of the virtues that dissolve each karma.

Manuals list over one hundred special *taps* that can be done on special occasions.[25] They usually have a special purpose, connected with numerology, as in the case of the *siddhi tap* and the dissolution of the eight kinds of karma. In addition to the number of days of *upvās*, sometimes broken by *beāsans*, the authors list precise numbers of Jain *svastikas* to be made, *khamāsamas*, *kāüssaggs* of *Logass*, recitations of a *mantra*, and occasionally circumambulations of the inner shrine of a temple to be done each day. One can easily see that a faster performing morning and evening *pratikraman̩*, temple worship, listening to a sermon, and performing anywhere from five to fifty each of these other rites, will have a very busy day.

An example of one of these special *taps* detailed in the manuals is the *khīr samudra tap* (milk ocean fast). It is of shorter duration than *updhān*, *varṣī*, or *siddhi tap*, but is more strenuous during the time of fasting. It is described by both Jinendravijaygaṇi (1982:154) and Bhuvanvijaygaṇi (1981b:137); my description is based on that of a Patan woman living in Bombay. She performed it on her own, unlike many of the group fasts, although she was still under the guidance of a *sādhu*. She has in her possession an album of photographs taken on the occasion of the first feeding after the *tap*.[26] For seven days she did *caūvihār upvās*, that is, neither ate nor drank anything. On the eighth day, she filled a platter with liquid *khīr* (a pudding made of milk and rice), and placed it on a small table before the *sādhu*, who had come to her house for the occasion. She placed a toy boat on the *khīr*, and made it circle around the edge of the platter five times. This, she explained, symbolized renunciation, which leads one to liberation. She then removed the boat from the platter, and drank some of the *khīr* to break her fast. This was the only food she ate on the eighth and final day.[27]

Asceticism for Liberation, Asceticism for Wellbeing

In an essay entitled "The Greatness of the Dharm of *Tap*," reprinted in a Jain magazine in 1959, the reformer Ācārya Vijay Dharmsūri (1868–1923) wrote the following, captioned "The Pretty Benefits from the Dharm of *Tap*":

> Both outer and inner riches are gained from the glory of *tap*. *Tap* is an unequaled bridge for crossing the ocean of existence. *Tap* has miraculous powers to avert both physical and mental illness. *Tap* is the extraordinary cause of fruitful wearing away of karma (*nirjarā*.) *Tap* is an unfailing means to remove stubborn obstacles. *Tap* is like an inconceivable *mantra* for subduing the very clever sense organs. *Tap* is the crest-jewel holy (*maṅgal*) of all holies. *Tap* is an otherworldly wishing-pot for success in desire-based activities. From the glory of *tap* the gods remain near at hand. *Tap* is an invincible weapon for defeating the army of the god of lust (*Kāmdev*). (Dharmsūri 1959:10)

This passage emphasizes the efficacy of *tap* for one who is treading the *mokṣa-mārg*. *Tap* carries one across the ocean of existence, that is, it is a means for achieving liberation. It results in the wearing away of karma. *Tap* leads to subduing the sense organs and therefore to the mental equanimity required for spiritual advancement.

But this passage indicates other benefits of *tap*. It gives one mental and physical health. *Tap* removes obstacles to both spiritual and worldly pursuits. It is like a wishing-pot, which grants all that we desire.

This formula is familiar to students of Indian religion. Through the pursuit of ascetic practices, one not only advances toward liberation, one also gains spiritual powers that allow one to achieve a wide variety of worldly goals. Asceticism results directly in worldly wellbeing. The language itself is sufficiently multivocal to allow for multiple interpretations. For example, the following verse is found in the seventeenth-century *Jñānasāra* (3.14) of Mahopādhyāya Yaśovijaya:

> Knowledgeable ascetics who engage in good practices
> have a continual increase of bliss (*ānanda*) due to the sweetness of their goal.

In a similar vein, a contemporary mendicant writes of the benefits that derive from the practice of *sāmāyik*, one of the principle constituents of the inner spiritual life according to the *mokṣa-mārg* ideology: "*Sāmāyik* is a great gift the Lord Tīrthaṅkar gave to the world. It rewards the entire world with joy (*sukh*), peace (*śānti*), fearlessness (*abhay*), and bliss (*ānand*)" (Kalāpūrṇsūri 1987:71).

Here the multivalent terms are the overlapping *ānand*, "bliss," and *sukh*, "joy" (I will discuss *śānti*, "peace," in chapter 7). From the perspective of the *mokṣa-mārg*, they refer to the bliss of enlightenment and liberation, the infinite joy that is one of the four characteristics of the pure soul. But from the perspective of the realm of wellbeing, they can just as easily mean pleasure and contentment in this lifetime.

We saw above the case of the woman who concluded a seven-day fast by floating a boat in a platter of *khīr*. She said that this symbolized renunciation and liberation. But an equally valid interpretation of this act is that it symbolized the wellbeing she earned from her fast, for, in the words of another Gujarati (non-Jain) woman, "Because it is both sweet and made with rice (both symbols of happiness and good fortune), kheer [*khīr*] is an important part of many religious feasts and special occasions" (Sacharoff 1972:117).

Some ideologues would deny the wellbeing interpretation of the fruits of asceticism, but the validity of this interpretation can be seen in the practices and intentions of Jains themselves. Josephine Reynell (1985b:30–31) tells of a family of Jaipur Jains in which the father had turned over the family business to his son, and spent his time in extensive meditation and fasting. Under the son's direction, the business flourished. This was credited, however, not to the son's business acumen but rather to the father's *tap*. Elsewhere Reynell states, "It is believed that *puṇya* accumulated through religious action invariably results in worldly fortune" (1985a:55).

As in the cases of *pūjā* and devotion to mendicant gurus, many Jains when they perform a *tap* or follow the proper dietary rules are not single-mindedly focused upon liberation. Anyone who performed *tap* solely for egregious worldly self-advancement would be criticized by his or her fellow Jains, for purity of intention is always an important part of any ascetic act, as seen in the central role played by *pacckkhāṇ*. But the line between what is and what is not acceptable is at best blurred. People perform *tap* for such goals as passing school exams or success in financial speculations. That *tap* leads to bodily and mental health is recognized by all. One layman recommended *upvās* to cure fever, and told the story of a man who had performed a sixteen-day *upvās* to cure himself of kidney stones. Similarly, one laywoman from Bombay performed an *aṭhṭham tap* at Shankheshvar for the health of her father, who was suffering from chronic illness. Since she did not want to perform the *tap* alone, she was joined by a friend from Patan. When I asked the latter woman, who had suffered several misfortunes in the previous months, why she performed the *aṭhṭham*, she simply answered, "for peace (*śānti*)." Such an intention was echoed by another layman, who said of his daily ascetic practices, "This brings us mental peace. Anything else, we do not know. But it brings us great mental peace." In 1995 a caste-based Jain organization in Ahmedabad sponsored a one-day "collective observance of *āyambil tap*" for, in the words of the printed invitation letter, "the purpose of generating welfare (*kalyāṇ*) and peace (*śānti*) for all souls in the entire universe," after untimely deaths of several young people over the previous several years. Kuśalcandravijay (1983:IX.3) quotes a Sanskrit maxim to illustrate the same point: "What is distant, what is difficult to obtain, and what is beyond reach—all that can be obtained by *tapas*, for *tapas* removes the effects of wrong actions."

There are limits, however, to the use of *tap* for worldly ends. Josephine Reynell (1985a:56) reports that the Jains of Jaipur distinguish between two types of merit (*puṇya*) derived from *tap*: that which brings only worldly benefits, and that which brings both worldly and spiritual benefits. Whereas *tap* performed with spiritual intentions brings the latter, multivalent form of merit, *tap* performed for worldly ends brings only worldly merit. Many Jains criticize Hindu fasts precisely because they are perceived as being too exclusively focused on the worldly concerns encapsulated in the concept of *saubhāgya*. By this is understood the health and wellbeing of a woman's husband and (male) children, without whom a woman's place in Hindu society and the family is often quite precarious. *Strī-dharm* (women's normative religion) as enunciated in the Brāhmaṇical tradition places ultimate value on a woman's *saubhāgya*.[28] But the Jain ideology sees *saubhāgya* as too exclusively a matter of *saṃsār*, the world of suffering and rebirth, and so opposed to the *mokṣa-mārg*. Jain women do, of course, perform some *tap*s for *saubhāgya*. One woman listed Oḷī, *aṭhṭham*, fifteen-day, and thirty-day among *tap*s some women do for *saubhāgya*, and another mentioned the *rohiṇī tap*.[29] Another *tap* she mentioned is the *gāllā* (treasure), performed by young girls for good future husbands: for five years, starting on Āṣādh Bright 14, they perform one *ekāsan*, three *beāsans*, and another *ekāsan*. But the general attitude of Jains toward such activity is encapsulated in the following conversation on the subject:

JEC:	"What do Jain women do in order to have sons?"
JAIN WOMAN 1:	"They can do the same things that Hindus do."
JEC:	"Do they do Hindu *vrats*?"
JAIN WOMAN 2:	"No, but some go to their *kuḷdevī* (family goddess)."
WOMAN 1:	"Some go to Ambājī [a major Gujarati goddess who is a *kuḷdevī* of many Jains, whose shrine is near Abu], some do a *bādhā* to Ambājī. But true Jains don't do that."
JEC:	"But true Jains are rare in this world."
WOMAN 1:	"Yes, that's true. But look at me. After I had four daughters, a friend of my husband said that I should go to Laṭiyā Mahādev [Śiva] near Harij. But I didn't go, and look, I got two sons anyways!"

By wearing away existing karma, and by limiting the occasions for the influx of new karma, *tap* reduces the total amount of karma binding one's soul and thereby advances one toward the ultimate goal of liberation. At the same time, *tap* primarily wears away demeritorious karma (*pāp*), and thereby improves one's karmic balance in favor of the remaining meritorious karma (*puṇya*). Hence in the discourse on *tap*, its fruits are frequently described in terms of attaining happiness (*sukh*), wealth (*sampatti*), enjoyment (*bhog*), success (*lakṣmī*), welfare (*kalyāṇ*), merit (*puṇya*), peace (*śānti*), accomplishment (*ṛddhi*), and destruction of obstacles (*vighnano nāś*).[30] According to Jain cosmology, liberation is unattainable at present from this earth. This results in a system in which the best one can achieve in this lifetime is some slight improvement of one's position within *saṃsār*. This improvement can advance one toward eventual liberation from *saṃsār*, but more immediately it will increase one's wellbeing within *saṃsār*, and most Jains view this as a good thing.

Regardless of the conceptual framework within which one views *tap*, uncontrolled consumption is seen to be a problem. Whether one is reducing one's dietary intake to advance oneself along the *mokṣa-mārg* or to improve one's wellbeing (or both), one is concerned to control interaction with the biological world. As we saw in chapter 3, a synonym for liberation is *anāhārī pad*, which can be translated as "the state of not consuming." The liberated soul is freed from all consumption of karma, and from the entire, ever-fluid cycles of life and death, the cycles of transactions and interactions. Similarly, the ideal of the Jain layperson is to be independent of all others, to be in a position where one can give freely to others and not have to receive anything. Although the goals of liberation from the world and wellbeing in the world may appear at first glance to be contradictory, the ascetic tools used to achieve them are basically the same.

6

Remembrance and Celebration

The Jain Religious Year

In the previous three chapters we have explored the ritual culture of the Mūrtipūjak Jains by focusing separately on three areas of ritual action: veneration and worship of the Jinas, veneration and worship of mendicants, and an array of actions, gathered together under the rubric of asceticism, that are intended to transform the relationship between the individual's eternal self and socially constructed self. Discussions of these three areas of ritual were kept as separate as possible in order to help see the distinctive characteristics of each. But in any one discussion references to the other two were inevitable. The Jains do not experience these discretely, but rather as interrelated facets of their lives. In this chapter we will see how these areas of ritual together create a distinctive Mūrtipūjak ritual culture by looking at the round of festivals and observances that make up the religious calendar (see Table 6.1).

Festivals are occasions of collective ritual activity that play a vital part in the identity of a community. Participation in a specifically Jain milieu reaffirms the individual in his or her identity as a Jain. Public display of the community's identity through events such as a procession helps to define the religious community within the larger social sphere. The sight of a procession of Jains, led by a *sādhu*, the living embodiment of renunciation and the *mokṣa-mārg*, and a cart carrying a Jina image, the physical representation of the spiritual goal of *mokṣa* (and, as we have seen, the *sādhu* and the image being at the same time important sources of wellbeing), followed by lay men and women carrying banners, singing songs, and shouting slogans, allows the wider public audience (and the researcher) to observe clearly an expression of what Jains feel to be central to their tradition (see Figure 6.1). All these are forms of *prabhāvnā*, the public glorification of the Jain tradition and its teachings. Structures of religious belief, which are interwoven with other values in the day-to-day life of the members of the community, on such public occasions are crystallized and made obvious. The researcher cannot observe a belief or worldview; but such an occasion allows him or her to observe a public statement about that belief. Victor and Edith Turner (1982:203–4) have spoken of three ways by which the sacra of a religious tradition are communicated in a religious celebration: exhibition of sacred objects,

Table 6.1 Śvetāmbar Mūrtipūjak Annual Festivals (All dates are according to the Gujarati calendar.)

Kārtak (October–November)	
Bright 1	New Year / Gautam Svāmī Enlightenment
Bright 5	Knowledge Fifth (Jñān Pañcamī)
	Wealth Fifth (Lābh Pañcamī)
Bright 14	Four-monthly Fourteenth (Kārtak Caudaś)
Bright 15	Kārtak Full Moon (Kārtak Pūnam)
Māgsar (November–December)	
Bright 11	Silence Eleventh (Maun Agyāras)
Dark 10	Poṣ Tenth (Poṣ Daśamī)
Poṣ (December–January)	
Māgh (January–February)	
Fāgan (February–March)	
Bright 14	Four-monthly Fourteenth (Fāgan Caudaś)
Dark 8	Beginning of Varṣītap
Caitra (March–April)	
Bright 7–15	Āyambil Oḷī
Bright 13	Mahāvīr Jayantī
Vaiśākh (April–May)	
Bright 3	Immortal Third (Akhā Trīj)
Jeṭh (May–June)	
Āṣāḍh (June–July)	
Bright 14	Four-monthly Fourteenth (Āṣāḍh Caudaś)
Bright 15	Beginning of Comāsu
Śrāvan (July–August)	
Dark 12/13	Beginning of Paryuṣaṇ
Bhādarvā (August–September)	
Bright 4/5	Saṃvatsarī
Āso (September–October)	
Bright 7–15	Āyambil Oḷī
Dark 13	Wealth Thirteenth (Dhan Teras)
Dark 14	Black Fourteenth (Kāḷī Caudaś)
Dark 15	Dīvāḷī / Accountbook Worship / Mahāvīr Liberation

actions, and instruction. Most Jain festivals involve all three, and the sacra being communicated are readily accessible both to members of the religious community and to the researcher.

Participation in festivals also provides a scale by which to measure the depth and extent of religious commitment. In most religious traditions, there are one or two events that are seen as so important that participation in them provides a minimum definition of adherence to the tradition. If one does not participate in these observances, one's membership in a community as religiously defined becomes

Figure 6.1. Procession on the occasion of mendicants changing residence at the end of *comāsu* on Kārtak Full Moon; boys in front carry banner from a local religious school. Patan, November 1985.

questionable. Just as there are "Easter Catholics," so there are "Paryuṣaṇ Jains." Whereas participation in other festivals is optional, not obligatory, Paryuṣaṇ is viewed by the *mokṣa-mārg* ideology (and by almost all Jains) as a duty. The extent to which an individual participates in other festivals is in part a measure of religious commitment; but other factors such as practicality, economic necessity, and family or neighborhood tradition may also determine the extent of one's participation.

Most religious rituals and festivals occur within some sort of temporal cycle. At one extreme are events that occur only once in a life, the life-cycle rites at birth, maturity, initiation, and death. At the other extreme are events that occur daily, usually dietary and cleansing rituals and other regular cultic activities. In between in the Jain tradition are ritual cycles based on annual, four-monthly, monthly, fortnightly, or weekly repetition. In this chapter I look at annual (and, to some extent, semi-annual and four-monthly) rituals; discussion of the more frequently revolving ritual cycles will be found in the discussions of worship and asceticism in chapters 3 and 5.

A perusal of the Jain and Hindu annual ritual calendars (*pañcāṅg*) reveals a certain amount of overlap and parallelism.[1] Some festivals, such as Dīvāḷī and Akhā Trīj, are celebrated by both traditions, although with different understandings of the origin and meaning of the festival. Others, such as the Hindu Navrātrī and the Jain Oḷī, show certain structural or temporal overlap. Clearly, there has been much interaction historically between Hindu and Jain festivals, and between Hindu and

Jain understandings of the same festivals. But I would hesitate to say that the Hindu festivals are necessarily the older ones, and that the Jain festivals are mere borrowings. The Hindu ritual calendar itself gives clear evidence of the accretive nature of Hinduism, as myriad local and sectarian traditions have interacted. Festivals evolve over time, and in some cases such as Dīvāḷī the Jain interpretation of the festival is as old as Hindu interpretations. Borrowings and interactions over time have been in multiple directions. Furthermore, discussions of the origins of a festival do little to help us understand the subsequent history of that festival in the religious lives of the people involved.

Any festival, as an event crowded with symbolically charged activity, is open to multiple levels of interpretation. In the following discussion, I will counterpoint my description of the rituals and interpretation of the observed activity with *mokṣa-mārg* ideological interpretations of the festivals as found in texts and sermons. This chapter involves a back-and-forth motion between the texts on the one hand and the descriptions of the festivals and their contexts on the other; or, to put it another way, between the written texts and the living texts. These shifts in source material are signaled in part by shifts in verb tense, present tense being used for the more general material, and past tense for descriptions of specific events observed during fieldwork. Correct understanding of the annual festivals according to the ideology of the *mokṣa-mārg* has long been a major concern within the Jain community. Most festivals involve morning sermons by the *sādhus* on the "true meaning" of the festival within the Jain tradition. This very concern for meaning indicates that these festivals involve a significant amount of activity that is oriented toward wellbeing and not toward *mokṣa*. Concern for meaning exists only when there are multiple and competing meanings; ideologies as contestations of the truth imply that there are alternative understandings of the world.

At the core of the sermon is the retelling of the paradigmatic event upon which the contemporary observance of the event is to be based. The *sādhu* usually bases his sermon on an older textual telling. The best-known example is the description of Paryuṣaṇ found in the third section of the *Kalpa Sūtra*; the public reading of this description is one of the major activities of Paryuṣaṇ itself. Whenever possible, I have chosen the texts employed by the *sādhus* for their sermons for my presentation of the *mokṣa-marg* interpretation. I do not mean to imply that there is a single ideological interpretation for each event; rather, I aim to present ideological interpretations that closely correspond to those I encountered in Patan.

The term used to denote a day of special religious observance is *parv*. In technical parlance, the *parvs* are the ten or twelve *tithis* in the month that are especially auspicious for fasting and other religious behavior.[2] The ten *parvs* are the second, fifth, eighth, eleventh, and fourteenth, of each fortnight, that is, every third day.[3] Some people include the full and new moon days to come up with a total of twelve. The term *parv* also is applied to other festival days, even if they do not fall on one of the regular *tithis*.

The paradigmatic event behind the Jain understanding of a festival is frequently from the life of one of the twenty-four Jinas. In the life of every Jina there are five *kalyāṇaks*, or events that generate religious benefit. These are the Jina's conception, birth, renunciation of worldly life, enlightenment, and final liberation at bodily death. The days on which these *kalyāṇaks* occurred are said to be so holy that even the suffering inhabitants of hell rejoice.[4] Although a description of the ritual year based on the *kalyāṇaks* is useful in showing one structure underlying the ritual year,[5] I feel it does not adequately represent the flow of the year as actually experienced. I therefore follow a linear calendrical approach. From the perspective of the Jain laity, the most important period of festivals is that of the *comāsu*, the four-month rainy-season retreat, so I begin my description there.

Comāsu, the Four-Month Rainy Season

The major distinction in the Jain religious year is between *comāsu* (Sanskrit: *cāturmāsa*), the four-month period when mendicants must remain in residence in one place, and the eight months when they must maintain their peregrinations. Since annual festivals are community occasions, it is not surprising that the major festivals fall within the *comāsu*, when the residence of the mendicants ensures the presence of the entire fourfold *saṅgh* of *sādhus*, *sādhvīs*, *śrāvaks*, and *śrāvikās*.

As we have seen above in chapter 1, among the five great vows of the mendicant is nonpossession (*aparigrah*). Residing in one place would imply possession of and attachment to that place, so *aparigrah* has always been understood to require that the mendicant not reside in one place. Although there is no single fixed rule governing how long a mendicant can remain in one residence,[6] common practice has been that he or she should change residence after a maximum stay of one month. But for a mendicant to travel during the monsoon would involve violation of another great vow, that of *ahiṃsā*, nonharm. It is impossible for even the most mindful mendicant to walk along a traditional Indian unpaved road during the monsoon and maintain the spirit of *ahiṃsā*, for the rains turn the roads into thick mud, which teems with insect and other life that the mendicant would inevitably walk upon and kill. Therefore, all mendicants are required to stay in one place for the four-month period of the rainy season.[7]

Comāsu begins on Āṣāḍh Bright 14 (mid-July), a day known as Four-monthly Fourteenth (Caumāsī Caudaś). The mendicants have known for several months where they will spend *comāsu*. Some four to six months before *comāsu*, leaders of lay congregations issue invitations to *sādhus* to spend *comāsu* with them. Only very rarely is a particularly renowned Tapā Gacch *sādhvī* specifically invited. Since Tapā Gacch *sādhvīs* are supposed to travel with *sādhus*, inviting a *sādhu* also commits the *saṅgh* to the responsibility of hosting the accompanying *sādhvīs*. Usually, the lay followers of a *sādhu* have been consulting with the *sādhu* concerning the *comāsu* for several months (and some charismatic *sādhus* plan their *comāsus* several years in advance), and the *sādhu* has been consulting with his own preceptor, so at the time of the formal invitation everyone knows what the answer will be. The *sādhus* of a *parivār* (chapter 2) are usually distributed among the towns and villages in an area, with at least two *sādhus* in any one group as a matter of mendicant discipline. This way as many laity as possible will have a *sādhu* present with whom to observe Paryuṣaṇ, and no one congregation has to undertake the financial and social burden of looking after the entire *parivār*. For example, in 1986 the *sādhus* of one *parivār* were distributed in the towns of Unjha, Patan, and Chanasma; two other groups in the *parivār* were further away in Surat and Indore. The *sādhus* of another *parivār* were divided among five suburban congregations of Ahmedabad and nearby Gandhinagar.

The *sādhu* plans his travel so that he approaches the village or town soon before *comāsu* begins. He may enter the town as much as several weeks before *comāsu*, or else on the morning of Āṣāḍh Bright 14. The day of his entry is the "city entrance" (*nagar praveś*). In the morning, the lay congregation meets the *sādhu* and his party at the outskirts of town, officially welcomes him to the town, and then escorts him to the *upāśray* with a procession, complete with band, banners, horses, all the laity dressed in their finest, and perhaps even an elephant in the case of an important *sādhu*. The civil administration of the city may also greet the *sādhu*; illustrations of medieval city entrances show the local king coming outside the town to greet the *sādhu*.

The *sādhu* is taken to the *upāśray*, where he delivers a sermon.[8] In 1986, the *sādhu* stressed the importance of *comāsu* for the *sādhus* as a time of study, and an opportunity for the laity to hear sermons regularly. He announced the two texts on which he would be basing his daily sermons during that *comāsu*,[9] as well as the time for the daily morning sermon. Further, he stressed, *comāsu* is a time when the laity should elect to keep certain *niyams*, or restrictions on behavior. He told the story of the *niyam* that Kumārapāla observed at the instruction of Hemacandra, not to leave the royal court except to go to the temple or *upāśray*. Finally, because Āṣāḍh Bright 14 is one of the three annual four-monthly *pratikramaṇs* (chapter 5), the time for that evening's *pratikramaṇ* was set. In the afternoon, there was performance of *dev-vandan* in the *upāśrays*.[10] At the major temples in town, there were special ornamentations of the images in celebration of the day.

For the laity, *comāsu* is a time of restrictive dietary practices. The more religiously motivated laity practice long fasts. Most fasts are scheduled to end on the final day of Paryuṣaṇ. The days for beginning the long fasts of thirty-one and fifteen days are marked in all the Jain almanacs in order to have the fasts end on this day.

Paryuṣaṇ

Paryuṣaṇ is one of the oldest Jain festivals, as well as the most important Śvetāmbar one.[11] It lasts for eight days. In the Tapā Gacch, the final day, Saṃvatsarī, is observed on Bhādarvā Bright 4. If no days are missing from the ritual calendar, the first day of Paryuṣaṇ is therefore Śrāvaṇ Dark 12. Other Mūrtipūjak *gacchs*, as well as the Sthānakvāsīs and Terāpanthīs, observe Saṃvatsarī on Bhādarvā Bright 5, and so start the festival one day later (Cort 1999a).

In Patan nowadays, *sādhus* generally stay for *comāsu* only in the two main *upāśrays* in the city, Sāgar and Maṇḍap. Here they can obtain food from the nearby *bhojanśāḷā* and *āyambilśāḷā*, and laity can come to hear their sermons. But since Paryuṣaṇ is the one festival observed by almost every single Jain, it is the custom for neighborhood congregations to invite *sādhus* from Sāgar and Maṇḍap to come to a local *upāśray* and preside over the Paryuṣaṇ observances.[12] In 1985, *sādhus* from

Maṇḍap were invited by the congregations of Bhāratī Society and Rājkā Vāḍo. Paryuṣaṇ in 1986 was marked by an acrimonious dispute, which resulted in Paryuṣaṇ being observed on different days by the *sādhus* and congregations of Sāgar and Maṇḍap (Cort 1999a). To prevent the importation of this divisive dispute into the local congregation, Bhāratī Society decided to invite *sādhus* from neither group, but instead to sponsor sermons on all nine days (covering both observances) by Bhānuvijay, an ex-*sādhu* who runs a social service organization outside of Patan, and who is well known for his powerful sermons. The other suburban congregation, Āśīṣ Society, invited *sādhus* from Maṇḍap. Although there were only two *sādhus* in the group at Sāgar, and many more at Maṇḍap, the Rājkā Vāḍo congregation sided with Sāgar in the dispute and so invited the junior *sādhu* from Sāgar.

Lay men observed *pratikramaṇ* and *poṣadh* (chapter 5) in the *upāśrays*; lay women observed them at various *upāśrays* throughout the city where *sādhvīs* were staying for *comāsu*. Several dozen men and women—older, retired or semi-retired people, students, or especially religious-minded young people perhaps intending to renounce the world and become mendicants—took the vow of *poṣadh* or temporary mendicancy for the duration of all eight days, and stayed at an *upāśray*. Men did this mostly at Maṇḍap and Sāgar, because of the presence of the *sādhus* and others observing the vow, and also the proximity of the *āyambilśāḷā* and *bhojanśāḷā*. The Sthānakvāsīs observed Paryuṣaṇ in their own *upāśray*, where two *sādhvīs* were staying for *comāsu*. The Terāpanthī laity, who form too small a congregation to support *sādhus* or *sādhvīs* for the entire *comāsu*, observed Paryuṣaṇ amongst themselves in the Terāpanthī Bhavan.

The two main elements of each day of Paryuṣaṇ are sermons by the *sādhus* and fasting by the laity and mendicants. Image worship, a major element of lay Jain life, is not a centrally conspicuous element, although the number of people performing *pūjā* in the temples every day is certainly greater than at other times. For the first three days, there are sermons only in the morning; thereafter, due to the large amount of material to be recited and commented upon, there are sermons twice daily, in the morning and mid-afternoon. The days of largest attendance are the first, fourth, fifth (afternoon), and last, as well as the congregational feast the day after Paryuṣaṇ ends. Attendance on the other days is limited to women, retired men, a few religiously minded younger men, and foreign scholars. Most Jains do some limited fasting on one or more days of Paryuṣaṇ; the more enthusiastic will do fasts of up to thirty-one days (especially if a charismatic *sādhu* who encourages people to fast is in residence), and a few take the vow of *poṣadh* for one or more days. As during any sermon, there are also some people who take the vow of one or more forty-eight-minute periods of *sāmāyik* during the sermon. Some people perform evening *pratikramaṇ* every day.

The sermons for the first three days are based on the eighteenth-century *Paryuṣaṇāṣṭāhnikā Vyākhyāna* of Ācārya Vijaya Lakṣmīsūri.[13] The subjects of these sermons are the five duties for Paryuṣaṇ and the eleven annual duties enjoined on every Jain, which together map a *mokṣa-mārg* vision of an ideal layman. For each of these duties, the *sādhu* giving the sermon provides stories from Jain history of laity and *sādhus* whose actions have exemplified the duties.

The first of the duties for Paryuṣaṇ is to stop killing (*amārī pravārtan*). Almost all Jains know the story of how Ācārya Hemacandra convinced King Kumārapāla to forbid all animal slaughter in his kingdom during Paryuṣaṇ. Even more popular is the example of the sixteenth-century Ācārya Hīravijayasūri, who traveled to Akbar's court and is credited by the Jains with convincing the Mughal emperor to forbid slaughter during Paryuṣaṇ. Smaller Hindu kings have often issued such edicts, in recognition of the influence of the Jains as both financiers and administrators of the kingdoms (Majmudar 1970). In 1986, a *pāñjrāpoḷ* (animal shelter) operated by a Jain congregation in Jamnagar district took out an advertisement in the Ahmedabad newspaper *Sandeś* requesting donations to help meet the monthly expense of Rs. 150,000 for feeding the over 2,000 animals in the *pāñjrāpoḷ*. (Due to a severe drought, in 1985–1987 most *pāñjrāpoḷs* in Gujarat were overcrowded with cattle and faced severe financial strains.) A notice in the same newspaper on the same day said that the organizational minister for one of the state's political parties, who was himself a Hindu, had publicly requested both the Ahmedabad mayor and the Gujarat chief minister to close all slaughterhouses on the final day of Paryuṣaṇ.

Amārī pravārtan is one of the few instances in which Jains attempt to extend their notion of *ahiṃsā* to the larger, non-Jain society.[14] In line with the Indian tendency to view ethics as contextualized according to caste and situation, Jains are usually content to observe *ahiṃsā* as an ethic suitable for themselves, but not expected of everyone else. But according to the *mokṣa-mārg* ideology, *ahiṃsā* is a universal ethic, and this is expressed through the duty of *amārī pravārtan* during Paryuṣaṇ.[15]

The second duty is affection or devotion to fellow Jains (*sādharmik vātsalya* or *sādharmik bhakti*). This refers to the noonday meal for all members of the *saṅgh* on the day after Paryuṣaṇ ends, which emphasizes congregational unity.

The third duty is *kṣamāpanā*, a formulaic statement that all faults committed during the previous year should be of no lasting karmic consequence. This is enacted through the ritual of annual *pratikramaṇ* on the final day, and through saying the Prakrit formula "micchāmi dukkaḍaṃ" ("may my improper actions be inconsequential") to each other after the annual *pratikramaṇ*, and mailing cards printed with *micchāmi dukkaḍaṃ* or similar expressions to all relatives and acquaintances who reside elsewhere.[16] The thirteenth-century Devendrasūri in his *Śrāddhadinakṛtya* (202–3) says that arguing with or holding a grudge against a fellow Jain is a moral fault (*āśātnā*) toward the Jinas themselves. A person cannot avoid the original negative effects of the karma generated by an action; but through the conscious expression of *kṣamāpanā*, one can avoid further negative effects.

The fourth duty is *aṭhṭham tap*. As discussed in chapter 5, this is a three-day fast. wherein the faster omits eight meals. The majority of Jains do not actually perform *aṭhṭham* during Paryuṣaṇ. Businessmen insist that it is impossible to continue one's daily work while engaging in such a strenuous fast, and others say that they do not have the inner strength. Almost everyone observes some sort of dietary restriction, either performing a one-day total fast, or eating a restricted diet for one or more days. Some people perform *ekāsan*, or eating only once in a day, on the second, fifth, and seventh days. The required minimum is neither to eat nor drink from the commencement of *saṃvatsarī pratikramaṇ* until forty-eight minutes after sunrise the following day. Paryuṣaṇ is the time of the most concentrated and extended fasting among Jains, and every day the vernacular newspapers in the larger cities print the photographs and names of individuals who have done the "spiritual discipline of fasting" and successfully completed a "fierce penance." Between September 4 and 8, 1986, the two main Gujarati dailies in Ahmedabad, *Sandeś* and *Gujarāt Samācār*, carried photographs of 168 people (with some overlap between the two newspapers)—44 lay men, 119 lay women, and 5 *sādhvīs*—who had done fasts ranging in length from eight to fifty-one days. Of these, 64 had done a month-long fast, and 29 had fasted for sixteen days.

The fifth duty is *caitya paripāṭī*, pilgrimage to a sequence of temples. In Patan, the major *caitya paripāṭī* occurs during the five days following Dīvāḷī. During Paryuṣaṇ, it is observed by a small procession on the last day, sometimes to specific temples but oftentimes by just a parade around the neighborhood. In 1995, the Bhāratī Society congregation sponsored a special *caitya paripāṭī* that consisted of a one-day group pilgrimage to the nearby village of Charup, site of a Pārśvanāth shrine important in twentieth-century north Gujarat Jain history.

We see in these five duties a twofold emphasis, on the one hand on asceticism and nonharm to improve one's karmic balance, and on the other hand on reinforcing the unity of the Jain community. The five duties all have aspects of personal practice, but they are even more corporate, public activities. *Amārī pravārtan*, through actively reducing *hiṃsā* in the world, improves the karmic position of the individual; it also spreads nonharm from a Jain-specific context into the larger social sphere, and reinforces the Jains' preferred social stance of being identified as the promoters of *ahiṃsā* par excellence. *Sādharmik vatsalya*, through its expression of *anumodan* or sympathetic praise of the righteous activities of others, generates *puṇya* and decreases harmful karma in the person; in the form of a congregational meal it also expresses the unity of the *saṅgh*. *Kṣamāpanā* leads directly to the diminishment of harmful karma, and publicly requesting forgiveness from all relatives and associates is conducive to the long-range unity of the *saṅgh*. *Aṭhṭham tap* also directly results in the wearing away of karma; public honoring of fasters, through newspaper announcements and rites of first-feeding and felicitating the fasters, expresses to the wider society the centrality of asceticism for the Jains. As we saw in chapter 3, the ritual of *caitya-vandan* that occurs in the temple in the *caitya paripāṭī* is understood to generate *puṇya* and wear away harmful karma through the praising and *anumodan* of the central religious ideals crystallized in the images of the Jinas; and a public procession from the *upāśray* to one or more temples is a public display of the Jains' faith.

I will simply list the eleven annual duties discussed in the *sādhus*' Paryuṣaṇ sermons. They overlap in part with the five Paryuṣaṇ duties, and are aimed at the same goals: advancing the individual along the *mokṣa-mārg* by enjoining conduct appropriate for a layperson, and simultaneously strengthening the unity of the *saṅgh* through shared activities. These eleven duties are as follows:

1. *saṅgh pūjā*: worship of the congregation, performed by giving every participant at some public religious function a small amount of money (usually a one-rupee coin) and a red forehead mark as a token of respect
2. *sādharmik vātsalya/bhakti*: a congregational meal
3. *yātrā*: processions of three kinds: during the twice-annual festivals of Oḷī (see below); with a chariot (*rath*); and to a pilgrimage shrine (*tīrth*)

4. *snātra*: ritual bathing of the images in the temple
5. increase of *dev-dravya*, the funds used for building and renovating temples
6. *mahāpūjā*: the annual *pūjā* on the anniversary of the main image of a temple
7. *rātrī jāgaraṇ*: night-long observance on special occasions
8. *pūjā-bhakti* of *śruta-jñān*: worship of knowledge that leads one along the Jain *mokṣa-mārg*, by either donating money to scholarly pursuits[17] or the worship of *jñān* on Jñān Pañcamī
9. *tap udyāpan*: fasting
10. *prabhāvnā* of *Jin-śāsan*: glorifying the Jain teachings, including glorifying pilgrimage shrines and publicly welcoming *sādhus* when they enter a town
11. *ālocanā*: cleansing of harmful karma through avowal of past misdeeds, through *pratikramaṇ*.

On the fourth day, the *sādhus* begin the *Kalpa Sūtra* recitation.[18] Fischer and Jain (1977:15), Folkert (1993:192), and Laidlaw (1995:276) have described how in some communities a copy of the *Kalpa Sūtra* (sometimes written in letters of gold leaf) is taken out in a procession. A young girl dressed in pure clothes carries the book in a tray atop her head, while water from the morning *pūjā* at the temple is sprinkled before her to purify the ground. The book is taken to the house of a man who won the public auction for the honor of presenting the book the next day.[19] It is kept at his house overnight, and worshiped with devotional songs. The next morning the book is taken, again in a small procession, to the *upāśray*. But this is by no means a required or universal activity. In Patan, such processions are held only at the larger downtown *upāśrays*, if they are held at all, and are not observed with much pomp. I did not observe any procession in Patan in 1985 or 1986, nor in Ahmedabad in 1995, nor did people seem concerned about the absence of any procession when I inquired. We see here the extent to which many elements in the observance of a festival are matters not of ideological prescription, nor of a pan-Indian Jain ritual culture, but rather of regional and even local style.

If there is not a formal procession, then a copy of the *Kalpa Sūtra* is brought into the sermon hall of the *upāśray*, either from the *saṅgh*'s collection of books or from the *sādhu*'s own collection. The following description of the commencement of the reading from the *Kalpa Sūtra* is from 1986 in Sāgar Upāśray.

The copy of the *Kalpa Sūtra* was placed in front of the *sādhu*, and a low table was placed on the floor in front of the book. On the table was a rice *nandyāvart*, a coconut, and a two-paise coin. A small group of thirty men and women was present, two-thirds of whom were doing *poṣadh* or *sāmāyik*. Before the sermon everyone sang several hymns in praise of knowledge (*jñān*) itself, reading from booklets in a manner that can only be called cacophonous. Four women dressed in silk saris stood in the front of the women's section. Each held in front of her a metal tray, one with a coconut, another some white sweets, a third a lit lamp and a red hybiscus, and the fourth a small dish with smoking incense. One of the two hymns they sang was the following, from Paṇḍit Vīrvijay's 1826 *Pistālīś Āgam Pūjā* (Worship of the Forty-five Scriptures):

> Now I will describe the forty-five [scriptures], our support in the Kali Yug.
> The scriptures hold a deep meaning. Among them are the eleven Aṅgs.
> Offer up the sandalwood skillfully, put it on the serpent hood [over Pārśva].

Wealth, the Jina-speech is wealth.
King Udāyī sings the qualities of the lord, and Queen Padmāvatī dances.
Wealth, the Jina-speech is wealth.
Time always destroys its foes, but enlightenment uproots time.
Wealth, the Jina-speech is wealth.
The *Ācārāṅga* is the first teaching. Singing its name one praises the other scriptures.
Wealth, the Jina-speech is wealth.[20]

In this case they were singing an unfamiliar hymn, sung only when worshiping the scriptures. No one knew it by heart, so the singing was disorderly and unspirited. In many cases the hymns are well known, so that people do not need to sing from a hymnal, and can sing with great feeling (*bhāv*). In her study of the hymns sung by Tapā Gacch women in Pune, Whitney Kelting (1996) has shown the importance of such hymns for an adequate understanding of Jain practice and belief. Most Jain rituals are accompanied or punctuated by the singing of vernacular hymns. It is the rare Jain who does not know at least a few hymns from his or her childhood, and many have memorized dozens. Many of the hymns have been composed by *mokṣa-mārg* ideologues; Vīrvijay, for example, was one of the handful of *saṃvegī sādhus* in the early nineteenth century who composed elaborate image-oriented congregational rituals designed to replace the magical rituals performed by *yatis*. Although these hymns often suffer from all the faults of sermons set to music in any language, they are expressive of a broad range of ideological and nonideological understandings of Jainism. Symbols of both *mokṣa-mārg* and wellbeing frequently are found side by side. In this case, in the refrain "the Jina-speech is wealth" Vīrvijay contrasts the Jain merchant's vocational pursuit of worldly wealth with what this ideologue says is true wealth, the saving knowledge found in the words of the Jina. The author employs a common South Asian trope, that wealth and knowledge are in the end incompatible. A well-known saying repeated to me often by Jains holds that Lakṣmī, goddess of wealth, and Sarasvatī, goddess of knowledge, cannot live in the same house. But one can just as easily interpret the refrain to mean that the holy Jina-speech is itself the only true source of that wealth which is worldly wellbeing.

When the singing was finished, the four women presented the copy of the *Kalpa Sūtra* to the *sādhu*. They worshiped the book by waving the four trays in front of it, and sprinkling onto it *vāskep* they received from the *sādhu*. Everyone thrice sang four verses in praise of the *Kalpa Sūtra*, bowing to it in between each repetition. The *sādhu* then commenced his sermon.

The recitation of the *Kalpa Sūtra* lasts for four days. The *sādhu* recites the Gujarati translation of Vinayavijaya's seventeenth-century Sanskrit *Subodhikā* commentary on the *Kalpa Sūtra* along with the root text, and expounds upon the commentary according to his interest and ability. Due to the time required for these sermons, each day there is a two-hour afternoon sermon in addition to the morning sermon. Few people attend all the sermons. Most *sādhus* rush through both the Prakrit root text and the Gujarati commentary in a sing-song manner. Rarely is much attention given to a clear exposition of the text.

In 1986, after a grueling two-hour session listening to a spiritless sermon in the afternoon heat, I asked a layman why people bothered to come, since they could hear and understand so little. His first response was that most of the people had been going to these sermons for many years, so they already knew what was going to be said, and it was sufficient that they gain just a little additional understanding. In response to my continued skepticism, he shifted from an explanation based upon communication of knowledge to one based upon liturgical logic. He said that since the *sādhus* must recite every syllable of the *Kalpa Sūtra* (meaning here both root text and Vinayavijaya's commentary) in these few days, they had no choice but to rush through it, and only a very skilled *sādhu* could clearly explain things in the short time available. When I repeated that this did not explain the attendance of any of the laypeople in the audience, he said that many people believe that anyone who listens to the whole of the *Kalpa Sūtra* will attain *mokṣa* within two or three lifetimes.

The objections I raised against the formalized, sing-song style of recitation can also be heard from many laity, especially those who are younger and better educated. The 1986 sermons at Bhāratī Society by Bhānuvijay were well attended in large part because of his eloquence as a speaker. Dissatisfaction with the traditional style of sermons has led to modern lecture series for the general public on the themes of Paryuṣaṇ in big cities such as Ahmedabad and Bombay.

The *Kalpa Sūtra* is a central text in the *mokṣa-mārg* ideology. It contains the sacred history of the twenty-four Jinas, the holy saviors who showed the path to liberation; the lineage of mendicants who followed Mahāvīr and perpetuated the holy Jain teachings; and the rules for mendicant conduct that advances one along the *mokṣa-mārg*. To listen to the *Kalpa Sūtra*, therefore, is to listen to a key exposition of the *mokṣa-mārg* ideology, and it is for this reason that it was one of the first Jain texts to be translated into English, by the Rev. J. Stevenson in 1847. Over the centuries, as the Prakrit of the root text became increasingly unintelligible to most Jains, commentators translated the knowledge contained in the text into a vernacular that would allow listeners to understand, reflect upon, and act upon that knowledge. This is not, however, what has happened. The recitation of the *Kalpa Sūtra* and commentary is not a matter of a lucid lecture upon the *mokṣa-mārg* ideology, but rather more of a magico-religious ritual, in which the saving knowledge contained in the words of the text is fused into the very sound of these words, syllable by syllable, in the form of an extended *mantra*. The recitation of the *Kalpa Sūtra* is not a communication event but rather a performance event. Language in this case does not carry meaning from the speaker to the listener. Jains believe that the sounds themselves constitute an active force that creates an ontological transformation in the listener's soul. Listening to the many hours of recitation effects a transformation not by the listener meditatively reflecting upon the meaning of the words, but by the sounds acting directly upon the listener's soul.

Late on the morning of the fifth day, the *sādhu* in his recitation of the *Kalpa Sūtra* came to the description of the birth of Mahāvīr, and the fourteen dreams seen by his mother upon his conception. There he stopped, for this passage was to be recited in the afternoon. The entire *saṅgh* showed up for the afternoon sermon, dressed in their finest, most expensive clothes. The women's section of the *upāśray* was a sea of brightly colored silk saris and gold jewelry, and the men wore the traditional *dhotīs* and long shirts of Gujarati businessmen, in this case usually of freshly washed and starched silk, with pearl or diamond buttons, and the traditional merchants' caps showing bits of colored embroidery. The first year I attended the recitation, my wife was told that she must wear a silk sari, as even a fashionable cotton sari was insufficiently festive. The few people wearing the somber quasi-mendicant clothes for *poṣadh* formed a stark sartorial contrast. In the *upāśray* were hung garlands of auspicious *āsopalav* leaves. Although the actual anniversary of Mahāvīr's birth falls in the spring on Caitra Bright 13, this day when his birth is recited saw a much larger and more emotionally charged celebration.

The main event of the afternoon was the display of silver replicas of the fourteen dreams (see Figure 6.2). As befits auspicious dreams that presage the birth of an extraordinary son, these dreams are a catalogue of pan-Indian emblems of wellbeing:

Figure 6.2. Silver replicas of the dreams seen by the mother of a Jina upon his conception, prior to auctioning of various rites. Ahmedabad, August 1995.

1. an elephant
2. a bull
3. a lion
4. the goddess Lakṣmī anointed by two elephants
5. a flower garland
6. the moon
7. the sun
8. a Jina temple
9. a full pot
10. a lotus lake
11. the milky ocean, depicted by a ship
12. a heavenly vehicle in which deities travel
13. a heap of jewels
14. a flame[21]

An auctioneer solicited bids for the honor of performing each act. There were four rights for each dream: to swing the dream, to garland it with *āsopalav* leaves or flowers, to garland it with a gold or silver necklace, and to place the dream on a table in the center of the *upāśray*.[22] Each man who won a bid first bowed before the *sādhu*; in response, the *sādhu* sprinkled *vāskep* on the head of the bidder, as well as his wife and children, who were usually the ones to perform the acts. The silver replicas were lowered from either a hole in the ceiling or an upper level (representing the dreams "coming down" to the mother) and received by a child. Two children swung the dream back and forth (see Figure 6.3). The dream was garlanded, and another child placed the dream atop his or her head and carried it to a centrally located table. Since there were dozens of people involved, including many excited young children, the scene was increasingly chaotic. Throughout the afternoon the noise level grew, people were confused as to which action to perform, and men tried to restore order by shouting and gesticulating. The late monsoon heat and humidity increased in the crowded *upāśray*. One friend commented in advance that this is always a "two-handkerchief occasion," as by the end of the day both handkerchiefs were soaked with sweat from mopping his brow. The celebration of Mahāvīr's birthday provides a contrast to most Jain events, where excess is avoided in favor of control, which is valued as an important social and religious principle. Through it all, the mendicants sat, silently observing the noise, confusion, and merriment, intervening only on occasions when their encouragement was needed to raise the level of the bids.

The bids for the first several dreams were low.[23] These were won by young men who were just starting their careers and their families; it was a chance for them to earn some merit and social credit. The bidding became heated for the fourth dream, Gajālakṣmī, the goddess Lakṣmī anointed by two elephants. As the bidding increased, one man leaned over to me and explained in English, "She is the goddess of wealth and prosperity." After Gajalakṣmī, the bids returned to a lower level, with much good-natured banter among the men of the *saṅgh*. The job of auctioneer usually goes to a man who is skilled at gently coaxing up the bids. If someone bid 181 *pān-śers*, the auctioneer might accept it as 201 *pān-śers*, and yet all the while keep people smiling and laughing at his jokes and public accusations of parsimony.[24] The entire event was marked by camaraderie and joyful playfulness. The *sādhu* also

Figure 6.3. Layman and children swinging silver replica of dream of the sun. Photograph by Kendall W. Folkert, 1985.

got involved in the process, asking how much some important bids such as Gajalakṣmī went for, and, if he felt that the bids were too low, chiding the men of the *saṅgh* for not being willing to contribute to a worthy cause.[25] Women rarely bid, but when the bidding slowed they sang songs that also accused the men of miserliness.

The largest bids in Patan were for the silver lotus lake. The family of the man who won the right to place the lotus lake on the table also got to sprinkle several bottles of rose water over the audience.[26] Different reasons were given by laymen concerning why this was the highest bid. One man said that the winner received the gain (*lābh*) of the peace (*śānti*) of the entire congregation. Another remarked that the sprinkling of rose water served to cool down the entire congregation, which had presumably become overheated due to the strenuous bidding.

After the last dream was lowered from the upper floor, the hole in the ceiling was closed and the bidding was held for the last three actions: to garland a small silver cradle of Mahāvīr with flowers, to rock the cradle, and to place Mahāvīr's baby toys in the cradle. At the conclusion of these bids, there were several minutes of noise and bustle as the people who won the bids came forward and rice was handed out to everyone present. The male leaders of the congregation then tried in vain to quiet everyone down, so that the *sādhu* could read the last few verses from the *Kalpa Sūtra*. All afternoon his role had been minimal: he sprinkled *vāskep* on those who won bids, and occasionally tried to increase the level of the bids, but in general he just sat on the dais, smiling at all the activity. This was the laity's occasion, not the *sādhu*'s. In 1985, as the *sādhu* began to recite the verses, he stopped, and started to give a short sermon on the significance of Mahāvīr's birth according to the *mokṣa-mārg* ideology. He was gently interrupted by a lay leader, and asked to get on with the recitation. This happened several times; every time he stopped reciting and started expounding, the layman asked him to return to the recitation. Again, the role of the *sādhu* in this was clearly the functional one of reciting the text. Any attempts on his part to remind people of the *mokṣa-mārg* interpretation of the occasion were blocked. As he finally recited the verse describing the birth of Mahāvīr, the barely constrained pandemonium of the crowd broke out. Everyone shouted in Gujarati, "Say it: victory of Lord Mahāvīr Svāmī!," threw rice at the cradle, and rushed forward to swing it (see Figure 6.4). One *sādhu* was quite explicit in his explanation to Kendall Folkert (1993:200) that people swing the cradle in order to procure children. At the same time, people broke open coconuts, another act symbolic in South Asia of fertility and wellbeing, and pieces of coconut were given to everyone as they left. People crowded in front of the *sādhu* to be blessed with *vāskep*; in 1986, the crowd was so large that the *sādhu* stood up on the platform and threw handfuls of *vāskep* over the crowd. Then everyone left the *upāśray* to hurry home. It was Paryuṣaṇ, so everyone was observing the prohibition on eating after dark, and since the ceremony ended in the late afternoon, there was not much time left to eat. Due to Paryuṣaṇ, there were no green vegetables in the meal, emphasizing the ascetic side of Jain diet. At the same time, it was a festive occasion, so instead of the usual breads there were sweet *laḍḍus*, the favorite of the infant Mahāvīr.

Paryuṣaṇ, the holiest of Jain festivals, is a time of fasting, austerities, and mendicant-like behavior on the part of the laity. It is the one time during the year when almost every Jain observes some of the precepts of the *mokṣa-mārg*. In the middle of these observances falls the recitation of the birth of Mahāvīr, the last of the twenty-four Tīrthaṅkars of this age, who established the fourfold congregation in which all Jains now reside. The *mokṣa-mārg* as presently constituted was established and taught by Mahāvīr. But the recitation of his birth is not an occasion

Figure 6.4. Laity swinging cradle of infant Mahāvīr (represented by silver coconut). Ahmedabad, August 1995.

dedicated to further commitment to the *mokṣa-mārg*; rather, it is an occasion for a joyous celebration of the this-worldly fruits of wellbeing that ensue from his birth. As we have seen earlier, the hierarchical ranking of mendicants over laity is in many ways nearly absolute. But on this occasion the *sādhu* is present merely to fulfill the role of reading aloud the passage, a role he is best suited to play because of his skill in recitation and the power that emanates from a mendicant's reading of the sacred words. When he attempted to assert his superiority over the laity, and to assert the superiority of the *mokṣa-mārg* ideology over the realm of wellbeing, he was politely but firmly reminded of his circumscribed role and requested to get on with the recitation. This reversal is in some ways reminiscent of the reversal of caste hierarchy among Hindus during Hoḷī as described by McKim Marriott (1966).

But it is more than that, for not only social hierarchy is reversed. This is a vivid demonstration of the temporary encompassment of the *mokṣa-mārg* ideology by the value of wellbeing. For most of the year, the two exist in an unsteady equilibrium. During Paryuṣaṇ, the *mokṣa-mārg* comes to the fore, and encompasses wellbeing. So it is not surprising that in the middle of this temporary disequilibrium there should be a drastic reversal, and wellbeing should in turn encompass the *mokṣa-mārg*.

The sixth and seventh days of Paryuṣaṇ involve lengthy, sparsely attended sermons in which the *sādhu* recites the final sections of the *Kalpa Sūtra*, which treat of the successors to Mahāvīr and the rules of Paryuṣaṇ. The sermon on the morning of the eighth and final day consists of the *sādhu* reading aloud the Prakrit root-text of the *Kalpa Sūtra*.[27] The text read aloud on this day is known as the *Bārsā Sūtra*, literally the "Twelve Hundred Verses," referring to the length of the Prakrit root-text.[28] The sermon in 1985 at Bhāratī Society began with a small crowd. Eight auctions were held: one to present the *sādhu* with a copy of the *Bārsā Sūtra* to be recited, five to worship it with *vāskep*, one to perform eightfold *pūjā* to it, and one to hold aloft illustrations during the recitation. After the auctions, everyone present sang from the same hymns to knowledge as on the fourth day. The presentation copy of the *Bārsā Sūtra* nowadays tends to be a printed edition illustrated with reproductions of medieval manuscript paintings;[29] formerly, wealthy laity would arrange for a copy to be hand-copied (sometimes with gold ink) and illustrated for presentation on this occasion.[30]

As the *sādhu* recited the Prakrit text, a young boy (ideally dressed in pure clothes; at a minimum covering his mouth with a *muhpattī*) held aloft for all to see an illustration of the portion of the text being recited. Another *sādhu* prompted the boy as to which picture to show. Most of the people bowed their head to each picture as it was shown.[31] The full recitation took a little over two hours. When only a few verses remained, the *sādhu* stopped, and a leader of the *saṅgh* announced the time for the afternoon's *saṃvatsarī pratikramaṇ*, for the next day's ceremonial feeding of all those who had fasted during Paryuṣaṇ, and the *saṅgh* feast that is one of the Paryuṣaṇ duties. In 1985 at Bhāratī, donations to pay for the *saṅgh* feast were collected at this time. In 1986 at Sāgar, the rights to perform the various functions in the *saṅgh*'s procession to nearby temples (another duty) were also auctioned off. After unbroken uncooked rice grains had been distributed to everyone present—and by now the *upāśray* was full—the *sādhu* resumed and finished the recitation. As he concluded, everyone threw the rice as a blessing in the direction of the *Bārsā Sūtra*.

The reciting of the *Bārsā Sūtra* is often followed by a small procession of the *sādhus* and some laity, perhaps accompanied by a small brass band, to a nearby temple, where they perform *caitya-vandan*. In 1985, the Bhāratī Society *saṅgh* did not have a procession, but many people went on their own to one of the major downtown temples for *darśan* of the ornamented Jina images.

Those people who were not accustomed to fasting ate a big noontime meal, as well as a mid-afternoon snack.[32] In the late afternoon, everyone dressed in pure clothes and went to the *upāśrays*, men with *sādhus* and women with *sādhvīs*, to perform the hour-and-a-half-long *saṃvatsarī pratikramaṇ*.[33] As part of the vow of temporary renunciation taken on this occasion, one can neither eat nor drink until forty-eight minutes after sunrise on the following day. Almost all Jains perform *pratikramaṇ* on this occasion, and its performance marks one minimal definition of who is and is not a Jain. After *pratikramaṇ*, everyone bowed to each other (and children touched their elders' feet) and said, "micchāmi dukkaḍaṃ" ("may my improper actions be inconsequential"). For several weeks many shops in the bazaar had been selling postcards printed with *micchāmi dukkaḍaṃ*, *kṣamāpanā*, and other similar expressions, which people sent to all their friends, relatives, and business associates (see Figure 6.5). Those who cared to be extravagant could even send telegrams, using the postal service's precoded English or Hindi *micchāmi dukkaḍaṃ* message, number 28, "Greetings on the occasion of 'Paryushan' a day of universal forgiveness." Jains in the United States also send e-mail messages; in 1998, a Jain friend e-mailed me the following message:

> Dear Friends,
> During this year, other times in this life or in other previous lives, if I have caused you any pain, suffering, or discomfort, either knowingly or unknowingly, in the manner of physical, verbal, or mental activities, directly by me or through others or by encouraging others, then on this auspicious occasion of Paryushan Parva I ask for your forgiveness. At the same time I forgive everyone who may have caused me the same. I extend my friendship to all.

Early the next morning, the *sādhus* returned to the *upāśrays* where they were staying for *comāsu*. The festival continued for the laity for at least one more day.

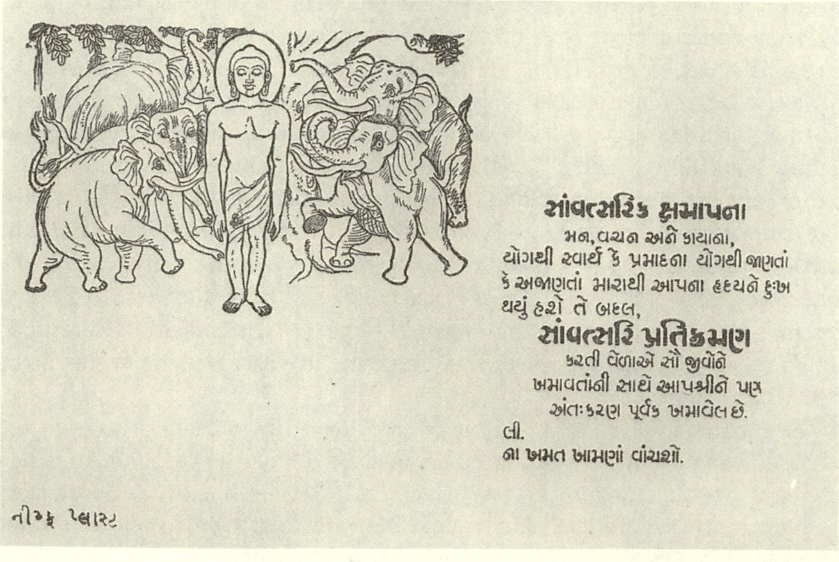

Figure 6.5. Printed card on occasion of Paryuṣaṇ. The text requests forgiveness on occasion of the annual *pratikramaṇ* for any suffering caused knowingly or unknowingly by thought, speech, or action. Author's collection, purchased in Patan, August 1986.

Those who had undertaken any fast during Paryuṣaṇ, whether a one-day fast or a thirty-one-day fast, were invited to ritual fast-breaking feedings given by individual families on the morning after Saṃvatsarī. The fasters were fed mostly sweet dishes, with some protein-rich lentil dishes. Each was given a red mark on the forehead and a one-rupee coin as signs of respect (Folkert 1993:illustrations 14 and 16). At midday everyone gathered at the *upāśray* (unless it was an *upāśray* where mendicants were still staying, in which case they went to another, vacant building) for the feast attended by all the members of the *saṅgh*; for anyone not to show up for this would be a public expression of disrespect to the entire *saṅgh*. It would in essence mark the person's resignation from the *saṅgh*, and also result in breaking off other forms of social and economic interaction. Finally, either on this day or soon afterward (depending in part on people's schedules, but mostly on the availability of horse carts, a band, and the other accessories necessary for a procession), the large *saṅghs* held public processions.[34]

The following description is of the 1986 procession of the Sāgar *saṅgh*. Before the start of the procession, all the participants went for *darśan* and *caitya-vandan* to the nearby temple of Pañcāsar Pārśvanāth. The large open area outside the wall surrounding this temple is used as the staging area for processions. The procession was led by a man on a horse carrying a triangular red-and-white flag, called the "flag of religion" (*dharm dhajā*). He was followed by a bullock cart on which were seated two men playing drums, as an auspicious sound to lead the procession. Next came a cart with a tall, beflagged pole, the Indra *dhajā*.[35] Following this was a hand-pushed cart with seated musicians playing a *śenāī* (a reed instrument) and a small drum, again as auspicious music. Then came two boys dressed as princes riding horses. They were followed by two drummers and another *śenāī* player, this time on foot. Since some children were too small to ride a horse, there were several rickshas filled with dressed-up boys and girls. Behind them was a loud marching band, consisting of one trombone, one tuba, three large baritone horns, two trumpets, two snare drums, one bass drum, a man playing maracas, a man singing devotional songs set to *filmī* tunes through a loudspeaker, and an electric "banjo" on a cart.[36] In some processions, there are frequent interruptions for men or boys to do rhythmic, circular dances in which they rap foot-long wooden sticks against each other in front of the band (Folkert 1993:illustration 9). In this case, the dancing was done by a dozen young boys from Sāgar Jain Pāṭhśāḷā (religious school), who marched with a banner behind the band. The boys danced in front of the *sādhus*, who came next, to display their devotion to them. Behind the *sādhus* walked the laymen of the *saṅgh*, on this occasion numbering only about a dozen. After four more boys on horses came three silver-covered chariots carrying metal Jina images, each drawn by a pair of bullocks covered with brightly colored embroidered caparisons. Each image was accompanied by two people waving yak-tail fans, and a married couple seated behind it, representing Indra and Indrāṇī, the king and queen of the gods.[37] In front of the chariots walked four *pujārīs*: two poured an unbroken stream of water from the morning's water *pūjā* on the road in front of the chariots, to ensure the purity of the road (several assistants carried pots of water on their heads, from which the pouring pots were replenished); one carried a lamp; and one threw on the ground on either side of the road handfuls of mixed grains for *rāśikaraṇ*, to persuade ill-tempered spirits not to disturb the procession.[38] After the chariots walked the *sādhvīs* and several dozen laywomen. One laywoman carried a silver plaque of the goddess Lakṣmī, with a lamp set into a tray at the base of the plaque; this auspicious object is also carried in wedding processions. The women loudly sang devotional songs, while the men shouted slogans in Gujarati such as "Hail Mahāvīr!," "Say it: Victory of the god of the Jain teachings!," and "Say it: Victory of Lord Mahāvīr Svāmī!" The procession lasted for about an hour, and slowly wound its way down the main bazaar street and through the Jain-dominated merchant bazaars in the center of town. Whenever the procession came to one of the many mosques in town, the band was quieted, people stopped singing, and the procession hurried past, so as not to antagonize or insult the Muslims. There was no attempt to circumambulate either the entire town or the Jain area, as is done in the procession connected with an image-installation ceremony, but the wellbeing generated by the procession was distributed through the Jain area.

Oḷī

A month after Paryuṣaṇ, from Āso Bright 7 to 15, is the festival of Oḷī. There are two Oḷīs annually, in Āso and Caitra (also Bright 7–15). Of these, the autumnal Oḷī in Āso is more broadly observed because of the *comāsu* residence of mendicants. It is marked by extensive *āyambil* fasting. *Oḷī* (Sanskrit *avalī*) means "line" or "series," so Oḷī is a line of nine days. Each day is devoted to the worship of and meditation upon one of the nine *pads*, or petals, of the *siddhcakra*, also known as the *navpad* (nine petals): the five supreme lords of Jainism, the Jina, *siddha*, *ācārya*, *upādhyāya*, and *sādhu*; the three jewels of correct faith, understanding, and conduct; and the fourth jewel of correct asceticism. Margaret Stevenson (1912:877) has aptly said of the *siddhcakra* that it "bears on its surface a complete summary of Jainism" (see Figure 5.1).

In Patan, a couchwork embroidered cloth of a *siddhcakra* under a glass covering was set up on the porch of the temple of Pañcāsar Pārśvanāth, and people worshiped the *siddhcakra* with *vāskep*. People also performed bathing *pūjās* to a metal Jina image on a bathing stand next to the *siddhcakra*.

Sādhus gave sermons on one of the nine *pads* each morning. These sermons involved the telling of the story of King Śrīpāl, his wife Mayaṇāsundarī, and her saving devotion to him through her worship of the nine *pads*, followed by a description of the qualities of the *pad* under discussion that day. This story, well known both through sermons and the many painted depictions of it on temple walls and popular prints (Pal 1994:illustration 120), indicates the extent to which Oḷī has rightly been called primarily a women's festival.[39]

> Śrīpāl was the young prince of Campa. After his father's death, his uncle Ajitsen seized the throne, and tried to kill Śrīpāl and his mother by preparing a harmful *yantra* or magical diagram. The two escaped him and took refuge in a village of 700 lepers. There Śrīpāl also contracted leprosy, and was selected as the leper's leader. He eventually married Mayaṇāsundarī, a princess from Ujjain. She accepted that such a marriage was due to the fruition of her own karma. At the instruction of a Jain *ācārya*,

she worshiped a *siddhcakra yantra* he had prepared, and undertook an *āyambil* fast, in order to counteract her bad karma. By lustrations of the water used to bathe the *siddhcakra*, she cured not only her husband but all the other lepers.

This story provides the charter for the observance of Oḷī by Jain women. The goal of their worship is not liberation but rather to ensure the health of their husbands. As Josephine Reynell says concerning Oḷī, "the *puṇya* a woman accumulates is thought to safeguard the health of her children and, more particularly, her husband" (1985a:127). In other words, the worship of the *siddhcakra*, an image symbolizing the basic teachings of the *mokṣa-mārg*, is efficacious in the realm of worldly wellbeing. Further, the worship of the Jain *siddhcakra yantra* is clearly contrasted to the ineffectual use of a Hindu *yantra* by Ajitsen.

Not many non-Jains are aware of the observance of Oḷī. Nor does it have much noticeable impact on the daily lives of the men of families in which one or more of the women observe it. It is not so much a time of universal Jain religious activity as a time when women's practices are intensified. The total number of *āyambil* meals taken from the *āyambilśāḷā* during the ten days (nine days plus post-fast feeding) of the Caitra Oḷī in 1986 was 2,250. The total number for the Āso Oḷī in 1986 was 1,800 laity and 700 mendicants. This means that between 5 and 10% of the lay Jain population of Patan ate *āyambil* meals from the *āyambilśāḷā*. I encountered little evidence that many people prepared and ate *āyambil* meals at home. The festival was observed almost exclusively by *sādhus*, *sādhvīs*, and lay women. Many men with whom I spoke were only vaguely aware of Oḷī, and could not tell me what happened during Oḷī other than that people observed *āyambil*. In Caitra 1986, the sermons at Maṇḍap were attended by 75–100 people daily. Three-quarters of them were women, and the average age of those attending was probably over sixty. But many people observed some dietary restrictions during Oḷī, whether it was a limited fast or not eating after dark. Some followed the *mokṣa-mārg* prescription. This involved morning and evening *pratikramaṇ*, reciting twenty rounds of the *Nokār Mantra* daily on a rosary, doing three *dev-vandan*s daily in a temple, and doing as many offerings of rice *svastika*s as there are virtues of that day's *pad* in a different temple each day. All of this is carefully outlined in widely available booklets (see *Navpad* n.d.).

Some people observe nine successive Oḷīs, starting with the autumnal Āso Oḷī. According to one mendicant, this latter observance brings two types of benefit (*lābh*): the immediate one of mental contentment (*ānand*), and the long-term one of rebirth in a place and time where *mokṣa* is attainable. We see here another example of how a properly observed religious practice benefits a person according to both the wellbeing and *mokṣa-mārg* ideologies. In recent decades, a Bombay-based organization, the Navpad Oḷī Ārādhak Samāj, has sponsored group observance of Oḷī at various Jain pilgrimage shrines under well-known *sādhus*. In 1986, for example, the Samāj sponsored the observance of Caitra Oḷī at the Jain shrine of Delvada on Mount Abu. In addition to the daily sermons and the fasting, there were daily congregational temple rituals, and on the full moon of Caitra, described by Muni Bhuvanvijay (1981a:130) as "the most merit-increasing of all the full moons," there was an elaborate congregational ritual in worship of the *siddhcakra* conducted by a renowned lay Jain ritual specialist.

Dīvāḷī to Knowledge Fifth

Two weeks after the autumnal Oḷī, and two weeks before the end of the *comāsu*, is the festival of Dīvāḷī (line of lights, also known as Dīpāvalī). In Gujarat it marks the calendrical new year. It is actually a cluster of festivals, beginning with the worship of wealth as Lakṣmī on Wealth Thirteenth (Dhan Teras) on Āso Dark 13. The next day sees a reversal of focus, from celebration of what is desired to protection from what is feared, with the worship of the powerful Ghaṇṭākarṇ Mahāvīr on Black Fourteenth (Kāḷī Caudaś). The emphasis returns to the positive on the new-moon day of Dīvāḷī proper, with the worship of Lakṣmī in the form of Sarasvatī for wealth. The morning of Kārtak Bright 1, the first day of the new year according to the western Indian calendar, is taken up with rites to guarantee wellbeing in the coming year. Kārtak Bright 2 is Brother Second (Bhāī Bīj), another day for protection, this time of sister by brother. Finally, the cycle ends on Kārtak Bright 5 with Knowledge Fifth (Jñān Pañcamī) or Profit Fifth (Lābh Pañcamī), a day with simultaneous emphases on liberating knowledge and gain of wellbeing.[40]

On Wealth Thirteenth the goddess Lakṣmī was worshiped as *dhan*, or wealth incarnate. There is no *mokṣa-mārg* interpretation of this event, and customs varied widely from family to family. In recent years most Jain families have observed the day only minimally, and performed the formal *pūjā* to Lakṣmī two days later on the evening of Dīvāḷī. This *pūjā* involves sprinkling auspicious red powder and *pañcāmṛt* or "five nectars" of milk, curd, clarified butter, honey, and sugar onto silver coins. Wealth Thirteenth is considered to be an auspicious day for buying silver, which many people did in the bazaar. On this day many merchants bought new account books for the coming year. Many Jains and non-Jains in Patan went to the Mahālakṣmī temple in Mahālakṣmīno Pāḍo for *darśan*.[41] Most people at noon ate a special sweet dish known as *lāvsī* or *kansār*, which is considered to be a *śukan* (Sanskrit *śakuna*). This term literally means "omen," in the sense of a passive indicator of future developments, but in actual use it has a more active sense.[42] Not only does *śukan* indicate future wellbeing, it also indicates anything that helps to ensure that wellbeing. In the villages, peasants and herders adorned their animals by painting their horns, and in many cases painted joyous slogans in bright colors on their sides.

Black Fourteenth (Kāḷī Caudaś), also known as Hell Fourteenth (Narak Caudaś), is a day of dangerous inauspiciousness, and so is carefully contained between two auspicious days, Wealth Thirteenth and Dīvāḷī. It is a special day for Hindu Tantrics, who "believe the night of Kali Chaudash to be particularly propitious for invoking spirits and call it Maharatri [Great Night]" (Trivedi 1965:64). Tantrics spend the night in a burning ground, and there make offerings of food to potentially malevolent beings. This is also a day for worshiping the powerful male deities Bhairav and Hanumān; Hanumān in particular "is worshipped on this day with oil and red lead as this is believed to free people from terrors of disease and evil spirits" (Trivedi 1965:64).

For contemporary Jains of Patan and Gujarat, the observance of Kāḷī Caudaś is intimately connected with the fire sacrifice (*havan*) to Ghaṇṭākarṇ Mahāvīr, the Jain equivalent of Hanumān.[43] He is the muscular, mustachioed male deity worshiped by Jains as a fellow Jain who can assist them within the worldly realm of wellbeing (see Figure 6.6). Since the early years of this century, the worship of Ghaṇṭākarṇ Mahāvīr has been particularly associated with the Jain temple in the town of Mahudi, on the Sabarmati River near Vijapur in the eastern part of Mehsana district.

In 1985, I joined tens of thousands of Jains and others from all over Gujarat who went to Mahudi for the fire sacrifice. In 1986, I observed the worship of Ghaṇṭākarṇ in Patan. The Gujarati verb for such worship is *caḍāvũ*, "to offer up," a term used in the context of deities other than the Jina because it implies that what is offered to the deity can be returned to the worshiper as *prasād* or blessed leftovers. In the household I observed, there was a brief mid-morning worship of Ghaṇṭākarṇ. A lamp was placed before a photograph of the Mahudi image of

Figure 6.6. Image of Ghaṇṭākarṇ Mahāvīr in Patan. November 1986.

Ghaṇṭākarṇ. While reciting a hymn, the worshipers offered a bowl of the auspicious sweet *sukhaḍī*. This is Ghaṇṭākarṇ's favorite dish, and also his famous *prasād* offered and received by pilgrims to Mahudi. A coconut (itself a symbol of fertility and wellbeing) was broken open, and both the coconut and *sukhaḍī* were distributed to family members as *prasād*.

In Patan, there was also a midday fire sacrifice at the Ghaṇṭākarṇ Mahāvīr shrine attached to the Sīmandhar Svāmī temple in Lakhiār Pāḍo in Rājkā Vāḍo.[44] Many people did short *pūjās* to photographs of Ghaṇṭākarṇ Mahāvīr in their homes.

The sacrifice in Patan, like the one at Mahudi, started at 12:39 P.M., the "time of victory," which is always auspicious for beginning a task. The basic structure of the sacrifice was essentially the same in Mahudi and Patan, as it was performed according to a booklet written by Ācārya Buddhisāgarsūri (1983–1984; see also 1953), the mendicant who established the cult of Ghaṇṭākarṇ in its present form.[45] In Patan it was performed by several Jain laymen, assisted by the temple *pujārī*. The ritual consisted of 108 identical offerings. For each offering a Sanskrit *mantra* was recited, and at the utterance of "svāhā" concluding each *mantra*, a bell was rung once,[46] a spoonful of *pañcāmṛt* (in this case milk, curd, clarified butter, sugar, and saffron) was poured into the fire,[47] a stick of wood was placed on the fire, and a black ball made of incense, wood, herbs, fragrance, coconut, and clarified butter was offered into the fire. At the same time, a flower was placed at the base of the image of Ghaṇṭākarṇ. The *mantra* is:

> *Oṃ* Ghaṇṭākarṇa Mahāvīra! Destroyer of all ailments! Protect protect those in mighty fear of boils, Greatly Strong!
>
> Wherever you stand, O deity, diseases and gout are destroyed by the written lines of letters.[48]
>
> Instantly from the recitation in the ear there is no fear of kings. Witches, ghosts, vampires, and demons do not arise.
>
> There is no untimely death, nor are snakes seen, nor is there fear of fire or thieves, *hrīṃ* Ghaṇṭākarṇa! Homage to you *ṭhaḥ ṭhaḥ ṭhaḥ svāhā*![49]

The one significant difference between the rituals at Mahudi and Patan was that at Mahudi with each offering everyone also tied one knot in a long red and yellow tie-dyed thread. It was taken home to help ensure the person's protection and wellbeing.[50] This practice was omitted in Patan.

At the conclusion of the 108 offerings, coconuts were broken open, and both coconut and *sukhaḍī* distributed as *prasād* to everyone. In Patan, the Jain layman who had recited the *mantra* then recited a long Sanskrit hymn to Ghaṇṭākarṇ. It contains many of the same requests as the *mantra*, for protection from disease, hostile kings, anxiety, hostile beings, rabid dogs, scorpion stings, snake bites, and other manner of misfortunes. It also requests positive benefits, such as wealth, success, increase of Lakṣmī, peace, satisfaction, pleasure, health, glory, and holiness (*maṅgala*). Further, the hymn requests that Ghaṇṭākarṇ protect the fourfold Jain congregation and show them the *mokṣa-mārg*. The benefits requested of Ghaṇṭākarṇ, while overwhelmingly related to very worldly concerns, are thus placed in the encompassing context of the concern for liberation.

> Ghaṇṭākarṇa Mahāvīra, give me universal power. Protect me in times of distress, protect my fame.
>
> Always be near me with your universal power. Protect the fourfold Jain congregation everywhere.
>
> *Oṃ kraumṃ droṃ drīṃ* create welfare Mahāvīra Ghaṇṭākarṇa! Destroy boils and other illnesses in the body of your devotee.
>
> *Aiṃ jhraumṃ sraumṃ hrīṃ* Mahāvīra Ghaṇṭākarṇa Greatly Strong! Give knowledge, give power, give me purity and wisdom.
>
> Embodiment of power, remove knots and worries. Show the path to liberation by the gift of pure knowledge.[51]

There are two very different understandings of the day of Dīvāḷī proper, on the new moon of Āso, and the actions performed by the Jains on this day oscillate between the two understandings. The *mokṣa-mārg* understanding is that on this day Mahāvīr attained his final liberation. In the words of a contemporary mendicant ideologue, "The worship on this *parv* is chiefly devotion to Lord Mahāvīr" (Jinendravijaygaṇi 1980:i). It is also celebrated as the day of the enlightenment of Gautam Svāmī, the chief disciple of Mahāvīr. The Jain understanding of the nearly ubiquitous practice among Hindus and Jains of lighting lamps on Dīvāḷī is found in the biography of Mahāvīr in the *Kalpa Sūtra*:[52]

> On the night when Lord Mahavir breathed his last and became liberated, reaching a state beyond pain, many gods and goddesses glided up and down the skies, shedding luster in the dark.
>
> On that night, as countless gods and goddesses glided resplendently in ascending and descending movements, there was a great bewilderment all around and a mighty tumult of wonder arose in the world.
>
> And on that night Gautam Svāmī, a homeless mendicant of the Jñātā clan and the chief disciple of Lord Mahāvīr, was at last freed of all the bonds of attachment and attained the boundless, ultimate enlightenment.
>
> On that moonless night, eighteen princely chiefs—nine Mallakas and nine Licchavis—of Kāśi and Kauśala, illuminated their doors and observed *poṣadh*. They exclaimed: "The lamp of inner light is extinguished; let us now burn lamps of ordinary clay."

Because Dīvāḷī is also the last day of the calendrical year in Gujarat, it is an important time of transition. It is the chief day in the year for the worship of the goddess Lakṣmī, and so an important day for focusing on wellbeing. Lakṣmī is the patron deity for all merchants; her worship on this day is of vital importance to their continued prosperity. For Jain merchants it is thus a day of differing, and sometimes conflicting, religious emphases, which must be carefully balanced.

As with any Jain festival, there was a sermon in the morning in the *upāśray*. The subject of it was Mahāvīr's life and liberation, and Gautam Svāmī's enlightenment. This sermon is usually based upon the *Dīpālikā Kalpa* of Jinasundarasūri.[53] Particularly learned *sādhus* base their sermons on the *Uttarādhyayana Sūtra*, the canonical text that contains the final sermon given by Mahāvīr on this day.

The observance of Dīvāḷī by the mendicants, who have renounced the realm of worldly affairs and especially wealth and Lakṣmī, consisted simply of the performance of *dev-vandan* in the *upāśrays* at midnight, the time when Mahāvīr attained liberation, and again in the predawn hours when Gautam Svāmī attained enlightenment.[54] The story of these two linked events was also the subject of the sermons given by *sādhus* on the previous morning.

The principle observance for the laity was the book *pūjā* performed in the evening. This is also known as Śāradā *pūja*, for the principal goddess worshiped is in fact not Lakṣmī but Śāradā or Sarasvatī, although she is perceived by Jains as being identical with Lakṣmī on this occasion. Many Jains are aware that the aims of the book *pūjā* run directly counter to the *mokṣa-mārg* interpretation of Dīvāḷī. Whereas the latter emphasizes renunciation and enlightenment, the former emphasizes attachment and profit. As a result, the performance of Lakṣmī *pūjā* on Dīvāḷī was included among the non-Jain observances to be avoided in the resolutions passed by the reformist All-India Śvetāmbar Jain Conferences in the early years of the century.[55] Although the effort to abolish this observance was unsuccessful, the effort to have Jains perform the *pūjā* according to more orthodox Jain ideology has been successful, at least in part. Many Jains possess small pamphlets that give in detail the "proper" Jain ritual, and refer to it during their performance of the ritual.[56]

In the office of the family business, at an auspicious time chosen according to the religious almanac,[57] the head of the family with whom I observed the book *pūjā* set up a temporary shrine, with poster-prints and photographs of images of various deities: three of Śaṅkheśvar Pārśvanāth, one of Śatruñjay Ādeśvar, one of Padmāvatī, one of both Ghaṇṭākarṇ Mahāvīr and Buddhisāgarsūri, two of Lakṣmī, and two of the *Nokār Mantra* (see Figure 6.7). Auspicious *āsopalav* leaves were hung over all the doorways and windows in the office. After lighting a lamp and incense, red protective strings were tied around the right wrist of everyone present. Strings were also tied around the new bamboo pens that were used in the rite. A Brāhmaṇ performed the first *pūjā*, the Gaṇeś *pūjā*, by speaking *mantras* that invoked the presence in the ritual space of Gaṇeś and the various rivers of India. While these *mantras* were being recited, the head of the family made offerings of milk, *pañcāmṛt*, water, red saffron powder, mixed flowers, and white, pink, and orange powders onto a betel nut placed on a betel leaf.[58] At the conclusion of the invocations, everyone present bowed to the leaf, in which the deities had been invoked, and the leaf was placed on the portable shrine.

The second *pūjā* was the Mahālakṣmī *pūjā*, the worship of wealth otherwise performed on Wealth Thirteenth. Five silver coins with representations of Lakṣmī were worshiped in the same way as the betel nut, and then also placed on the shrine. Next came a series of offerings to both the betel nut and the Lakṣmī coins: red saffron powder, unbroken rice, a flower, pink, white, red, and orange powders, a mixture of nuts and seeds, a red thread, a small fruit, and water. Red paste and rice were dabbed on the foreheads of all the deity pictures. The Mahākāḷī *pūjā* was performed by the Brāhmaṇ by reciting *mantras* over the bottle of black ink. Then the Mahāsarasvatī *pūjā* was performed to the account books.[59] Using the bamboo pens and ink made of red paste, the head of the family wrote in one account book while his eldest son wrote the same things in a second book. At the top of the first page each drew five red dots, and then they wrote the following:

Figure 6.7. Jain layman worshiping new account books at shrine in office of family business on Dīvāḷī. Patan, October 1995.

praise to śrī God
praise to śrī teachers
praise to śrī Sarasvatī
may there be the magical powers of śrī Gautam Svāmī
may the storehouse of śrī Keśarīyājī be full
may there be the wealth of emperor śrī Bharat
may there be the strength of śrī Bāhubali
may there be the wisdom of śrī Abhaykumār
may there be good fortune of śrī merchant Kayavannā
may there be the joy [or compassion] of śrī Ratnākarsāgar
may there be the success of śrī Dhannā and Sālibhadra
may there be the glory of śrī Jainism[60]

śrī
śrī śrī
śrī śrī śrī
śrī śrī śrī śrī
śrī śrī śrī śrī śrī
śrī śrī śrī śrī śrī śrī
śrī śrī śrī śrī śrī śrī śrī

Figure 6.8. Auspicious Pyramid.

Still using the red ink, in each book they then wrote a pyramid of seven lines of "śrī" (synonymous with Lakṣmī; see Figure 6.8).

Beneath the pyramid they drew a red *svastik*. Finally, they wrote the date and time.[61] The books were then piled on top of each other on the shrine, a betel leaf and betel nut placed atop them, and another series of offerings made, similar to the series made in the invocation of the rivers. The Brāhmaṇ sang a hymn containing the names of the goddess. The head of the family read out from the pamphlet a Sanskrit invocation of the following eight names of the goddess as follows:

Praise to Primal (Ādya) Lakṣmī
Praise to Wisdom (Vidyā) Lakṣmī
Praise to Good-fortune (Saubhāgya) Lakṣmī
Praise to Immortality (Amṛta) Lakṣmī
Praise to Desire (Kāma) Lakṣmī
Praise to Truth (Satya) Lakṣmī
Praise to Enjoyment (Bhoga) Lakṣmī
Praise to Asceticism (Yoga) Lakṣmī

Again from the pamphlet, the head of the family read out a hymn to Mahālakṣmī. While everyone present performed *āratī*, he read out an *āratī* hymn. Finally, he read from the book a hymn to Gautam Svāmī, before giving the Brāhmaṇ five rupees as the latter left. Everyone silently recited the *Nokār Mantra* thrice. The head of the family sprinkled a small amount of *vāskep* over the account books, which he had gotten from his guru earlier the same evening. The ritual concluded with one of the women reciting the auspicious Jain hymn *Moṭī Śānti* (Sanskrit *Bṛhacchānti*). This hymn evokes peace on the entire universe and is frequently sung on occasions calling for wellbeing. At the conclusion of the ritual, everyone ate candy and ice cream. Finally, after a visit to the Mahālakṣmī temple for *darśan*, everyone went home to sleep.

This ritual provides a dense representation of various values within the Jain tradition. The very altar, with its mixture of Jinas, a Jain goddess (Padmāvatī), a merchant goddess (Lakṣmī), a Jain unliberated deity (Ghaṇṭākarṇ), a Jain guru (Buddhisāgarsūri), and the *Nokār Mantra*, encapsulates this variety. A Brāhmaṇ was present, not because his presence was felt to be necessary but because the family wanted to demonstrate the complete ritual to the visiting scholar, and they felt that he would pronounce the *mantras* properly and therefore most efficaciously. His expertise was needed to invoke the unliberated deities, and this invocation was an additional benefit to the basic ritual performed by the Jain men. The men wrote into their account books a series of *mantras* designed to convey into their worldly business concerns the holy power inherent in the Jain religion. The *mantras* demonstrate clearly the way in which this power operates on both the planes of the *mokṣa-mārg* and wellbeing: in the series of invocations, there is praise for enlightenment, wisdom, spiritual strength, and the glories of Jainism, as well as for wealth, a full storehouse, and good fortune. The eight names of Lakṣmī demonstrate a similar multivalency: she is the goddess of both enjoyment (*bhoga*) and asceticism (*yoga*), of both desire (*kāma*) and truth (*satya*).

The ritual ends with hymns to both Mahālakṣmī, the giver of wealth and prosperity, and Gautam Svāmī, the enlightened renouncer. Yet even the praise of Gautam Svāmī here is polysemous. In this context, the Jain Gautam stands in for the god Gaṇeś, who is invoked by Hindus at all beginnings to remove obstacles in the way of attaining wellbeing, just as Gautam is invoked in the new account books immediately after God, the gurus, and Sarasvatī. From the *mokṣa-mārg* perspective, Gautam is important as the foremost disciple of Mahāvīr, whose enlightenment on this day is commemorated. From the wellbeing perspective, he is a rotund, well-fed mendicant famous for the magical power of his "unfailing kitchen" by which he multiplied a small quantity of food to feed 500 mendicants. He is worshiped by Jains because doing so, in the words of a Gujarati hymn by the seventeenth-century Lāvaṇyasamay, "prevents disease . . . brings increase . . . provides whatever is pleasing" and "brings all desired success" (Cort 1995a:92).[62] Auspiciousness and prosperity are associated with sweet things, so after the ritual everyone ate ice cream, even though both ice cream and eating after dark are to be avoided according to the *mokṣa-mārg* ideology. The *mokṣa-mārg* values of *ahiṃsā* and *tap* are superseded by the wellbeing values of sweetness and auspiciousness. The contrast of the evening is heightened when one remembers that all the while the town was illuminated with lamps, candles, and electric lights, and the night was filled with the constant roar of firecrackers—all the sort of excess needed to ensure an excess of wellbeing during the coming year—and at the same time in the darkened *upāśrays* the mendicants recited a lengthy *dev-vandan* in praise of Mahāvīr's liberation from the worldly concerns and joys so evident all around them. *Mokṣa-mārg* ideologues are clearly aware of the differing emphases given to the day: Ānandsāgarsūri, for example, in his printed sermon for Dīvāḷī contrasts spiritual and physical pleasure (*sukh*), and asks, "Are you consuming pleasure or is it consuming you?" (1971:18). In a similar vein, Bhuvanvijay in his printed sermon says that a fast performed on this day results in one thousand times as much *puṇya* as a fast done on any other day; since everyone is pursuing sensual pleasure on this day, it is a day of extensive binding of karma, and therefore a fast results in great destruction of karma (1981a:56).

The new year begins with sunrise on the following day, Kārtak Bright 1. Early in the morning, after only a few hours of sleep, all the Jains in Patan went to the temple of Śāmḷā Pārśvanāth for *darśan*. Outside the temple two men played auspicious music on a drum and a *śenāī*, instruments of auspicious beginnings. Most people just took *darśan*, but many performed *caitya-vandan*. Women were dressed in silk saris and adorned with gold jewelry. Everyone greeted friends, neighbors, and acquaintances with "Happy New Year." Outside the temple a line of non-Jain women sold salt and *coḷā*, a special kind of pulse: this was the auspicious first purchase of the year, to be eaten at the midday meal.

From the temple everyone then went to their neighborhood *upāśrays* to hear a *sādhu* recite the new year's *māṅgaḷik*, or holy verses. These consist of the medieval Prakrit and Sanskrit hymns known as the *Navasmaraṇ* (Nine Remembrances), which are considered to be especially efficacious both for advancing along the *mokṣa-mārg* and ensuring the wellbeing of the Jain community. One year, the *sādhu* also recited the fourteenth-century Gujarati *Gautam Svāmī Rās* of Mahopadhyāya Vinayprabh (Vinaya Sāgar 1987). Both years, the *sādhus* attempted to give brief sermons concerning the importance of the day. They said that on this day people should remember the liberation of Mahāvīr and the enlightenment of Gautam Svāmī. In 1985, the *sādhu* talked about the true definition of *maṅgaḷ kām* (holy work): the real *maṅgaḷ*, he said, is *ahiṃsā*, and therefore one need not be concerned whether or not the day is an auspicious one (*maṅgaḷ tithi*) in order to perform *tap*. He intentionally played off two connotations of *maṅgaḷ*, on the one hand as something holy on the *mokṣa-mārg*, and on the other as something auspicious within the world. The people were present to hear the *māṅgaḷik* because the recitation ensured an auspicious beginning to the new year; but the *sādhu* stressed the other meaning of *maṅgaḷ*, in order to remind the audience of the centrality of the *mokṣa-mārg* and its hierarchical superiority to the worldly realm of wellbeing. Both years, the people quickly got restless with the sermonizing, and in 1986 they started to leave the *upāśray* before the *sādhu* had even finished; the women had to get home to start cooking, and the men wanted to go to the temple to perform *pūjā*. This was also the first day of the month, and so in every temple there was the monthly auspicious bathing *pūjā* to the images.

At home, everyone ate a spoonful of yogurt as the first food of the new year. This is also the last thing someone eats before departing on a long trip, and so has connotations of wellbeing at times of transition. At midday, the men briefly opened their businesses at the auspicious time of 12:39, and then returned home, as the real opening of business was not until four days later, on Knowledge Fifth. New Year's is also the one day of the year when all Jains give money to beggars, and money is also given according to social rank by fathers to sons and daughters and by employers to servants.[63]

The three-day *caitya paripāṭī*, or procession to all the Jain temples in Patan, also began on Kārtak Bright 1. The *sādhus* staying at Maṇḍap and Sāgar led processions to the temples in the downtown area on the first day. Some years, *sādhus* led groups of laity on a tour of all the temples in Patan.

Most people, however, went to the temples in small groups of family or friends. In a number of groups, *sādhvīs* led their relatives and acquaintances. The women were dressed in fine silk saris. Only a few people performed *caitya-vandan* in any of the temples; most people took *darśan* of the ornamented images, sang a few verses to the main image,[64] quickly drew a Jain *svastik* in rice on the offering box, bowed to the images, and left for the next temple. The whole process took no more than two or three minutes per temple. In some neighborhoods residents served boiled sugar-water to the pilgrims. Others invited friends into their homes for tea, cold drinks, and snacks, reestablishing relationships with people perhaps not seen since the previous year's procession. The neighborhood *saṅghs* decorated the temples and arranged for special ornamentation of the images. Because there are about eighty Jain temples in Patan, the procession was spread out over three days. The procession on the first day went to the temples in the central section of town, on the second day to those in the southern section, and on the third day to those in the western section. In recent years, a fourth day has been added for the procession to the two temples in the new eastern suburbs, Bhāratī Society and Āśīṣ Society. In neighborhoods that no longer have a Jain population but still have a Jain temple, this was the only day of the year when any people came to the temples, and one of only two days in the year when they were opened (the other being the annual flagdays for each of these temples). The procession was also the only occasion when many people went to other parts of town; for example, it was the only time when many Vāṇiyā Jains went to Sāḷvī Vāḍo, and people who could walk blindfolded through the labyrinthine alleys downtown felt very much out of place in the straight alleys of Sāḷvī Vāḍo. The procession thus plays an important role in reinforcing the sense of the unity of all Patan Jains in a single *saṅgh*.

Kārtak Bright 2 is Brother Second (Bhāī Bīj), which was observed by Jains in the same way as by Hindus. This festival reaffirms the importance of the brother-sister blood relationship even after marriage. On this day, a married woman invites her brother(s) to her home. Some men travel to nearby towns and villages to fulfill their obligations. He brings her sweets and some money, and in return she feeds him. There is a Jain ideological explanation for the day: on this day Mahāvīr's sister Sunandā invited her surviving brother Nandivardhana to her house to console him of his grief at their brother's death (Trivedi 1965:67). But I rarely heard this explanation given by any Jain.

The Dīvāḷī sequence ends with Knowledge Fifth (Jñān Pañcamī) on Kārtak Bright 5. Both Jains and Hindus observe it as Good-Fortune Fifth (Saubhāgya Pañcamī) and Profit Fifth (Lābh Pañcamī) (Trivedi 1965:67), but it is more centrally important in the Jain tradition. It is a day on which the Jains' involvement in the realm of religious knowledge (*jñān*) again interacts with their involvement as merchants in the realm of wealth and commercial intercourse (*lābh*), and when the interaction of the *mokṣa-mārg* ideology and wellbeing can be clearly seen. On this day merchants ritually reopened their shops and offices, which in theory (and in many cases in practice as well) had been closed since before Dīvāḷī. One merchant explained the day as follows, clearly giving precedence to the *mokṣa-mārg* understanding of the day over the wellbeing understanding: "This day is both Jñān Pañcamī and Lābh Pañcamī, but the former is more important, for *jñān* is a virtue of the soul.[65] Therefore one should first do *jñān pūjā*, and only then celebrate Lābh Pañcamī by starting work." As a day for the worship of *jñān*, it was also a day when school children bought pencils and notebooks.

The morning sermon at the *upāśray* is based on any one of a number of *Jñāna Pañcamī Kathās* that have been composed in Prakrit and Sanskrit over the past thousand years.[66] In addition to the sermon, the laity took advantage of the occasion to announce and felicitate publicly the *jñān*-promoting activities undertaken during the *comāsu* that was coming to an end, especially the texts studied by the young children in the schools under the supervision of the resident *sādhus*.

The most popular story for the sermons nowadays is that of Vardatt and Guṇmañjarī:[67]

> Guṇmañjarī, the daughter of a millionaire, was very sickly. Her father asked the Jain *sādhu* Vijaysen the cause and cure of her illness. He explained that in a former life she had shown disrespect to *jñān* in thought, speech, and deed. Through such disrespect, shown, for example, by mistreating books, one accrues knowledge-obscuring karma.[68] To rid herself of the karma, and therefore cure herself of the disease, he told her to observe *Jñān Pañcamī*, a fast lasting for five years and five months to be performed on every *jñān tithi*, the fifth of the bright half of every month, or at the very least annually on *Jñān Pañcamī*. He explained, "Ignorance and illness are removed by the ritually proper observance of Jñān Pañcamī; through that observance the girl will get every kind of pleasure (*sukh*)."
>
> Similarly, Vardatt was a prince in the same city who was also sickly. His father also asked Vijaysen for help. He explained that when Vardatt was an *ācārya* in a former life he had shown disrespect to *jñān* by refusing to give teachings. Vardatt also accepted the *jñān* fast. Both he and Guṇmañjarī were cured, lived successful lives (Vardatt married a thousand wives, a clear indicator of wellbeing), became mendicants, were reborn in heaven, and finally were reborn in Mahāvideha, where after again leading successful lives they took initiation under Sīmandhar Svāmī and attained enlightenment.

This story, as with most prescriptive, exemplary stories told by *sādhus* in their sermons, recommends what we might call a maximalist strategy, that is, it prescribes a maximum ascetic observance according to the ideology of the *mokṣa-mārg*. But few people follow such a maximalist strategy; I never heard of anyone performing the full sixty-five-month *jñān* fast, and I would suspect that most of those who do are mendicants. Most laity instead follow a minimalist strategy, by following the most basic observance on Jñān Pañcamī itself. Many people perform *āyambil* or *upvās* on this day. A moderate-sized crowd attends the morning sermon. Most people do *jñān pūjā* by worshiping the five kinds of *jñān* at five different places.[69]

There were several dozen places in Patan where one could perform this *pūjā*, including all the *upāśrays* and religious schools, and the Hemacandra Jñān Mandir, the Jain manuscript library. Most people performed the *pūjā* in the morning, after the sermons in the *upāśrays*. At each location a table was set up with a tiered display of religious books. Standing before the display, people first recited some verses to *jñān*. Then they put some money on a platter containing *vāskep*, and sprinkled some more *vāskep* onto the books. As one layman explained, "*vāskep pūjā* is done in devotion to *jñān*, as a prayer to the Lord to give me *jñān*." Some people drew a rice *svastik* (the maximal observance was five *svastiks*, each of a different grain) on the table, and offered *āratī* with a five-wick lamp. Some also did *caitya-vandan* (see Figure 6.9). Many people on this occasion visited in the *upāśray* with mendicants whom they knew. In addition to going five places to perform *jñān pūjā*, most people also went to Pañcāsar Pārśvanāth and other temples for *darśan*. In the afternoon, a few people performed *dev-vandan* with the mendicants in the *upāśray*.[70] But since this was also the day for resuming business after the new year break, most men opened their shop or office after the *jñān pūjā*. An auspicious time was selected for opening the shop, either by consulting an almanac or asking an astrologer. One businessman in Patan opened his office at the ever-auspicious time of 12:39 P.M. This was the favorite time of the *sādhu* of whom he was a special devotee; he said that by opening his business at the time favored by his guru, he was ensuring his continued prosperity for the coming year.

Kārtak Full Moon

Two weeks after the beginning of the new year, the *comāsu* comes to an end. On Kārtak Bright 14 is the four-monthly *pratikramaṇ*. In the morning, the *sādhus* concluded the *comāsu* with a final sermon. In 1986 at Sāgar, the *sādhu* summarized the two texts on which he had lectured during the *comāsu*. He explained the importance of the mendicants "changing *cāturmās*": it is a ritual action (*kriyā*), and

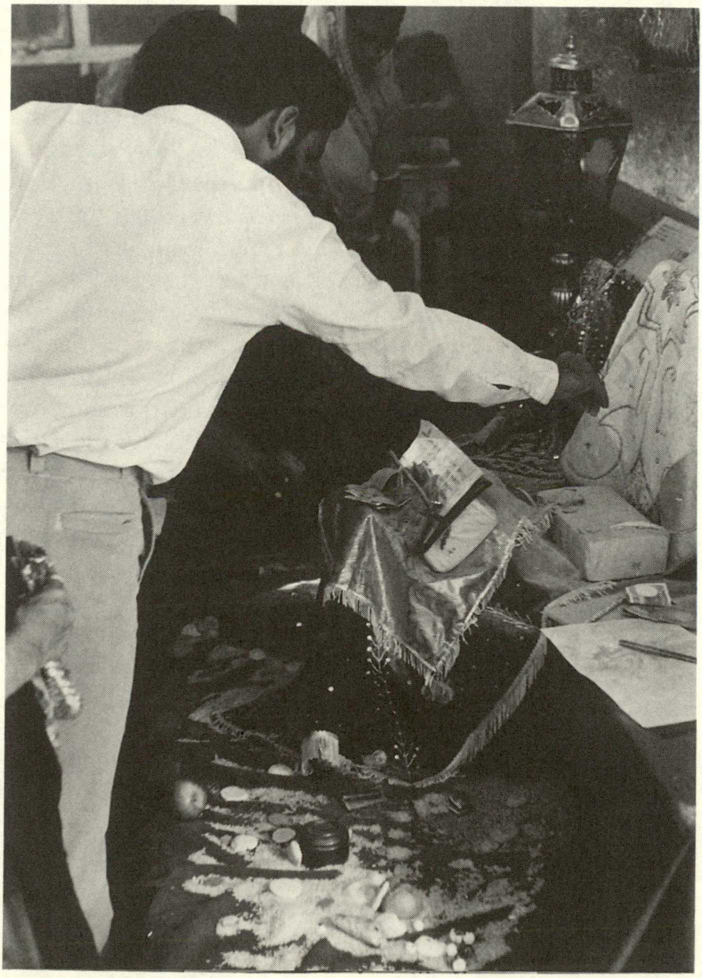

Figure 6.9. Layman worshiping books on Jñān Pañcamī. Patan, November 1986.

like all ritual actions in Jainism its purpose is to break the bondage of karma and attain liberation. At the end of the sermon, a man from the Rājkā Vāḍo *saṅgh* formally invited the *sādhus* to come to Rājkā Vāḍo on the following day. The *sādhu* announced the results of the examination he had given the boys who had been studying under him, and had them recite the pedagogical hymns they had memorized so that all present could get the benefit of their *jñān*. There was then formal honoring of the students; the *sādhu* explained that since the students had studied *jñān*, honoring the students was really honoring the virtues of the nine principles (*navpad*), and such honoring leads to reduction of karma in those who are doing the honoring. This is a statement of the classic Jain karma doctrine, that approval (*anumodan*) of correct action results in a positive karmic result, just as does the actual performance of the correct action. Finally, the *sādhu* said that this was the last chance to settle all affairs from the concluding *comāsu*, and stressed the importance of settling them. The Jains as good merchants do not like to be in debt of any sort, whether financial or social; for example, I was told by one Jain woman that if she were in debt when she died, she would surely be reborn in an infernal realm. At noon there was *dev-vandan* in the *upāśrays*, and that evening there was *pratikramaṇ*.

The following day, Kārtak Full Moon, is highly auspicious in both the Jain and Hindu traditions (Trivedi 1965:69–71; Underhill 1921:95–96). According to Hindu mythology, four days earlier, Kārtak Bright 11 marks the day every year when the gods end their four months of sleep and again become active in the world. Kārtak Full Moon marks the end of the four-month rainy season in the Hindu ritual calendar, and many dietary restrictions and other forms of asceticism—undertaken for the four months in order to counteract the potential negative effects of the gods' slumber—end on this day. Kārtak Bright 11 through Full Moon sees over 100,000 pilgrims, both laity and mendicants (especially those of the Nāth order), circumambulate Mount Girnar in Saurashtra, an event known as the Līlī Parikramā or "Green Circumambulation," so named because it celebrates the successful end to the rainy season (Trivedi 1965: 216–20). There are also sectarian Hindu understandings of the day. For Vaiṣṇavs, it is centrally important in the divine sports of Kṛṣṇa and Rādhā, and so is observed in Kṛṣṇa temples. For Śaiva Hindus it is Tripurārī Full Moon, in celebration of Śiva's slaying of the demon Tripura. There are more fairs held on this day in Gujarat than on any other day; many of them are held at Śiva temples, giving evidence of the old Śaiva layer of Gujarati Hinduism.

In addition to the fair organized by the Moḍh Ghāñcī (oil-presser) caste in Patan at Khān Sarovar, an artificial lake on the southern edge of town, and one just outside Patan at the Padmanābh Śiva temple, fairs were held at the nearby towns of Sidhpur and Mehsana. All of these were dedicated to Śiva, although many who attend do so for commercial and entertainment reasons.

Many Jains go to Mount Shatrunjay at Palitana, for on this day the mountain is "reopened" after being closed for the *comāsu*. One can climb the mountain during *comāsu*, but the trust managing the mountain does not provide facilities for the worshiper during these four months. Jains believe that climbing the mountain during this period results in much killing of the plants that grow due to the rains, and is therefore inappropriate conduct. The merit (*puṇya*) from climbing Shatrunjay on

Kārtak Full Moon is believed to be much greater than on almost any other day. Muni Bhuvanvijay (1981a:75) quotes a Sanskrit verse that indicates the conjoined wellbeing and *mokṣa-mārg* benefits from this act: "He who meditates on the Jina here on the full moon of Kārtak attains all worldly pleasures in his life and then attains liberation." He quotes another verse with a similar intent: "By performing just one *upvās* on the full moon of Kārtak atop Shatrunjay, a man is freed from the bad karma of killing a learned man, woman, or child." The story of Kārtak Full Moon as told in sermons concerns Drāviḍ and Vālikhill, two grandsons of Ṛṣabhnāth, who were reconciled after a long and bloody war, took initiation as *sādhus* and on this day attained liberation atop Shatrunjay with fifty million other *sādhus*.[71]

Kārtak Full Moon is also important as the birthday of the great medieval scholar-saint Ācārya Hemacandra, the "omniscient one of the dark age." Some *sādhus* briefly recounted his life in sermons on this day, especially in Patan, where he spent most of his life, first as advisor to Emperor Jayasiṃha Siddharāja, and then as the personal preceptor to Emperor Kumārapāla.

In the morning, all *sādhus* changed their residence. To celebrate the conclusion of the *comāsu*, there was usually a procession. Members of the new *saṅgh* came to the *upāśray* and formally escorted the *sādhus* to their new residence. The distance involved in the change of residence was not great, as little as a few minutes' walk to another neighborhood, and often after a day or two they returned to the first *upāśray*. The size and pomp of the procession was directly proportional to the importance of the *sādhus*. The 1986 procession from Sāgar to Rājkā Vāḍo, for two relatively unimportant *sādhus*, consisted of only fifty or sixty laity, the two *sādhus*, and half a dozen *sādhvīs*, led by a *śenāī* and two drums. The 1985 procession for a much more renowned *sādhu* was larger. In addition to the musicians, there were boys from the Sāgar school carrying dancing sticks and banners, and young girls carrying auspicious full pots of water on their heads. The procession also included an *Indra-dhajā*, the auspicious banner of Indra found in many larger processions. The procession went from Sāgar to the temple of Pañcāsar Pārśvanāth, where everyone took *darśan* and performed *caitya-vandan*. Everyone then went for *darśan* of the Shatrunjay painting (see below) in the compound next to the temple. The procession resumed and wound its way through the alleys on either side of the main bazaar, several times retracing its route, and finally after an hour and a half arrived at Kanāsāno Pāḍo, which is normally only a five-minute walk from Sāgar. The *sādhus* were venerated at the gate into the neighborhood; more young girls with full pots of water on their heads lined up at the gate, and a small table with a rice *nandyāvart* on it was placed on the ground under the gateway. The *sādhus* entered the neighborhood, and went into the temple for *darśan*. Because of the size of the crowd, which would not comfortably fit into the neighborhood *upāśray*, a pavilion had been erected in the center of the neighborhood in front of the temple. There the *sādhus* sat on a platform, and after the leading men of the *saṅgh* did *guru pūjā* to the chief *sādhu*, the latter delivered a sermon on the importance of Kārtak Full Moon.

In the afternoon, almost all the Jains of Patan went to the fair at Khān Sarovar, where in addition to the Śaiva fair there was also a display of two large cloth paintings of Shatrunjay[72] (see Figure 6.10). Most Jains would like to go to Shatrunjay on this day; but since only a few can go, paintings of Shatrunjay are installed in

Figure 6.10. Laity performing *vandan* to cloth paintings of Shatrunjay. Photograph by Thomas A. Zwicker, © 1989 The University of Pennsylvania Museum Archives.

almost every town and village. In Patan, these paintings have traditionally been erected near Khān Sarovar, outside the gates of the town to the south, in the direction of Shatrunjay. In recent years, a painting has also been erected in the compound next to Pañcāsar Pārśvanāth for people who are unable to go the several miles to Khān Sarovar. At Khān Sarovar, people circumambulated the painting in imitation of circumambulation of the mountain and performed *caitya-vandan* to the paintings. Many of the vernacular hymns composed for inclusion in *caitya-vandan*, such as the following, are addressed to Shatrunjay:

> Bad rebirth is eliminated at blessed Shatrunjay, the land of perfection.
> Maintain the proper sentiment (*bhāv*) and cross over the ocean of rebirth.
> This is the sacred field of conduct of infinite perfected souls. This is the king of all shrines.
> Ṛṣabh came here ninety-nine times. Here are the footprints of the Lord.
> The Sun Tank is lustrous. Kavaḍ Yakṣ is attractive.
> King Nābhi is the crown of his lineage. Bow down to the excellent Jina.[73]

Many people offered flowers at the base of the paintings. There was also a metal Jina image atop a bathing stand next to the paintings for those who wanted to make offerings to it. The *saṅgh* from one of the neighborhoods in Rājkā Vāḍo provided sweetened boiled water for people to drink. All around the temporary pavilion that shelters the paintings was the Śaiva fair, so people went not only for *darśan* of Shatrunjay but also to enjoy themselves on an outing.

With Kārtak Full Moon, the steady procession of festivals that began two and a half months earlier with Paryuṣaṇ comes to an end. For the next eight months, the *sādhus* and *sādhvīs* travel from place to place. Without the settled continuity of the fourfold *saṅgh*, the festivals in these eight months tend to lack the same intensity of collective community observance. Participation is much more a matter of personal devotion and style, and the observances are of a much less highly visible nature. Many non-Jains would be aware of the Jain observance of Paryuṣaṇ, the *caitya paripāṭī* following Dīvāḷī, and the *darśan* of the Shatrunjay paintings on Kārtak Full Moon. Fewer would be aware of the observances I will discuss in the remainder of this chapter.

Silence Eleventh

Silence Eleventh (Maun Agyāras, Sanskrit Mauna Ekādaśī) falls soon after Kārtak Full Moon, on Māgsar Bright 11. Just as any bright fifth is a knowledge fifth, but Kārtak Bright Fifth is the important Knowledge Fifth (and, in the Hindu context, any dark thirteenth is a night of Śiva, *śiva rātrī*, but Māgh Dark 13 is the Great Night of Śiva, Mahā Śiva Rātrī), so any bright eleventh is a silence eleventh, but the main day of its observance during the year is in the month of Māgsar. This day is especially holy, and religious activities especially meritorious, because five *kalyāṇaks* fall on this day: the renunciation *kalyāṇak* of Aranāth, the birth, renunciation, and enlightenment *kalyāṇaks* of Mallināth, and the enlightenment *kalyāṇak* of Nemināth. But it is believed that there are in total 150 *kalyāṇaks* that fall on this date, and so fasts done on this day earn 150 times more *puṇya*.[74]

The observances for this day were followed mostly by mendicants. Many mendicants and some laity took a vow of silence for the day. A few people took the vow of *poṣadh* and spent the entire day in the *upāśray*. In the morning, there were special sermons by the *sādhus*, in which was told the story of how Kṛṣṇa performed the Silence Eleventh fast in accord with the teaching of his cousin, the Jina Nemināth.[75] At midday there was *dev-vandan* in the *upāśrays*,[76] and some laity also performed *pratikramaṇ* in the evening. At most temples there were special decorations of the images, and many people went for *darśan*. People were also more scrupulous about observing Jain dietary restrictions, such as not eating after nightfall.

Poṣ Tenth

Two weeks later, on Māgsar Dark 10, is Poṣ Tenth, the birth *kalyāṇak* of Pārśvanāth. The name of the day is Poṣ Tenth, but in Gujarat it falls in the month of Māgsar, due to the different calendrical systems in use in north and south India. In Gujarat, the south Indian calendar is in use; this calendar begins with the bright half of the month, and ends with the new moon. The north Indian calendar, in use in Banaras where Pārśvanāth was born and in Marwar whence many Gujarati Jains migrated, begins with the dark half of the month and ends with the full moon. Therefore every dark fortnight is in one month according to the south Indian calendar, but in the following month according to the north Indian calendar. This can be clearly seen in Table 6.2.

Table 6.2 Corresponding Months in North Indian and South Indian Calendars

North		South
Māgsar	dark 1–15	Kārtak
Māgsar	bright 1–15	Māgsar
Poṣ	dark 1–15	Māgsar
Poṣ	bright 1–15	Poṣ
Māgh	dark 1–15	Poṣ
Māgh	bright 1–15	Māgh

In Patan, there was little that was special about the observance of Poṣ Daśamī. There were morning sermons, in which the *sādhus* narrated in brief the life story of Pārśvanāth.[77] The images in most temples (and in many temples the main images are of Pārśvanāth) were decorated with special ornamentations, and the evening *āratī* at many Pārśvanāth temples included a special 108-wick lamp.[78]

Those who wanted to observe Poṣ Tenth in a fuller fashion performed the three-day fast known as *aṭhṭham*, under a well-known *sādhu*. The favorite place in Gujarat to perform this is Shankheshvar, for it was here that Kṛṣṇa performed *aṭhṭham* in accord with the teaching of Nemināth in order to obtain the image of Śaṅkheśvar Pārśvanāth and defeat Jarāsandha (Cort 1988). Every year, several thousand people go to Shankheshvar to perform *aṭhṭham* on Poṣ Tenth. Other pilgrimage shrines of Pārśvanāth are also efficacious for this fast, and people from Patan went to nearby shrines such as Charup and Bhildi, or any shrine where a well-known *sādhu* was leading the observance of *aṭhṭham tap*.

Hoḷī

In general, *mokṣa-mārg* ideologues encourage lay Jains to observe Jain festivals and avoid observance of Hindu festivals, but are not overly strident in their condemnation of participation in Hindu festivals. The major exception to this is the spring festival of Hoḷī. Bhuvanvijay (1981a:113) cites the following Sanskrit verse:

> Hoḷī is a worldly observence full of bad karma which increases the cycle of rebirth. Therefore it is to be avoided by those who know the transcendent religion.

The celebration of Hoḷī really consists in two parts: Hoḷī proper, or Hutāśinī, on Fāgan Bright 15, on which the Hoḷī fire is lit in commemoration of the burning of the demoness Holikā;[79] and Dhuleṭī (Dusty Day), on Fāgan Dark 1, when people throw colored powders and other less appealing substances on each other in the morning, sing bawdy songs, and engage in abusive repartee. The Jain *mokṣa-mārg* objection is specifically to the burning of the Hoḷī fire, since this involves large-scale destruction of insects and other minute creatures. Several narratives in Sanskrit and Gujarati explain why Jains should not participate in this observance. These relate the woeful consequences of observance of Hoḷī, and explain the proper, Jain observance. Bhuvanvijay (1981a:129) concludes his condemnation of Hoḷī by saying: "The Jain *ācāryas* have preached that from speaking one irrelevant sentence, or being abusive, a soul is bound to enjoy bad karma for many lives. In the end one will suffer the fruit of this negative babble. One must abandon the physical (*dravya*) Hoḷī, speak positive words full of discrimination and wisdom in the spiritual (*bhāv*) Hoḷī, and burn the logs of karma in the fire of *tap*."

The reformist Jain Śvetāmbar Conferences in the early years of the twentieth century listed several festivals observed by non-Jains that should not be observed by Jains, but over the centuries Hoḷī has been the focus of the most strident condemnation. The resolutions passed at the conferences noted that instead of Hoḷī, Jains should only observe the four-monthly *pratikramaṇ* to be performed on Fāgan Bright 14 (Cort 1995b).

In Patan, few Jains participated in the Hoḷī fires, for social as well as religious reasons. The fires tended to be rather rowdy occasions, the sort of occasion usually avoided by the average, restrained Jain. Children participated in the color-throwing on Dhuḷeṭī; but this was as much a secular as a Hindu activity, and in Gujarat was certainly quite restrained in comparison to the very physical activity in Rajasthan and north India. On the afternoon of Dhuḷeṭī most Patan Jains went for *darśan* to the Ṛṣabhnāth temple on the campus of Jain Boarding, the school on the western outskirts of town run by the Pāṭan Jain Maṇḍaḷ. For many years the students of the school organized a Fun Fair on this day, and although this had been discontinued, there were still many vendors on the road outside the school selling snacks and cold drinks. Like the *darśan* of the Shatrunjay paintings at Khān Sarovar on Kārtak Full Moon, this was a religious occasion that was also an excuse for a pleasant family outing.

Mahāvīr Jayantī

Mahāvīr Jayantī, on Caitra Bright 13, the birth-*kalyāṇak* of Mahāvīr, is the one Jain festival that is also a national holiday. In part this follows an Indian government practice of observing the birthdays of the "founders" of different religions as official holidays. Mahāvīr's birth *kalyāṇak* is also one of the few dates on which the Digambar and Śvetāmbar calendars agree, and so it is one of the few Jain festivals that the government can recognize as a holiday without stirring up a sectarian dispute. It was not, however, an important day for Jains in Patan. The few temples in which the main image is of Mahāvīr had special ornamentations on the images, and some people went to Pañcāsar Pārśvanāth for *darśan*, but otherwise there were no special observances. Emotionally and ritually the celebration of the birth of Mahāvīr is on the day of the recitation of his birth during Paryuṣaṇ; Mahāvīr Jayantī is thus an extraneous day.

The Patan nonobservance of Mahāvīr Jayantī contrasted sharply with that in a major metropolis such as Ahmedabad, where in 1987 a large procession was sponsored by the Samast Jain Sevā Samāj (All Jain Service Society). It went from the Mahavir Vidyalay, a Mūrtipūjak school in Paldi, several miles up Ashram Road to Gujarat Vidyapith, where some 25,000 people of all four Jain sects listened to speeches by Jain industrialists, the (Jain) state minister of finance, and two Digambar *sādhus*. The only mendicants who participated were Digambar, although at a similar cross-sectarian public program the year before there had been speeches by a Mūrtipūjak *ācārya* and a Terāpanthī *sādhvī*.

Immortal Third

The final festival in our survey of the calendar year is Immortal Third (Akhā Trīj, Sanskrit Akṣaya Tṛtīya) on Vaiśākh Bright 3. This day commemorates the occasion when King Śreyāṅs of Hastinapur offered Ṛṣabhnāth some sugarcane juice, and thus allowed him to break a fast of more than a year. Śreyāṅs received imperishable merit (*akṣaya puṇya*) for this act. In commemoration of this event, in some temples images of Ṛṣabhnāth are bathed in sugarcane juice. Due to uneasiness at the large number of insects attracted by and subsequently drowned in the sweet juice, in clear violation of the *mokṣa-mārg* ideological emphasis on *ahiṃsā*, in recent years this has been replaced by bathing the images in water to which a small amount of sugarcane juice has been added.

The main event on this day was the first feeding of people who, in imitation of Ṛṣabhnāth's fast, had undertaken the thirteen-and-one-half-month-long *varṣī tap* (one-year fast), described in chapter 5. The fasters are fed sugarcane juice by family members. People especially try to go to Palitana at the base of Mount Shatrunjay for this event, since it is sacred to Ṛṣabhnāth.[80] Sopher (1968:417) reports that some 12,000 people came to Palitana for Immortal Third in 1966. Those who cannot go all the way to Shatrunjay will often go to a nearby pilgrimage shrine to observe the first feeding with a *sādhu* who has also undertaken the *varṣī tap*. In 1986, many people from Patan went to Charup, where a well-known *sādhu* ended his *varṣī tap*. The *sādhus* were led around the village in a procession, complete with a band from Patan, and then the assembled *saṅgh* heard a sermon on the importance of the day,[81] before the two *sādhus* who had performed *varṣī tap* accepted sugarcane juice from some lay devotees.

Annual Temple Celebration

One other annual event is the *varṣgāṇṭh*, or annual celebration of the installation of the main image at each temple. The date for the installation of an image is set by the *saṅgh* in consultation with an astrologer, who determines a suitably auspicious date and time. Every year on this date the installation is celebrated again. This is one of the eleven annual duties discussed in the Paryuṣaṇ sermons. Following is a brief description of the *varṣgāṇṭh* at a neighborhood temple in Patan in June 1986.

In the morning there was a bathing *pūjā*, identical to that performed on the first day of every month. After the morning *pūjā* (and some people performed *pūjā* on this day who rarely performed it during the year), a Jain ritual specialist came to perform a more elaborate *pūjā* called a *sattarbhedī pūjā* (seventeen-fold *pūjā*) to a metal Jina image on a bathing stand in the temple pavilion.[82] This is a purification rite aimed at cleansing the temple of karmic impurities accumulated over the preceding year by the inevitable ritual faults (*āśātnā*) committed in the course of regular worship. This *pūjā* was timed so that the ninth offering, the offering of the flag, occurred at the auspicious time determined by the astrologer as suitable for laying a foundation stone and so also for renewing the temple. At the conclusion of the ninth offering, the couple who had earlier won the bid to perform the flagpole rite, both dressed in pure clothes, thrice circumambulated the metal image, with the wife carrying the new flag on a metal tray atop her head. Led by a man banging steadily on a metal gong to scare away potentially malevolent beings, the couple and the temple *pujārī* climbed onto the roof of the temple. There the man did a *pūjā* of water, sandalwood, and incense to the top of the small platform atop the flagpole, and together with the *pujārī* took down the old flag and raised the new flag. The old flag was carefully and respectfully disposed of later by the *pujārī*; this is often done in a well. After the couple thrice circumambulated the flag pole, everyone returned inside the temple where the *sattarbhedī pūjā* was resumed (see Figure 6.11).

At midday there was a feast for everyone in the *saṅgh* (most of whom had not attended the *pūjā*) and for all the non-Jain residents of the neighborhood, since they also are believed to benefit from the presence of the temple. In some downtown neighborhoods, from which most people have migrated to Bombay, many people return to Patan for the *varṣgāṇṭh* of the neighborhood temple. Most *varṣgāṇṭhs* occur during the particularly auspicious months of Vaiśākh and Jeṭh. Since this also happens to be the popular vacation time of May and June, many people combine their annual vacation to their native place with attending the *varṣgāṇṭh*.

Concluding Observations

Several points emerge from this lengthy description of the Jain religious year. The *parvs*, or days of heightened religious observance, are frequently days when for a limited time some laity approximate the daily behavior of the mendicants, and the mendicants themselves engage in added ritual behavior in accordance with the *mokṣa-mārg* ideology. The rituals of *pratikramaṇ* and *caitya-vandan* (of which *dev-vandan* is an expanded version) are part of the daily necessary (*āvaśyak*) routine of a mendicant; the vast majority of laity perform them only on *parvs*. Fasting and concern for dietary restrictions are major components of the mendicant's life; although almost all Jains observe certain dietary prohibitions, these prohibitions approach the strictness of the mendicant's diet only on *parv* days. The festivals of Immortal Third and Paryuṣaṇ involve public feeding and public meals, in both cases precisely to celebrate the successful completion of fasts. Fasting is not part of the common observance of Dīvāḷī; but then this festival, with its emphasis on the wellbeing values of wealth, increase, and auspiciousness, in many ways provides a counterpoint to the *mokṣa-mārg* emphasis on renunciation. The *parvs* are also days

Figure 6.11. Changing the flag at the annual celebration of a temple in Patan. June 1986.

of heightened lay-mendicant interaction. A few laity become temporary mendicants through the vow of *poṣadh*, or otherwise engage in mendicant-like behavior. Among the majority of Jains who do not imitate the mendicants, many are still likely to attend a sermon by a *sādhu*. Many laity never enter an *upāśray* or have other contact with a mendicant except on a *parv*.

At the same time, image worship, the defining ritual for Mūrtipūjak Jains, is not a prominent activity on all *parvs*. The only annual festival on which image worship is an essential part of the observance is the *varṣgāṇṭh* of a temple. Image worship performed on the occasion of other *parvs*, such as Immortal Third, Oḷī, or Paryuṣaṇ is not a necessary part of the observance according to the *mokṣa-mārg* ideological formulation, which would have all *parvs* be days of mendicant-imitating conduct by laity. However, although *pūjā* is not necessarily enjoined, many Jains who do not perform *pūjā* on a daily basis are more likely to do it on a *parv*. *Saṅghs* arrange for the main temple images to be specially ornamented on *parvs*, and many Jains who might not otherwise go to the temple will make a special trip for *darśan* on these days.

If we looked only at the *mokṣa-mārg* interpretations of the Jain religious year, there is much that we would miss. Mendicants observe most festivals and *parvs* by additional ascetic and venerational ritual actions. But the stories told to and the actions enjoined of the laity by the *mokṣa-mārg* ideologues in their sermons and writings are themselves multivalent, pointing toward both the *mokṣa-mārg* and wellbeing, and so are understood to be efficacious for both. It is the rare festival that does not include clear indications of wellbeing values. The enthusiasm with which Jains celebrate festivals such as Mahāvīr's birthday during Paryuṣaṇ and the days of Divāḷī is evidence that many Jains see the special days of the religious year as occasions to acquire, preserve, and maximize wellbeing. In this the observance of the festivals is of a piece with all the other ritual activities we have explored, in which symbols and statements of wellbeing are nearly omnipresent. In the concluding chapter, I turn to a more focused discussion of the religious value of wellbeing within the Mūrtipūjak Jain ritual culture.

7

Ideologies and Realms of Value

In the preceding chapters we have explored, as a thread running through Jain practice and discourse, the tension between the *mokṣa-mārg* ideology and the range of values that I have called "wellbeing." This latter realm involves a mix of health, contentment, peace, and prosperity, designated by a galaxy of overlapping concepts such as *śri*, *lakṣmī*, *lābh*, *fāydā*, *śreyas*, *hit*, *kalyāṇ*, *bhadra*, *śubh*, *puṇya*, *maṅgaḷ*, and *śānti*.[1] This realm is not unique to the Jain tradition; recent scholarship has highlighted the importance of similar values within the Hindu tradition.[2] The term "wellbeing" as I use it is obviously closely allied to the term "auspiciousness" as used in previous scholarship. I have chosen to use wellbeing rather than auspiciousness because it covers a wider range of concerns, and so more adequately denotes the particular realm of value within the Jain tradition. In addition, I feel that wellbeing is more a readily accessible term in English than is auspiciousness.

No religious tradition speaks with a single voice. One feature of an ideology is that it is presented as the single true representation of reality; in contrast, all other values are presented as, at best, less than adequate. Ideologues encourage both members of the religious tradition and the students of that tradition to focus on the ideology and not waste time with other values "mistakenly" expressed elsewhere in the tradition. But the student of a religion whose aim is to understand lived experience must be attentive to all voices within the tradition, not just those propounding a hegemonic ideology.

We have seen the manifold ways in which the *mokṣa-mārg* ideology and the value of wellbeing interact within the Śvetāmbar Mūrtipūjak Jain tradition in contemporary north Gujarat. The *mokṣa-mārg* ideology as explicitly spelled out some two thousand years ago in *Tattvārtha Sūtra* chapter 1 and *Uttarādhyayana Sūtra* chapter 28 has remained remarkably consistent throughout subsequent Jain history. (Since ideologies present themselves as timeless and unchanging, further research on Jain intellectual history is needed to determine whether this perception of ideological univocality is accurate, or is merely a projected self-identity of the ideology itself.) Its power and influence in large part derive from the clear and conscious ideological expression it has found in these two texts, in dozens of subsequent texts, and in sermons delivered by thousands of ideologues over the centuries. But as with any ideology, it is not expressed and understood solely in explicit formulations; it, too, draws upon the rich multivalent and multileveled meanings of symbols. Core concepts such as *jñān*, *darśan*, *cāritra*, and *tap* are investigated and spelled out in great detail by the *mokṣa-mārg* ideologues; but they are also symbols, and thereby stand for and point to meanings and significances outside of and beyond themselves.

The value of wellbeing is not an explicit ideology as is the *mokṣa-mārg*. Much of the *mokṣa-mārg* ideology is readily accessible and even obvious to the Jains, for a defining feature of an ideology is precisely that it is consciously and publicly enunciated. Wellbeing, however, is not consciously and publicly enunciated on a regular basis, and the tendency of *mokṣa-mārg* ideologues to denigrate wellbeing means that when it is discussed it is often in order either to dismiss it or to relegate it to a marginal, unimportant position. Because the value of wellbeing is not systematically expressed, the student must investigate the various elements constituting this value that are implicitly expressed within the tradition, and then extract these elements for scholarly analysis.

In the above chapters, I have intentionally avoided giving a precise definition of wellbeing in order to allow the reader to perceive some of its components and ramifications without being burdened by a prematurely presented level of abstraction. Because it is an implicitly expressed value, not an explicitly expressed ideology, there is a significant extent to which it is intractable to precise definition. Nonetheless, we can identify a galaxy of related concepts such as those listed in the beginning of this chapter, which together can be used to demarcate the rough boundaries of wellbeing. These concepts frequently overlap in Jain usage, and I found that attempts to get Jains to elucidate precise distinctions between any two closely related concepts rarely if ever resulted in clarity, and any clarity that did emerge was usually of an ad hoc and ex post facto nature. The similarities among the different concepts that together point to the value of wellbeing can be characterized in terms of what Ludwig Wittgenstein has called "family resemblances," in which there is "a complicated network of similarities overlapping and criss-crossing: sometimes overall similarities, sometimes similarities of detail. . . . I can think of no better expression to characterize these similarities than 'family resemblances'; for the various resemblances between members of a family: build, features, colour of eyes, gait, temperament, etc. etc. overlap and criss-cross in the same way" (Wittgenstein 1958:32e). At the same time, we must be careful not to overemphasize similarities at the expense of differences and thereby elide the concepts into one another as synonyms. David Tracy (1987:94–95) has rightly remarked that families are marked by differences as well as by similarities, and these differences are by no means insignificant.

It would be a grave interpretive error to essentialize the concepts discussed below into a single transcendent value termed "wellbeing." The concepts I discuss under the general rubric of wellbeing may profitably be viewed as an example of what Rodney Needham, borrowing from the natural sciences, has called a "polythetic" grouping, which "places together organisms that have the greatest number of shared features, and no single feature is either essential to group membership or is sufficient to make an organism a member of the group" (Needham 1975:356, quoting Sokal and Sneath 1963:14).

I should emphasize again that I use the English word "wellbeing," for which there is no single Indian gloss, precisely because there is no single indigenous term to cover this family of concepts, and this multivocality is important to keep in focus. (The same is true of "Jainism" as well; this English term has a different semantic field than any indigenous terms such as Jain dharma or Jain *saṃskṛti.*)[3] As Needham (362) points out, a polythetic grouping—or a grouping sharing family resemblances—is not amenable to a single definition due to the imprecision that results when there is neither a shared core nor a shared boundary among the features under consideration.

If there were a single Indic term, wellbeing would not be only a symbolically expressed value. It would be a consciously expressed ideology like the *mokṣa-mārg*. The following catalogue is not intended to be comprehensive, but it should be adequate to give a sharper focus to the contours of wellbeing that we have already encountered throughout the book.

A Family of Wellbeing Values

Śrī or Lakṣmī is the goddess of wealth and prosperity (see Figure 7.1). She is the fourth of the fourteen dreams seen by the mother of a Jina upon his conception, the

Figure 7.1. Image of Lakṣmī being annointed by two elephants, atop gateway to Jain temple in Patan. October 1995.

celebration of which was a high point of Paryuṣaṇ. The rights to perform the various actions in worship of the silver replica of this dream received among the highest bids; with the exception of the lotus lake, which seems to have a local importance in Patan, the bids for Lakṣmī were many times larger than those for any other dream. In Patan in 1985 they totaled Rs. 7,304, whereas the next largest total, for the thirteenth dream, a heap of jewels, was only Rs. 1,604 (Cort 1989:510). Similarly, these bids were more than seven times the amount of the next highest sum (for the fourteenth and final dream, a flame) in the nearby town of Sami (Folkert 1993:209), and almost eight times that of the next highest bid (for the lotus lake) in the village of Ved (Zwicker 9/16/85.5). Manuscript illustrations of the dreams in copies of the *Kalpa Sūtra* feature Lakṣmī prominently in the middle of the painting, with the other dreams ranged around the goddess in much smaller size.[4] In these illustrations she is portrayed as Gajalakṣmī, Lakṣmī anointed with life-giving waters by two auspicious elephants.

We also saw the importance of Lakṣmī in the Jain observance of Dīvāḷī. She was worshiped as wealth itself embodied in the form of five silver coins, and the head of the family wrote a triangular diagram made up of the word *śrī* in the new account book. Later he read aloud the eight names of Lakṣmī. These eight names indicate that the goddess transcends any narrow categorization as wealth alone, and extends into a broader context of success in all endeavors. She is the primal force (*ādya*), wisdom (*vidyā*), immortality (*amṛta*), and truth (*satya*); at the same time she is worldly good fortune (*saubhāgya*, often associated specifically with a woman's good fortune to have her husband alive) and physical desire (*kāma*). Her last two names provide a mediation between two values seen as contradictory in South Asian culture, *bhoga* and *yoga* or enjoyment and asceticism. This broad range of understanding of the sphere of Lakṣmī, as not just wealth but as any form of success, is also seen in Mānatuṅga's medieval *Bhaktāmara Stotra*, one of the "Nine Remembrances" and a text memorized by many Jains, both mendicants and laity, in which the poet culminates this most popular of Jain hymns by asserting that devotion to the Jina results in the attainment of Lakṣmī:

> O Jina King,
> Lakṣmī comes quickly
> to this proud man
> who forever wears around his neck
> your garland of praise,
> woven from the qualities
> of my devotion
> and adorned by multihued flowers
> of radiant color.[5]

In his commentary, the fourteenth-century Guṇākara gives six readings of this verse, with different meanings of Lakṣmī as the goddess Śrī who resides in the royal heaven, splendor, the wife of Kṛṣṇa, the wealth of the whole universe, the flower-bearing goddess, and a woman as beautiful as the goddess.[6] Similarly, the Sthānakvāsī editors of a contemporary edition gloss Lakṣmī here as four kinds of successful attainment: royalty, heaven, liberation, and fine poetry.[7]

The word *śrī* is contained in the ritual term for a coconut, *śrīphal*, "the fruit of Śrī." The everyday word for coconut is *nāriyeḷ*; *śrīphal* is restricted to religious contexts. The *śrīphal* is a pan-Indian symbol of fertility and success, which is why, as mentioned in chapter 3, at Shankheshvar they should be offered only to the goddess Padmāvatī and not to the Jina. *Śrīphals* are much in evidence in the celebration of Mahāvīr's birth during Paryuṣaṇ. They are also essential in the ritual known as *Śānti Kalaś*, "The Full Pot of Peace," which will be discussed below.

Related to Lakṣmī are several terms that one often hears in terms of gain, benefit, profit, or advantage, in particular *lābh* and *fāydā*. The latter word, of Arabic origin, tends to be used in more strictly secular settings, in the sense of "what is the advantage of following a particular course of action?" *Lābh* has connotations of both profit in the world, as when used to designate profit in a business deal, or in the context of Lābh Pañcamī, the fifth day of the new year when businesses open; and also profit in the religious sphere, as when a mendicant, in return for being given food, blesses the householder by saying, "dharm lābh," "[may you have] the profit of religion." *Lābh* is a synonym for *phal*, "fruit," in the sense of the fruit of any action. These terms tie wellbeing into an everyday understanding of karma: the fruit of an action is directly related to the purity of the actor's intentions, words, and deeds, and so *lābh* is an expression of good karma.

Also closely related to these notions of gain are *śreyas* and *hit*, which are often given as synonyms of *lābh* and *fāydā* in dictionaries. But these two tend to indicate a sense of more generalized welfare than do *lābh* and *fāydā*, without quite the same connotations of numerically measured gain. *Śreyas* in particular usually refers to one's spiritual welfare, not one's financial welfare. In many manuscript colophons, image inscriptions, and inscriptions for the construction of religious buildings, in addition to the name of the donor one finds the name of a departed ancestor for whose *śreyas* the manuscript was commissioned, the image installed, or the building constructed. Thus, the inscription on a metal image of the Jina Śreyāṅsnāth presently in a temple in Tharad north of Patan informs us that the image was consecrated in Patan by a layman named Gaṇiyāka in 1468 "for the welfare of his mother and father" (Yatīndrasūri 1983:108). Many recent images in Patan record that the image was consecrated for the welfare of the soul (*ātmaśreyas*) of a departed ancestor, with the occasional variant forms that the installation was for the merit (*puṇyaśreyas*) or gain (*lābhaśreyas*) of the departed ancestor. This is not a recent phenomenon, as the formula is found in inscriptions and colophons from throughout the past millennium. *Hit* is also found in early image inscriptions from Mathura, not in terms of the karmic welfare of a specific person but rather the general wellbeing of the entire universe.[8]

These terms slide into *kalyāṇ* and *bhadra*. The latter term is found less often in Jain contexts than in Hindu contexts (such as the goddesses Bhadrakālī and Subhadrā), but does occur frequently in mendicants' names, of which several examples are found in the bibliography. We encountered *bhadra* in the context of the funeral of a mendicant, where it is coupled with *nandā* (joy) in the celebratory shouts of the laity in the procession to the cremation site. Similarly, *bhadra* is found in the names of the three longest fasts undertaken by Mahāvīr during his ascetic career (chapter 5). A modern Prakrit dictionary gives *maṅgaḷ* and *kalyāṇ* as synonymns for *bhadra*, and cites the *Samyaktvasaptatikā* (167) of Haribhadra that the preaching of the Jina, which is devoid of wrong faith and is like the nectar of immortality, is *bhadra* (Śeṭh 1963: 643–44).

Kalyāṇ was discussed in chapter 6 in the context of the five *kalyāṇaks* of each Jina, the five events that generate *kalyāṇ* or welfare for the entire Jain universe, and the discussion of these events in the *Kalpa Sūtra* is replete with references to *kalyāṇ*. Although *kalyāṇ* is usually understood as a condition of existence made possible by prior holy actions, its occasional equation with *kṛpā*, the grace of the Jina or guru, indicates that it can also be understood as having an active aspect. The first of these *kalyāṇaks*, the conception of the Jina, is accompanied by his mother's vision of fourteen dreams, which are described in the *Kalpa Sūtra* (4) as "illustrious, producing welfare, auspicious, rich, holy, and full of bounty."[9] This list is a veritable catalogue of wellbeing values. Elsewhere (*Kalpa Sūtra* 51) the Jina's future mother describes the dreams as indicating that she had gained some special welfare-generating karmic fruit. Her husband, upon hearing of the dreams, replies that they obviously are indicators that she has received auspiciousness, wealth, holiness, bounty, health, satisfaction, long life, welfare, and sacredness—another catalogue of wellbeing.[10] Although the conception of the Jina is essential for the establishment of the *mokṣa-mārg*, clearly it is an event that is not without its wellbeing aspects. The following *Kalpa Sūtra* narrative recounts that the Jina's conception resulted in a great increase in the worldly wellbeing of his family, which is why his parents named him Vardhamāna, "The Increaser":

> Since the night Śramaṇa Bhagavān Mahāvīra was brought to the clan of the Jñātṛs, the clan began to increase in manifold ways: its gold increased, its gold-ornaments increased, its wealth, agriculture, kingdom, imperial power along with its armies, carriages, treasuries, ware-houses, towns, women's apartments and its subjects—all increased bountifully. The Jñātṛs increasingly multiplied in wealth, gold, gems, precious stones, pearls, mother-of-pearls, coral and rubies—they multiplied in every valuable that they possessed. Their happiness and their honour grew increasingly.
>
> Then the parents of the Śramaṇa Bhagavān Mahāvīra reflected, and formed this resolution: "Ever since this child, our son, has entered the womb, we and ours have increased in every way. Therefore, when our son will see the light of the day, we shall name him Vardhamāna (the Increasing One), a noble name and a name befitting his supreme merits."[11]

It is no wonder that the observance of the *kalyāṇak* of the birth of this riches-generating Lord is celebrated so joyously, when this and similar passages are read during Paryuṣaṇ.

Śubh and its opposite *aśubh* in their most general senses mean simply "good" and "bad." But they are also semantically loaded terms in the Jain and Hindu traditions. In both traditions, *śubh* has a general meaning of "auspicious," and its usage by Jains in this sense differs little if at all from its usage by Hindus as discussed by T. N. Madan (1987:48–71). In this sense one also finds words such as *kuśal* and *bhāgya* (especially *saubhāgya*). But *śubh* also has a more technical meaning within the Jain *mokṣa-mārg*, as something that is good but that nonetheless binds one to the world of rebirth. In particular, it here refers to beneficial karma, which, while desirable in the wellbeing context, is detrimental in the *mokṣa-mārg* context, and hence is ultimately to be renounced. I quoted in chapter 3 the statements of two contemporary mendicants that on the *mokṣa-mārg* one must go from what is *aśubh* to what is *śubh*, and then from what is *śubh* to what is *śuddh*. Here *śuddh* is defined not in Brāhmaṇical terms as a state of ontological purity required to perform many rituals, but in *mokṣa-mārg* terms as freedom from the bondage of karma. In this sense, *śubh* and *aśubh* are synonyms for *puṇya* and *pāp*. This equation is made by Umāsvātī in the *Tattvārtha Sūtra* (6.3–4), where he explains that conjunction of the soul with *śubha* karma is the influx of *puṇya*, and conjunction with *aśubha* karma is the influx of *pāpa*.

Jean Filliozat (1991:239) has noted that *puṇya* usually has connotations of wellbeing that has been earned by the recipient: "*puṇya* is above all 'wellbeing' but it is linked to the merit of works." He elucidates on this comment as follows: "if one felicitates someone for some gain or good fortune that has come his way, one would tell him admiringly: 'What *puṇya* you must have!' and it means literally 'what good fortune!' or 'What good luck!'. But it signifies more deeply that this good fortune or luck are not fortuitous but are held to be the fruit of good acts that have been performed."

The ontological status of *puṇya* and *pāp* would appear to have been the subject of some disagreement in the early Jain tradition, as there was no ideological consensus on the role or even utility of conduct (*cāritra*) (or of asceticism, *tapas*) in attaining liberation. According to Umāsvātī in his *Tattvārtha Sūtra* (1.4), there are seven *tattvas* or universal "reals": sentient soul, insentient matter, karmic influx, bondage, stopping karmic influx, wearing away of accumulated karma, and liberation. In this list, *puṇya* and *pāpa* are understood to be included under bondage, for they are both forms of karma, and karma itself is bondage.[12] Other Śvetāmbar ontologies, however, such as those found in *Sthānāṅga* 9, *Uttarādhyayana Sūtra* 28.14, and *Navatattva Prakaraṇa*, elucidate *puṇya* and *pāpa* as separate *tattvas*,[13] and therefore of independent significance.[14] I have been unable to discover any discussion within the Jain tradition on this difference between seven and nine *tattvas*, but I suspect that the separate lists of seven and nine were the result of differing views on the positive or negative valuation of *puṇya*, and on the relative importance of moral action within the realm of bondage.[15] If *puṇya* and *pāp* are considered only within the framework of karmic bondage, then they are viewed in a wholly negative light. If they are considered as universal principles independent of their classification under bondage, then action that is karmically binding yet morally valuable is not viewed so negatively. In other words, an ontology of just seven *tattvas* accords value only to the *mokṣa-mārg* goal of liberation from the world by eliminating all karmic bondage, whereas an ontology of nine *tattvas* allows room for a positive valuation of action within the world by distinguishing among forms of karmic bondage, and therefore accords some importance to wellbeing.

Śubh is often considered to be roughly synonymous with *maṅgaḷ* in its meaning as auspicious. Scholarship on auspiciousness in the Hindu context has not indicated any significant difference in usage between the two, and many Jains whom I asked also were unable to say how they differed.[16] An analysis of the language of printed invitations to a range of Jain rituals reveals that *maṅgaḷ* tends to have a more generalized usage referring to the event as a whole ("on this *maṅgaḷ* occasion"), although one will also find *śubh* and *pāvan* (pure) used less frequently for this, whereas *śubh* tends to be used in the more specific contexts of time, place, and actor ("at the *śubh* time of . . . at the *śubh* place of . . ."). But the distinction between the two is not firm.

Maṅgaḷ also has a special usage within the Jain tradition, as a multivalent term that at times has different meanings according to the *mokṣa-mārg* ideology and wellbeing. We can see this in three doctrinal statements of cardinal importance for Jains. The first verse of the *Daśavaikālika Sūtra*, the most important text of mendicant praxis, reads as follows:

> Dharma is the highest *maṅgala*;
> it consists of nonviolence, equanimity, and asceticism.
> Even the gods worship him
> whose mind is always on dharma.

The second text is the *Nokār Mantra*, which we have already encountered in chapter 3.[17] This is the best known of all Jain sacred utterances and is recited daily by millions of Jains. In it the Jain praises the fivefold spiritual hierarchy of the Jinas, all other liberated souls, *ācāryas*, *upādhyāyas*, and all other mendicants in the world and then concludes the mantra by stating, "This fivefold praise destroys all bad karma [*pāp*], and of all holies [*maṅgalas*] it is the foremost holy [*maṅgala*]."

The third is a verse frequently recited as the final *māṅgalik* at the end of a sermon, and also found as the last verse of two important liturgical texts that will be discussed below, *Bṛhacchānti* or "Big Peace" and *Laghu Śānti* or "Little Peace":

> The *maṅgal*-ness of all *maṅgals*, the cause of all goodness,
> the foremost of all religions, victory to the Jain teachings.

All three of these texts make argumentative assertions concerning *maṅgaḷ*. They speak of one *maṅgaḷ*—dharma, the *Nokār Mantra*, the Jain teachings—among many, indicating that there are multiple *maṅgaḷs*, or at least multiple perspectives as to what is *maṅgaḷ*. These contested understandings of *maṅgaḷ* were also seen in chapter 6 in the contexts of the sermon delivered by the *sādhu* on the occasion of the celebration of Mahāvīr's birth during Paryuṣaṇ, and especially the recitation of the *māṅgaḷik* on New Year's morning.

Similarly, we find an ancient verse in the *Āvaśyaka Sūtra* (12), a verse usually recited as part of the *māṅgaḷik* or blessings at the beginning and end of a sermon, which states that there are four *maṅgaḷs*:

> Four *maṅgalas*: the *Arhats* are *maṅgala*, the *Siddhas* are *maṅgala*, the *sādhus* are *maṅgala*, and the dharma taught by the enlightened ones is *maṅgala*.

The meaning of *maṅgaḷ* here is amplified in the next two verses, also recited as part of *māṅgaḷik*, in which the same four are described as being the best things in the world to which one should go for refuge, that is, as the only basis for a religious life:

> Four supreme things in the world: the *Arhats* are supreme in the world, the *Siddhas* are supreme in the world, the *sādhus* are supreme in the world, and the dharma taught by the enlightened ones is supreme in the world.
>
> I go to the four for refuge: I go to the *Arhats* for refuge, I go to the *Siddhas* for

> refuge, I go to the *sādhus* for refuge, and I go to the dharma taught by the enlightened ones for refuge.[18]

We see here the ideological assertion that true *maṅgaḷ*, the *maṅgaḷ* which is supreme in the world and which leads to liberation, consists of the tripartite hierarchy of the enlightened souls who taught the *mokṣa-mārg*, the liberated souls who have traveled it, and the unenlightened mendicants who are now traveling it, as well as the teachings of the path itself. Haribhadra, in his commentary on the *Āvaśyaka Sūtra*, gives a lengthy analysis of *maṅgaḷ*, in which he employs false etymologies to indicate that *maṅgaḷ* is the perfection of welfare, the cause of following the teachings, and that which is liberated from rebirth.[19]

Another verse recited as *māṅgaḷik* reinforces this understanding of *maṅgaḷ*, here by asserting that the Jain tradition taught by Mahāvīr and continuing after him with his chief disciple Gautam Svāmī and the important mendicant leader Sthūlabhadra (claimed by the Śvetāmbars to have been the last person who knew by heart all the oral teachings of Mahāvīr), as well as the teachings themselves, are all *maṅgaḷ*:

> *Maṅgala* is God Mahāvīra, *maṅgala* is Lord Gautama,
> *maṅgala* is Sthūlabhadra and the others [mendicants], *maṅgala* is the Jain tradition.

These are not the only things in the Jain tradition that are *maṅgaḷ*. An ancient set of eight symbols depicted frequently in Jain art are known collectively as the *aṣṭamaṅgala* (U.P. Shah 1955b:109–12, Wayman 1989). These are as follows: 1. the *svastika* or "good thing"; 2. the *śrīvatsa* or "favorite of Śrī," a diamond-shaped lozenge found from early medieval times onward on the chest of Jina images; 3. the *nandyāvarta* or "auspicious turning," an extended *svastika*; 4. the *varddhamānaka* or "increaser," a powder flask; 5. the *bhadrāsana* or "auspicious seat," a throne; 6. the *kalaśa*, a full pot; 7. the *darpaṇa* or mirror; and 8. the *matsya-yugma* or pair of fish (see Figures 7.2, 7.3). These symbols of increase and fertility are ubiquitous in the Jain tradition. They are embroidered on the cloths that are wrapped around the handles of mendicant brooms (Pal 1994:125) and on manuscript covers (Pal 1994:218). They are carved on temple doors and above temple doorways, and painted at the beginning of manuscripts. One of the rituals in the consecration of a new temple, the *Aṣṭamaṅgaḷpūjā*, invokes their presence. This ritual begins with a Sanskrit verse outlining another range of what is holy within Jainism:

> The blessed Jinas are *maṅgala*, the Jain teaching is *maṅgala*.
> The entire congregation is *maṅgala*, this worshiper is *maṅgala*.[20]

Laity who are skilled at drawing will draw the eight maṅgaḷs with rice grains as part of their temple worship; others merely draw a *svastika* in rice on a small table with the eight *maṅgaḷs* embossed in silver on the top. In art, the eight *maṅgaḷs* are frequently linked with the fourteen dreams seen by the mother of a Jina upon his conception, since both sets indicate an abundance of wellbeing.

We see here a range of meanings of *maṅgaḷ* encompassing both the *mokṣa-mārg* ideology and the wellbeing value, both liberation from rebirth and birth-giving fertility. I have translated *maṅgaḷ* as "holy" in this book precisely to indicate its multivalency, which would have been obscured by the more standard translation

Figure 7.2. Eight *maṅgaḷs*, from nineteenth-century painting in collection of the Hemacandra Jñān Mandir, Patan, March 1987.

of "auspiciousness." Holy and holiness, of course, have a long history in Western scholarship on religion, and the sacred or the holy has become what John Carman (1985:117) has termed a "super-category" in the study of religion.[21] It has been a central category in the study of religion since Rudolf Otto's *The Idea of the Holy* (1917).[22] Otto emphasized the wholly otherness or transcendence of holiness, speaking of it as a *mysterium tremendum*, something that inspired awe or religious dread, and therefore absolutely unapproachable. He spoke of the might, power, and majesty of the holy. He also described it as fascinating and wonderful, and therefore associated with love, mercy, pity, and comfort. *Maṅgaḷ* differs, though, from holiness as defined by Otto in one significant way. Holiness for Otto involves an ambiguity and tension between wholly positive and wholly negative or fearful aspects; *maṅgal*, on the other hand, for the Jains involves only an unambiguously positive attitude and valuation. Even the *mokṣa-mārg* ideologues who criticize the wellbeing understanding of *maṅgal* are not afraid of it in Otto's sense of something that is powerfully dreadful, but rather as a beguilingly desirable entrapment. Holy is an attractive translation of *maṅgal* precisely because both of them are "value-plus" terms, meaning that they refer to a range of values greater than themselves.

Otto's conclusions were repeated and expanded upon in *The Sacred and the Profane* by Mircea Eliade (1959), who was interested in the process by which the holy or the sacred simultaneously reveals and conceals itself.[23] These tensions found in holiness, between revelation and concealment, between immanence and transcendence, and between involvement in the world and removal from the world, are found also in the Jain usage of *maṅgal*.[24] On the one hand, *maṅgal* denotes holiness in the world, a physical and spiritual state of wellbeing and satisfaction in which the person is in harmony with the rhythms of society and the cosmos. On the other, *maṅgal* is a matter of striving for a moral purity that is removed from the affairs and the staining passions of this world, and in which one strives to reach a condition of absolute ontological stability and rest that cannot be swayed by the transient rhythms of society and the universe.

A final concept that exhibits a similar multivalency as *maṅgal* in its ability to refer to both the *mokṣa-mārg* and wellbeing is *śānti*, "peace." Just as *ahiṃsā* has a different range of applications among Jains than does nonviolence in contemporary

Figure 7.3. Images of eight *maṅgaḷs* on gateway to Jain temple at Shatrunjay. October 1986.

Euro-American society, so for the Jains, and in general in India, *śānti* does not have the socio-political connotations that "peace" has had in this century in the West. "Peace" in Euro-American culture has referred to the absence of war and to social efforts to eliminate warfare, as in the American designation of the Brethren, Mennonites, and Quakers as "historic peace churches" whose members have been exempt from armed military service. It overlaps in significant ways with the concept of "justice."

In India, *śānti* refers on the one hand to inner spiritual and emotional quietude, and on the other to social harmony. This is quite clearly seen in the following range of translations for both *śānti* and the related adjective *śānt* (Deśpāṇḍe 1974:839–40): "*śānt* . . . peaceful, quiet, calm; . . . *śānti* . . . peace, stillness, quietude; silence; absence of clash, quarrel or war; recovery from mental or physical ailment; patience; retirement; satisfaction (of hunger, etc.); rest." *Śānti* in Jainism refers on the one hand to the pacification of karma-generating activity, and therefore advancement along the *mokṣa-mārg*. As defined by two *mokṣa-mārg* ideologues, *śānti* is "victory over lust, hatred, and other passions, a state devoid of sensory fluctuation that precludes all troubles."[25] *Śānti* also refers to a state of calm, control, and equilibrium, a state highly desired by the Jain businessman as necessary to maneuver successfully and profitably among the obstructions in life. For the layperson, *śānti* refers to the sense of inner peace and quietude one gets from performing a fast, from the attention of one's mendicant guru, or from taking *darśan* of an image in a temple.

One comes across *śānti* frequently in the Jain tradition. One of the most popular Jinas is the sixteenth, Śāntināth. Roughly 20% of the Jain temples in Patan have Śāntināth as the main image, a total exceeded only by Pārśvanāth and Ādīnāth.[26] The popularity of Śāntināth is directly due to his name, as he is invoked to spread *śānti* in the world. Thus the fifteenth-century poet Munisundarasūri in his Prakrit *Santikara* sings,

> The person of right faith who thrice daily
> remembers Śāntinātha for protection
> will become devoid of all troubles
> and obtain the supreme state of happiness.[27]

In most temples there is an image of the goddess Śāntidevī, usually located in the base of the altar directly beneath the main image. She is responsible for maintaining the peace and safety of the temple. She shares this role with the local male protector deity (*khetarpāl*); but whereas the latter is rarely found in the main shrine, Śāntidevī's central location indicates her priority over the *khetarpāl*.[28]

Several Prakrit and Sanskrit hymns, including three of the widely recited collection known as the *Navasmaraṇa* or "Nine Remembrances," are addressed to Śāntināth because of the power of his name to bring about both social and personal peace.[29] The hymns frequently assert that invoking Śanti eliminates *upadrava*, a word for troubles in general.

The *Santikara* or "Peace Maker" was composed in the fifteenth century by Munisundarasūri, then head of the Tapā Gacch.[30] According to Jain history, the Jain congregation of Delvada on Mount Abu was afflicted by a plague created by malevolent goddesses. Munisundarasūri composed this fourteen-verse Prakrit hymn to eliminate the disease. It is still recited for relief from such worldly problems, as clearly stated by a contemporary mendicant: "This hymn if sung with pure intention (*bhāv*) and pure body can destroy illness, suffering, and fear, and allow one to attain one's desires."[31] Munisundarasūri in the hymn says that Śāntināth provides peace for his devotees, and specifies that this peace consists of protection from all sorts of troubles. Munisundarasūri requests that other deities also protect him, but does not restrict the protective power to them:

> May Śānti Jinacandra, together with the host of deities who have right faith,
> protect the *saṅgha* and me by the glory of this hymn by Munisundarasūri.[32]

The *Śāntistava* of Mānadevasūri was composed under similar circumstances. Although this hymn is technically not one of the *Navasmaraṇa* texts, it is closely associated with them, and is recited in *pratikramaṇ*, as are *Santikara* and *Bṛhacchānti*. According to Jain history, Mānadevasūri was head of the undivided Śvetāmbar community in the third century C.E. When he was at Nandol in Rajasthan, he was visited by representatives of the Jain congregation of Takshashila. The people there were suffering from an epidemic, and had been informed by a Jain goddess that only Mānadevasūri could help them. He thereupon composed the Sanskrit *Śāntistava*, and told the Jains from Takshashila that those who recited the hymn and sprinkled around the perimeter of their houses water over which the hymn had been recited would be saved from the epidemic. Mānadevasūri calls upon Śāntināth, and indicates that Śāntināth can protect his devotees from a wide array of problems:

> Hail hail to God Śānti, worshiped by the triple world,
> praiseworthy, possessed of great affluence and all superhuman qualities.
>
> He destroys the mass of all troubles, pacifies all problems,
> destroys bad planets, ghosts, goblins and witches.[33]

The Sanskrit *Bṛhacchānti* (or *Moṭī Śānti*, "Big Peace," in contrast to which Mānadevasūri's hymn is generally known as *Laghu Śānti* or "Little Peace") is attributed to the eleventh-century mendicant Vādivetāla Śāntisūri, who also authored a commentary on the canonical *Uttarādhyayana Sūtra*, and the *Jīvavicāra*, an important *mokṣa-mārg* textbook on Jain biology (see chapter 1). This hymn also invokes peace in the world, starting out with the following statement of intention:

> May those who are full of devotion to the career of the *Jinas*,
> the gurus of the triple world,
> have that peace which by the glory of the Jinas
> is the source of health, wealth, joy, and wisdom,
> and is the end of all affliction.[34]

The poet invokes the twenty-four Jinas, the sixteen Tantric goddesses of magical wisdom (*vidyādevī*; see Cort 1987:237–40), the nine planets (*graha*, who exercise considerable influence over the karmic efficacy of time), and the eight earth guardians (*lokapāla*, who exercise considerable influence over the karmic efficacy of space) to protect the congregation. He then invokes Śāntināth, asking for peace in the homes of all his devotees, and asserts that the mere recitation of Śāntināth's name negates all sorts of bad omens and grants the successful completion of tasks.

The poet invokes the peace of Śāntināth and the Jain religion upon the entire universe:

> May there be peace in the blessed congregation.
> May there be peace in the blessed land.
> May there be peace for the blessed king.
> May there be peace in the blessed royal encampment.
> May there be peace in the blessed assembly.
> May there be peace for the city's blessed leading citizens.
> May there be peace for the blessed townsfolk.
> May there be peace in blessed heaven.

He attributes this peaceful condition to the worship of the Jina:

> Troubles are destroyed and series of hindrances are cut off;
> the mind is at peace from worshiping the Lord Jina.

The poem ends with the *māṅgaḷik* verse discussed above which asserts that the Jain religion is the holiness of all holy things, the cause of all goodness, and the best of all religions.

The authors of these hymns were all either important ideologues or leaders of the Jain community, which reminds us that the interplay of *mokṣa-mārg* ideology and the value of wellbeing is often found within a single person's experience. Mānadevasūri was leader of the undivided Śvetāmbar community, and Munisundarasūri was leader of the Tapā Gacch. Śāntisūri also wrote a *mokṣa-mārg* textbook and a commentary on a central canonical text. Munisundarasūri was the author of the *Traividyagoṣṭhi*, a text on logic that taught Jains how to engage in formal debate with Brāhmaṇs.

These hymns are recited in a wide variety of contexts: by mendicants as part of the regular *pratikramaṇ* and as part of the New Year's *māṅgaḷik*, and by laity as part of their daily devotions. They are also recited in the context of several popular congregational rituals. The *Śānti Snātra* or "Peace Ablution," which includes portions of the texts of *Bṛhacchānti*, *Laghu Śānti*, and *Santikara*,[35] is performed, according to the first verse of the liturgy itself, "on the occasion of an image consecration, a pilgrimage, an eight-day festival, or other observance, for the sake of pacifying nagging troubles."[36] It is most frequently performed at the conclusion of a major observance to ensure that there are no lingering troublesome consequences of the faults inevitably committed during the ritual performances. The *Śānti Snātra* is also performed by some Jains on the anniversary of a death for the welfare of the soul of the departed, so that the soul in its new embodiment can find added peace through the removal of karmic troubles.

The *Śānti Kalaś* or "Full Pot of Peace" is performed at the end of some congregational rituals for the wellbeing of the worshipers, in particular for the fertility of the couple who perform it, as is obvious from the symbolism of the ritual elements. A metal pot is placed on the linked hands of a married couple. Other worshipers pour the water from a bathing *pūjā* of a Jina image into the pot in an unbroken stream while one or more worshipers recite *Bṛhacchānti*. When the pot overflows, it is covered with auspicious green leaves and the opening closed with a coconut (*śrīphal*). These are wrapped in bright green cloth, which is secured around the neck of the pot by auspicious red thread. The pot is garlanded with auspicious marigold flowers, and the woman places it atop her head. She leads a small procession (in some cases with her sari tied to her husband's lower wrap, in clear imitation of the marriage rite) in three circumambulations of the Jina image on its bathing stand in the middle of the temple pavilion. Sometimes the pot is left in the temple, but usually the couple takes it home and establishes it on their home altar for the night before discarding the water in a well or other pure location.

One evening early in my stay in Patan, a Jain man from Maharashtra was taking *darśan* at several of the downtown temples, going quickly from one to another for as many holy viewings as possible. We met in the temple of Pañcāsar Pārśvanāth. As he was talking to me of the beauty of the old images in the temple, and the carvings on the recently renovated temple walls, he suddenly stopped. He opened his arms wide, gestured to the temple surrounding us, and exclaimed, "*Śānti śānti śānti*. The hubbub of the world is not *śānti*. *This* is *śānti*."

He was expressing an attitude in which the cares and concerns of the world are left outside the temple, and the worshiper can focus his mind solely upon the Jina in a proper spirit of devotion. The peace that the worshiper gains is, of course, multivalent. It is a salvific peace that is totally other than the daily life of business and family. It is also a peace that one can take back to that daily life. Peace refers both to the subduing of passions that lead one astray on the path to liberation, and the subduing of obstacles on the path of worldly success.

Ideology and Value, Liberation, and Wellbeing

The *mokṣa-mārg* ideology and the value of wellbeing are held in an unresolved tension because of the multivocality of the symbols by which the two are expressed. According to the *mokṣa-mārg* ideology, an individual has to make a choice between wellbeing and the *mokṣa-mārg*. In practice, the two are held in tension, and people act and live on the assumption that one can have it both ways: following practices of the *mokṣa-mārg* brings wellbeing, and pursuit of wellbeing (within certain boundaries) advances one at least a small way along the *mokṣa-mārg*.

These two realms are not equal within the Jain tradition; the tension between the two is imbalanced. This is not to affirm the assertions of the *mokṣa-mārg* ideologues that the *mokṣa-mārg* is "true Jainism," and wellbeing marginal or wrong. The imbalance is a matter of how they are articulated, and therefore how they are perceived. As we have seen, the *mokṣa-mārg* exhibits all the characteristics of systematic expression one would expect of an ideology, whereas wellbeing is expressed in unsystematic ways through actions and symbols. The ideologues of any ideology will strive to have it occupy a privileged position within the tradition's discourse, and in this the *mokṣa-mārg* ideologues have been highly successful, especially in the context of the reform movements of the past hundred years. Thus the *mokṣa-mārg* might appear at first impression to constitute the core or essence of Jainism. But we have seen that this claim can be maintained only by ignoring or denigrating much that is vital to the lived experience of Jains.[37]

Ideologues claim for their ideology a monopoly on the truth, saying that only it accurately explains the world and how one should live. An ideology, in other words, is an attempt to bring order to life. The *mokṣa-mārg* ideology, with its vast cosmographical and soteriological schemes and its ready answer of how a true Jain should respond to any situation, is just such an attempt to impose coherence. For many ideologues, and others who accept the *mokṣa-mārg* as the one truth, this totalizing strategy is successful. But for others it is clearly not compelling. The majority of Jains vacillate between the two positions. No ideology is ever completely successful, for life is too various, too shaped by ambiguities and imprecisions, to be reduced to a single formula, no matter how complex and inclusive. Thus the realm of wellbeing remains a vital aspect of the lives of most Jains.

Justification for the existence and even necessity of wellbeing is found in the very nature of the *mokṣa-mārg*. If it were possible to attain liberation in this time on this earth, then all the activities aimed at wellbeing would be wrong, as they would lead away from the attainable goal of liberation. But according to Jain cosmography, liberation is not attainable here and now. The impossibility of attaining liberation in this lifetime radically undercuts the universality and urgency of the *mokṣa-mārg* ideology. Since one is certainly going to be reborn, actions aimed at generating wellbeing in this and the next lifetime are not wrong. Of course, the ideologues argue that becoming a mendicant and traveling along the *mokṣa-mārg* is the best way to ensure one's better status in the next life. But short of that drastic step, and even for those who have taken it, other activities focused on wellbeing will also improve one's condition, as long as they do not transgress the boundaries of Jain morality and thereby result in a worsening of one's karmic balance.

But wellbeing is more than just a concession to the exigencies of unliberated existence. Mendicants are expected to minimize their involvement in the world of physical things, and in a very real sense are prohibited from practicing the skills needed just to stay alive in the world. The Jain laity, therefore, is essential for the survival of the fourfold Jain congregation and the Jain teachings. Attaining physical wellbeing, earning wealth, and spending that wealth for the greater glory of the Jain religion are both necessary and laudable. A wealthy layman (and a well-known *mokṣa-mārg* spokesman who frequently addresses Jain audiences in Gujarat, Bombay, the United Kingdom, and North America) said to me once, "Wealth is our birthright." His life as a wealthy, important Jain was to him proof that he had lived righteously and successfully in his previous lives. Now he was able to live a comfortable life, to pursue the wellbeing of himself, his family, and his community, and to spend time and money in support of the *mokṣa-mārg*, as well. Without wellbeing there could be no *mokṣa-mārg*.

We have seen that activities on the *mokṣa-mārg* are also producive of wellbeing. By worshiping the Jina, gifting to mendicants, performing ascetic acts upon oneself, and observing Jain festivals, one can generate *puṇya* that manifests itself in one's life as wellbeing. These actions are fully efficacious only because of the *kalyāṇ* generated by the five *kalyāṇaks* in the lifetimes of the Jinas. Wellbeing is thus derived from the holy nature of the Jain religion itself. From this perspective, both the *mokṣa-mārg* and wellbeing spring from the same source, much as God is the ultimate source of both salvation and worldly auspiciousness for a Hindu (Carman 1974; Narayanan 1985). Just as without wellbeing the *mokṣa-mārg* would not survive, without the *mokṣa-mārg* there would be no wellbeing. Jain ideologues may argue that the only thing which is truly valuable is liberation from the world, but it is the possibility of striving for liberation that also provides the possibility of wellbeing within the world. The two are joined in a relationship of mutual dependence. The Jain ideologues argue that the relationship between the two is absolutely hierarchical, with the *mokṣa-mārg* superior to wellbeing. The student of the Jains must see this claim as just that, a claim, and avoid reifying this one ideological position within Jainism as the whole of Jainism. To study only the *mokṣa-mārg* ideology is to study only part of the world in which Jains live their full and complex lives.

Hymn to Pañcāsar Pārśvanāth

Lord Pās, God of Pañcāsar,
shining among all the gods.
Lord, you are a silver coin among the planets,
shining with a thousand victorious rays.

Lord, you are the staff of dharma, the wheel of dharma,
the divine message in the sky.
Lord, you help not just a single species
but those in all four realms of birth.

Lord, the gods ring the bell,
like a wish-granting cow on earth and sea.
Lord, with your foot resting on a golden lotus,
who can imagine your glorious bodily signs?

Lord, you are grand from your toes to your head.
Drums resound in the firmament.
Lord, your knees are like a welcome rain,
like a five-colored fruit from a wish-granting cow.

Lord, the thorn has been removed,
even the trees bow down to you.
Lord, in the procession of the six seasons
we offer the fly-whisk and lamp as we circumambulate you.

Lord, with your golden form outlined by gems,
you are a jewel on the lion throne.
Lord, you are seated in the shade of the *aśoka* tree,
surrounded by gods holding a parasol and fly-whisks.

Lord, from your four mouths you preach the fourfold dharma
to all four realms of birth.
Lord, your play is imperishable and endless.
Experience of you grants the reward.

Lord, your teachings shower on all alike
just like rain from the clouds.
Lord, you are the shelter for faithful hearts.
Even a little creeper sprouts right faith.

Lord, you purify the people of Patan
who take *darśan* of you in the morning.
Lord, those who see your enchanting gesture
remember the goal of this birth.

Lord, why should a servant of the supreme lord
bow to anyone else?
Lord, churning milk produces ghee,
why would anyone eat what's left over?

Lord, those who neglect the physician of this era
are like those who sow seeds of poisonous weeds.
Lord, you liberate your servants,
so why should they worship Viṣṇu, Śiva, or Brahmā?

Lord, we think of sons, wife, family,
wisdom, happiness, fame and wealth.
Lord, from you comes the supreme pleasure,
in you we can forever sport with the wife who is success.

Lord, you are the lord of the homeless virtues,
so homeless mendicants bow to your feet.
Lord, observe the glance of your servant,
who wanders in birth after birth.

Lord, I stayed in Patan for *comāsu*
in this year 1791 [= C.E. 1735].
Lord, I sing to Pañcāsar Pās:
effect the pleasure of Kṣāmāvijay!

Kṣamāvijay, *Pañcāsarā Pārśvanāth Jin Stavan*, in *Jinendra Stavanādi Kāvya Saṅgrah*, pp. 167–68.

Glossary

Terms are given in their Gujarati form. This is usually identical with the Hindi, and differences between the two have not been indicated. When the Sanskrit form is significantly different, it has also been included, and indicated by "S."

abhakṣya	foods that are not to be eaten
abhigrah	a resolution taken by a mendicant that determines the conditions under which he or she will break a fast
abhiṣek	rite of anointing an image
ācārya	mendicant leader
Ādināth	"First Lord," the first Jina of this time period; also Ādīśvar, Ādeśvar, Ṛṣabhnāth
agra pūjā	part of *pūjā* in which offerings are placed in front of a Jina image
āhār-dān	Digambar mendicant's ritualized food-gathering round
ahiṃsā	nonharm
anāhārī pad	"the state of not consuming," definitive of a liberated soul
ānand	bliss
anant-kāy	food containing infinite bodies
aṅg pūjā	part of *pūjā* in which offerings are made directly onto a Jina image
anumodan	approval of the performance of a meritorious action by another person
aparigrah	nonpossession
āratī	rite of offering a five-wick lamp to a Jina image
arhat	Jina
āśātnā	an expiable moral fault committed in a temple
aṣṭaprakārī pūjā	rite of eightfold worship to a Jina image
aśubh	bad karma, *pāp*
aṭhṭham tap	three-day fast
ātmā	soul; also *jīv*
āvaśyak	six obligatory rites of a mendicant

āyambil (S. *ācāmāmla*)	fast in which one eats only certain sour foods
āyambilśāḷā	building for eating *āyāmbil*
bādhā	lay voluntary pledge to engage in some form of asceticism; also *niyam*
bahu-bīj	food containing many seeds
beāsan	"two sittings," fast in which one eats twice per day
ben	"sister," commonly appended to a woman's name
Bhagvān	God
bhāī	"brother," commonly appended to a man's name
bhakt	devotee of a particular mendicant guru
bhakti	devotion
bhāv	sentiment, spiritual attitude
bhāvnā	intentionally generated meditational sentiment
bhāv pūjā	spiritual worship of the Jina, in which no physical objects are offered
bhojanśāḷā	eating house
brahmacarya	celibacy
caitya	Jina image
caitya-vandan	rite of veneration, including the *caturviṃśati-stava*, of a Jina image
camatkār	"wonder," referring to wonder-working Jina images
caturviṃśati-stava	hymn of veneration to the twenty-four Jinas; also *Logass*
caūvihār	fast involving total abstinence from food and water
comāsu (S. *cāturmāsa*)	four-month rainy season period, when mendicants cease their travels
dakṣiṇā	in Hinduism, gift to a superior person
dān	ritual gifting
darśan	1. perception or intuition; 2. the rite of viewing a Jina image or other superior being
dev	God
dev-vandan	rite of veneration of the twenty-four Jinas
dharmśāḷā	pilgrim resthouse
Digambar	"Sky-Clad" or naked sect of Jains
dravya pūjā	worship in which physical objects are offered to a Jina image
ekāsan	"one sitting," a fast in which one eats only once per day
gacch	"those who travel together," the basic Mūrtipūjak mendicant subdivision
gaṇi	"group leader," a *sādhu* rank
gocarī	Mūrtipūjak mendicant's ritualized food-gathering round
guṇ	virtue
guṇasthān	the fourteen-rung ladder to liberation
guru	spiritual teacher, in the Jain case almost always a mendicant
guru pūjā	lay rite of worship of a mendicant
guru-vandan	rite of veneration of one's mendicant leader

havan	fire-offering, made to an unliberated deity
hiṃsā	harm
Jina	"Conqueror," the twenty-four enlightened teachers of each time period; also Tīrthaṅkar
jñān	knowledge, especially religious knowledge
kaivalya	enlightenment; also *keval-jñān*
kalyāṇ	welfare
kalyāṇak	five welfare-generating events in the life of a Jina
karma	the subtle material substance that binds the soul
kāüssagg (S. *kāyotsarga*)	"abandoning the body," a form of standing meditation
keval-jñān	enlightenment; also *kaivalya*
khamāsamaṇ	part of *caitya-vandan*, in which the worshiper recites a Prakrit phrase and performs a five-limbed prostration
kriyā	any ritual action
kṛpā	grace
kṣamāpanā	formulaic statement that all faults committed should be of no lasting karmic consequence
lābh	gain, benefit, profit
Logass	*caturviṃśati-stava*, the hymn to the twenty-four Jinas
Mahāvideha	part of the universe where liberation is currently possible
Mahāvīr	the twenty-fourth and final Jina of this era
mahāvrat	five great vows of a mendicant
maṅgal	holiness, auspiciousness; eight holy symbols
maṅgal dīvo	"holy lamp," a single-wick lamp offered as part of *āratī*
māṅgalik	auspicious verses recited at new year and other times of beginning
mantra	spell, performative utterance
māryadā	customary practice
micchāmi dukkaḍaṃ	Prakrit expression meaning "may my improper actions be inconsequential," said to fellow Jains at conclusion of *saṃvatsarī pratikramaṇ*
mokṣ	liberation; also *nirvāṇ*
mokṣa-mārg	the path to liberation
muhpattī	cloth tied to cover the mouth
mūrti Mūrtipūjak	temple image of a deity image-worshiping Śvetāmbar sect
nandyāvart	holy symbol, an expanded *svastik*
navkārsī	time that falls forty-eight minutes after sunrise
navpad	"nine petals," also *siddhcakra*
Nemināth	the twenty-second Jina of this era
nirjarā	wearing away of karma
nirvāṇ	liberation; also *mokṣ*
nisīhi	"it is abandoned," phrase uttered in *pūjā*
nīvi	fast in which one avoids food containing any of ten modified substances
niyam	lay voluntary pledge to engage in some form of asceticism; also *bādhā*

Nokār Mantra (S. *Namaskāra Mantra*)	praise of the five supreme lords
pacckkhāṇ (S. *pratyākhyāna*)	vow to perform certain karmically efficacious acts, especially fasts
paḍilehaṇ (S. *pratilekhana*)	mendicant's ritual inspection of clothes for insects and other minute organisms
paṇḍit	professional lay intellectual
paṅnyās	a *sādhu* rank, often simultaneous with *gaṇi*
pāp	demerit, bad karma
Paramātmā	God
parivār	"family," a mendicant group within a *samudāy*
parv	days in each month that are especially auspicious for fasting and other religious behavior
Pās (S. Pārśvanāth)	the twenty-third Jina of this era
poṣadh	temporary renunciation; also *pauṣadh*
poṣadhśāḷā	technically a building for laity to perform *poṣadh*, but in practical terms an *upāśray*
prasād	in Hindu ritual, food offerings that are offered to the deity and returned as blessings
pratikramaṇ	rite by which person ritually negates the karmic impact of words, thoughts, and deeds
pratiṣṭhā	the rites of installing an image in a temple
pravacan	sermon given by a mendicant; *vyākhyān*
pūjā	rites of worship of Jina images and other superior beings
pujārī	temple employee, usually non-Jain
puṇya	merit, good karma
ratnatraya	the three jewels that constitute the *mokṣa-mārg*: *samyag-cāritra*, *samyag-darśan*, and *samyak-jñān*
rātrī bhojan bandh	prohibition on eating at night
sādhu	male mendicant
sādhvī	female mendicant
sāmāyik	form of meditation
saṃsār	world of rebirth
samudāy	"those with the same origin," a mendicant lineage within a *gacch*
saṃvar	stopping influx of new karma into contact with the soul
saṃvatsarī	annual *pratikramaṇ* performed at conclusion of Paryuṣaṇ; also *sāṃvatsarī*
saṃvega	shock at hopelessness of life in the world, which impels one to renounce the world and seek liberation
saṃvegī	"liberation-seeking" full-fledged *sādhu*

samyag-cāritra	correct conduct
samyag-darśan	correct faith; also *samyaktva*
samyak-jñān	correct knowledge and understanding
samyak-tap	correct asceticism
samyaktva	correct faith; also *samyag-darśan*
saṅgh	1. as *caturvidh* or *sakaḷ*, the totality of the Jain community; 2. as *sādhu* or *sādhu-sādhvī*, the totality of the mendicant community; 3. a neighborhood or city-based lay congregation
saṅghaḍā	group of mendicants temporarily traveling together
śānti	peace
Śāntināth	the sixteenth Jina of this era
śenāī	auspicious reed instrument
siddha	a perfected soul
siddhcakra	"circle of perfection," a diagram with a figure of a Jina in the center, and in eight surrounding petals figures of the *siddha*, *ācārya*, *upādhyāya*, *sādhu*, and words honoring correct faith, knowledge, conduct, and asceticism; also *navpad*
Sīmandhar Svāmī	Jina currently living and preaching in Mahāvideha
śraddhā	faith
śrāvak	layman
śrāvikā	laywoman
śrīpūjya	*ācārya* who heads a lineage of domesticated mendicants
Sthānakvāsī	Śvetāmbar sect that eschews worship of Jina images
sthāpanācārya	"established *ācārya*," a ritual prop that symbolically represents the mendicant hierarchy
śubh	good karma, *puṇya*
śuddhatā	purity; in the *mokṣa-mārg*, refers to liberation
sukh	joy, bliss
svastik	holy Jain symbol, representing the rounds of rebirth and the path to liberation
Śvetāmbar	"White-clad" sect of Jains
tap (S. *tapas*)	asceticism
tattva	the nine verities of the Jain worldview
Terāpanthī	Śvetāmbar sect that broke off from Sthānakvāsīs
tīrth	1. pilgrimage shrine; 2. any Jain temple
Tīrthaṅkar	"Ford-Maker" or "Congregation-Founder," the twenty-four enlightened teachers of each time period; also Jina
tithi	a liturgical day, commonly measured from sunrise to sunrise
tivihār	fast involving abstinence from food only
upādhyāya	mendicant teacher
upāśray	hall where mendicants stay
updhān tap	collective program of fasting and textual study
upvās	any kind of fast; a day of fasting
vandan	rite of veneration, directed toward either a Jina image or a mendicant

Vāṇiyā	merchant caste
varṣgāṇṭh	annual festival of renewal of a temple
varṣī tap	year-long fast
vāskep	sandalwood powder that has been charged by a mendicant saying a *mantra* over it
vīrya	power
vītrāg	freed from all desire, an adjective descriptive of a liberated soul, especially a Jina
vrat	twelve lay vows
vyākhyān	sermon given by a mendicant; *pravacan*
yakṣ	male deity who attends upon a Jina
yakṣī	female deity who attends upon a Jina
yantra	magical diagram used in worship
yati	domesticated *sādhu*

Notes

Introduction

1. Padmasāgarsūri's style can be clearly seen in several scenes in Paul Kuepferle's excellent 1986 film, *The Frontiers of Peace: Jainism in India*.

2. John Carman 1985 has used the term "axis of sacred value." I prefer "realm" to "axis" to indicate that wellbeing is not a linear path, but rather an interpenetrating galaxy of concerns.

3. This sentence betrays the profound change Jain studies have undergone in the past fifteen years as a result of a number of excellent fieldwork-based studies. See Cort 1986, 1997a.

4. Within this voluminous literature, some surveys of the history of the term that I have found helpful are Drucker 1974, Eagleton 1991, Larrain 1979, and McLellan 1986. See also Madan 1997:2–4 for a definition of ideology that is very consonant with the one I use.

5. See Olivelle 1993:244–46 for a related discussion, based in part on the work of the sociologists Peter Berger and Thomas Luckmann and the historian of religion Jonathan Z. Smith, of ways in which the common perception of Brāhmaṇical religion and culture as unchanging is itself a product of an exegetical process by which change has been reinterpreted as the uncovering of preexisting Vedic truths.

6. To an extent, that book is the multiauthored *Open Boundaries* (Cort 1998a).

Chapter One

1. The mendicant curriculum is that approved as resolution 2 at the conference of Tapā Gacch mendicants in Ahmedabad in April 1988, and found in *Jain* 85.16–17 (April 1988), pp. 92–94. The *paṇḍit* curriculum is that of the Śrīmad Yaśovijayjī Jain Saṃskṛt Pāṭhśāḷā in Mehsana, the main school for Mūrtipūjak *paṇḍits*. Information on this curriculum comes from a September 1995 interview with the principal of the school. See also Cort forthcoming-d. Most of these texts are not from the Jain "scriptural canon," but rather from what I have termed a "canon-near" (Cort 1992). See also Dundas 1996.

In a brilliant essay, Charles Hallisey 1995 discusses the consequences attendant on the interpretive choices of privileging "original scriptures" or vernacular commentaries for the study of Theravāda Buddhism. The same arguments, mutatis mutandis, could be made for the study of Jainism.

In this chapter I use Sanskrit spellings of most terms, as that is the language privileged by *mokṣa-mārg* ideologues.

2. The dating of the *Tattvārtha Sūtra* has been the subject of much debate in recent years; it is safest to say that it dates from the early centuries C.E.

3. This wheel of rebirth is contrasted with the ideology of the path to liberation most clearly in Buddhaghosa's *Visuddhimagga*, "The Path of Purification." On the key role of such "path ideologies" within Buddhism, see Buswell and Gimello 1992. Path ideology is also found in Hinduism in the concept that there are three paths (*mārga*; the *Bhagavadgītā* uses the similar language of yogas or disciplines): of action (*karma*), knowledge (*jñāna*), and devotion (*bhakti*); according to this ideology, the three constitute the totality of religious experience.

4. As will be discussed in chapter 5, correct asceticism (*tapas*) is often added to these three.

5. See Folkert 1993:41–84 on the many problems inherent in talking of a Jain "canon" of scripture.

6. See Cort 1989:474–81 and Jacobi 1895:152–57 for translations of this chapter.

7. There is an alternate but not contradictory characterization of the universe as consisting of six fundamental facts or existents (*dravya*). These six are: sentient existents (*jīva*); material existents (*ajīva*); and four types of neither sentient nor material existents; space (*ākāśa*); the principle of motion (*dharma*); the principle of rest (*adharma*); and time (*kāla*). See Jaini 1979:97–106.

8. Neither the author nor the date of this text is known. Its role in Jain education is seen in the hundreds of copies of it in Jain manuscript libraries, and it was the subject of many commentaries; Mehtā and Kāpaḍiyā 1968:182 list seven dating from the fourteenth through the seventeenth century, and add that there are others. This was also one of the first two Jain texts translated into English, by Rev. J. Stevenson in 1847.

9. *Pāpa* is often translated as "sin." Although I will use this translation on occasion, it carries with it inappropriate preunderstandings from Jewish and Christian theology, and translating *puṇya* and *pāpa* as "merit" and "sin" occludes the Jain understanding of these as essentially mirror opposites, an understanding seen more clearly when using the synonymous terms of *śubha karma* (good karma) and *aśubha karma* (bad karma).

10. Most contemporary Śvetāmbar ideologues study their karma theory through the thirteenth-century *Karmagranthas* of Devendrasūri, and more advanced students also read the *Pañcasaṃgraha* attributed to the ninth-tenth century Candrarṣi Mahattara. See von Glasenapp 1942 and Jaini 1979:107–33. Lay knowledge of *mokṣa-mārg* karma theory is mediated through the *Cosaṭh Prakārī Pūjā*, a devotional ritual text composed by Paṇḍit Vīrvijay in 1818.

11. For the Jain cosmography, see Caillat and Kumar 1981, who include many of the wonderfully detailed cosmographical paintings used to study and teach this material. Most contemporary Śvetāmbar ideologues learn this material through the twelfth-century *Bṛhatsaṃgrahaṇi* of Maladhārī Candrasūri and the *Jambūdvīpa Saṃgrahaṇi*, also called the *Laghusaṃgrahaṇi*, attributed to Haribhadrasūri. (In the opinion of Mehtā and Kāpaḍiyā 1968:170, the author is a different Haribhadrasūri from either of the two well-known Jain authors of the same name.) More advanced students will also read the sixth-century *Kṣetrasamāsa* and *Bṛhatsaṃgrahaṇi* of Jinabhadragaṇi Kṣamāśramaṇa.

For the Jain universal history, see Cort 1993b. The standard Śvetāmbar source is Hemacandrasūri's twelfth-century *Triṣaṣṭiśalākāpuruṣacaritra*.

12. The Jain cosmography is obviously at variance with the Copernican cosmography of the modern worldview, and many Jains accept that the latter is scientifically more accurate. But the cosmographical differences have been the source of much reflection among Jains, and some ideologues have aggressively tried to defend Jain cosmography on what they claim to be scientific grounds. In part, this defense is driven by the fact that many aspects of the cosmography are described in texts that Jains believe to be fully authoritative since they

transmit the teachings of Mahāvīra. These teachings are understood to be timeless truths cognized by the omniscient Jina, and so are not open to questioning, lest one lose correct faith. As Paul Dundas (1992:77) pointed out, the Jain assumption that these scriptures are fully authoritative due to the omniscience of Mahāvīra has the result that Jainism in many ways resembles a revealed faith of the Abrahamic mode. Certainly the Jain defense of their traditional cosmography in the face of the claims of modern science bears fruitful comparison with some Christian defenses of Biblical cosmology.

One well-known Tapā Gacch ideologue, the late Paṅnyās Abhaysāgargaṇi (d. 1986), arranged for the construction of a working model of Jain cosmography at the Jambūdvīp temple in Palitana. He also founded several institutions such as the Earth Rotation Research Institute in Mehsana, and arranged for the publication of a number of magazines and books. These publications had titles such as *Is the Earth Round?* (Abhaysāgargaṇi 1968) and *Did Apollo Go to the Moon?* (Tripāṭhī 1970). The Digambar nun Āryikā Jñānmati engaged in similar activity from the Digambar Jain Triple World Research Institute in Hastinapur, Uttar Pradesh (Balbir 1990). An overview to these issues is found in a special issue of the monthly magazine *Tīrthaṅkar* (12.4, August 1982) devoted to Jain cosmography. This issue includes a lengthy interview with Abhaysāgargaṇi.

13. The principal texts by which contemporary Śvetāmbar ideologues study Jain biology are the eleventh-century *Jīvavicāra* of Vādivetāla Śāntisūri and the sixteenth-century *Daṇḍaka Prakaraṇa* of Gajasāra Muni. See also von Glasenapp 1942:51–62; *Tattvārtha Sūtra*, chapters 2–4; and *Uttarādhyayana Sūtra*, chapter 36.

14. We see here that in terms of the four states of rebirth there is a clear distinction between humans and plants-and-animals, whereas in classifying beings in terms of sense organs the two lie along a continuum.

15. The characterization of a human birth as difficult to attain is shared by Jainism, Buddhism, and Hinduism, and is a frequent trope in *mokṣa-mārg* discourse.

16. The introduction of Kierkegaard into the discussion also hints at the extent to which all salvation-oriented religious traditions function as ideologies.

17. One also finds him called Ādīśvara and Ādeśvara, also meaning "First Lord."

18. Only the last two Jinas, Pārśvanātha and Mahāvīra, are accepted as historical persons by scholars. According to the Jain tradition, Mahāvīra lived in the 6th century B.C.E. Many scholars would have his dates somewhat later than this with opinions ranging from the fifth to the third centuries B.C.E. See Bechert 1983 and 1991.

19. This statement simplifies a very complex issue within Jain theology, and one that has been a source of disagreement between Śvetāmbars and Digambars (Dundas 1985).

20. Muni Nyāyvijay (1890–1970), one of the more important Mūrtipūjak ideologues of the twentieth century, explains the Jain understanding of God in his *Jain Darśan*, an oft-reprinted summary of Jain doctrine that has been used as a textbook in some Jain schools (Nyāyvijay 1986:37, translation at 1998:31): "The position of a *tīrthaṅkara* is more exalted than that of an ordinary omniscient one (*sāmānyakevalin*), because the former is attended with miraculous events . . . [and] also because he is a greatly powerful propounder of Religion. But they are on the same plane so far as the degree of their spiritual development is concerned. As they have attained omniscience and the state of highest purity, they are absolutely equal; hence both of them are supreme souls, God."

21. The three unenlightened lords constitute the living and historical mendicant hierarchy, whose conduct is studied in the many texts on mendicant praxis, especially the "canonical" *Daśavaikālika Sūtra*, the anonymous *Pañcasūtraka*, and the fourteenth-century *Yatidinacaryā* of Bhāvadevasūri. The nature of liberated divinity is the subject of the many devotional hymns written in all languages spoken by Jains. For the purposes of study, among the most important are the twelfth-century *Vītarāga Stotra* by Hemacandrasūri, the collection of nine Prakrit and Sanskrit hymns known as the *Navasmaraṇa* or "Nine Remembrances,"

and two collections of Gujarati hymns, the *Jinguṇpadyāvalī* and the *Sudhāras Stavan Saṅgrah.*

22. The loci classici of the five great vows are *Ācārāṅga Sūtra* 2.15.1–5 (Jacobi translation 1884:202–10) and *Daśavaikālika Sūtra* 4.11–15 (Schubring translation 1932:84–86; Lalwani translation 1973:29–36). The latter text is memorized by most mendicants soon after initiation.

23. The *āvaśyakas* will be discussed at greater length in chapters 3 through 5. The ideological schema behind the *āvaśyakas* can be seen more clearly when one considers that there are four textual clusters studied by the ideologues. The performance of *pratikramaṇa* is detailed in a large number of manuals, some giving the rite for just the morning and evening performances (*Devasia-Rāïa Pratikramaṇa Sūtro*), others giving the rite for all five (*Pañca Pratikramaṇa Sūtro*). The *caturviṃśati-stava* (here called *deva-vandana*, "veneration of God"), *guru-vandana*, and *pratyākhyāna* are studied in three commentaries on the basic liturgies, known collectively as the *Bhāṣyatraya*. These were composed by Devendrasūri, who in the thirteenth century provided the intellectual basis for the Tapā Gacch. These and other rites are also detailed with Prakrit liturgy and Gujarati explanation in *Śramaṇakriyānā Sūtro.*

24. The text through which most contemporary ideologues study and understand the *guṇasthānas* is the second chapter of Devendrasūri's *Karmagrantha*. See von Glasenapp 1942:68–92.

25. "What does a true Jain do? He must become a mendicant! . . . If he doesn't become a mendicant, then he must become a true *śrāvak*." Muktiprabhvijay n.d.:9, 14.

26. For a lengthier discussion of the ideal Jain layman, based upon the description given by Hemacandrasūri in his *Yogaśāstra*, and contrasted with the ideals depicted in biographies of twentieth-century Jain merchant-princes, see Cort 1991c.

Jain literature is replete with narrative depictions of ideal laypeople. A popular text for examples used in sermons by mendicants is Śubhaśīlagaṇi's *Bharateśvarabāhubalivṛtti*, also known as the *Kathākośa*, composed in 1453 C.E. (Upadhye 1983:33–34). It provides edifying stories of fifty-three laymen and forty-seven laywomen.

27. The vows are also mentioned in section 57 of the *Aupapātika Sūtra.*

28. For classical understandings of the twelve *vratas*, see Williams 1963:55–171; representative modern interpretations are found in Hitajñāśrī 1985, Kuśalcandravijay 1977:VI, and Muktiprabhvijay n.d.:131–59.

29. For example, Margaret Stevenson (1910:42) reported that her *paṇḍit* vowed in his lifetime never to go further west than England, further east than Japan, further north than the Himalayas, or further south than Ceylon.

30. Closely related to the twelve lay vows is another explicit path ideology, in this case that of the eleven stages (*pratimā*) of the layman's path. This path was first described in the *Upāsakadaśāḥ*, and so is of great antiquity in the Jain tradition. But it is much less alive in the ideology of the *mokṣa-mārg*, and so is referred to far less frequently than the twelve vows. See Cort 1991c:396 and Williams 1963:172–81.

Chapter Two

1. Verses 13–14 of *Vijñapti Mahālekha* sent by the Kharatara Gaccha mendicant Jinodayasūri from Patan to Lokahitācārya in Ayodhya in 1375 C.E.

2. Only by comparing the history and social structures of the Jains of Patan with Jains of other regions will it be possible to move to a level of more generalized statements concerning Jain history and social structure. This latter task is not attempted here, but the material in this chapter will provide one basis for future efforts in such a direction. The recent work of other scholars in Jaipur (Babb, Humphrey, Laidlaw, Reynell), Sirohi (Singhi), Jamnagar (Banks), Kholapur (Carrithers), and Pune (Kelting) is beginning to provide the kind of regionally specific ethnographic data on the Jains that will make comparisons and therefore valid generalizations possible.

3. The significant Muslim presence in Patan (11.21% of the population in 1971) is largely missing from this study. This is indicative more of the Jain perceptions of Muslims as profoundly "other" than of any accurate reflection of the place of the Muslims in Patan. It has long been an important city for Gujarati Muslims. For example, Ali Muhammad Khan in his eighteenth-century *Mirat-i-Ahmadi* (pp. 91–101) listed thirty-two Muslim saints buried in Patan, more than in any other city of Gujarat.

4. That is, 3,648 out of 64,519 (Doctor 1975:224). They made up only 1.15% of the population of the district as a whole (24,046 out of 2,092,466 [Doctor 1975:18–19]), indicative of the largely urban location of contemporary Jains. The last census for which I have found religious demographic data is 1971.

5. That is, 4,801 out of 31,402 (Dalal 1902:II.12–13).

6. That is, 3,318 out of 29,830 (Mukerjea 1932:II.12–13).

7. See Folkert 1993:44–49 on the problematic nature of exactly what was accomplished at these councils.

8. U. P. Shah 1955–1956a and 1955–1956b, and R. C. Agrawala 1968 have published a number of Jain image inscriptions from Bhinmal from the seventh through twelfth centuries.

9. The major literary sources for the history of medieval Gujarat are almost exclusively Jain, and so our understanding of that history is highly sectarian. My concern here is not with issues of strict historicity or factuality, but rather with the Jain narration of their own history. See also Cort 1995c and 1998c.

10. According to chapter 26 of Jinaprabhasūri's *Vividhatīrthakalpa* (Cort 1990b:265–66), a temple of Neminātha had existed in Lakkharama for several centuries before Vanarāja founded Anahillapura. There is also archaeological evidence of a Brāhmaṇical presence from the mid-eighth century; see Goetz 1949–1950 and Dhaky 1965–1966.

11. On Vanarāja, Śīlaguṇasūri, and the founding of Patan, see Dave 1976:11–26, Majmudar 1960:222–26, and Tripuṭī Mahārāj 1952:468–71, 493–99.

12. On Mūlarāja, see Majumdar 1956:23–24.

13. Inden 1982 discusses a contemporary idealized portrait of Patan during the time of Jayasiṃha and Kumārapāla.

14. See Bühler 1936:ix–xi, 1–5 for the extensive sources for the lives of Hemacandra and Kumārapāla.

15. Ghīvālā 1987. The existing marble image of Lakṣmī could conceivably date from the twelfth century or earlier. The images of Sūrya and his spouse Ratnādevī are made of sandalwood; although it is unlikely that the extant images date from the twelfth century, the fact that they are made of wood does indicate a certain antiquity to their history. At the same time, two inscriptions from Bhinmal from 1249 C.E. record grants to the temple of Jagatsvāmī (V. K. Jain 1990:144). There are obviously multiple understandings of what occurred in 1147.

16. There are many accounts of Vastupāla and Tejaḥpāla, some of them by authors who were their contemporaries, such as Arisiṃha. The best English source on the brothers is Sandesara 1953. Steven Heim of the University of Chicago is finishing a doctoral dissertation on the contemporary biographies of Vastupāla.

17. The figures in the residence list are not comprehensive, as the president of the Maṇḍaḷ himself admitted to me in 1986. From my extensive use of the list, however, I have found very few people not listed in it, and would estimate that it is 90–95% complete. It should be noted that this list includes only Mūrtipūjak Jains, not Sthānakvāsīs or Terāpanthīs.

18. The relevant social and cultural tables for Gujarat from the 1981 and 1991 censuses have not been published. The total population of Patan increased from 64,519 to 96,109 between 1971 and 1991. I would estimate the Jain population of Patan during that time to have remained stable or to have increased slightly, but certainly not to have increased at a larger rate than the population of Patan as a whole.

19. I have discussed the internal organization of the mendicant orders much more fully in Cort 1991b.

20. The work of Paul Dundas (1987–1988, 1993, 1999) into the late medieval history of the Tapā Gacch marks an important beginning in such historical investigation. The situation is much better in Indian-language scholarship, but, as Padmanabh Jaini 1976 has perceptively observed, this scholarship all too infrequently interacts with European-language scholarship on the Jains.

21. For other areas of doctrinal and cultic difference between the Śvetāmbars and Digambars, see Dundas 1985, Jaini 1991, and Premī 1956:468–77.

22. As Paul Dundas notes (1992:217), the history of the Sthānakvāsī movement is still inadequately understood. See Flügel n.d. for a beginning.

23. On the Terāpanthīs, see Dundas 1992:218–24, Flügel 1994 and 1995–1996, and Vallely 1999.

24. Dharmasāgaragaṇi, *Svopajñavṛtti* on *Tapāgacchapaṭṭāvalī*, p. 48; see also Tripuṭī Mahārāj 1952:304–6.

25. Various lists of these eighty-four *gacchs* exist, some of them paralleling lists of eighty-four Jain castes (Sangave 1980: 108–16), but the lists only partially overlap with the names of *gacchs* as known from inscriptions and text-dedications. Kendall Folkert 1993:43 has observed that eighty-four is a number emblematic of a totality in the Jain tradition, and therefore not to be taken literally.

26. See Cort 1989:491–94 for a summary of the demography of the Śvetāmbar Mūrtipūjak mendicant community as of 1986.

27. Dharmasāgaragaṇi, *Svopajñavṛtti* on *Tapāgacchapaṭṭāvalī*, p. 57, and Klatt 1882:254–55.

28. See the many references in *Kharataragaccha Bṛhad Gurvāvalī*.

29. The memorial temple also contains the footprints and dedicatory inscription, dated 1602, of an Añcal Gacch *sādhu*. Babb 1996 and Laidlaw 1995 suggest that such shrines are focused on the four Dādāgurus or greatly venerated monks of the Khartar Gacch. Although the dates of the inscriptions (1602, 1614, 1623) of the Patan shrine indicate activity around the time of Dādāguru Jincandrasūri II (1541–1613), none of the footprints is dedicated specifically to a Dādāguru. Two are dedicated to disciples of Jincandrasūri.

30. One must beware of the change in the meaning of the word *yati* over time. As observed by Schubring (1962:71–72), in medieval times *sādhu* and *yati* were used interchangeably. Only later did *yati* come to refer to a mendicant who followed laxer practices.

31. See *Tapāgacchapaṭṭāvali* of Dharmasāgaragaṇi, pp. 57–58 and 69; and Ratna Prabha Vijaya 1950:74–77, 135–43, and 186–87.

32. I use the past tense here, as this is appropriate for discussing *yatis* in north Gujarat. The situation is different in parts of Rajasthan, Malwa, and Kacch, where many *yatis* still live.

33. This does not mean that *saṃvegī sādhus* were or are totally unattached to specific locations. In 1804 (or 1809, according to Śāh 1996:36), lay followers of Paṇḍit Vīrvijay, one of the leading *saṃvegī sādhus* of Ahmedabad, built an *upāśray* in Bhaṭhṭhī Poḷ for his use whenever he was in Ahmedabad; this *upāśray* is now known as Vīrvijay Upāśray (Kāpaḍiyā 1991:16). Similarly, Mahopādhyāya Yaśovijaya, an important seventeenth-century *saṃvegī sādhu* and *mokṣa-mārg* ideologue, seems to have had a special connection with an *upāśray* in Nāgorī Sarāy, near Ratanpol Crossing, in Ahmedabad (Kapadia 1966:13, Koṭhārī 1993:12). Some *sādhus* reside principally in one *upāśray*, moving away on occasion for a day or two to maintain the letter of the prohibition on fixed residence. Although some of these *sādhus* are criticized by laity for exhibiting signs of attachment to a specific *upāśray*, others who have been resident in one place for extended times, such as the scholar Puṇyavijay, who stayed in

Sāgar Upāśray for many years while cataloguing the Patan Jain libraries, have been highly revered.

34. To my knowledge, nowadays there is only one *śrīpūjya*, a Khartar Gacch *śrīpūjya* who resides in Rol, a village outside of Bikaner.

35. Buddhivijay's innovation was an imitation of a similar change in apparel instituted by Paṅnyās Satyavijaygaṇi in 1653, during another time of struggle between *saṃvegī sādhus* and *yatis* (Cort 1995b:17–18).

36. Miles 1835, Burgess 1884b, Bühler 1936:8. Dayā 1849, Singh 1995:94–96 and 1895:228–29, and Ḍuggaḍ 1979:341–45 also provide excellent descriptions from Gujarat, Marwar, and Panjab, respectively.

37. Jinvijay 1921 gives texts of ten similar letters of instruction from Tapā Gacch *śrīpūjyas*, dating between 1718 and 1857. See also Ḍuggaḍ 1979:343–45 for two similar documents, dating from 1815 and 1824, relating to *yatis* of the Lāhaurī Uttarārdh branch of the Loṅkā Gacch. The second of these documents also provides a valuable description of the rite of installation of a *śrīpūjya*.

38. In large part as a result of this reform, it is somewhat difficult to obtain information about the *yatis*. My informants were mostly elderly men, who remembered the *yatis* from their youth, and written sources. Because the *yatis* are now considered to represent an undesirable side of Jainism, clearly in contrast to the *mokṣa-mārg* ideology, I also encountered resistance to talking about them on the part of some Jains.

39. See Śivprasād 1992 for the medieval history of this branch, from 1464 through 1742.

40. In Rajasthan also I found that most of the descendants of married *yatis* were ostracized by the merchant-caste Jains.

41. In his biography of Ācārya Nemisūri, one of the great reformist mendicants of the early twentieth century, Śīlcandravijay (1973:6) estimated the number of *saṃvegī sādhus* in the period 1845–1865 to be no more than twenty-five to thirty. Although it is not clear if he means only within the Tapā Gacch, or in all the Mūrtipūjak *gacchs*, the number is still very small.

42. Information on dates is readily available from many sources; I have used Nityānandvijay 1976 and 1981. Maṇivijaygaṇi was tenth in pupilic succession to Paṅnyās Satyavijaygaṇi.

43. His name then changed to Ācārya Vijay Ānandsūri. *Sūri* is always added to the name of a mendicant who becomes an *ācārya*. As a matter of common practice in the Tapā Gacch, the "personal" name (Ānand) and the lineage name (Vijay) are reversed. Nonetheless, he continued to be most commonly known as Ātmārāmjī.

44. See also Reynell 1985a:249, 268–69 and Shântâ 1985:336.

45. See also Shântâ 1985:418. This is not the case in other *gacchs*. Khartar Gacch *sādhvīs* preach, which may in part be a result of the paucity of *sādhus* in the *gacch*. Some Tapā Gacch *samudāys*, especially those centered on rural areas of Kacch, in which there is a predominance of *sādhvīs* and shortage of *sādhus*, do allow *sādhvīs* to preach.

46. I must stress that these comments are restricted to the Tapā Gacch in Gujarat. James Laidlaw 1995 clearly indicates that the situation is very different in the Khartar Gacch, as it is also among Sthānakvāsīs and Terāpanthīs.

47. The various aspects of the Jain definition of *saṅgh* differs sharply from the Buddhist definition of *saṅgh* as referring only to the mendicant community. The rootedness of the Jain community in the laity, and the inclusion of the laity in the fundamental organizational structures of the tradition, help explain the persistence of the Jain tradition in India in contrast to the disappearance of Buddhism.

48. In Gujarati, *derāsar* (from the Sanskrit *deva-gṛha-āśraya*) is used exclusively for Jain temples, while the more common north Indian term *mandir* is used for Hindu temples. In

Marwar, Jains also use the term *mandir*. In more elevated discourse, the terms *caitya* and *prāsād* are also used for a Jain temple.

49. This was quite clear in an acrimonious debate over a seemingly small calendrical issue in the mid-1980s; see Cort 1999a.

50. The term most often used for a strictly orthoprax Jain is *cust*, which has all the negative and positive connotations, depending on context, of the English "stern and unbending."

51. People did not speak of membership in either *saṅgh*, but rather of going to one or the other for the performance of Saṃvatsarī Pratikramaṇ during Paryuṣaṇ (see chapter 6). Each *upāśray* has a membership list and charges a small annual fee, although in recent years Sāgar has eliminated the fee thanks to a single large donation.

52. Jñānsundar 1927:87–88 gives several examples of ways in which *yatis* would contrive to get the names of laity listed in their own offices. Such competition was not restricted to *yatis*. In 1802, Paṇḍit Vīrvijay, an important nineteenth-century *saṃvegī sādhu*, compiled a list of the Ahmedabad laity attached to his guru Śubhvijay (Kāpaḍiyā 1991:63).

53. These terms are used interchangeably. Strictly speaking, an *upāśray* (also *apāsro*) is a place where *sādhus* and *sādhvīs* stay, whereas a *poṣadhśāḷā* (also *pauṣadhśāḷā* and *pośāl*) is a building for laity to perform the rite of *poṣadh*, but there is no difference between them in actual usage.

54. What is striking about this list is the nearly total absence of caste names, in sharp contrast to both Jamnagar (Banks 1992) and Jaipur (Laidlaw 1995).

55. Eighty is my own count on the three *caitya-paripāṭīs* (see chapter 6) in which I participated in 1985, 1986, and 1995. By adding the 9 nonneighborhood temples downtown, and the one attached to the Jain Boarding School, I arrive at a total of 90 temples in Patan. A. P. Śāh 1953:135–52, writing before the construction of five of these temples, and omitting Śāmḷā Pārśvanāth, listed 106 temples; his list included 31 house-temples. K. H. Dośī 1981:9, omitting only one temple, said "in 85 main temples there are 134 separate temples," by which he means distinctive areas of worship with their own main images. The 1907 tabulation by the Jain Śvetāmbar Conference (Conference 1907:4–15, appx. 8–15) listed 93 public temples and 123 house temples in Patan, whereas a 1911 directory (M. L. Śā 1911) listed 85 public temples. This fluidity is not unique to the twentieth century. R. N. Mehta's 1995 study of four listings of Patan temples, from 1520, 1592, 1673, and 1903 (found in Kalyāṇvijaygaṇi 1928), shows great divergence in each list, indicating that the neighborhood residence and temple patterns of Patan have not been stable over the centuries. Most Patan Jains will say that there are 125 Jain temples in Patan, 125 being an auspiciously round number indicative of prosperity and growth. What constitutes a temple, and how many there are, obviously depend on who is counting.

56. See Lodrick 1981 for a study of the *pāñjrāpoḷ* and the related Hindu institution of the *gośālā* (cow shelter).

57. This school was closed in the early 1990s due to internal troubles.

58. Jains believe that *pūjā* should be done daily to an image that has been fully consecrated. Not to do so is considered a moral fault.

59. This is actually a simplification of a much more complicated issue. Whether or not *pujārīs* can be paid out of the *dev dravya* account has been a hotly contested issue throughout the twentieth century, and ideologues have debated the precise boundaries and suitable uses of *dev dravya* for hundreds of years.

60. Elsewhere in Gujarat, and in Marwar, I also came across Bhārwaḍs (shepherds), Rājputs, as well as other castes of Brāhmaṇs as *pujārīs*. Babb 1996:202n3 reports that in Ahmedabad, too, most of the *pujārīs* came from middle-ranking Hindu castes. Stevenson 1910:95 reports Kaṇbīs (Patels, farmers) and Bāroṭs (bards) as also being *pujārīs*.

61. *Jñātī* (also spelled *nāt* and *nyāt*) is the Gujarati term for the social unit called *jātī* in

north India. The relationship between Jains and caste is covered in greater detail in Cort n.d.; see also Banks 1986 and 1992, and Laidlaw 1995:83–119.

62. *Vāṇiyā* is the Gujarati word for merchant castes that corresponds to the Hindi word *baniyā*, although there is a subtle semantic difference in the way the two terms are used by Gujarati speakers. See Cort n.d. and Thoothi 1935:125n2.

63. Marcus Banks 1992:51–52 and James Laidlaw 1995:114–16 describe the twenty-ten distinction as working in slightly different ways in Jamnagar and Jaipur. This is only one of a number of aspects of the caste "system" that in fact are highly localized, rendering suspect almost all generalizations about caste in India.

64. *Śāh* is a Gujarati word from the Sanskrit *sādhu*, literally meaning "good."

65. Von Stietencron 1966:243 has argued quite convincingly that this is a false etymology; instead, Bhojak should be derived from the Middle-Iranian **bōžak*, "healer, savior."

66. *Paṇḍits* are not very highly respected by Mūrtipūjak Jains because being a *paṇḍit* is a fixed-salary occupation. Greater social prestige attaches to being an independent businessman, with all the attendant risks and possibilities.

67. The relationship between caste ranking and sectarian division among the Jains is an unexplored area. Although I do not have adequate data on the subject, I suspect that one element in the spread of the Sthānakvāsī movement was the attraction for lower-caste Jains such as Bhāvsārs and Ramīs of a new sect less dominated by higher-caste Vāṇiyās. Dharmdāsjī (1645–1703), one of the "founders" of the Sthānakvāsīs, was a Bhāvsār. There is some evidence that Bhāvsārs in Patan were formerly Mūrtipūjaks; Buddhisāgarsūri 1917:63 records an inscription on a Jina image consecrated by a Bhāvsār in 1412 C.E. Baakza 1962:33 mentions the objections of Mūrtipūjak Vāṇiyās to dining with Bhāvsārs at an intra-Jain meal. He does not say where this occurred, but it seems to have been in Saurashtra, where there is a pattern of local *saṅghs* being identified by caste. At the other end of the Jain caste spectrum, it seems clear that the Terāpanthī movement has appealed to the sense of superiority among Vīśā Osvāḷs in certain rural areas of Marwar; certainly initiation as a Terāpanthī mendicant was for many decades restricted to Vīśā Osvāḷs (Goonasekera 1986:117), and only Vīśā Osvāḷs could become full-fledged members of the lay Terāpanthī *saṅgh* (Flügel 1995–1996:145).

68. In 1901, the caste as a whole in Gujarat was 65.5% Hindu, 20.0% Jain, and 14.5% Muslim (Enthoven 1975:I.147–49). In Patan, the Bhāvsārs are almost exclusively Jain.

Chapter Three

1. "He Śaṅkheśvar Svāmī," in *Sudhāras Stavan Saṅgrah*, p. 132.

2. In this chapter I generally use the Indic word *mūrti*, since there is no English translation that is fully adequate. Jains writing in English use the word "idol," and Humphrey and Laidlaw (1994:57–58) in their recent study of Jain temple ritual have followed them in this. I prefer not to use "idol," due to its negative connotations in American and British English, stemming from the prohibition on the worship of graven idols found in Genesis, and the subsequent long history of critiques of idols and idolatry in all three Abrahamic traditions (see Halbertal and Margalit 1992). The word "icon" calls up associations with two-dimensional Eastern Orthodox Christian icons, whereas a *mūrti* is three-dimensional. The most common translation of *mūrti* is "image," which I do use on occasion. This term also presents problems, for whereas "image" refers to a mental construct, *mūrti* refers specifically to something which has form. Some sources use the more elevated words *pratimā* or *bimb*. Similarly, I have usually retained the Indic word *pūjā*. I use "worship" to refer to the entire complex of actions and relationships indicated by terms such as *pūjā*, *vandan*, *darśan*, and *kriyā*. I am sure that I have not been totally

consistent in my usage, and in this slippage reflect the ways these terms and concepts slide into each other in Jain usage, as well.

3. *Caitya* sometimes refers to either a temple or a small shrine within a temple; in this case, however, it specifically refers to a *mūrti* of the Jina. For a detailed discussion of *caitya*, with many relevant Prakrit and Sanskrit passages quoted in full, see Rājendrasūri (1913–1934:III.1205ff.).

4. My treatment of image worship differs in many significant ways from that in Humphrey and Laidlaw's 1994 *The Archetypal Actions of Ritual.* Although I agree with much of their book on a theoretical level, I find that their analysis of an ultimate lack of fixed meanings in *pūjā* does not adequately represent the understandings and pre-understandings of worship I encountered in Gujarat. By disregarding the extensive written discourse on ritual, they also omitted much that is essential for an adequate understanding of Jain practice of and attitudes toward ritual. See also Cort 1997a:107–8 and Babb 1996:198n7.

5. This description is based on Ratnasenvijay 1983, with consultation of the following sources: Bhuvanbhānusūri 1991, Candraśekharvijay 1995, Guṇratnavijay n.d.:8–19, Jinendravijaygaṇi 1981, Kamalratnavijay 1986:4–8, and Nirvāṇa Sāgara 1986:210–11. I have not indicated areas of difference, which usually consist of either a slightly different order or a different number of repetitions of a particular act. Another translation is in Cort 1995f.

6. This is part of the rite of *pratikramaṇ* discussed in chapter 5. It is understood that a silent dialogue takes place here. The person requests permission to perform the rite. Permission is silently received, as if from a mendicant guru, and confirmed aloud. The pattern, which is repeated below in terms of *caitya-vandan*, is modeled directly upon *guru-vandan*, in which permission is actually received.

7. See chapter 5 on *kāüssagg.*

8. In place of Śāntinātha, one can also recite Pārśvanātha.

9. These are the three continents from which it is possible to attain liberation.

10. Pās is vernacular for Pārśva.

11. I have used the following sources: Amityaśvijay 1995:38–42, Candraśekharvijay 1995:16–31, Divyakīrtivijay and Puṇyakīrtivijay 1995, Hemratnavijay 1983:48–79, Kamalratnavijay 1986:28–41, Khokar 1986, Kuśalcandravijay 1983:V.12–18, Manojitāśrī n.d., Muktiprabhvijay n.d.:42–65, and Ratnasenvijay 1983:4–29. Other sources that give interpretations of specific aspects of the *pūjā* will be cited as appropriate. In recent years the *aṣṭaprakārī pūjā* has been the subject of extensive scholarly discussion. See Babb 1988 and 1996, Cort 1991a, 1994b, and 1997a, Humphrey 1985, and Humphrey and Laidlaw 1994.

12. There are also restrictions after a death in the family. The restrictions apply to doing *mūrti-pūjā*, but not other rites such as *pratikramaṇ* and *darśan*. These prohibitions have been the subject of varied opinions by ideologues over the past centuries, ranging from a position with varied restrictions after the births or deaths of animals and slaves in one's house, to a position that pollution applies only to the birth mother; see Dānsūri 1927:210–14, Divyakīrtivijay and Puṇyakīrtivijay 1995:42, Jambūsūri 1957:42–43, and Rāmsūri 1978:193–96.

13. In practice, worshipers try to leave previous offerings on the *mūrti* lest they offend the previous worshiper. As a result, the water *pūjā* is done to the main images only by the first worshipers of the day, and subsequent worshipers do it to smaller metal images, if they do it at all. The flowers and other offerings are removed later by the *pujārī*.

14. This is a matter of some slight controversy. Khokhar 1986 says, "The second *pūjā* to the Lord is the sandalwood *pūjā*. The term 'saffron *pūjā*' is not mentioned anywhere [in the scriptures]." On the other hand, Muktiprabhvijay (n.d.:53) says, "Some people say that there is no instruction to do saffron *pūjā* in the scriptures. But this argument is incorrect."

15. The nine gods who preside over the eight directions and the zenith in the Brahmaloka (Caillat and Kumar 1981:25).

16. Khokhar 1986 says that this is an unnecessary folk custom, and many of the other sources omit the camphor *pūjā* altogether.

17. Because the worshiper remains in the shrine for the incense and lamp *pūjās*, some people regard them as *aṅg pūjās*.

18. See Fuller 1992:57–82 and the many sources cited therein.

19. The word actually used here is *sūr*, meaning an unliberated god; I have translated it in the song as "devotee" for the sake of clarity. As Babb 1996:79–82 has so clearly shown, Indra and the other unliberated gods are the model worshipers for Jain laity.

20. *Sevā pūjā* is commonly used by Puṣṭimārg Vaiṣṇavs to describe their rituals to Kṛṣṇa; the Jain use of this term is quite likely a borrowing.

21. I have directly quoted several explanations he gave for the intention behind parts of the ritual. In Gujarati, *bhāī* (brother) and *ben* or *bhen* (sister), which I use here, are frequently added to the names of men and women in everyday usage as a sign of respect.

22. I received various answers as to why *pūjā* clothes should be unstitched. One *sādhu* said that it is merely a matter of tradition: Ṛṣabhnāth's son Bharat wore unstitched clothes when he instituted the tradition of *pūjā*, and so *pūjā* clothes have been unstitched ever since. Upon further reflection, he added that wearing unstitched clothes both prevents worldly fashion from entering into the choice of clothes, and serves as a reminder that one is engaged in religious, not worldly, activity. See also Tarlo 1996:28–29, who writes, "some Hindus . . . opposed the introduction of tailored garments on the grounds that they were ritually defiling. . . . Uncut, unstitched cloth was considered less permeable to pollution and was preferred for all ritual performances."

Jains are careful to maintain the purity of *pūjā* clothes. One must never eat, drink, urinate, or defecate while wearing them, nor should a woman wear her *pūjā* clothes during her menstrual period. One must also be careful to protect *pūjā* clothes from accidental pollution while they are not being worn. *Pūjā* manuals often recommend that after performing *pūjā* one should go straight home and remove one's *pūjā* clothes, in order to prevent accidental and/or unwitting pollution. Should any of these prohibitions be violated, the clothes are considered permanently unfit for *pūjā*. See Kelting 1996:342–49 for an excellent extended discussion of *pūjā* clothes.

23. On this goddess, see U. P. Shah 1982:281–86. Whereas the *yakṣ* and *yakṣī* are considered to preside over the teachings (*śāsan*) of the Jina with whom they are associated (and therefore are also known as *śāsandevatās*; see Cort 1987), Śāntidevī is considered to protect the temple and neighborhood. She is usually located either in the base of the throne of an image or in the altar itself, as is the case here.

24. Many Jains are aware of this ritual and theological distinction, but I have also observed many do the full nine-limbed sandalwood *pūjā* to images of unliberated gods. To remind Jains not to do this, many images of goddesses are draped with a cloth that covers the body below the waist.

25. *Sudhāras Stavan Saṅgrah*, p. 5.

26. See Babb 1996:93–96 for a discussion of *dev-dravya*.

27. These are *mūrtis* of important *sādhus* in the *samudāy* of the *ācārya* who consecrated and installed the temple. *Guru mūrtis* are by no means rare in Tapā Gacch temples, but they do not play the important role of the Dādāgurus of the Khartar Gacch (Babb 1996, Laidlaw 1995).

28. These are a set of well-known devotional texts in Prakrit and Sanskrit, believed to be highly efficacious and meritorious. They are the Prakrit *Navakāra* (*Nokār*, *Namaskāra*) *Mantra*, the Prakrit *Uvasaggaharaṃ Stotra* of Bhadrabāhu Svāmī, the Prakrit *Santikaraṃ Stotra* of Munisundarasūri, the Prakrit *Tijayapahutta Stotra* of Mānadevasūri, the Prakrit *Namiūṇa Stotra* of Mānatuṅgasūri, the Prakrit *Ajita Śānti Stavana* of Nandiṣeṇa, the Sanskrit *Bhaktāmara Stotra* of Mānatuṅgasūri, the Sanskrit *Kalyāṇa Mandira Stotra* of Siddhasena Divākara, and the Sanskrit *Bṛhacchānti* (*Moṭī Śānti*) *Stotra* of Śāntisūri. Śāntibhāī recites the *Nokār Mantra*, *Uvasaggaharaṃ Stotra*, *Bhaktāmara Stotra*, *Moṭī Śānti Stotra*, and *Ajita Śānti Stavana*.

29. In most temples the water from the water *pūjā* is kept in a small pot by the door into the temple. People can dab their fingers in the water, and touch it to their eyes, throat, and the top of their head, for health and protection. This water is also used in processions, when it is sprinkled on the ground in front of the chariot bearing the *mūrti* in order to purify the ground. Any water that is not used in either of these two ways should be carefully disposed of on a plot of earth where people will not step on it.

30. Many ideologues give a list of eighty-four *āśātnās*, which range from spitting, vomiting, and washing to tethering horses, transacting business, failing to concentrate the mind, and wailing. See Williams 1963:225–29. In practice, the use of the term is not restricted to these eighty-four.

31. Bhadrabāhuvijay 1994, Bhadraguptvijaygaṇi 1983:2 and Guṇratnavijay n.d.:6–8.

32. *Namrattā*, p. 237.

33. *Sudhāras Stavan Saṅgrah*, p. 96.

34. The parents of Ṛṣabhnāth.

35. Kumārpāl was the great Jain emperor of medieval Gujarat (chapter 2); he is invoked here as an icon of a golden age of Jainism (Cort 1998c).

36. "Established form" is *sthāpnā nikṣep*. The *nikṣeps* are an ancient Jain hermeneutical technique (Alsdorf 1973, Bhatt 1978) that has been employed by defenders of *mūrtipūjā* for many centuries. See Bhadraṅkarvijaygaṇi n.d.:61–77.

37. See Babb 1996 for an excellent discussion of the "transactional neutrality" of the Jina.

38. This is an interview; I have omitted the questions.

39. *Aśubh*, sometimes rendered in English as "inauspicious," and in general parlance often meaning simply "bad," refers here to negative, harmful karma, or *pāp*, whereas *śubh* refers to positive, meritorious karma, or *puṇya*. *Śuddhatā*, normally rendered as "purity," and in common parlance understood to have distinctly Brāhmaṇical connotations, has a more technical meaning in the Jain *mokṣa-mārg* as the spiritual purity that results from eliminating accumulated karma (see Jaini 1985b:88).

40. Māṇibhadra Vīr, whose three principal shrines are at Magarvada and Aglor in north Gujarat and Ujjain in Madhya Pradesh, is the protector (*adhiṣṭhāyak*) of the Tapā Gacch (Cort 1997b). His cult has been eclipsed in recent decades by those of Ghaṇṭākarṇ Mahāvīr (Cort 1997b and forthcoming-e) and Nākoṛā Bhairav (Babb 1996:95–96, Bhaṇḍarī 1991, Laidlaw 1995:71–74).

41. Mahāvīr here refers to the Jain analogue of Hanumān, not the twenty-fourth Jina. Information on the history and practices of this cult is based on interviews with *sādhus* of the Buddhisāgar Samudāy and the manager and several trustees of the temples at Mahudi. See Cort 1997b and forthcoming-e, in addition to chapters 6 and 7.

42. Ghaṇṭākarṇ is defined as passionate because he is within the realm of rebirth, in contrast to the liberated Jina who is defined as totally dispassionate.

43. See Zydenbos 1993 for another discussion of this topic.

44. The Jain position that God did not create the universe is by no means unique in India. Many theologies and cosmologies view God and the universe as separately eternal and uncreated, rather than one deriving from the other. See Cort 1995e for a more extended translation of this passage.

45. Bhadraṅkarvijaygaṇi 1986:26–31 repeats this list, and adds a further sixteen epithets.

46. Jinraṅg, "Śāntināth Jin Stavan," in *Sudhāras Stavan Saṅgrah*, p. 51.

47. *Oṃ dharaṇendra-padmāvatī-paripūjitāya śrī śaṅkheśvara-pārśvanāthāya namaḥ*.

48. See Cort 1995e for a lengthier translation of this passage.

49. See Kelting 1996:321–78 for an extended discussion of *bhāv*, as well as Humphrey and Laidlaw 1994:220–25.

50. Translation by Helen M. Johnson, *Triṣaṣṭiśalākāpuruṣacaritra* 10, Vol. 6, p. 67.

51. This connection between the power of an image and the charisma of the *sādhu* who installed it only partially accounts for which images are most popular. Although the connection is stressed in the stories told of some images, the most popular images tend to have miracle-working powers that are independent of any human agency.

52. Excepting, of course, Sthānakvāsī and Terāpanthī Jains, who oppose all image-related practices on ideological grounds.

Chapter Four

1. Nearly identical passages are at Jambūvijay 1997:29 and Ratnasenvijay 1984:31.

2. The first part of this chapter overlaps with Cort 1999b.

3. I use Sanskrit forms in this paragraph, since it deals with an ideological depiction of mendicant praxis.

4. For a Śvetāmbar layperson to observe either function is considered an impropriety. This contrasts sharply with the invitation Michael Carrithers (1989:233n7) received to observe a Digambar mendicant defecating.

5. This is in the Tapā Gacch; conch shells are not used by all *gacchs*.

6. Dānsūri 1927:12–13, citing the sixth chapter of the *Vyavahārabhāṣya*, says it is a sign of vanity for an *ācārya* to perform *gocarī*, and as a result is a major fault (*doṣ*).

7. The precise timing and number of *paḍilehaṇs* and *gocarīs* vary, depending on which particular ascetic practices each mendicant has committed him or herself to perform in the recitation of *pacckkhāṇ*.

8. As noted in chapter 2, most Tapā Gacch *sādhvīs* cannot give public sermons as a matter of customary practice (*māryadā*). They only give private instruction and advice to laity, mostly women, in the *upāśrays*.

9. Gautam Svāmī was the chief disciple of Mahāvīr, and is also the focus of later devotion as a wonder-working *sādhu* (see Dundas 1992:33–34 and Laidlaw 1995:376–80). Sthūlabhadra was an early *ācārya* who, according to the Śvetāmbar version of Jain history, was leader of the community when the Digambars split off. His exploits are often told in Jain story literature. The reference to these two essentially encapsulates the Śvetāmbar mendicant lineage.

10. See Williams 1963:242–44 and 149–66 for detailed textually based discussions of *veyāvacc* (Sanskrit *vaiyāvṛtta*) and *dān*.

11. *Svopajñavṛtti* on *Yogaśāstra* 3.119 (p. 564). According to contemporary understanding of the fields, the seven are ranked hierarchically, as money given in a lower field can be transferred to a higher field, but not vice versa. This hierarchical understanding is not found in Hemacandra's text.

12. *Svopajñavṛtti* on *Yogaśāstra* 3.119 (p. 576). I use the English noun "gift" and verb "to gift," instead of the more common "donation" and "to give" in order to indicate the formal, ritual status of such transactions. This usage accords with that found in other recent discussions of *dān*, such as Haynes 1987.

13. See Laidlaw 1995:309–13 for a description and illustrations of the process of food gathering and gifting in Jaipur.

14. There should be no pollution due to death, birth, or menstruation. Should the mendicant accidentally enter a polluted house, he or she has to perform a penance, usually some sort of abstention from food.

15. Although I have observed the ritual in Delhi, my description here is based primarily upon that of Mahias, with additional or different details from Shântâ as appropriate. Bālyogī n.d. gives a prescription for the ritual. See also Fischer and Jain 1977:74–76 for twelve photographs of it.

16. The technical term for such a resolution is *abhigrah*. They are less common, but by no means rare, among Śvetāmbars, where they are an optional, not a mandatory, practice.

Tatia and Kumar 1981:57–58, citing the c. sixth century C.E. *Bṛhatkalpasūtrabhāṣya* of Saṅghadāsagaṇi, give a detailed synopsis of the Śvetāmbar understanding of this topic, which they translate as "secret resolve."

The biographies of the Jinas are replete with such resolutions. A famous example comes from the biography of Hemacandra's biography of Mahāvīr in his *Triṣaṣṭiśalākāpuruṣacaritra* (Vol. 6, p. 112). Mahāvīr took an *abhigrah* to break a fast only if he were offered unspiced boiled lentils by "a princess, who has been reduced to slavery, her feet bound by iron chains, shaven, fasting, weeping from distress, one foot inside the threshold, the other one outside . . . [and who has] turned away from the house all [people] seeking alms." (I have slightly altered Johnson's translation for clarity).

In the course of my fieldwork, one *sādhu* vowed to break his *varṣī tap* (chapter 5) only if three requirements were met: 1. there should be only nine rickshas and nine jeeps present in the *upāśray* compound; 2. on his *gocarī* he should meet any two women who had just come from a specific nearby town bringing sugarcane juice for his fast-breaking; and 3. he should meet any three men who had come from another specific nearby town and were at the time wearing their *pūjā* clothes. All three requirements were met, and so he broke his fast.

Thomas Zwicker (1984–1985:5/27–29.17) reported that once a teenage Jain girl in a small village vowed not to eat until both he and a certain *sādhu* stood before her. Since such an *abhigrah*, if carried to its logical conclusion, could result in death, there was much frantic scurrying to try to meet the girl's unstated requirements. At the same time, everyone was peeved at the girl's willful demand.

I encountered various explanations for such *abhigrahs*, but no one was confident of their response, and they were clearly uncertain as to the rationale behind such practices. Some said that it exhibited the willpower or telepathic powers of the *sādhu*. Nor do Tatia and Kumar provide any rationale. But it seems evident that the *abhigrah* helps prevent any unconscious intentionality behind the mendicant's *gocarī*; intentionality could involve the mendicant in the karmically harmful violence involved in the food preparation, and could also lead to the establishment of emotional attachments (even if only fondness or preference) between mendicants and laity. See also note 29 below.

17. Slight variants of the formula are found in different written sources. This variation is typical of most Jain rituals.

18. *Antarāy* (hindrance) is that form of karma in Jain theory which blocks the innate energy of the soul (Jaini 1979:123). In other words, the impurity is a sign of a hindrance in the mendicant's karmic status that should be addressed by added asceticism, in this case a further restriction on the intake of food.

19. See Babb 1996 for an extended discussion of Jain and Hindu ritual cultures.

20. As I noted in chapter 1, "sin" is a rather problematic English translation for the Indic term *pāp*. Sin is an extremely weighted term in Christian and Jewish theology, and these preunderstandings can obscure an adequate understanding of *pāp* for many Euro-American readers. Nor does the word "sin" fully indicate the extent to which *pāp* is the binary opposite of *puṇya*, "merit," an opposition seen clearly in the synonymous pairing of *śubh-aśubh*.

21. See also Toffin's 1990 and Parry's 1994:135–39 pointed critiques of parts of Raheja's thesis, Laidlaw 1996 on Parry, and the exchange between Madan 1991 and Parry 1991.

22. Parry 1994:130 notes that *dakṣiṇā* is not completely free of perilous side-effects, either. Whereas *dān* is widely used for all forms of gifting, one finds many texts and informants who distinguish *dān* as gifting to socio-moral inferiors from other forms of gifting, such as *dakṣiṇā*, to socio-moral superiors. In the Jain case, this is reflected in the frequently heard comment that *supātra dān*, or gifting to a superior recipient, and which by definition must be given to mendicants and Jina images, is in fact not a form of *dān* at all. On this see also Laidlaw 1995:316.

23. There is a degree of overlap in Hindu and Jain understandings of the effects of *dān* to world-renouncing mendicants. Parry 1994:129–30 observes of "the *bhiksha* (or *bhikh*) given in alms to an ascetic (or beggar), and the *chanda* donated towards the upkeep of a monastery" that "neither of them is said to contain the sins of the donor." See also Babb 1986:64–70, 210–14.

24. See also Babb 1988:80.

25. As discussed in chapter 3, karma accrues to the soul through three mechanisms: the actions one performs, the actions one causes others to do, and approval (*anumodan*) of the actions of others. Thus the mendicant has to be careful not to appear to approve of the way a householder has prepared the food.

26. Similarly, a Brāhmaṇ in theory can accept *dān* without endangering himself if he is a *supātra* or superior recipient, that is, if he lives a life that closely approximates to that of an ascetic renouncer; but since the Brāhmaṇ by definition is a householder, he cannot fully embody the required ascetic and renunciatory practices. The very fact of accepting the *dān* "irretrievably compromises this ideal of ascetic autonomy" (Parry 1994:131), and indicates that he is not truly a *supātra*.

27. *Svopajñavṛtti* on *Yogaśāstra* 3.119 (p. 572).

28. Josephine Reynell found similar Jain attitudes to *dān* and merit among Khartar Gacch Jains in Jaipur. She has written (1987:355), "*dān* is seen as indicative of inner spiritual purity but this is not achieved through the donor's sins leaving with the donation. Any accumulated sin must bear its fruit. The only way that *dān* can affect sin is that the act of *dān* accumulates *puṇya* which may then modify the future consequences of any sin already accumulated."

29. We also see the transactional logic behind the otherwise sometimes puzzling *abhigrahs* discussed in note 16: by establishing a random set of preconditions upon the food-gathering round, the mendicant ensures against any even unconscious intentionality (and therefore desire) entering into his or her *gocarī*.

30. This analysis also sheds light on the moral force behind the decision of the early Buddhist (and some early Jain) renouncers to adopt consciously the epithet "beggar" (*bhikṣu*, *bhikkhu*). To accept willingly a title indicative of one who is the unwilling recipient of worldly *pāp* is an even stronger expression of the renunciation of worldly values than we see in the carefully controlled renunciation in the practice of most Buddhist, Jain, and Hindu renouncers.

31. The situation of the food offered before the image of the Jina may reflect a slightly different understanding. As Babb 1996:186 notes, this food becomes a sort of "hot potato," the disposal of which presents a dilemma to the Jains. Orthoprax and orthodox Jains cannot accept this food, and so it is either passed on in the form of salary (not *dān*) to the non-Jain temple servants, or else sold in the market to non-Jains. The stringency of restrictions encircling this food would seem to indicate that it is in fact a bearer of some *pāp*. Taking all these different forms of transaction together, the net increase in *puṇya* within the Jain world might be in part a result of the beneficial effects of the Jina's actions while alive; in part a result of the pious, ascetic acts of contemporary Jain mendicants; and in part a result of the passing on of *pāp* to non-Jains. In other words, the Jains do not operate in a zero-sum economy for two reasons: first, the abilities of the Jain *supātras*, the Jinas and the Jain mendicants, both to create *puṇya* and to eliminate *pāp*; and second, the presence of non-Jain receptacles for *pāp*.

32. *Sarva-kalyāṇa-kāraṇa*.

33. Similarly, the human recipients in the cases reported by Parry and Raheja are in all instances married householders. By definition, householders are involved with possessions and desires. In the words of T. N. Madan 1987, they are involved not with renunciation but with nonrenunciation. Since householders are possessive accumulators, the *pāp* attached to

any *dān* sticks to the recipient. Higher-caste, more orthodox Brāhmaṇs, as indicated by Parry, try to circumvent this occurrence, by insisting on the acceptance only of nondangerous *dakṣiṇā* instead of dangerous *dān*, and by the observance of as ascetic and renunciant a lifestyle as possible within the householder's state. I suspect that an investigation of the moral effects of donations to Hindu renouncers would uncover a situation quite similar to what we see with Jain mendicants. See also Laidlaw 1996.

34. My description is taken from Jinendrasūri 1986:3–9, Muktiprabhvijay n.d.:34–35, and Nirvāṇa Sāgara 1986:210.

35. This stanza is also used in the performance of *caitya-vandan*. Since the *caitya-vandan* is addressed to the Jina, a being superior to the mendicant, in that rite the worshiper bows thrice.

36. See in particular a rather scurrilous attack upon Rāmcandrasūri in the Bombay edition of the Gujarati daily *Sandeś*, May 17, 1986, p. 12.

37. At most large public congregational rituals, the person sponsoring it personally marks the forehead of everyone attending with red paste as a mark of respect and appreciation. A cloth is almost always held between the Jina and the individual receiving the mark, again to avoid the offence of honoring an unliberated person in the presence of the liberated Jina.

38. For examples of Gujarati Vaiṣṇav worship of the guru as god, see Barz 1976:22 on the Puṣṭimārg, and Williams 1984:58–85 and 1985 on the Swāmīnārāyaṇ tradition.

39. This is particularly evident in Gujarati, in which the polite, plural forms common in Hindi and Marwari are almost never used in everyday speech.

40. "Mahārāj" (great king) is the most common term of respect used by laity to refer to a mendicant. It is appended to the name of a known mendicant as indicative of respect, and is used generically to refer to any mendicant.

41. The use of *vāskep* is documented at least as early as the twelfth century *Triṣaṣṭiśalākāpuruṣacaritra* of Hemacandra (Vol. 1, p. 210n274). It does not appear to possess the overt thermal powers of either the cooling grey Śaivite *vibhuti* or the heating red Vaiṣṇavite *vāsyog* used at Hoḷī, although the use of sandalwood as a cooling substance fits in with a general Jain emphasis on coolness and control. See Burgess 1884a:191 for a description of how it is made.

42. See Zwicker (1984–1985:5/23/85) for a description of the procession and cremation of an important *ācārya* in Ahmedabad in 1985.

43. On the occasion described by Zwicker, this rite was auctioned for Rs. 461,000. In 1985, this was equal to roughly $38,500.

44. In Unjha, this was next to one of the two Jain temples in town, where a *samādhi* or guru temple was later built. In the case of the death of the famous *sādhu* Paṅnyās Bhadraṅkarvijaygaṇi in Patan in 1980, a layman donated some land just outside the western town wall for the cremation and the guru temple. The cremation ground used by Jains outside the north gate of Patan has several memorials to *yatis*, indicating that they were cremated there.

45. See Babb 1996 and Laidlaw 1995.

Chapter Five

1. Parts of this chapter also appear in Cort forthcoming b, albeit within a very different theoretical framework. For a discussion of ways in which some Jain ideologues have understood the self as also being "other," see Cort 1998b. See also Laidlaw 1995:151–286 for an extended discussion of the ways in which asceticism demonstrates various Jain attitudes toward the body and the soul, what he terms "topographies of the self."

2. Yaśovijay, *Navpad Pūjā*, p. 202.

3. The sources of this and similar lists are the medieval commentaries on the more

generalized descriptions of Mahāvīr's dietary and other austerities in the *Ācārāṅga Sūtra* 1.8.4 and *Kalpa Sūtra* 120. See Vinayavijaya's *Subodhikā Ṭīkā* on the *Kalpa Sūtra*, pp. 329–30, for a slightly different list.

4. See Cort 1989:233–34 for the details on these last three fasts.

5. For the Śvetāmbar Mūrtipūjak Jains, *vrat* always retains this restricted, technical meaning, unlike the more generalized Hindu sense of *vrat* as any woman's fast (Wadley 1983, McGee 1987 and 1991).

6. On the *āvaśyaks*, see Balbir 1993, Dundas 1992:146–49, and Williams 1963:184–215. Laidlaw provides a detailed discussion of some of the *āvaśyaks*. He notes that although the six are conceptually separable, in practice they are thoroughly intertwined, as will be evident in the course of discussions of and references to the *āvaśyaks* throughout this book.

7. I have given the first four in their Sanskrit forms, and the last two in their Prakrit forms, and all six as reflecting Gujarati pronunciation. Laidlaw's 1995:195 list reflects a similar heteroglossia in Jaipur, with the Sanskrit and Prakrit overlaid by Hindi.

8. *Svopajñavṛtti* on *Yogaśāstra* III.82 (p. 477).

9. See Laidlaw 1995:204–15 for a good fieldwork interpretation of *pratikramaṇ*, and Sanghavi 1993 for a good discussion by a leading twentieth-century *mokṣa-mārg* ideologue.

10. Harmful karma (*pāp*) is frequently used as a shorthand for all forms of karmic attachments in *mokṣa-mārg* discourse.

11. For example, those listed in the bibliography under *Pratikramaṇa Sūtra*.

12. See Nityānandvijay 1966 and *Dīkṣāvidhi tathā Vratvidhi*, which give the similar rites for both mendicant initiation through taking the five *mahāvrats* and lay adoption of the twelve *vrats*.

13. The tension between *kriyā* and *jñān* is an important one in the *mokṣa-mārg* ideology, and shows how this ideology is neither homogenous nor static. Many "reformers" in Jain history, such as the founders of the various Śvetāmbar *gacchs*, have insisted on a return to the proper performance of *kriyā*, whereas others, such as Banārsīdās, Raycandbhāī, and Kānjī Svāmī (Dundas 1992:165–68, 224–32) have either derided or downplayed *kriyā* and instead stressed *jñān*.

14. The best treatment of Jain foodways is Mahias 1985.

15. For lists of the twenty-two, see Cort 1989:269–70, forthcoming-b, and Williams 1963:110–13.

16. See chapter 6, note 2, Cort 1989:280–82 and Cort 1999a for fuller discussions of the *tithis*. Each month in the Indian lunar calendar consists of two fortnights of fourteen or fifteen days. Gujarat follows the southern Indian calendar which ends at the new moon. The month consists of a bright half (*sud*) ending on the full moon and a dark half (*vad*) ending on the new moon.

17. See chapter 3, note 21, on the usage in Gujarati of *bhāī* (brother) and *ben* or (sister).

18. Reynell (1985a:44) reports that three-quarters of sixty-nine married women whom she interviewed in Jaipur performed *sāmāyik* every morning upon rising. I did not find such a ubiquitous practice in Patan.

19. Reynell (1985a:52–53) also reports Jains in Jaipur saying that it is difficult to fast and work at the same time.

20. See the explanation by M. C. Modi, *Antakṛddaśāḥ*, pp. 120–21.

21. Dharmasāgaragaṇi, *Svopajñavṛtti* on *Tapāgacchapaṭṭāvalī*, p. 57.

22. Reynell 1985a describes much more such congregational fasting in Jaipur than I observed in Patan. I suspect that congregational fasting is more of a big-city phenomenon, as a form of "modern Jainism" in the metropolitan centers.

23. See Abhaycandravijay 1982 for a detailed description of the *tap*, and Kalyāṇvijaygaṇi 1966:74–89 for a detailed historical discussion of it. Laidlaw 1995:175–79 also describes the performance of the *updhān* in Jaipur. He relates that at its conclusion many laity formally

adopt one or more of the twelve *vrats*. I did not encounter this in Gujarat, nor have I seen it mentioned in any printed discussions.

24. Laidlaw 1995:217–18 describes a different performance of this *tap* in Jaipur, one that I encountered neither in practice nor in written materials.

25. For example, the *Taporatna Mahodadhi* (Ocean of the Jewel of *Tap*) of Jinendravijaygaṇi (1982) and the *Tapaḥ Parimal* (Fragrance of *Tap*) of Bhuvanvijay (1981b). Vernacular collections are based on medieval sources, in these cases primarily two texts by Khartar Gacch authors, the early-fourteenth-century *Vidhimārgaprapā* of Jinaprabhasūri and the early-fifteenth-century *Ācāradinakara* of Vardhamānasūri.

26. Reynell 1985a has perceptively noted that such photograph albums made in connection with a *tap* are analogous to, and seen as extensions of, albums of wedding photographs.

27. Bhuvanvijay and Jinendravijaygaṇi say that the faster should fill a platter with *khīr*, sugar, and ghee, and offer the platter before a Jina image in a temple. The faster then makes a gift to the *sādhu*, and performs *jñān pūjā* (chapter 6).

28. On Hindu understandings of *strī-dharm*, see McGee 1991 and Young 1987.

29. On the *rohiṇī tap*, see Laidlaw 1995:224–29. Jinendravijaygaṇi 1982:114–15 says that the fruit of this *tap* is *saubhāgya*.

30. These are all taken from Jinendravijaygaṇi 1982.

Chapter Six

1. See Cort 1989:497–501 for a chart listing the major annual Jain and Hindu holidays in Gujarat.

2. A *tithi* "is the time required by the combined motions of the sun and moon to increase (in the bright fortnight) or to diminish (in the dark fortnight) their relative distance by twelve degrees of the zodiac" (Jacobi 1888:145). Because a *tithi* is measured according to how long it takes the moon to traverse a certain distance against the fixed map of the stars, and the moon's orbit is elliptical, a *tithi* can vary in length between 21.5 and 26 hours. For the purposes of this discussion, I will follow the common practical understanding that a *tithi* is a solar day (sunrise to sunrise), designated by the *tithi* in effect at the first sunrise. See Cort 1999a for a fuller discussion of what is a rather complicated and technical astronomical matter.

3. See chapter 5, note 16.

4. Hemacandra, *Vītarāga Stotra* 10.7.

5. This is the approach of Fischer and Jain 1978:I.

6. Tatia and Mahendra Kumar 1981:49; see also Shântâ 1985:423n2.

7. The four months of the mendicant *comāsu*, mid-Āṣāḍh through mid-Kārtak, do not correspond to the actual monsoon season, which in Gujarat is roughly Jeṭh through Bhādarvā. The vernal equinox annually moves slightly backward through the zodiac, so the calendar must be corrected periodically in order to keep the lunar and solar calendars synchronized. Indians ceased to do this in the late sixth century C.E., with the result that the lunar and solar calendars are growing increasingly unsynchronized. (Gary Tubb, personal communication. See also Kane 1968–1977:V. 645ff.)

8. In 1986, the sermon I heard was based on the *Āṣāḍha Cāturmāsika Vyākhyāna* of Ācārya Vijaya Lakṣmīsūri (1741–1802). For a Hindi translation, see Bhuvanvijay 1981a:1–14.

9. These were Śubhaśīlagaṇi's 1453 C.E. *Bharateśvarabāhubalivṛtti* (see chapter 1) and Śubhavardanagaṇi's 1496 C.E. *Vardhamāna Deśanā* (Mehtā and Kāpaḍiyā 1968:218–19), both compilations of edifying stories of pious laity.

10. *Dev-vandan* is a two-hour-long ritual recitation of praises to each of the twenty-four Jinas of the present age, the *śāsvatā-aśāsvata* Jinas, and the five *tīrthas*. The four *śāsvata*

(eternal) Jinas—Ṛṣabh, Candrānan, Vārīṣeṇ, and Vardhamān—are so called because their names occur in every era in one of the fifteen *karmabhūmīs* where enlightenment is possible (U. P. Shah 1987:100). The *aśāsvata* (noneternal) Jinas are the millions of transient images of Jinas in the various realms. The five *tīrthas* are the most sacred pilgrimage shrines for the Śvetāmbar Jains: Shatrunjay and Girnar in Saurashtra, Abu in the Aravalli Hills of southern Rajasthan, Sammet Shikhar in Bihar, and Ashtapad, identified by some with Mount Kailash in the Himalayas. Twenty Jinas attained *mokṣa* on Sammet Shikhar, Nemināth on Girnar, and Ṛṣabhnāth on Ashtapad. The latter is also the site of the first temple built in this era.

The *dev-vandan* is based on the shorter *caitya-vandan* ritual. See *Devvandan Mālā*, pp. 121–220, for popular Gujarati *Caumāsī Dev-vandans* by Ācārya Jñānvimalsūri (early eighteenth century), Paṇḍit Vīrvijay (early nineteenth century), and Paṇḍit Padmavijay (late eighteenth century).

11. Although the Gujarati form is Pajjuṣaṇ, in recent years use of the more Sanskritized form Paryuṣaṇ has come into vogue. For other detailed accounts of Paryuṣaṇ, see Banks 1992:176–84, Folkert 1993:189–211, and Laidlaw 1995:275–86. Laidlaw reports that in Jaipur the observance of Paryuṣaṇ is counterpointed with the observance of the simultaneous Hindu festival of Gaṇeś Caturthī, and his analysis revolves around this counterpoint. Whitney Kelting (personal communication) reports a similar counterpoint in Pune, which is not surprising, given the prominence of the worship of Gaṇeś in Maharashtra. But the worship of Gaṇeś by Jains was noticeably absent in both Patan and Ahmedabad, nor does Banks report it in Jamnagar.

In the early centuries C.E., Paryuṣaṇ was observed by the *sādhus* reciting the *Kalpa Sūtra* among themselves. According to the eleventh-century *Kalpasūtra Ṭippaṇaka* by Pṛthvīcandrasūri (cited by Vinaya Sāgar 1984:xxvii), the present custom of public reciting of the *Kalpa Sūtra* began in 457 C.E. in Anandapura (modern Vadnagar), when Kālakācārya publicly recited the *Kalpa Sūtra* before a large audience to celebrate the completion of his copying the Jain scriptures. In another commentary, the 1640 C.E. *Kalpasūtra Subodhikā* (pp. 15–16), Upādhyāya Vinayavijaya says that the first recitation was done in either 454 or 467 to console King Dhrūvasena of Anandapura upon the death of his young son.

12. In recent years, the Vīr Sainik (Soldiers of Mahāvīr), an organization established by the activist ideologue Paṅnyās Candraśekharvijaygaṇi, has been training young laymen to lead congregations in the observance of Paryuṣaṇ, and sending them to villages and small towns where no *sādhus* are staying for *comāsu*. The concern of the Vīr Sainik is that Paryuṣaṇ be observed properly, according to the *mokṣa-mārg* ideology.

13. Because of its annual liturgical use, there are many vernacular versions of this text. See Bhuvanvijay 1981a:15–48 and Rāmcandrasūri 1974.

14. They have not, for example, been a notable pacifist presence in terms of issues of war and peace (Sanghavi 1950).

15. The Sanskrit phrase "nonviolence is the foremost ethic" (*ahiṃsā paramo dharmaḥ*), first found in the Hindu *Mahābhārata*, has been adopted by the Jains as a motto. See also Jaini 1987 and Dundas 1992:138.

16. *Kṣamāpanā* is also an integral part of the twice-daily *pratikramaṇ* performed by all mendicants.

17. Almost all congregations have a separate account for such purposes.

18. For another discussion of the worship and recitation of the *Kalpa Sūtra*, see Cort 1992:175–79.

19. The rights to perform most rites in a festival or public ritual are auctioned, with the money going into the *saṅgh* account.

20. Paṇḍit Vīrvijay, *Pistālīś Āgam Pūjā*, p. 409. Kali Yug in Jain parlance refers to the current time period, when liberation is not possible in one lifetime. The eleven *Aṅgs*, of which the *Ācārāṅga* is the first, are the holiest of the Śvetāmbar scriptures. The serpent

hood being worshiped is that of Dharaendra, the serpent deity who protects Pārśvanāth, indicating that this hymn is dedicated to the worship of Pārśvanāth. I think that Udāyī is King Udayana, the subject of many Indian stories (Adaval 1970). In the Jain tradition he was a king of Kosambi and contemporary of Mahāvīr. He was famous as a musician, and Padmāvatī was one of his queens.

21. See also Folkert 1993:illustration 11. The Digambars add two dreams to the list, a throne and a pair of fish. There is also a popular Hindu enumeration of fourteen auspicious objects that emerged from the churning of the milky ocean (Wilson 1972:66–67), which partially overlaps with the Jain list of fourteen dreams. The fourteen Hindu auspicious objects are carved in the modern marble surround of the main image in the Mahālakṣmī temple in Patan, in imitation of the frequent Jain use of the fourteen dreams to ornament temples.

22. Each of the four celebrations of Mahāvīr's birth I have observed (Patan in 1985 and 1986, at different *upāśrays*; Boston in 1992; and Ahmedabad in 1995) has been marked by a number of highly localized customs, affecting the order and number of actions, the number of bids, and even the relative size of the bids.

23. See Banks 1991, Cort 1991c:408–10, and Laidlaw 1995:334–51 for other accounts of the bidding process. See Cort 1989:510 and Folkert 1993:209–11 for detailed lists of bids at two congregations in 1985. See also C. W. Smith 1989 for a general description of auctions in Euro-American culture that is quite germane to the Jain case.

24. The unit of bidding is *pān-śer*, or five *śers* of ghee. The price is calculated on a set scale, reflecting prices from many decades ago. Margaret Stevenson (1910:96) reported the same value for a *pān-śer* at Girnar in the early years of the century that I encountered in Patan in 1985, and stated that even then it was "a price which must have prevailed long ago, as the present market value is ten times that amount." Since there are forty *śer* to one *maṇ* (eighteen and two-thirds kilograms), and one *maṇ* of ghee was worth two and a half rupees in the bidding in 1985, one *pān-śer* of ghee was roughly equal to one-third of a rupee. This ritual monetary value of one *pān-śer* varies in different parts of the country, but in all cases bears little relation to current market prices for ghee. In 1999, prices of ghee ranged from roughly Rs. 120 to 170 per kilogram, or roughly Rs. 270 to 385 per *pān-śer*.

25. In most *saṅghs*, this money is *dev-dravya*, and so can be used only for religious purposes, in particular, the renovation and building of temples.

26. These high bids for the lotus lake seem to be a Patan tradition. I have not seen similar bids in Ahmedabad or Boston. Neither does Laidlaw report them from Jaipur, nor Folkert from Sami, a town west of Patan. Zwicker (1984–1985:9/16/85.5), however, found high bids for the lotus lake in Ved, a village southwest of Sami. Here again we see how some aspects of Jain ritual culture are highly localized.

27. This probably constituted the original observance of Paryuṣaṇ, as the mendicants gathered to reaffirm orally their universal history, teacher-disciple succession, and mendicant rules. Then, as people became increasingly unfamiliar with Prakrit, four days of reading a vernacular commentary were added to the celebration. A further three days of sermons on the duties of the faithful were added to make the total number of days add up to the desired eight, an eight-day festival being common in the *mokṣa-mārg* ideology.

28. See Cort 1992:177–78 for a fuller discussion of the distinction between *Kalpa Sūtra* and *Bārsā Sūtra*.

29. See *Kalpasūtram (Bārasāsūtram) Sacitram*.

30. See Brown 1934, and Nawab 1956 and 1978.

31. See Folkert 1993:illustration 13. As another example of the way in which these practices are highly localized, James Laidlaw 1995:280–81 says that in Jaipur the pages were passed around the room, whereas in Patan and Ahmedabad the young boys holding the pages remained seated next to the reciting *sādhu*.

32. The minimal observance in both Patan and Ahmedabad, which was followed by the

vast majority of Jains, was to fast from after the midday meal on the Fourth until after sunrise on the Fifth. Laidlaw 1995:279–84 reports that in Jaipur most Jains fasted from the evening of the Third until after sunrise on the Fifth.

33. Laidlaw reports that in Jaipur people were not concerned to wear pure clothes for either *pratikramaṇ* or *sāmāyik*. Although I certainly observed people in Gujarat performing these rites wearing clothes that did not appear to have been set aside for ritual purposes, the vast majority of Jains I knew were careful that the clothes they wore for these rites met the purity standards for *pūjā* clothes.

34. Two terms are used for processions: *rath yātrā* (procession with a chariot) and *varghoḍo* (men on horses). The former is used only if the procession includes a bullock-drawn chariot bearing a Jina *mūrti*; the latter term is used to refer to any procession, regardless of whether or not it includes horses. For a fuller discussion of the Jain *rath yātrā*, along with photographs, see Jyotindra Jain 1979.

35. Among the earliest accounts of Indian processions are those of the Indramāha, or Indra festival, in which an Indra banner was paraded through the town. See V. S. Agrawala 1970:50–60 and *Bṛhatsaṃhitā* 43.

36. This last is like a Western slide guitar; it plays the melody to the songs. In recent years it has been replaced by the synthesizer.

37. See Babb 1996:79 on the significance of the frequent representation of the worshipers as Indra and Indrāṇī.

38. Ill-tempered spirits are believed to be voraciously greedy. They scramble after the seeds and thereby ignore the chariots.

39. Dozens of tellings of the story of Śrīpāl have been composed, the earliest extant of which is the Prakrit *Sīrivāla Kahā* of Ratnaśekharasūri composed before 1372 C.E. The one usually used as the basis for the sermons is the Gujarati *Śrīpāl Rājāno Rās* of Upādhyāy Vinayvijay and Mahopādhyāy Yaśovijay, composed in 1682 C.E. See also Laidlaw 1995:226 and Cort forthcoming-c.

40. See also Laidlaw 1995:364–87 for an excellent description and analysis of Dīvāḷī in Jaipur, noting in particular the different activities on the Fourteenth.

41. The image in this temple is mentioned in chapter 2. Mahālakṣmī is not an exclusively Jain goddess. This particular Lakṣmī image is the most important one in Patan. It is patronized by both Hindus and Jains, although the running of the temple is in the hands of the Bhojak *pujārī*s, who claim to have come to Patan with the goddess in the twelfth century. The temple was renovated in 1986, with the money for the renovation coming from both Hindus and Jains. In the late 1980s a new Mahālakṣmī temple was built in the wholesale market on the eastern edge of town, because the merchants there felt that the downtown temple was too far away.

42. Śāstrī (1976–1981:2,142) defines it as "the sign (*cihn*) or suggestion (*aṇsār*) of auspicious indications (*śubh sūcak*).

43. See Cort 1997b and forthcoming-e.

44. Sīmandhar Svāmī is the Jina currently living in the region of Mahāvideha (Dundas 1992:255–56). Although there is no theological connection between Sīmandhar Svāmī and Ghaṇṭākarṇ Mahāvīr, in the twentieth century both their cults have been promoted by mendicants of the Buddhisāgarsūri Samudāy, and so the location of the Ghaṇṭākarṇ Mahāvīr shrine in the Sīmandhar Svāmī temple in Patan comes as no surprise.

45. This description is based on the *havan* I observed in Patan in 1986. I also observed the *havan* at Mahudi in 1985, but due to the large crowd I could only see it on one of the television screens set up around the temple courtyard.

46. Ghaṇṭākarṇ literally means Bell-Ears, and hence the bell is an important part of his cult.

47. Every Ghaṇṭākarṇ shrine (as well as most other shrines to *vīr*s, powerful unliberated

male deities) has a small fire pit in front of the image for the performance of the annual *havan*. It is covered for the rest of the year.

48. Images, paintings, and photographs of Ghaṇṭākarṇ Mahāvīr usually include *yantras* (diagrams) consisting mostly of letters.

49. Buddhisāgarsūri 1953:16. The final syllables are typical of the performative utterances of *mantras*; they are pure sound devoid of communicated content, aimed at effecting a result.

50. Such red and yellow tie-dyed threads are common in northern and western India as amulets charged with the power of a protective deity, usually the goddess, but also of other deities.

51. Vimalacandra, *Ghaṇṭākarṇamahāvīramantrastotra* 16–17, 23–25, in Buddhisāgarsūri 1953:34–35.

52. Adapted from Mukund Lath's translation of verses 124–27. There are various Hindu interpretations of Dīvāḷī, all revolving around the birth or rescue of Lakṣmī and her subsequent coming into the homes of her devotees (Trivedi 1965:65–66, Underhill 1921:59–62).

53. This 434-verse Prakrit text was composed in 1427 C.E., although most *sādhus* know it through one of several Gujarati paraphrases. See Ānandsāgarsūri 1971:1–26 and Jinendravijaygaṇi 1980.

54. Ācārya Jñānvimalsūri (1638–1726), *Dīvālīnā Dev-vandan*, in *Devvandan Mālā*, pp. 1–9.

55. For example, a resolution was passed at the Fifth Jain Śvetāmbar Conference held in Ahmedabad in 1907 listing harmful customs that Jains should avoid. Among these was the observance of the customs and practices of the followers of other religions on holy days, including specifically the performance of Lakṣmī *pūjā* on Dīvāḷī. See Conference 1908 and Cort 1995b. See also Śāradā 1985, a liturgy published in a popular Jain monthly magazine, in which the editor says (p. 5), "Jains should worship according to the Jain liturgy on Dīvāḷī. We are therefore publishing the Jain liturgy."

56. See Anūpcandra 1972, Śāradā n.d., and Śāradā 1980. James Laidlaw (1995:368n2), however, says that he did not see such pamphlets in evidence in Jaipur. My description is based on my observances of book *pūjās* in 1985 and 1986, the first performed with reference to Śāradā n.d., the second with reference to a copy of Śāradā 1980 that I myself had brought to Patan from Bhavnagar. In both cases, a Brāhmaṇ who was otherwise an employee of the family business was specially requested to perform part of the ritual because of my presence as researcher. The family indicated that without the Brāhmaṇ there would not have been the elaborate preliminary invocation of Gaṇeś, the rivers, and the goddesses. The manipulation of such unliberated deities was seen to be one of the special qualifications of a Brāhmaṇ. I observed the ritual with the same family in 1995. By then they had reverted to doing it without a Brāhmaṇ, but still followed a pamphlet.

57. Every almanac has a chart for determining auspicious and inauspicious times of the day. Each of the seven days of the week is divided into sixteen units, known as *coghaḍiyā*. There are eight each for the day and night, the length of each unit determined by dividing the day or night into eight equal units. Each unit is assigned one of seven astrological qualities: *udveg* (disquiet), *cal* (unsteadiness), *lābh* (gain), *amṛt* (immortality), *kāḷ* (death), *śubh* (auspiciousness), and *rog* (illness). These can then be used by anyone for determining the relative auspiciousness or inauspiciousness of times for conducting various affairs. For more important undertakings, a more detailed horoscope is needed, and so people consult a professional astrologer, most of whom are Brāhmaṇs, although in earlier times many of them were *yatis*. I have also known Jains to consult an astrologer for a more precise reading if the only auspicious times in the *coghaḍīyā* chart fall at inconvenient times in terms of regular household activities. One year the auspicious *coghaḍīyā* times for the book *pūjā* were either too early or too late in the evening, whereas the most convenient time, between 8:00 and

9:00 P.M., fell in an inauspicious *coghaḍīyā*. The astrologer was consulted, and he said that by his more detailed calculation this time was appropriate.

58. Several days earlier, the head of the family had left an order with a stationery store for a kit that included all the ingredients needed in the ritual, along with the account books he would need for the coming year.

59. An alternate interpretation of the three days from Wealth Thirteenth through Dīvāḷī is that they involve the sequential worship of the goddess in her three forms as Lakṣmī, Kāḷī, and Sarasvatī.

60. The first three lines are in Sanskrit. The rest are in Gujarati; in Anūpcandra 1972:2 they are in Hindi. Gautam Svāmī is famous for his magical powers (*labdhi*). Keśarīyājī is a shrine of Ṛṣabhnāth in southern Rajasthan that is famous for its desire-fulfilling powers. Bharat was the first world emperor (*cakravartin*) of the current era of time. Bāhubali was Bharat's half-brother, famed for his martial prowess, who could have defeated him in battle but instead chose to renounce the world and become the first man to attain enlightenment in the current era of time (Hemacandra, *Triṣaṣṭiśalākāpuruṣacaritra*, Vol. 1, pp. 215–326). Abhaykumār was a wise prince who lived during the time of Mahāvīr (*Triṣaṣṭiśalākāpuruṣacaritra*, Vol. 10, pp. 147–313). Kayavanna (Sanskrit Kṛtapuṇya) was a merchant who, due to his perfect gifting of food to a *sādhu*, was able to consume the pleasures of heaven in this world; his story is told in narrative texts such as Nemicandrasūri's *Ākhyānakamaṇikośa*, pp. 20–24, Śubhaśīlagaṇi's *Bharateśvarabāhubalivṛtti*, Vol. 1, pp. 156–67, and Vijayalakṣmīsūri's *Upadeśaprāsāda*, story 167. Ratnākarsāgar is probably the same as Ratnākarsūri, whose story is told by Muni Jambūvijay 1997:III.205 in a sermon on Dīvāḷī: he ground to dust several diamonds, pearls, and other precious stones, to demonstrate to a layman that real value lies only in knowledge, not money. One printed text listed the compassion (*maher*) of Ratnākarsāgar rather than his joy (*laher*). Dhanna and Sālibhadra were two friends who symbolize both great worldly wealth and eventual renunciation of that wealth (see Bloomfield 1923, and the versions in *Ākhyānakamaṇikośa*, pp. 30–35, *Triṣaṣṭiśalākāpuruṣacaritra*, Vol. 6, pp. 254–62, and *Śālibhadra-Dhanna-Carita*). Laidlaw 1995:374–84 gives an extended discussion of a slightly different list from Jaipur, which he aptly calls a "catalogue of virtues."

61. Some people also made a symbolic first entry into the book, entering both a credit and a debit of the auspicious amount of one and one-quarter rupees. Khare 1976b:211n8 has also noted that this is an auspicious amount because it "calls for completion."

62. See also Dundas 1992:33–34 and 1998, and Laidlaw 1995:375–80.

63. I do not know if this transaction is termed *dān*, but Laidlaw 1995:373 reports that in Jaipur it was not. This is not an example of gifting in order to transfer inauspiciousness, as are the *dān* transactions analyzed by Raheja 1988. Rather, it seems to entail the understanding that only by freely giving to start the new year will one be assured of income during the course of the year. In a similar spirit, Hindu men I knew when I lived in Banaras insisted on gambling on Dīvāḷī; they said that anyone who did not gamble on this day would not gain any wealth in the coming year. See also Laidlaw 1995:384.

64. In many temples, the name of the main image is written either above the doorway into the central shrine or on the back wall of the shrine above the image. In the temples where the name was not written, people often had to ask a local resident the name of a particular image; and if there was no one to ask, they sang a generic song, not addressed to any particular Jina.

65. This is an ancient formulation within the Jain tradition. Ācārya Ānandsāgarsūri 1971:27 in his sermon on the importance of Knowledge Fifth cites the *Uttarādhyayana Sūtra* as saying, "The chief virtue of the soul is the virtue of *jñān*." See *Uttarādhyayana Sūtra* 28.11.

66. For a partial list of texts composed between the eleventh and nineteenth centuries, see A. S. Gopani's introduction to Maheśvarasūri's *Jñānapañcamīkathā*, pp. 1–7.

67. See Ānandsāgarsūri 1971:65–66 and Bhuvanvijay 1981a:62–74. Ānandsāgarsūri cites as his source story 215 in the *Upadeśaprāsāda* of Ācārya Vijaya Lakṣmīsūri, composed in 1787.

68. At one congregational ritual I attended, a woman was concerned that I neither place my copy of the liturgical manual on the floor of the temple nor place my notebook on top of the manual while writing my notes. She said, in English, "It's a holy book."

69. The five types of *jñān* are (Jaini 1979:121–22) as follows:

1. *matijñāna*: functioning of the six senses (Western five plus mind)
2. *śrutajñāna*: reasoning
3. *avadhijñāna*: clairvoyance and other limited supersensory perception
4. *manaḥparyayajñāna* or *manaḥparyavajñāna*: awareness of thought forms of others
5. *kevalajñāna*: absolute omniscience

70. See *Devvandan Mālā*, pp. 10–31, for *Jñān Pañcamīnā Dev-vandan* of Ācārya Vijay Lakṣmīsūri.

71. Ānandsāgarsūri 1971:100–6 and Bhuvanvijay 1981a:75–80. After hearing this story in a sermon, one young man jokingly wondered aloud what this had done to the population of India. His father replied that one simply has to believe such stories, "one has no choice."

72. For examples of such paintings, see Pal 1994:illustrations 117a-c.

73. "Śatruñjaynū Caityavandan," in *Sudhāras Stavan Saṅgrah*, pp. 8–9. Kavaḍ or Kapardin Yakṣ is the protector deity of Shatrunjay; see *Vividhatīrthakalpa* 30, Chojnacki 1995:512–16, and Granoff 1990:185–86. King Nābhi is Ṛṣabhnāth's father. On Shatrunjay, see also Burgess 1869, Cort 1990b:246–51, and J. Jain 1980.

74. The calculation is based on Jain cosmography. These five *kalyāṇaks* occur in each of the five Bhārat and five Airāvat countries, and since these *kalyāṇaks* occur in each of the past, present, and future cycles of Jinas, the total number of *kalyāṇaks* is 150 (Bhuvanvijay 1981a:82):

5 *kalyāṇaks* x 5 Bhārat countries = 25 *kalyāṇaks*
5 *kalyāṇaks* x 5 Airāvat countries = 25 *kalyāṇaks*
50 *kalyāṇaks* x 3 times = 150 *kalyāṇaks*

75. Ānandsāgarsūri 1971:107–22 and Bhuvanvijay 1981a:81–91.

76. See *Devvandan Mālā*, pp. 40–62 and 62–78 for *Maun Ekādaśīnā Dev-vandans* by Paṇḍit Rūpvijay (?–1849) and Ācārya Jñānvimalsūri.

77. Ānandsāgarsūri 1971:123–34 and Bhuvanvijay 1981a:92–100.

78. Approximately 30% of the main images in Patan are Pārśvanāth, far more than any other Jina. This pattern is replicated throughout India. Pārśvanāth is also the Jina who most tends to have geographical or other qualifiers added to his name, such as Pañcāsar Pārśvanāth, Śaṅkheśvar Pārśvanāth, or Śāmḷā Pārśvanāth. Partly as a result of this localization of Pārśvanāth, there is a sense of there being 108 important Pārśvanāth images (and therefore shrines) in India.

79. Trivedi 1965:77 gives four stories that recount the origin of the event, and Underhill 1921:44–45 gives five.

80. Further north in Rajasthan and north India, many Jains try to go to Hastinapur (near Delhi) for the first feeding, since this was where Śreyāṅs fed Ṛṣabhnāth.

81. Ānandsāgarsūri 1971:153–68 and Bhuvanvijay 1981a:137–42. See also Hemacandra, *Triṣaṣṭiśalākāpuruṣacaritra*, Vol. 1, pp. 176–83, for a medieval telling of the mythic charter for Immortal Third.

82. Ātmārāmjī, *Sattarbhedī Pūjā*, in *Vividh Pūjā Saṅgrah*, 457–74.

Chapter Seven

1. Hemacandra in his *Abhidhānacintāmaṇi* (1.86) gives fourteen synonymous terms in this context, which provide an alternative list: *śvaḥśreyasa, śubha, śiva, kalyāṇa, śvovasīyasa, śreyas, kṣema, bhāvuka, bhavika, kuśala, maṅgala, bhadra, madra*, and *śasta*.

2. In particular, see Carman and Marglin 1985, Das 1982, Khare 1976a and 1976b, Madan 1987, Marglin 1985, and Raheja 1988.

3. See Fuller's 1992:10 discussion of the need to use the term "Hinduism" despite critiques that it has no indigenous equivalent: "Anthropological or sociological analysis abstracts from the empirical data and also attempts to make them intelligible by using concepts and deploying generalizations that are formulated comparatively and rarely correspond precisely to indigenous categories in any particular society. That 'Hinduism' is not a traditional, indigenous category, concept, or 'cultural reality'—albeit an important negative fact—in no way nullifies an analysis that demonstrates that Hinduism is a relatively coherent and distinctive religious system founded on common structures of relationships."

4. In addition to Brown 1934, see the illustrations included in the Vinaya Sāgar edition and in *Kalpasūtram (Bārasāsūtram) Sacitram*.

5. Mānatuṅga, *Bhaktāmara Stotra* 44 (Śvetāmbar recension). The phrase "proud man" (*mānatuṅga*) is a play on the author's name, and serves as a signature line for the poem as a whole.

6. In Sanskrit these are *rājyasvārgāpavargasatkā śrī, śobhā, vārdhikanī, sakalabhūmi śrī, puṣpadā*, and *śrīsamarūpā strī*.

7. *Rājya, svarg, mokṣ*, and *satkāvya*. Bogāvat and Bhaṇḍrī, p. 104. In place of "good poetry," the English translator has "dignity," so *satkāvya* may be a misprint for *satkārya*.

8. For example, the famous image of Sarasvatī and various Jina images were installed "for the benefit and pleasure of all beings," the inscriptions giving variants of *sarvvasatvānāṃ hitasukhāya* (Bühler 1892:391 and 1894:203, 208, 210).

9. In Prakrit, *orāla, kallāṇa, siva, dhanna, maṅgalla*, and *sassirīa*.

10. In Prakrit, *siva, dhanna, maṅgalla, sassirīa, ārugga, tuṭṭhi, dīhāu, kallāṇa*, and *maṅgallakāraga*.

11. *Kalpa Sūtra* 85–86, Lath translation, pp. 131–33.

12. Nathmal Tatia, in his translator's note (pp. 6–7) to this verse, remarks that the Śvetāmbar commentator Siddhasenagaṇi includes *puṇya* and *pāpa* under only bondage, whereas the Digambar commentator Pūjyapāda includes them under both influx and bondage.

13. The *Sthānāṅga* uses the term *padārtha*. On the use of the terms *tattva* and *padārtha*, see Folkert 1993:113–45.

14. A further list of ten is found in *Sūtrakṛtāṅga* 5.13–17, which includes the nine that became standard plus *vedanā*, feeling. A significant difference is that unlike the lists of seven and nine, the *Sūtrakṛtāṅga* list consists of five linked pairs of opposites. See Dixit 1978:39.

15. Dixit 1971:5–6 and 21, and Johnson 1995:49–51, 87–88, also see this categorization as implying a disagreement on doctrine, although Johnson sees Umāsvātī as supportive of lay conduct, whereas I see his formulation as not supportive.

16. See, among others, the works in note 2.

17. See Roth 1974 for an extended discussion of the *Nokār Mantra*.

18. The similarity between these verses and early Buddhist liturgy indicates that they derive from the broader early *śramaṇa* tradition.

19. See Vol. 1, pp. 2–5 of Sāgarānandsūri's edition, as well as Balbir 1993:219–21 and Mehtā 1967:139–40.

20. In *Śāntisnātrādividhisamuccaya*, p. 54.

21. These words reflect the dual parentage of the English language: "sacred" is cognate with French *sacré* and "holy" is cognate with German *heilige*. The two have been used by scholars as essentially interchangeable.

22. See also Durkheim 1912 and Söderblom 1913 for contemporaneous discussions of the sacred and the holy.

23. Eliade's formulations have not been without their critics; see in particular Jonathan Z. Smith 1978 and 1987.

24. I should note that Padmanabh Jaini has taken an opposing view, when he says, "Eliade's concepts of the sacred are deficient when we consider the religion of the Jains" (1985a:102).

25. Bhadraṅkarvijaygaṇi and Kalyāṇprabhvijay in *Subodhaṭīkā* on *Pratikramaṇa Sūtra*, p. 469.

26. This is according to A. P. Śāh 1953:35–52 and Dośī 1981:26–35. Dośī actually lists more temples of Śāntināth than of Ādināth. There are many fewer temples to Mahāvīr, between 5 and 7%.

27. *Santikara* 13.

28. U. P. Shah 1987:152 argues that her worship is directly tied to the rise of Jain Tantric practices, in particular the Tantric rite of *śānti-karma*.

29. I omit discussion of one of the three *Navasmaraṇa* hymns, the *Ajitaśānti* attributed to Nandiṣeṇa, in which praises of Śāntināth alternate with praises of the second Jina Ajitanāth, "The Invincible Lord."

30. Tellings of the lives of the authors of these poems are widely available; see Tripuṭī Mahārāj 1952, Ratna Prabha Vijaya 1950, and the editors' introductions to the texts themselves.

31. Dānvijay, *Navasmaraṇa*, p. 6.

32. *Santikara* 12.

33. Mānadevasūri, *Laghu Śānti* 3 and 5. Text in *Pratikramaṇa Sūtra*.

34. *Bṛhacchānti* 1b–d.

35. It also includes portions of the text of *Ajitaśānti*.

36. *Śāntisnātrādividhisamuccaya*, p. 82.

37. See the similar comments of Fuller 1992:27, who discusses the mistake committed by M. N. Srinivas 1952, and following him, many other scholars, in the interpretation of Hinduism, of converting "an indigenous, ideological distinction [the distinction between the Brāhmaṇical Sanskritic Hinduism of the great tradition and the non-Sanskritic Hinduism of the little tradition] into an analytical concept, and then appl[ying] it to the empirical evidence to try to divide what is actually united by common underlying themes and principles."

Bibliography

I. Prakrit [P], *Sanskrit* [S], *Gujarati* [G], *Old Gujarati* [OG], *Hindi* [H], *and Persian* [Pe] *texts*

In accordance with Jain practice, the names of Prakrit texts (except those in the *Navasmaraṇa*) are given in their Sanskrit forms.

Abhidhānacintāmaṇi [S] of Hemacandra, with *Maṇiprabhā Ṭippaṇa* [H] of Pt. Hargovind Śāstrī. Edited by Nemichandra Sastri. Varanasi: Chowkhamba Sanskrit Series Office. Vidyabhawan Sanskrit Series 109.

Ācārāṅga Sūtra [P]. Edited by Hermann Jacobi. London: The Pali Text Society, 1882.

———. Edited by Walther Schubring. Leipzig: F. A. Brockhaus, 1910.

———. English translation in Jacobi 1884, 1–213.

Ākhyānakamaṇikośa [P] of Nemicandrasūri, with *Vṛtti* [P] of Āmradevasūri. Edited by Muni Puṇyavijay. Varanasi: Prakrit Text Society, 1962. Prakrit Text Series 5.

Antakṛddaśāḥ [P]. Edited with English translation by M. C. Modi. Ahmedabad: Gurjar Granth Ratna Karyalay, 1932. Prakrit Granth Mala 1.

Aupapātika Sūtra [P]. Edited by Ernst Leumann. Leipzig: G. Kreysing, 1882.

———. *Uvavāiya Suttam*. English translation by Kastur Chand Lalwani, Hindi translation by Rameś Muni Śāstrī, edited by Ganesh Lalwani. Jaipur: Prakrit Bharati Academy; and Mewanagar: Shri Jain Shwetambar Nakoda Parshwanath Teerth, 1988.

Āvaśyaka Sūtra [P]. With *Niryukti* [P] of Bhadrabāhu and *Ṭīkā* [S] of Haribhadra. Edited by Ācārya Sāgarānandsūri [Ānandsāgarsūri]. 2 volumes. Bombay: Āgamoday Samiti, 1916–1917. Reprint Bombay: Bherulāl Kanaiyālāl Koṭhārā Dhārmik Ṭrasṭ, 1982.

———. Edited by Muni Puṇyavijaya and Pt. Amritlāl Mohanlāl Bhojak. *Dasaveyāliyasuttaṃ, Uttarajhayaṇāiṃ and Āvassayasuttaṃ*. Bombay: Shri Mahāvīra Jaina Vidyālaya, 1977. Jaina Āgama Series 15.

———. *See* Balbir 1993.

Bhagavatī Sūtra [P] with *Ṭīkā* [S] of Abhayadeva, Sanskrit translation by Rāmacandragaṇi, and Gujarati translation by Meghrājgaṇi. Edited by Ṛṣi Nānakcand. Banaras: Rāy Dhanpatisiṃh Bahādur Āgam Saṃgrah, 1882.

———. *See* Deleu 1970.

Bhaktāmara Stotra [S] of Mānatuṅga. With *Vivṛtti* [S] of Guṇākara, *Vṛtti* [S] of Mahopādhyāya Meghavijaya, and *Vṛtti* [S] of Kanakakuśalagaṇi. Edited by Hīrālāl Rasikdās Kāpaḍiyā. *Bhaktāmarakalyāṇamandiranamiūṇastotratrayam*. Surat: Śeṭh Devcand Lālbhāī Jain Pustakoddhār Saṃsthā, 1932. Devcand Lālbhāī Jain Pustakoddhār Granth 79.

———. *Bhaktāmara, Ratnākara Paccīsī, Sāmāyika Pātha*. Edited by Premrāj Bogāvat and Prem Bhaṇḍārī. English translation by Himmat Sinha Sarupria. Jaipur: Samyagjñān Pracārak Maṇḍal, 1975.

Bharateśvarabāhubalivṛtti [P] of Śubhaśīlagaṇi. Edited by Paṅnyās Pradyumnavijaygaṇi. 2 volumes. Ahmedabad: Śrī Śrutajñan Prasārak Sabhā, 1987.

———. Gujarati translation by Paṅnyās Cidānandmuni. 3 volumes. Kadi: Candrakānt Ratīlāl Śāh, n.d.

Bhāṣyatraya [P] of Devendrasūri. Mehsana: Śrīmad Yaśovijayjī Jain Saṃskṛt Pāṭhśāḷā ane Śrī Jain Śreyaskar Maṇḍaḷ, 1977 (4th printing).

———. *Devavandana-Guruvandana-Pratyākhyāna-Bhāṣyatraya*. Edited by Ācārya Vijay Jinendrasūri. Lakhabawal: Śrī Harṣapuṣpāmṛt Jain Granthmālā, 1993. No. 255 in publisher's series.

Bṛhatsaṃgrahaṇi [P] of Maladhārī Candrasūri. With Gujarati translation by Paṇḍit Amṛtlāl Puruṣottamdās. Ahmedabad: Śrī Jain Prakāśan Mandir, n.d.

———. *Saṃgrahaṇiratnagrantha*. With Hindi translation by Ācārya Vijay Yaśodevsūri. Baroda: Śrī Muktikamalmohan Jain Jñānmandir, 1993.

Bṛhatsaṃgrahaṇi [P] of Jinabhadragaṇi Kṣamāśramaṇa. With *Vivṛti* [S] of Malayagiri. Bhavnagar, 1917.

Bṛhatsaṃhitā [S] of Varāhamihira. English translation by H. Kern. London: Trübner & Co., 1869–1874.

Bṛhacchānti (*Moṭī Śānti*) [S] of Vādivetāla Śāntisūri. In *Navasmaraṇa* (Navab edition), 617–22.

Cosaṭh Prakārī Pūjā [G] of Paṇḍit Vīrvijay. In *Vividh Pūjā Saṅgrah*, 321–77.

Daṇḍaka Prakaraṇa [P] of Gajasāra Muni. Mehsana: Śrīmad Yaśovijayjī Jain Saṃskṛt Pāṭhśāḷā ane Śrī Jain Śreyaskar Maṇḍaḷ, 1981 (5th printing).

Daśavaikālika Sūtra [P]. Edited by Ernst Leumann, with English translation by Walther Schubring. Ahmedabad: Anandji Kalianji, 1932.

———. English translation by Kastur Chand Lalwani. Delhi: Motilal Banarsidass, 1973.

Devvandan Mālā [G]. Ahmedabad: Jain Prakāśan Mandir, n.d.

Dīkṣāvidhi tathā Vratvidhi [P, G]. Bhavnagar: Śrī Yaśovijay Jain Granthmālā, 1928.

Jambūdvīpa Saṃgrahaṇi (*Laghusaṃgrahaṇī*) [P] of Haribhadrasūri. Mehsana: Śrīmad Yaśovijayjī Jain Saṃskṛt Pāṭhśāḷā ane Śrī Jain Śreyaskar Maṇḍaḷ, 1981 (5th printing).

Jinendra Stavanādi Kāvya Saṅgrah, Vol. 1 [G]. Edited by Muni Cāritravijay. Jamnagar: Jesaṅglāl Hīrālāl Lālaṇ, 1948.

Jinguṇpadyāvalī [G]. Mehsana: Śrīmad Yaśovijayjī Jain Saṃskṛt Pāṭhśāḷā ane Śrī Jain Śreyaskar Maṇḍaḷ, 1991 (9th printing).

Jīvavicāra [P] of Vādivetāla Śāntisūri. Mehsana: Śrīmad Yaśovijayjī Jain Saṃskṛt Pāṭhśāḷā ane Śrī Jain Śreyaskar Maṇḍaḷ, 1985 (10th printing).

———. Edited by A. Guérinot in *Journal Asiatique* (9th Series) 19 (1902), 231–88.

Jñānapañcamīkathā [P] of Maheśvarasūri. Edited by A. S. Gopani. Bombay: Siṅghī Jain Śāstra Śikṣāpīṭh and Bhāratīya Vidyā Bhavan, 1941. Siṅghī Jain Series 25.

Jñānasāra [S] of Mahopādhyāya Yaśovijaya. Edited by Pt. Girishkumar Parmanand Shah, translated by Amritlal S. Gopani. Bombay: Jaina Sāhitya Vikāsa Maṇḍala, 1986.

Kalpa Sūtra [P] of Bhadrabāhu Svāmī. Edited and Hindi translation by Mahopādhyāy Vinaya Sāgar, English translation by Mukund Lath. Jaipur: Prakrit Bharati, 1984.

———. *Kalpasūtram (Bārasāsūtram) Sacitram*. Surat: Śrī Bārasāsūtra Prakāśan Samiti, 1980.

———. English translation in Jacobi 1884, 215–311.

———. With *Subodhikā Ṭīkā* [S] of Upādhyāya Vinayavijayagaṇi. Surat: Devcand Lālbhāī Pustakoddhār Fund, 1911. No 7–9 in publisher's series.

Karmagrantha [P] of Devendrasūri. With *Stābukārth* [G] of Muni Jīvvijay. 3 volumes. Mehsana:

Śrīmad Yaśovijayjī Jain Saṃskṛt Pāṭhśāḷā ane Śrī Jain Śreyaskar Maṇḍaḷ, 1977 (4th printing).

Kharataragaccha Bṛhad Gurvāvali [S]. Edited by Muni Jina Vijaya. Bombay: Siṅghī Jain Śāstra Śikṣāpīṭha and Bhāratīya Vidyā Bhavan, 1956. Siṅghī Jain Series 42.

Kṣetrasamāsa [P] of Jinabhadragaṇi Kṣamāśramaṇa. Edited by Nityānandvijaygaṇi. 2 volumes. Cambay: Saṅghvī Ambālāl Ratnacand Jain Dhārmik Ṭrasṭ, 1978–1979.

Lalitavistarā [S] of Haribhadra Yākinīmahattarāsūnu, with *Pañjikā* [S] of Municandrasūri. Surat: Devcand Lālbhāī Jaina Pustakoddhāra, 1915. No. 29 in publisher's series.

Mahādeva Stotra [S] of Hemacandra. *Vītarāga-Mahādeva Stotra*. Edited by Muni Caraṇvijay. Bhavnagar: Śrī Jain Ātmānand Sabhā, 1935.

———. Paṅ. Śīlcandravijaygaṇi, *Śrī Hemacandrācārya ane temne racel Śrī Mahādeva Batrīśī-Stotra*. Cambay: Śrī Jain Granth Prakāśan Samiti, 1989.

Mahānisītha Sūtra [P]. Edited and translated by Jozef Deleu and Walther Schubring as *Studien zum Mahānisīha*. 2 volumes. Hamburg: Cram, de Gruyter, 1951–1963. Alt- und Neu-Indische Studien 6 and 10.

Mirat-i-Ahmadi Supplement [Pe] of Ali Muhammad Khan. Translated by Syed Nawab Ali and Charles Norman Seddon. Baroda: Oriental Institute, 1928. Gaekwad's Oriental Series 43.

Namrattā [G]. Bombay: Arihant Ārādhak Maṇḍaḷ, n.d.

Navpad Pūjā [G] of Mahopādhyāya Yaśovijay. In *Vividh Pūjā Saṅgrah*, 184–205.

Navasmaraṇa [P, S]. *Mahāprābhāvika Navasmaraṇa*. Edited by Muni Dānvijay. Palitana: Kāntilāl Ḍī. Śāh, n.d.

———. *Mahāprābhāvika Navasmaraṇa*. Edited by Sārābhāī Maṇilāl Navāb. Ahmedabad: Sārābhāī Maṇilāl Navāb, 1961. Shree Jain Prachina Sahityoddhar Granthavali Series 6.

Navatattva Prakaraṇa [P]. Mehsana: Śrīmad Yaśovijayjī Jain Saṃskṛt Pāṭhśāḷā ane Śrī Jain Śreyaskar Maṇḍaḷ, 1993 (7th printing).

———. *The Kalpa Sutra and Nava Tatva* [sic]. English translation by Rev. J. Stevenson. London: Oriental Translation Fund of Great Britain and Ireland, 1847. Reprint Varanasi: Bharat-Bharati, 1972.

Pañcasaṃgraha [P] of Candrarṣi Mahattara. With *Svopajñavṛtti* [S] and *Bṛhadvṛtti* [S] of Malayagiri. 2 volumes. Dabhoi: Muktābāī Jñānmandir, 1937–1938.

Pañcasūtraka [P] of Cirantanācārya. Edited by Muni Jambūvijay. Delhi: Bhogilal Leherchand Institute of Indology, 1986.

Pistāliś Āgam Pūjā [G] of Paṇḍit Vīrvijay. In *Vividh Pūjā Saṅgrah*, 405–22.

Prabandhacintāmaṇi [S] of Merutuṅga. Edited by Muni Jinavijaya. Santiniketan: Siṅghī Jaina Jñānapīṭha, 1933. Siṅghī Jain Series 1.

———. English translation by C. H. Tawney. Calcutta: Asiatic Society, 1899. Bibliotheca Indica 141.

Pratikramaṇa Sūtra [P, G]. *Devasia-Rāïa Pratikramaṇa Sūtro*. Mehsana: Śrīmad Yaśovijayjī Jain Saṃskṛt Pāṭhśāḷā ane Śrī Jain Śreyaskar Maṇḍaḷ, 1980 (15th printing).

——. *Pañca Pratikramaṇādi Sūtro*. Mehsana: Śrīmad Yaśovijayjī Jain Saṃskṛt Pāṭhśāḷā ane Śrī Jain Śreyaskar Maṇḍaḷ, 1983 (15th printing).

——. *Śrāddha-Pratikramaṇa-Sūtra (Prabodha Ṭīkā)*. Edited by Paṅnyās Bhadraṅkarvijaygaṇi and Muni Kalyāṇprabhvijay. 3 volumes. 2nd edition. Bombay: Jain Sāhitya Vikās Maṇḍaḷ, 1977.

——. *See* Jinendrasūri 1986.

——. *See* Nirvāṇa Sāgara 1986.

Ratnākara Paccīsī [S] of Ratnākara. *Bhaktāmara, Ratnākara Paccīsī, Sāmāyika Pātha*. Edited by Premrāj Bogāvat and Prem Bhaṇḍārī. English translation by Himmat Sinha Sarupria. Jaipur: Samyagjñān Pracārak Maṇḍaḷ, 1975.

Sālibhadra-Dhanna-Carita [OG] of Matisāra. Edited and translated by Ernest Bender as *The Sālibhadra-Dhanna-Carita: The Tale of the Quest for Ultimate Release by Sālibhadra and Dhanna.* New Haven: American Oriental Series, 1992. American Oriental Series 72.

Samarārāsu [OG] of Ambadevasūri. In *Prāchīna Gurjara-Kāvyasaṅgraha*, Part I, 27–38. Edited by C. D. Dalal. Baroda: Central Library, 1920. Gaekwad's Oriental Series 13.

Samyaktvasaptatikā [P] of Haribhadra with *Tattvakaumudī* [S] of Saṅghatilakasūri. Bombay: Śeṭh Devcand Lālbhāī Jain Pustakoddhār Fund, 1913.

Santikara [P] of Munisundarasūri. In *Navasmaraṇa* (Navāb edition), 257–92.

Śāntisnātrādividhisamuccaya [S]. Edited by Ācārya Vijay Jinendrasūri. Lakhabaval: Śrī Harṣapuṣpāmṛt Jain Granthamālā, 1985. No. 135 in publisher's series.

Śāntistava (*Laghu Śānti*) [S] of Mānadevasūri. In *Pratikramaṇa Sūtra.* (Bhadraṅkarvijaygaṇi and Kalyāṇprabhvijay edition) II: 464–537.

Sindūraprakara [S] of Somaprabhasūri with *Vṛtti* [S] of Harṣakīrtisūri. Edited and Gujarati translation by Paṅnyās Pradyumnavijaygaṇi. Ahmedabad: Śrī Śrutajñān Prasārak Sabhā, 1984.

Śrāddhadinakṛtya [P] with *Svopajñavṛtti* [S] of Devendrasūri. 2 volumes. Ratlam: Ṛṣabhdevjī Kesrīmaljī Jain Saṃsthā, 1938–1939. Reprinted Bombay: Śrī Jinśāsan Ārādhnā Ṭrasṭ, 1989.

Śramaṇkriyānā Sūtro Sārth [P, G]. Ahmedabad: Śrī Śrutajñān Prasārak Sabhā, 1982.

Śrīpālrājāno Rās [G] of Upādhyāya Vinayvijay and Mahopādhyāya Yaśovijay. Bhavnagar: Śrī Jain Ātmānand Sabhā, 1982.

Sthānāṅga Sūtra [P] with *Vṛtti* [S] of Abhayadeva. Edited by Ācārya Sāgarānandsūri, revised by Muni Puṇyavijay, further revised by Muni Jambūvijay. In *Sthānāṅga Sūtram and Samavāyaṅga Sūtram*, 1–411, Delhi: Motilal Banarsidass, 1985. Lala Sundarlal Jain Āgamagranthamālā 2.

Sudhāras Stavan Saṅgrah [G]. Palitana: Kāntilāl Ḍī. Śāh. (There have been several dozen printings of this collection in the twentieth century, most with slightly different contents. The version I have used was purchased in 1985.)

Sukṛtasaṃkīrtana [S] of Arisiṃha. Edited by Muni Puṇyavijay. Bombay: Siṅghī Jaina Śāstra Śikṣāpīṭha and Bhāratīya Vidyā Bhavan, 1961. Siṅghī Jain Series 32.

Sūtrakṛtāṅga Sūtra [P]. With *Niryukti* [P] of Bhadrabāhu and *Ṭīkā* [S] of Śīlāṅka. Edited by Ācārya Sāgarānandsūri, reedited by Muni Jambūvijay. Delhi: Motilal Banarsidass, 1978. Lala Sundarlal Jain Āgamagranthamālā 1.

——. English translation in Jacobi 1895, 233–435.

Tapāgacchapaṭṭāvalī [P] with *Svopajñavṛtti* [S] of Mahopādhyāya Dharmasāgaragaṇi. Edited by Muni Darśanvijay in *Śrī Paṭṭāvalī-Samuccaya*, Vol. 1. Viramgam: Śrī Cāritra Smārak Granthmālā, 1933. No. 22 in publisher's series.

Tattvārtha Sūtra [S] of Umāsvāti. Edited by Paṇḍit Pukhrāj Amīcand Koṭhārī. Mehsana: Śrīmad Yaśovijayjī Jain Saṃskṛt Pāṭhśāḷā ane Śrī Jain Śreyaskar Maṇḍaḷ, 1976.

——. Edited with *Svakṛta Bhāṣya* [S] attributed to Umāsvāti by Keshavlal Premchand Mody. Calcutta: Asiatic Society, 1903–1905. Bibliotheca Indica 159.

——. English translation by Nathmal Tatia as *That Which Is*. San Francisco: Harper Collins, 1994.

——. English translation and commentary in Sanghavi 1974.

Triṣaṣṭiśalākāpuruṣacaritra [S] of Hemacandrasūri. 6 volumes. Bhavnagar: Jaina Dharma Prasāraka Sabhā, 1905–1913.

——. English translation by Helen M. Johnson. 6 volumes. Baroda: Oriental Institute, 1931–1962. Gaekwad's Oriental Series 51, 77, 108, 125, 139, 140.

Upadeśaprāsāda [S] of Vijayalakṣmīsūri. 3 volumes. Bhavnagar: Jaina Dharma Prasāraka Sabhā, 1914–1923.

——. Gujarati translation by Ācārya Vijay Viśālsensūri. Palitana: Virāṭ Prakāśan Mandir, 1973.

Upāsakadaśāḥ [P]. Edited by A. F. Rudolf Hoernle. Calcutta: Asiatic Society, 1885.

——. *Uvāsagadasāo*. Translated by A. F. Rudolf Hoernle. Calcutta: Asiatic Society, 1890.

Uttarādhyayana Sūtra [P]. Edited by Jarl Charpentier. Uppsala: J.-A. Lundell, 1922. Archives d'Études Orientales 18:1–2. Reprint New Delhi: Ajay, 1980.

——. English translation in Jacobi 1895, 1–232.

Uvasaggaharaṃ Stotra [P] attributed to Bhadrabāhu. In *Navasmaraṇa* (Navāb edition), 156–83.

Vanarājavṛttam [S]. In *Purātanaprabandhasaṃgraha*. Edited by Jinavijaya. Calcutta: Siṅghī Jaina Jñānapīṭha, 1936. Siṅghī Jain Series 2.

Vāstusāra Prakaraṇa [P] of Ṭhakkura Pheru. Edited by Ācārya Jayantsensūri "Madhukar," and Gujarati translation by Paṇḍit Bhagvāndās Jain. Ahmedabad: Rāj-Rājendra Prakāśan Ṭrasṭ, 1989.

Vijñapti Mahālekha [S] of Jinodayasūri. In *Vijñapti-lekha-saṃgraha*. Edited by Jina Vijaya. Bombay: Siṅghī Jain Śāstra Śikṣapīṭha and Bhāratīya Vidyā Bhavan, 1960. Siṅghī Jain Series 51.

Vītarāga Stotra [S] of Hemacandrasūri. Edited with *Avacūrṇī* [S] of Somodayagaṇi, *Vivaraṇa* [S] of Prabhānandasūri, and Gujarati translation by Muni Candraprabhasāgara. Surat: Śeṭh Devcand Lālbhāī Jain Pustakoddhār Fund, 1949. Devcand Lālbhāī Series 95.

Vividh Pūjā Saṅgrah [G]. Ahmedabad: Śrī Jain Prakāśan Mandir, 1984 (12th printing).

Vividhatīrthakalpa [P, S] of Jinaprabhasūri. Edited by Jina Vijaya. Santiniketan: Siṅghī Jaina Jñānapīṭha, 1934. Siṅghī Jain Series 10.

——. Translation of selected chapters in Cort 1990b and Granoff 1990.

——. Partial translation by Christine Chojnacki. *Vividhatīrthakalpaḥ: Regards sur le saint Jaina*. 2 volumes. Pondichéry: Institut Français de Pondichéry; and Paris: École Française d'Extrême-Orient, 1995. Publications du Département d'Indologie 85.

Yatidinacaryā [P] of Bhāvadevasūri. With *Vivṛtta* of Matisāgarasūri. Ratlam: Ṛṣabhadevajī Keśarīmalajī Śvetāmbara Sansthā, 1936.

Yogaśāstra [S] of Hemacandrasūri. Edited with *Svopajñavṛtti* [S] of Hemacandrasūri by Muni Jambūvijay. 3 volumes. Bombay: Jain Sāhitya Vikās Maṇḍaḷ, 1977–1986.

II. Modern works

Abhaycandravijay, Paṅnyās. 1982. *Updhān Tap Vidhi*. Dhanera: Śrī Updhāntap Samiti.

Abhaysāgargaṇi, Paṅnyās. 1968. *Kyā Pṛthvī kā Ākār Gol Hai?* Kaparvanj: Jambūdvīp Nirmāṇ Yojnā.

——. 1985. Pūjā ke sāth Cāhiye Cāritra. *Tīrthaṅkar* 15.4/5, 128.

Adaval, Niti. 1970. *The Story of King Udayana as Gleaned from Sanskrit Pali & Prakrit Sources*. Varanasi: Chowkhamba Sanskrit Series Office. Chowkhamba Sanskrit Series 74.

Agrawala, R. C. 1968. An Unpublished Bronze from Bhinmal, Rajasthan. *Bulletin of the Museum and Picture Gallery* 20, 49–50.

Agrawala, V. S. 1970. *Ancient Indian Folk Cults*. Banaras: Prthvi Prakasan.

Alsdorf, Ludwig. 1973. Nikṣepa—a Jaina Contribution to Scholastic Methodology. *Journal of the Oriental Institute* 22, 455–63.

Amityaśvijay, Muni. 1995. *Bhakt kī Bhāvnā*. 3rd printing. Madras: Śrī Kalāpūrṇ Jain Ārādhak Maṇḍaḷ.

Ānandsāgarsūri, Ācārya. 1971. *Parv-Māhātmya*. Edited by Lābhsāgargaṇi. Surat: Śrī Jain Pustak Pracārak Saṅsthā.

———. 1979. Śrī Updhānnī Mahattā. *Āgam Jyot* 14, 15–36. Originally in *Siddhcakra* 4 (1934).

Ānandsūri, Ācārya Vijay (Ātmārāmjī). 1936. *Jaintattvādarś*. 2 volumes. Edited by Banārsīdās Jain. Ambala: Śrī Ātmānand Jain Mahasabhā Panjāb. First published in 1884.

Anūpcandra, Ṛṣi. 1972. *Jain Śāradā-Lakṣmī Pūjan Vidhi*. Bambora: Pt. Kāśīnāth Jain.

Baakza, A. H. A. 1962. *Half-hours with a Jain Muni*. Bombay: Jaico.

Babb, Lawrence A. 1975. *The Divine Hierarchy: Popular Hinduism in Central India*. New York: Columbia University Press.

———. 1981. Glancing: Visual Interaction in Hinduism. *Journal of Anthropological Research* 37, 387–401.

———. 1986. *Redemptive Encounters: Three Modern Styles in the Hindu Tradition*. Berkeley and Los Angeles: University of California Press.

———. 1988. Giving and Giving Up: The Eightfold Worship among the Śvetāmbar Mūrtipūjak Jains. *Journal of Anthropological Research* 44, 67–86.

———. 1993. Monks and Miracles: Religious Symbols and Images of Origin among Osvāl Jains. *Journal of Asian Studies* 52, 3–21.

———. 1996. *Absent Lord: Ascetics and Kings in a Jain Ritual Culture*. Berkeley and Los Angeles: University of California Press.

Balbir, Nalini. 1990. Recent Developments in a Jaina Tīrtha: Hastinapur (U.P.)—A Preliminary Report. In Hans Bakker, ed., *The History of Sacred Places in India as Reflected in Traditional Literature: Papers on Pilgrimage in South Asia*, 177–91. Leiden: E. J. Brill.

———. 1993. *Āvaśyaka-Studien: Introduction générale et Traductions*. Stuttgart: Franz Steiner Verlag. Alt- und Neu-Indische Studien 45.1.

Bālyogī. n.d. *Bālyogī Ādhyātmik Munirāj Ācārya Subāhusāgar Mahārāj Muni Saṅgh ke Cāturmās ke Uplakṣ mẽ Śrī Di. Jain Śāntināth Mandirjī, Śāntivīr Nagar, Śrī Mahāvārjī (Rāj.) par unke Caraṇõ mẽ Samarpit*. New Delhi (c. 1990).

Banks, Marcus. 1986. Defining Division: An Historical Overview of Jain Social Organization. *Modern Asian Studies* 20, 447–60.

———. 1991. Competing to Give, Competing to Get: Gujarati Jains in Britain. In Pnina Werbner and Muhammad Anwar, eds., *Black and Ethnic Leaderships in Britain: The Cultural Dimensions of Political Action*, 226–50. London: Routledge.

———. 1992. *Organizing Jainism in India and England*. Oxford: Clarendon Press.

Barth, A. 1882. *The Religions of India*. Translated by J. Wood. Boston: Houghton, Mifflin. French original Paris, 1879.

Barz, Richard. 1976. *The Bhakti Sect of Vallabhācārya*. Faridabad: Thompson Press.

Bechert, Heinz. 1983. A Remark on the Problem of the Date of Mahāvīra. *Indologica Taurinensia* 11, 287–90.

———, ed. 1991. *The Dating of the Historical Buddha*. Gottingen: Vandenhoeck & Ruprecht. Abhandlungen der Akademie der Wissenschaften in Gottingen, Philologisch-Historische Klasse; Folge 3, Nr. 189.

Bechert, Heinz, and Richard Gombrich, eds. 1984. *The World of Buddhism: Buddhist Monks and Nuns in Society and Culture*. London: Thames and Hudson.

Berger, Peter L. 1969. *The Sacred Canopy: Elements of a Sociological Theory of Religion*. New York: Doubleday.

Berger, Peter L., and Thomas Luckmann. 1967. *The Social Construction of Reality: A Treatise in the Sociology of Knowledge*. New York: Doubleday.

Bhadrabāhuvijay, Muni. 1994. *Jindarśan*. 4th printing. Mehsana: Śrī Viśvakalyāṇ Prakāśan Ṭrasṭ.

Bhadraguptvijaygaṇi, Paṅnyās. 1981. *Jay Śaṅkheśvar*. Mehsana: Śrī Viśvakalyāṇ Prakāśan Ṭrasṭ.

———. 1983. *Prārthnā*. Mehsana: Śrī Viśvakalyāṇ Prakāśan Ṭrasṭ.

Bhadraṅkarvijaygaṇi, Paṅnyās. n.d. *Pratimā Pūjan*. Bombay: Smṛti Granth Samiti. First published in 1941.

———. 1977. *Jain Mārgnī Pichān*. Anjar: Śrī Mahāvīr Tattvajñān Pracārak Maṇḍaḷ. First published in 1945.

———. 1978. *Dharmśraddhā*. Ahmedabad: Gurjar Granthratna Kāryālay. First published in 1942.

———. 1980. *Tattvadohan*. Ahmedabad: Vimal Prakāśan.

———. 1986. *Paramātmā-Darśan*. Edited with Hindi translation by Muni Ratnasenvijay. Madras: Svādhyāy Saṅgh. Gujarati original, *Dev Darśan*, published in 1941.

Bhaṇḍārī, Prem, ed. 1991. *Jain Tīrth Śrī Nākoṛā*. Jodhpur: Jñān Prakāśan.

Bhatt, Bansidhar. 1978. *The Canonical Nikṣepa: Studies in Jaina Dialectics*. Leiden: E. J. Brill.

Bhuvanbhānusūri, Ācārya Vijay. 1991. *Ārādhnā: Caityavandan Sūtra Prakāś*. Edited by Muni Bhuvansundarvijay. Dholka: Divyadarśan.

Bhuvanvijay, Muni. 1981a. *Parvakathādi Vividh Viṣay Saṅgrah*. Bhinmal: Śrī Rājendra Bhavan Jain Upāśray Samiti.

———. 1981b. *Tapaḥ Parimal*. Bhinmal: Śrī Rājendra Bhavan Jain Upāśray Samiti.

Bloomfield, Maurice. 1923. The Śālibhadra Carita: A Story of Conversion to Jaina Monkhood. *Journal of the American Oriental Society* 43, 257–313.

Brown, W. Norman. 1934. *A Descriptive and Illustrated Catalogue of Miniature Paintings of the Jaina Kalpasūtra as Executed in the Early Western Indian Style*. Washington, D.C.: Smithsonian Institution, Freer Gallery of Art.

———. 1940. The Basis for the Hindu Act of Truth. *Review of Religion* 5:1, 36–45.

———. 1963. Ṛg Veda 10.34 as an Act of Truth. In J. H. Dave, et al., eds., *Munshi Indological Felicitation Volume*, 8–10. Bombay: Bharatiya Vidya Bhavan. *Bharatiya Vidya* 20–21.

———. 1968. The Metaphysics of the Truth Act (**Satyakriya*). *Mélanges d'indianisme à la mémoire de Louis Renou*, 171–77. Paris: Boccard.

———. 1970. *Man in the Universe: Some Continuities in Indian Thought*. Berkeley and Los Angeles: University of California Press.

———. 1972. Duty as Truth in the Rig Veda. In J. Ensink and P. Gaeffke, eds., *India Maior*, 57–67. Leiden: E. J. Brill.

Buddhisāgarsūri, Ācārya. 1917. *Jain Dhātupratimā Lekh Saṅgrah*, Vol. 1. Bombay: Śrī Adhyātma Jñānprasarak Maṇḍaḷ, 1917.

———. 1953. *Maṅgaḷ Pūjā*. Sanand: Sāṇand Sāgar Gacch Committee.

———. 1978. *Jainsūtramā̃ Mūrtipūjā*. Bombay: Adhyātmak Jñān Prasārak Maṇḍaḷ. First published in 1906 and 1925.

———. 1983–1984. *Ghaṇṭākarṇ Mahāvīr Dev*. Mahudi: Śrī Mahuḍī Jain Śvetāmbar Karkhānā Ṭrasṭ. First published in 1924.

Bühler, Alfred, and Eberhard Fischer. 1979. *The Patola of Gujarat*. 2 vols. Basle: Krebs AG.

Bühler, G. 1892. New Jaina Inscriptions from Mathura. *Epigraphica Indica* 1, 371–93.

———. 1894. Further Jaina Inscriptions from Mathura. *Epigraphica Indica* 2, 195–212.

———. 1936. *The Life of Hemacandrācārya*. Translated by Manilal Patel. Santiniketan: Siṅghī Jaina Jñānapṭṭha. German original 1889.

Burgess, James. 1869. *The Temples of Śatruñjaya*. Bombay: Sykes & Dwyer.

———. 1884a. Papers on Śatruñjaya and the Jainas, VI. The Jaina Ritual. *Indian Antiquary* 13, 191–96.

———. 1884b. Papers on Śatruñjaya and the Jainas, VII. Gachchhas, Śrīpūjyas, Yatis, Nuns, &c. *Indian Antiquary* 13, 276–80.

Burghart, Richard. 1983. Renunciation in the Religious Traditions of South Asia. *Man* (NS) 18, 635–53.

Burlingame, Eugene Watson. 1917. The Act of Truth (Saccakiriya): A Hindu Spell and Its Employment as a Psychic Motif in Hindu Fiction. *Journal of the Royal Asiatic Society*, 429–67.

Buswell, Robert E., and Robert M. Gimello, eds. 1992. *Paths to Liberation: The Mārga and Its Transformations in Buddhist Thought*. Honolulu: University of Hawaii Press.

Caillat, Colette, and Ravi Kumar. 1981. *The Jain Cosmology*. New York: Harmony Books.

Candraśekharvijay, Paṅnyās. 1995. *Cālo Caityavandan Karīe*. Bombay: Śrī Vardhmān Saṃskṛtidhām.

Caraṇvijaygaṇi, Paṅnyās. 1950. *Śrī Jinpūjā Praśnottarī*. Reprint Bombay: Hīrsūri Jagadguru Śve. Mū. Pū. Jain Saṅgh Ṭrasṭ, 1984.

Carman, John B. 1974. *The Theology of Ramanuja*. New Haven: Yale University Press.

———. 1985. Conclusion: Axes of Sacred Value in Hindu Society. In Carman and Marglin 1985, 109–20.

Carman, John B., and Frédérique A. Marglin, eds. 1985. *Purity and Auspiciousness in Indian Society*. Leiden: E. J. Brill.

Carrithers, Michael. 1989. Naked Ascetics in Southern Digambar Jainism. *Man* (NS) 24, 219–35.

Conference. 1907. *Jain Śvetāmbar Mandirāvali*. Bombay: Śrī Jain Śvetāmbar Conference.

———. 1908. *Pañcamī Jain Śvetāmbar Conference Report*. Ahmedabad: Svāgat Committee.

———. 1909. *Jain Śvetāmbar Directory*, Vol. 1. Bombay: Śrī Jain Śvetāmbar Conference.

Cort, John E. 1986. Recent Descriptive Accounts of the Contemporary Jainas. *Man in India* 66, 180–87.

———. 1987. Medieval Jaina Goddess Traditions. *Numen* 34, 235–55.

———. 1988. Pilgrimage to Shankheshvar Pārshvanāth. *Center for the Study of World Religions Bulletin* 14:1, 63–72.

———. 1989. Liberation and Wellbeing: A Study of the Śvetāmbar Mūrtipūjak Jains of North Gujarat. Ph.D. dissertation, Harvard University.

———. 1990a. Models of and for the Study of the Jains. *Method & Theory in the Study of Religion* 2.1, 42–71.

———. 1990b. Twelve Chapters from *The Guidebook to Various Pilgrimage Places (Vividha Tīrtha Kalpa)* of Jinaprabhasūri. In Phyllis Granoff, ed., *The Clever Adultress and Other Stories: A Treasury of Jain Literature*, 245–90. Oakville, Ont.: Mosaic Press.

———. 1991a. Mūrtipūjā in Śvetāmbar Jain Temples. In T. N. Madan, ed., *Religion in India*, 212–23. Delhi: Oxford University Press.

———. 1991b. The Śvetāmbar Mūrtipūjak Jain Mendicant. *Man* (NS) 26, 549–69.

———. 1991c. Two Models of the Śvetāmbar Mūrtipūjak Jain Layman. *Journal of Indian Philosophy* 19, 391–420.

———. 1992. Śvetāmbar Mūrtipūjak Jain Scripture in a Performative Context. In Jeffrey R. Timm, ed., *Texts in Context: Traditional Hermeneutics in South Asia*, 171–94. Albany: State University of New York Press.

———. 1993. An Overview of the Jaina Purāṇas. In Wendy Doniger, ed., *Purāṇa Perennis: Reciprocity and Transformation in Hindu and Jaina Texts*, 185–206. Albany: State University of New York Press.

———. 1994a. Connoisseurs and Devotees: Lockwood de Forest and the Metropolitan Museum's Jain Temple Ceiling. *Orientations* 25.3, 68–74.

———. 1994b. Following the Jina, Worshiping the Jina: An Essay on Jain Rituals. In Pratapaditya Pal, ed., *The Peaceful Conquerors: Jain Art from India*, 39–56. Los Angeles: Los Angeles County Museum of Art.

———. 1995a. Absences and Presences: Ganesh in the Shvetambar Jain Tradition. In Pratapaditya Pal, ed., *Ganesh the Benevolent*, 81–94. Bombay: Marg Publications, 1995.

———. 1995b. *Defining Jainism: Reform in the Jain Tradition*. Toronto: University of Toronto, Centre for South Asian Studies.

———. 1995c. Genres of Jain History. *Journal of Indian Philosophy* 23, 469–506.

———. 1995d. The Jain Knowledge Warehouses: Libraries in Traditional India. *Journal of the American Oriental Society* 115, 77–87.

———. 1995e. Jain Questions and Answers: Who Is God and How Is He Worshiped? In Donald S. Lopez, Jr., ed., *Religions of India in Practice*, 598–608. Princeton: Princeton University Press.

———. 1995f. The Rite of Veneration of the Jina Images. In Donald S. Lopez, Jr., ed., *Religions of India in Practice*, 326–32. Princeton: Princeton University Press.

———. 1996a. Art, Religion, and Material Culture: Some Reflections on Method. *Journal of the American Academy of Religion* 64, 613–32.

———. 1996b. King or Ascetic? Ornamentation of Jain Temple Images. Paper presented at American Council for Southern Asian Art, Symposium 7, Minneapolis, May 12.

———. 1997a. Recent Fieldwork Studies of the Contemporary Jains. *Religious Studies Review* 23, 103–11.

———. 1997b. Tantra in Jainism: The Cult of Ghaṇṭākarṇ Mahāvīr, the Great Hero Bell-Ears. *Bulletin d'Études Indiennes* 15, 115–33.

———. 1998a. (Ed.) *Open Boundaries: Jain Communities and Cultures in Indian History*. Albany: State University of New York Press.

——— 1998b. Introduction: Contested Jain Identities of Self and Other. In Cort 1998a, 1–14.

———. 1998c. Who Is a King? Jain Narratives of Kingship in Medieval Western India. In Cort 1998a, 85–110.

———1999a. Fistfights in the Monastery; Calendars, Conflict and Karma among the Jains. In N. K. Wagle and Olle Qvarnström, eds., *Approaches to Jaina Studies: Philosophy, Logic, Ritual and Symbols*, 36–59. Toronto: University of Toronto, Centre for South Asian Studies.

——— 1999b. The Gift of Food to a Wandering Cow: Lay-Mendicant Interactions among the Śvetāmbar Mūrtipūjak Jains. In K. Ishwaran, ed., *Ascetic Culture: Renunciation and Worldly Engagement*, 89–110. Leiden: E. J. Brill.

———. Forthcoming-a. Bhakti in the Early Jain Tradition: Contested Understandings of Devotional Religion in South Asia. Manuscript submitted to *History of Religions*.

———. Forthcoming-b. Devotion of Asceticism among the Śvetāmbar Mūrtipūjak Jains. In Vasudha Narayanan, ed., *Ascetics and Asceticism in India*.

———. Forthcoming-c. Doing for Others: Merit Transfer and Karma Motility in Jainism. In Olle Qvarnström, ed., *Festschrift for Professor Padmanabh S. Jaini*. Lund: Almqvist and Wiskell. Lund Studies of African and Asian Religions.

———. Forthcoming-d. How Jains Know What They Know: A Lay Jain Curriculum. *Nirgrantha: Festschrift for Muni Jambūvijayjī*.

———. Forthcoming-e. Worship of Bell-Ears the Great Hero, a Jain Tantric Deity. In David Gordon White, ed., *Tantra in Practice*. Princeton: Princeton University Press.

———. n.d. Jains, Caste, and Hierarchy in North Gujarat. Manuscript.

Dalal, C. D. 1937. *A Descriptive Catalogue of Manuscripts in the Jain Bhandars of Pattan*, Vol. 1. Edited by L. B. Gandhi. Baroda: Oriental Institute. Gaekwad's Oriental Series 76.

Dalal, J. A. 1902. *Census of India, 1901*. Vol. 18, *Baroda*. Bombay: Government of Baroda.

Dānsūri, Ācārya Vijay. 1927. *Vividh Praśnottar*. Surat: Śeṭh Nagīnbhāī Muñchubhāī Jain Sāhityoddhār Fanḍ.

Das, Veena. 1982. *Structure and Cognition*. 2nd edition. Delhi: Oxford University Press.

Dave, Kanaiyālāl Bhāīśaṅkar. 1967. Gujarātnā Jñātipurāṇo tathā Tīrthmāhātmyo. *Svādhyāy* 5, 87–105.

———. 1976. *Pāṭaṇ*. Patan: Pāṭaṇ Nagarpālikā.

Dayā, Dalpatrām. 1849. *Bhut Nibandh*. Translated by Alexander Kinloch Forbes. Bombay: Guzerat Vernacular Society. Reprinted as *Demonology and Popular Superstitions of Gujarat*. Gurgaon: Vintage Books, 1990.

Deleu, Jozef. 1970. *Viyāhapannatti (Bhagavaī)*. Brugge: Rijksuniversiteit te Gent.

Desai, Govindbhai H. 1911. *Census of India, 1911*. Vol. 16, *Baroda*, Part 1, *Report*. Bombay: Government of Baroda.

Desai, Govindbhai H., and A. B. Clarke. 1923. *Gazetteer of the Baroda State*, Vol. 1, *General Information*. Bombay: Times Press.

Deśāī, Mohanlāl Dalīcand. 1989. *Jindevdarśan*. 3rd edition. Edited by Kāntībhāī B. Śāh. Bombay: Śrī Mahāvīr Jain Vidyālay. First published in 1910.

Desāī, Ratilāl Dīpcand. 1983. *Śeṭh Āṇandjī Kalyāṇjīnī Peḍhīno Itihās*, Vol. 1. Ahmedabad: Śeṭh Āṇandjī Kalyāṇjī.

Deśpāṇḍe, Pāṇḍuraṅg Gaṇeś. 1974. *Gujarātī-Aṅgrejī Koś*. Ahmedabad: Yunivarsiṭī Granth Nirmāṇ Borḍ.

Dhaky, M. A. 1965–1966. "Late Gupta" Sculptures from Patan Anhilwad—Reviewed. *Bulletin of the Museum and Picture Gallery* 19, 17–28.

———. 1968. Some Early Jaina Temples in Western India. *Śrī Mahāvīra Jaina Vidyālaya Suvaramahotsava Grantha*, Part 1, 290–347. Bombay: Shri Mahavira Jaina Vidyalaya.

Dharmsāgar, Muni, ed. 1929. *Vidhipakṣ (Añcal) Gacchīya Mhoṭī Paṭṭāvalī*. Gujarati translation by Paṇḍit Hīrālāl Haṅsrāj. Jamnagar: Vidhipakṣ (Añcal) Gacch Sthāpak Āryarakṣitasūri Pustakoddhar Khātā.

Dharmsūri, Ācārya Vijay. 1959. Tapodharmno Mahimā. *Jain Yug* (NS) 2, 10–12.

Divyakīrtivijay, Muni, and Muni Puṇyakīrtivijay. 1995. *Darśan-Pūjan Vidhi ane Praśnottrī*. Patan: Bhārtī Sosāyṭī Jain Saṅgh.

Dixit, K. K. 1971. *Jaina Ontology*. Ahmedabad: L. D. Institute of Indology. L. D. Series 31.

———. 1978. *Early Jainism*. Ahmedabad: L. D. Institute of Indology. L. D. Series 64.

Doctor, C. C. 1975. *Census of India 1971*. Series 5, *Gujarat, A Portrait of Population*. Delhi: Controller of Publications.

Dośī, Kulcand Haricand. 1981. *Pāṭaṇ Tīrth Darśan*. 2nd printing. Patan: Śrī Hemcandrācārya Jain Sabhā.

Drucker, H. M. 1974. *The Political Uses of Ideology*. London: Macmillan.

Ḍuggaḍ, Hīrālāl. 1979. *Madhya Eśiyā aur Panjāb Mẽ Jain Dharm*. Delhi: Jain Pracīn Sāhitya Prakāśan Mandir.

Dumont, Louis. 1980. *Homo Hierarchicus*. Revised edition. Translated by Mark Sainsbury, Louis Dumont, and Basia Gulati. Chicago: University of Chicago Press.

Dundas, Paul. 1985. Food and Freedom: The Jaina Sectarian Debate on the Nature of the Kevalin. *Religion* 15, 161–98.

———. 1987–1988. The Tenth Wonder: Domestication and Reform in Medieval Śvetāmbara Jainism. *Indologica Taurinensia* 14, 181–94.

———. 1992. *The Jains*. London: Routledge.

———. 1993. The Marginal Monk and the True *Tīrtha*. In Rudy Smet and Kenji Watanabe, eds., *Jain Studies in Honour of Jozef Deleu*, 237–59. Tokyo: Hon-no-Tomosha.

———. 1996. Somnolent Sūtras: Scriptural Commentary in Śvetāmbara Jainism. *Journal of Indian Philosophy* 24, 73–101.

———. 1998. Becoming Gautama: Mantra and History in Śvetāmbara Jainism. In Cort 1998a, 31–52.

———. 1999. Jainism without Monks? The Case of Kaḍuā Śāh. In N. K. Wagle and Olle Qvarnström, eds., *Approaches to Jaina Studies: Philosophy, Logic, Ritual and Symbols* 19–35. Toronto: University of Toronto, Centre for South Asian Studies.

———. forthcoming. Some Jain Versions of the "Act of Truth" Theme. *Nirgrantha: Festschrift for Muni Jambūvijayjī*.

Durkheim, Emile. 1912. *The Elementary Forms of the Religious Life*. Translated by Joseph Ward Swain. Translation reprinted New York: Free Press, 1965.

Eagleton, Terry. 1983. *Literary Theory: An Introduction*. Minneapolis: University of Minnesota Press.

———. 1991. *Ideology: An Introduction*. London: Verso.

Eck, Diana L. 1980. *Darśan: Seeing the Divine in India*. Chambersburg, Pa.: Anima Books.

———. 1981. India's *Tīrthas*: "Crossings" in Sacred Geography. *History of Religions* 20, 323–44.

Eliade, Mircea. 1959. *The Sacred and the Profane*. Translated by Willard R. Trask. San Diego: Harcourt, Brace & World.

Emerson, Ralph Waldo. 1929. Self-Reliance. In *Essays, First and Second Series*, Vol. 1, 43–90. Boston: Houghton Mifflin. Originally published in 1841.

Enthoven, R. E. 1975. *The Tribes and Castes of Bombay*. 4 volumes. Delhi: Cosmo. Originally published in 1920–1922.

Falk, Nancy Auer, and Rita M. Gross, eds. 1989. *Unspoken Worlds: Women's Religious Lives*. Revised edition. Belmont, Ca.: Wadsworth.

Filliozat, Jean. 1991. Puṇya and Its Semantic Field. In Filliozat, *Religion, Philosophy, Yoga*, 233–51. Translated by Maurice Shukla. Delhi: Motilal Banarsidass. French original 1980.

Fischer, Eberhard, and Jyotindra Jain. 1977. *Art and Rituals: 2500 Years of Jainism in India*. Translated from German by Jutta Jain-Neubauer. New Delhi: Sterling.

———. 1978. *Jaina Iconography*. 2 volumes. Leiden: E. J. Brill.

Flügel, Peter. 1994. Askese und Devotion: Das rituelle System der Terapanth Svetambara Jains. Ph.D. dissertation, Johannes Gutenberg-Universität, Mainz.

———. 1995–1996. The Ritual Circle of the Terāpanth Śvetāmbara Jains. *Bulletin d'Études Indiennes* 13, 117–76.

———. n.d. Protestantische und Post-Protestantische Jain Reformbewegungen: Zur Geschichte und Organisation der Sthānakvāsī Jains. Manuscript.

Folkert, Kendall W. 1993. *Scripture and Tradition: Collected Essays on the Jains*. Edited by John E. Cort. Atlanta: Scholars Press.

Foucault, Michel. 1980. "Truth and Power." In Foucault, *Power/Knowledge*, 109–33. Edited by Colin Gordon, translated by Colin Gordon, Leo Marshall, John Mapham, and Kate Soper. New York: Pantheon Books.

Fuller, C. J. 1992. *The Camphor Flame: Popular Hinduism and Society in India*. Princeton: Princeton University Press.

Gāndhī, Lālcandra Bhagvān. 1952. Prastāvanā. In Muni Cāturvijay and Paṇḍit Lālcandra Bhagvān Gāndhī, eds., *Dvādaśāranayacakra of Śrīmallavādisūri*, 9–40. Baroda: Oriental Institute. Gaekwad's Oriental Series 116.

Geertz, Clifford. 1973. *The Interpretation of Culture*. New York: Basic Books.

Gellner, Ernest. 1979. Notes Towards a Theory of Ideology. In Gellner, *Spectacles and Predicaments: Essays in Social Theory*, 117–32. Cambridge: Cambridge University Press.

Ghīvālā, Sundarlāl Jīvrām, ed. 1987. *Śrī Mahālakṣmī Mātājī Punaḥ Prāṇ Pratiṣṭhā Mahotsav Smṛti Aṅk ane Devonī Bhūmi-Pāṭaṇ*. Patan: Śrī Mahālakṣmī Mātājīnū Mandir.

Gillion, Kenneth L. 1968. *Ahmedabad*. Berkeley and Los Angeles: University of California Press.

Glasenapp, Helmuth von. 1942. *The Doctrine of Karman in Jain Philosophy*. Translated by G. Barry Gifford. Bombay: Bai Vijibai Jivanlal Panalal Charity Fund.

Goetz, H. 1949–1950. "Late Gupta" Sculptures from Pātan-Aṇhilwāda: Archaeological Evidence of Vanarāja and the Chapotkata Dynasty. *Bulletin of the Baroda Museum and Picture Gallery* 7, 25–37.

Goonasekera, Ratna Sunilsantha Abhayawardana. 1986. Renunciation and Monasticism among the Jainas of India. Ph.D. dissertation, University of California, San Diego.

Gowda, M. S. L. 1944. *Economic and Political Life in H.H. the Gaekwad's Dominions*. Baroda: the author.

Granoff, Phyllis. 1990. Of Mortals become Gods: Two Stories from a Medieval Pilgrimage Text. In Granoff, ed., *The Clever Adultress and Other Stories: A Treasury of Jain Tales*, 182–88. Oakville, Ont.: Mosaic Press.

Guṇratnavijay, Muni. n.d. *Vidhi-ratna*. Bombay: Adhyātmik Jñān Śīkṣaṇ Saṅsthā.

Halbertal, Moshe, and Avishai Margalit. 1992. *Idolatry*. Translated by Naomi Goldblum. Cambridge: Harvard University Press.

Hallisey, Charles. 1995. Roads Taken and Not Taken in the Study of Theravāda Buddhism. In Donald S. Lopez, Jr., ed., *Curators of the Buddha: The Study of Buddhism under Colonialism*, 31–61. Chicago: University of Chicago Press.

Haynes, Douglas. 1987. From Tribute to Philanthropy: The Politics of Gift Giving in a Western Indian City. *Journal of Asian Studies* 46, 339–60.

Hemcandravijay, Muni. 1977. *Muktinū Maṅgal Dvār*. Bombay: B. A. Śāh.

Hemratnavijay, Muni. 1983. *Cālo Jinālaye Jaīe*. Ahmedabad: Arhad Dharm Prabhāvak Ṭrasṭ.

Hitajñāśrī, Sādhvī. 1985. *Bārvrat*. Bombay: Vipul Arts.

Hoernle, A. F. Rudolf. 1890. The Pattavali or List of Pontiffs of the Upakesa-Gachchha. *Indian Antiquary* 19, 233–42.

Humphrey, Caroline. 1985. Some Aspects of the Jain *Puja*: The Idea of "God" and the Symbolism of Offerings. *Cambridge Anthropology* 9.3, 1–19.

Humphrey, Caroline, and James Laidlaw. 1994. *The Archetypal Actions of Ritual: A Theory of Ritual Illustrated by the Jain Rite of Worship*. Oxford: Clarendon Press.

Inden, Ronald. 1982. Hierarchies of Kings in Early Medieval India. In T. N. Madan, ed., *Way of Life: King, Householder, Renouncer*, 99–125. New Delhi: Vikas.

Jacobi, Hermann. 1884. *Jaina Sūtras*, Vol. 1. Oxford: Clarendon Press. Sacred Books of the East 22.

———. 1888. Methods and Tables for Verifying Hindu Dates, Tithis, Eclipses, Nakshatras, etc. *Indian Antiquary* 17, 145–81. Reprinted in Bernhard Kölver, ed., Jacobi, *Kleine Schriften*, 911–47. Wiesbaden: Franz Steiner.

———. 1895. *Jaina Sūtras*, Vol. 2. Oxford: Clarendon Press. Sacred Books of the East 45.

Jain, Bābūlāl "Ujjval." 1994. *Samagra Jain Cāturmās Sūcī 1994*. Bombay: A. Bhā. Samagra Jain Cāturmās Sūcī Prakāśan Pariṣad.

Jain, Jyotindra. 1979. Rathayatra: The Chariot Festival of the Jainas. *art and archaeology research papers* 16, 15–18.

———. 1980. Spatial System and Ritual Use of Satrunjaya Hill. *art and archaeology research papers* 17, 47–52.

Jain, Kailash Chand. 1972. *Ancient Cities and Towns of Rajasthan*. Delhi: Motilal Banarsidass.

Jain, V. K. 1990. *Trade and Traders in Western India (AD 1000–1300)*. New Delhi: Munshiram Manoharlal.

Jaini, Padmanabh S. 1976. The Jainas and the Western Scholar. *Sambodhi* 5, 121–31.

———. 1977. Jina Ṛṣabha as an Avatāra of Viṣṇu. *Bulletin of the School of Oriental and African Studies* 40, 321–37.

———. 1979. *The Jaina Path of Purification*. Berkeley and Los Angeles: University of California Press.

———. 1980. Karma and the Problem of Rebirth in Jainism. In Wendy Doniger O'Flaherty, ed., *Karma and Rebirth in Classical Indian Traditions*, 217–38. Berkeley and Los Angeles: University of California Press.

———. 1985a. Jaina Concept of the Sacred. In S. K. Jain and K. C. Sogani, eds., *Perspectives in Jaina Philosophy and Culture*, 102–5. New Delhi: Ahimsa International.

———. 1985b. The Pure and the Auspicious in the Jaina Tradition. In Carman and Marglin 1985; 84–93.

———. 1987. Values in Comparative Perspective: Svadharma versus Ahiṃsā. In N. H. Samtani, ed., *Śramaṇa Vidyā: Studies in Buddhism. Prof. Jagannath Upadhyaya Commemoration Volume*, 111–22. Sarnath: Central Institute of Higher Tibetan Studies.

———. 1991a. *Gender and Salvation: Jaina Debates on the Spiritual Liberation of Women*. Berkeley and Los Angeles: University of California Press.

———. 1991b. Is there a Popular Jainism? In Michael Carrithers and Caroline Humphrey, eds., *The Assembly of Listeners: Jains in Society*, 187–99. Cambridge: Cambridge University Press.

———. 1993. Fear of Food? Jain Attitudes on Eating. In Rudy Smet and Kenji Watanabe, eds., *Jain Studies in Honour of Jozef Deleu*, 339–53. Tokyo: Hon-no-Tomosha.

Jambūsūri, Ācārya Vijay. 1957. *Praśnottar Śatavimśikā*. 2nd printing. Dabhoi: Ārya Jambūsvāmī Jain Muktābāī Jñānmandir.

Jambūvijay, Muni. 1997. *Guruvāṇī*. Edited by Sādhvī Jinendraprabhāśrī. Ahmedabad: Śrī Pārśva Kompyuṭars.

Jayantsensūri, Ācārya Vijay. 1985. Pūjā se Tire Tan, Tire Man. Interview by Nemicandra Jain, in *Tīrthaṅkar* 15.4–5, 103–16.

Jinendrasūri, Ācārya Vijay. 1986. *Shri Devasia Raia Pratikraman Sutro with English Transliteration etc*. Lakhabawal: Shri Harshapushpamrut Jain Granthamala. No. 152 in publisher's series.

Jinendravijaygaṇi, Paṇnyās [Ācārya Vijay Jinendrasūri]. 1980. *Dīpāvalī Parv Vyākhyān*. Lakhabawal: Śrī Harṣapuṣpāmṛt Jain Granthamālā. No. 96 in publisher's series.

———. 1981. *Shri Samayika Chaityavandanadi Sutro with English Transliteration etc*. Lakhabawal: Shri Harshap-shupamruta Jaina Granthamala. No. 97 in publisher's series.

———. 1982. *Taporatna Mahodadhi*. Lakhabawal: Śrī Harṣapuṣpāmṛt Jain Granthmālā. No. 101 in publisher's series.

Jinvijay, Muni. 1921. Kṣetrādeś Paṭṭak. *Jain Sāhitya Saṃśodhak* 1.3, 105–34.

Jñānsundar, Muni. 1927. *Jain Jāti Nirṇay*. Phalodi: Śrī Ratnaprabhākar Jñān-puṣpa-mālā.

Johnson, W. J. 1995. *Harmless Souls: Karmic Bondage and Religious Change in Early Jainism with Special Reference to Umāsvāti and Kundakunda*. Delhi: Motilal Banarsidass.

Jośī, Madanlāl, ed., 1963. *Dādāvāṛā-Digdarśan*. Bombay: Śrī Jindattsūri Sevāsaṅgh.

Kalāpūrṇsūri, Acārya Vijay. 1985. *Mile Man Bhītar Bhagvān*. Hindi translation by Mahopādhyāy Vinaysāgar and Nainmal Vinaycandra Surāṇā. Jaipur: Jain Śve. Tapāgacch Saṅgh.

———. 1987. *Sāmāyik Dharm: Ek Pūrṇ Yog*. Jaipur: Prākṛt Bhārtī Akādamī; and Mevanagar: Śrī Jain Śve. Nākoṛā Pārśvanāth Tīrth. Prākṛt Bhārtī Series 40.

Kalyāṇsāgarsūri, Ācārya. 1985. Ujjvalatar Bane. *Tīrthaṅkar* 15.4–5, 128.

Kalyāṇvijaygaṇi, Paṅnyās, ed. 1928. *Pāṭaṇ Caitya-Paripāṭī*. Ahmedabad: Śrī Haṃsvijay Jain Free Library Granthamāḷā. No. 28 in publisher's series.

———. 1966. Mahānisītha kī Parīkṣā. Kalyāṇvijaygaṇi, *Prabandh-Pārijāt*, 71–142. Jalor: Śrī Kalyāṇvijay Śāstra Samiti.

Kamalratnavijay, Muni. 1986. *Jinpūjā Darśan*. Bombay: Śā Rājmal Tilokcandjī.

Kane, P. V. 1968–1977. *History of Dharmaśāstra*. 5 volumes. Revised edition. Poona: Bhandarkar Oriental Research Institute.

Kapadia, H. R. 1941. *A History of the Canonical Literature of the Jainas*. Surat: the author.

———. 1966. *Yaśodohana*. Bombay: Śrī Yaśobhāratī Jain Prakāśan Samiti.

Kāpaḍiyā, Motīcand Girdharlāl. 1991. *Paṇḍit Śrī Vīrvijayjīnū Janmacaritra*. Ahmedabad: Paṇḍit Śrī Vīrvijayjī Jain Upāśray.

Kelting, M. Whitney. 1996. Hearing the Voices of the Śrāvikā: Ritual and Song in Jain Laywomen's Belief and Practice. Ph.D. dissertation, University of Wisconsin-Madison.

Khare, R. S. 1976a. *Culture and Reality*. Simla: Indian Institute of Advanced Study.

———. 1976b. *The Hindu Hearth and Home*. New Delhi: Vikas.

Khokhar, Campaklal T. 1986. Vītrāg-Prabhunī Dravya-Pūjānī Śāstrīya-Vidhi. One-page leaflet distributed by Śrī Jain Sevā Samāj, Unjha.

Klatt, Johannes. 1882. Extracts from the Historical Records of the Jainas. *Indian Antiquary* 11, 245–56.

———. 1894. The Samachari-Satakam of Samayasundara and Pattavalis of the Anchala-Gachchha and Other Gachchhas. *Indian Antiquary* 23, 169–83.

Koṭhārī, Jayant. 1993. Upādhyāya Yaśovijayjīnū Jīvanvṛtt: Saṃśodhanātmak Abhyās. In Muni Pradyumnavijay, Jayant Koṭhārī, and Kāntibhāī Bī. Śāh, eds., *Upādhyāy Yaśovijay Svādhyāy Granth*, 1–38. Bombay: Śrī Mahāvīr Jain Vidyālay.

Kuśalcandravijay, Muni. 1983. *Nemi-Vijñān-Kastūrsūri Smṛti Śreṇīnī Sacitra Daś Pustikā*. Bombay: Prārthnā Samāj. Hindi original published 1977.

Laidlaw, James. 1985. Profit, Salvation and Profitable Saints. *Cambridge Anthropology* 9.3, 50–70.

———. 1995. *Riches and Renunciation: Religion, Economy, and Society among the Jains*. Oxford: Oxford University Press.

———. 1996. The Uses and Abuses of Theology: Comments on Jonathan Parry's *Death in Banaras*. *South Asia Research* 16, 33–44.

Larrain, Jorge. 1979. *The Concept of Ideology*. Athens: University of Georgia Press.

Lewis, Bernard, ed., 1976. *The World of Islam: Faith, People, Culture*. London: Thames and Hudson.

Lodrick, Deryck O. 1981. *Sacred Cows, Sacred Places*. Berkeley and Los Angeles: University of California Press.

Madan, T. N. 1987. *Non-renunciation*. Delhi: Oxford University Press.

———. 1991. Auspiciousness and Purity: Some Reconsiderations. *Contributions to Indian Sociology* (NS) 25, 287–94.

———. 1997. *Modern Myths, Locked Minds: Secularism and Fundamentalism in India*. Delhi: Oxford University Press.

Mahias, Marie-Claude. 1985. *Délivrance et convivialité: Le système culinaire des Jaina*. Paris: Maison des Sciences de l'Homme.

Majmudar, M. R., ed., 1960. *Historical and Cultural Chronology of Gujarat*. Baroda: Maharaja Sayajirao University of Baroda.

———. 1970. Two Gujarati Documents Bearing on "Amāri" or Non-slaughter of Animals. *Journal of the Oriental Institute* 19, 286–88.

Majumdar, A. K. 1956. *Chaulukyas of Gujarat*. Bombay: Bharatiya Vidya Bhavan.

Malvania, Dalsukh. 1986. Bhaktimarga and Jainism. Translated by A. S. Gopani. In Malvania, *Jainism: Some Essays*, 76–88. Jaipur: Prakrit Bharati Academy.

Maniprabhāśrī, Sādhvī. 1985. Mūrti: Svarūp-Smaraṇ kā Saṭīk Ālamban. Interview by Nemicandra Jain. *Tīrthaṅkar* 15.4–5, 51–60.

Manojitāśrī, Sādhvī. n.d. *Aṣṭa Prakārī Pūjā (Duhāno Bhāvārth)*. Palitana: Somcand D. Śāh.

Marglin, Frédérique Apffel. 1985. *Wives of the God-King: The Rituals of the Devadasis of Puri*. Delhi: Oxford University Press.

Marriott, McKim. 1966. The Feast of Love. In Milton Singer, ed., *Krishna: Myths, Rites, and Attitudes*, 200–12. Chicago: University of Chicago Press.

McGee, Mary. 1987. Fasting and Feasting: The Vrata Tradition and Its Significance. Th.D. dissertation, Harvard Divinity School.

———. 1991. Desired Fruits: Motive and Intention in the Votive Rites of Hindu Women. In Julia Leslie, ed., *Roles and Rituals for Hindu Women*, 71–88. Rutherford, N.J.: Fairleigh Dickenson University Press.

McLellan, David. 1986. *Ideology*. Minneapolis: University of Minnesota Press.

Mehtā, Mohanlāl. 1967. *Jain Sāhitya kā Bṛhad Itihās*, bhāg 3: *Āgamik Vyākhyāē*. Varanasi: Pārśvanāth Vidyāśram Śodh Saṅsthān. Pārśvanāth Vidyāśram Granthmālā 11.

Mehtā, Mohanlāl, and Hīrālāl Ra. Kāpaḍiyā. 1968. *Jain Sāhitya kā Bṛhad Itihās*, bhāg 4: *Karm-Sāhitya va Āgamik Prakaraṇ*. Varanasi: Pārśvanāth Vidyāśram Śodh Sasthān. Pārśvanāth Vidyāśram Granthmālā 12.

Mehta, R. N. 1983. Anhilwad Pāṭan and Merutungāchārya. In A. V. Narasimha Murthi and B. K. Gururaja Rao, eds., *Rangavali: Recent Researches in Indology. Sri S. R. Rao Felicitation Volume*, 195–97. Delhi: Sundeep Prakashan.

———. 1995. Local History and Chaitya Paripati. In R. T. Vyas, ed., *Studies in Jaina Art and Iconography and Allied Subjects*, 83–86. Vadodara: Oriental Institute; and New Delhi: Abhinav.

Meister, Michael W. 1995. Seeing and Knowing: Semiology, Semiotics and the Art of India.

In Juana Gutierrez Haces, ed., *Los Discursos Sobre el Art*, 193–207. Mexico: Universidad Nacional Autonomo de Mexico Instituto de Investigaciones Esteticas.

Miles, William. 1835. On the Jainas of Gujerat and Marwar. *Transactions of the Royal Asiatic Society of Great Britain and Ireland* 3, 335–71.

Misra, S. C. 1982. *The Rise of Muslim Power in Gujarat*. 2nd edition. Delhi: Munshiram Manoharlal.

Mukerjea, Satya V. 1932. *Census of India, 1931*. Vol. 19, *Baroda*. Bombay: Government of Baroda.

Muktiprabhvijay, Muni. n.d. *Śrāvak ko kyā Karnā Cāhiye?* Translated from Gujarati by Ratilāl C. Śāh. Wadhwan: Kalyāṇ Sāhitya Prakāśan.

Naik, T. B. 1974. Social Status in Gujerat. In K. S. Mathur and B. C. Agrawal, eds., *Tribe Caste and Peasantry*, 230–36. Lucknow: Ethnographic and Folk Culture Society. Originally in *Eastern Anthropologist* 10 (1957), 173–81.

Narayanan, Vasudha. 1985. The Two Levels of Auspiciousness in Śrīvaiṣṇava Ritual and Literature. In Carman and Marglin 1985, 55–64.

Navāb, Sārābhāī Maṇilāl, and Muni Candrodayvijay, eds., 1985. *Śrī Ghaṇṭākarṇ-Māṇibhadra-Mantra-Tantra Kalpādi Saṅgrah (Sacitra)*. 4th revised edition. Ahmedabad: Mesars Sārābhāī Maṇilāl Navāb.

Navpad. n.d. *Navpad Oḷīnī Vidhi*. Palitana: Somcand D. Śāh.

Nawab, Sarabhai M. 1956. *Masterpieces of Kalpasutra Paintings*. Ahmedabad: Sarabhai M. Nawab.

———. 1978. *The Life of Lord Shri Mahavira as Represented in the Kalpasutra Paintings*. Ahmedabad: Sarabhai M. Nawab.

Needham, Rodney. 1975. Polythetic Classification: Convergence and Consequences. *Man* (NS) 10, 349–69.

Nevaskar, B. 1971. *Capitalists without Capitalism: The Jains of India and the Quakers of the West*. Westport, Conn.: Greenwood.

Nirvāṇa Sāgara, Muni. 1986. *Pratikramaṇa Sūtra (Hindī-English)*. Koba: Śrī Mahāvīra Jaina Ārādhanā Kendra.

Nityānandvijay, Muni. 1966. *Pravrajyā-Yogādi Vidhi Saṅgrah*. Dabhoi: Āryaśrī Jambūsvāmī Jain Muktābāī Āgam Mandir.

———. 1976. *Dān-Prem Vaṃś Vāṭikā*. Dabhoi: Āryaśrī Jambūsvāmī Jain Muktābāī Āgam Mandir.

———. 1981. *Guru Darśan Sampuṭ*. Dabhoi: Śrī Muktābāī Āgam Mandir.

Nyāyvijay, Muni. 1986. *Jain Darśan*. Patan: Śrī Hemacandrācārya Jain Sabhā. 12th printing.

———. 1998. *Jain Philosophy and Religion*. Translation of Nyāyvijay 1986 by Nagin J. Shah. Delhi: Motilal Banarsidas, Bhogilal Leharchand Institute of Indology, and Mahattara Sadhvi Shri Mrigavatiji Foundation.

Olivelle, Patrick. 1975. A Definition of World Renunciation. *Wiener Zeitschrift für die Kunde Südasiens* 19, 75–83.

———, tr. 1992. *Saṃnyāsa Upaniṣads: Hindu Scriptures on Asceticism and Renunciation*. New York: Oxford University Press.

———. 1993. *The Āśrama System: The History and Hermeneutics of a Religious Institution*. New York: Oxford University Press.

Oṃkārsūri, Ācārya Vijay. 1957. Updhān Tapnī Āvaśyaktā. Introduction to *Updhān Pauṣadh Mārgdarśikā*, 4–8. Vadaval: Jeśiṅglāl Tribhuvandās Śāh.

———. 1984. *Śrāvaknā Chatrīs Kartavyo*. Rohida: Rohiḍā Jain Saṅgh.

Otto, Rudolf. 1917. *The Idea of the Holy*. Translated by John W. Harvey. 2nd edition reprinted London: Oxford University Press, 1958.

Padmasāgarsūri, Ācārya. 1986. *Mokṣ Mārg mẽ Bīs Kadam*. Ahmedabad: Aruṇoday Foundation.

Pal, Pratapaditya, ed., 1994. *The Peaceful Liberators: Jain Art from India*. Los Angeles: Los Angeles County Museum of Art.

Parmar, Bhabhooti Mal N. 1990. *Cultural and Critical Study of Srimal Purana*. Jodhpur: J. S. Gahlot Research Institute.

Parry, Jonathan P. 1980. Ghosts, Greed and Sin: The Occupational Identity of the Benares Funeral Priests. *Man* (NS) 15, 88–111.

———. 1986. *The Gift*, the Indian Gift and the "Indian Gift." *Man* (NS) 21, 453–73.

———. 1991. The Hindu Lexicographer? A Note on Auspiciousness and Purity. *Contributions to Indian Sociology* (NS) 25, 267–85.

———. 1994. *Death in Banaras*. Cambridge: Cambridge University Press.

Pārśva. 1964. *Añcalgacchīya Lekh Saṅgrah*. Bombay: Śrī Anantnāthjī Mahārājnū Jain Daherāsarjī tathā tenu Sādhāraṇ Faṇḍ.

Pāṭaṇ Jain Maṇḍaḷ. 1982. *Pāṭaṇnā Jainonū Tṛtīya Vasati Patrak*. Bombay: Pāṭaṇ Jain Maṇḍaḷ.

Pocock, David F. 1972. *Kanbi and Patidar*. Oxford: Clarendon Press.

———. 1973. *Mind, Body and Wealth*. Oxford: Basil Blackwell.

Premī, Nāthūrām. 1956. *Jain Sāhitya aur Itihās*. 2nd edition. Bombay: Hindī-Granth-Ratnākar.

Raheja, Gloria G. 1988. *The Poison in the Gift: Ritual, Prestation, and the Dominant Caste in a North Indian Village*. Chicago: University of Chicago Press.

Rājendrasūri, Ācārya Vijay. 1913–1934. *Abhidhāna Rājendra*. 7 volumes. Ratlam: Śrī Saud-dharmabṛhattapogacchīya Jain Śvetāmbar Śrī Saṅgh.

Rajyagor, S. B., ed. 1975. *Gujarat State Gazetteers, Mehsana District*. Ahmedabad: Government of Gujarat.

Rāmcandrasūri, Ācārya Vijay. 1974. (Vyākhyānkār) *Paryuṣaṇāṣṭāhnikā Vyākhyan of Ācārya Vijay Lakmīsūri*. Edited by Ācārya Vijay Kanakcandra. Patan: Śrī Maṅgaḷ Prakāśan Mandir.

Rāmsūri [Ḍahelāvāḷā], Ācārya Vijay. 1978. *Śrī Jain Dharm Prakaraṇ Ratnākar*. Ahmedabad: Ācārya Śrī Surendrasūrīśvarjī Jain Tattvajñānśāḷā.

Ratna Prabha Vijaya, Muni. 1950. *Śramaṇa Bhagavān Mahāvīra*. Vol. 5, Part 2, *Sthavirāvali*. Ahmedabad: Śrī Jaina Siddhānta Society.

Ratnasenvijay, Muni. 1983. *Caityavandan Sūtra Vivecnā*. Falna: Śāradā Prakāśan.

———. 1984. *Śrāvak Pratikramaṇ Sūtra (Vandittu Sūtra) Vivecnā*. Falna: Śāradā Prakāśan.

———. 1990. *Aṅkhiyā Prabhu Darśan kī Pyāsī*. Madras: Svādhyāy Saṅgh.

Reynell, Josephine. 1985a. Honour, Nurture and Festivity: Aspects of Female Religiosity amongst Jain Women in Jaipur. Ph.D. dissertation, University of Cambridge.

——. 1985b. Renunciation and Ostentation: A Jain Paradox. *Cambridge Anthropology* 9.3, 20–33.

——. 1987. Prestige, Honour and the Family: Laywomen's Religiosity amongst the Śvetāmbar Mūrtipūjak Jains in Jaipur. *Bulletin d'études indiennes* 5, 313–59.

Ricouer, Paul. 1984. Ideology and Ideology Critique. In Bernhard Waldenfels, Jan M. Broekman, and Ante Pažanin, eds., *Phenomenology and Marxism*, translated by J. Claude Evans, Jr., 134–64. London: Routledge & Kegan Paul.

Rossi-Landi, Ferruccio. 1990. *Marxism and Ideology*. Translated by Roger Griffin. Oxford: Clarendon Press.

Roth, Gustav. 1974. Notes on the *Pamca-Namokkara-Parama-Mangala* in Jaina Literature. *Brahmavidya (Adyar Library Bulletin)* 38, 1–18.

Śā, Mohanlāl Lallubhāī. 1911. *Śrī Pāṭaṇnā Jin Mandironī Mandirāvaḷī*. Patan: Śrī Pāṭaṇ Jain Śvetāmbar Saṅghāḷunī Sarbharā Karnārī Kamīṭī.

Śā, Prāṇlāl Maṅgaljī. 1942. *Abhakṣya-Anantkāy-Vicār*. Hindi translation. Mehsana: Śrī Jain Śreyaskār Maṇḍaḷ.

Sacharoff, Shanta Nimbark. 1972. *Flavors of India: Recipes from the Vegetarian Hindu Cuisine*. San Francisco: 101 Productions.

Sādharmik Bhakti. n.d. Anonymous pamphlet. Ahmedabad: Camanbhāī Popatlāl Śeṭh.

Śāh, Ambālāl Premcand. 1953. *Jain Tīrth Sarva Saṅgrah*, Vol. 1. Ahmedabad: Śeṭh Āṇandjī Kalyāṇjī.

Śāh, Paṇḍit Dhīrajlāl. 1983. *Bhaktāmar-Rahasya*. Bombay: Narendra Prakāśan.

Śāh, Kavin. 1996. Paṇḍit Vīrvijayjī: Jīvan ane Kavipratibhā. In Kāntibhāī Bī. Śāh, ed., *Paṇḍit Vīrvijayjī Svādhyāy Granth*, 35–48. Ahmedabad: Śrī Śrutajñān Prasārak Sabhā.

Śāh, Narottamdās Nagīndās. 1972. *Śrī Ghaṇṭākarṃ Vīr Jaypatākā*. Bombay: Meghrāj Jain Pustak Bhaṇḍār.

Śāh, Ramanlāl C. 1985. *Jinatattva*. Bombay: Śrī Mumbaī Jain Yuvak Saṅgh.

Sandesara, Bhogilal J. [Sāṇḍesarā, Bhogilāl J.]. 1953. *Literary Circle of Mahāmātya Vastupāla*. Bombay: Singhi Jain Shastra Siksapith and Bharatiya Vidya Bhavan. Singhi Jain Series 33.

———. 1974. Kṣetrādeśapaṭṭaka Issued by Ācārya Vijayadharaṇendrasūri of Tapā Gaccha. *Journal of the Oriental Institute* 24, 228–33.

———. 1976a. Aṇahilapāṭak Pattan: Gujarātnī Prasiddh Rājdhānī. In Rasiklāl Choṭālāl Parīkh and Hariprasād Gaṅgāśaṅkar Śāstrī, eds., *Gujarātno Rājkīya ane Sāṃskṛtik Itihās*, Vol. 4; *Solaṅkī Kāl*, 1–14. Ahmedabad: Śeṭh Bhoḷābhāī Jesiṅgbhāī Adhyayan Saṃśodhan Vidyābhavan.

———. 1976b. Inscription of the Jaina Temple of Vāḍī Pārśvanātha at Pāṭaṇ and Genealogy of the Teachers of the Kharatara Gaccha. *Journal of the Oriental Institute* 25, 393–98.

———. 1987a. Letter to the author, 4 July.

———. 1987b. Letter to the author, 22 October.

Sangave, Vilas A. 1980. *Jaina Community*. 2nd revised edition. Bombay: Popular Prakashan.

Sanghavi, Pandit Sukhlal. 1950. *Pacifism and Jainism*. Banaras: Jain Cultural Research Society. Bulletin 25.

———. 1974. *Pt. Sukhlālji's Commentary on Tattvārtha Sūtra of Vācaka Umāsvāti*. Translated by K. K. Dixit. Ahmedabad: L. D. Institute of Indology. L. D. Series 44.

———. 1993. *Concept of Pratikramaṇa*. Translated by Nagin J. Shah and Madhu Sen. Ahmedabad: International Centre for Jaina Studies, Gujarat Vidyapith.

Sankalia, H. D. 1938. The Earliest Jain Sculptures in Kāthiāwār. *Journal of the Royal Asiatic Society of Great Britain and Ireland*, 426–30.

———. 1941. *The Archaeology of Gujarat*. Bombay: Natwarlal.

Śāradā. 1980. *Jain Śāradā Pūjan Vidhi*. Bhavnagar: Śrī Jain Ātmānand Sabhā.

———. 1985. Śubh Dīpāvalī Jain Pūjan Vidhi. *Vijayānand* 29.11, 5–9.

———. n.d. *Jain Śāradā Pūjan Vidhi*. Ahmedabad: Śrī Jain Prakāśan Mandir.

Sastri, Hiranand. 1939. *Annual Report of the Archaeological Department, Baroda State, for the Year Ending 31st July 1938*. Baroda: Baroda State Press.

Śāstrī, Keśavrām Kā. 1976–1981. *Bṛhad Gujarātī Koś*. 2 volumes. Ahmedabad: Yunivarsiṭī Granth Nirmāṇ Borḍ.

Sax, William S. 1991. *Mountain Goddess: Gender and Politics in a Himalayan Pilgrimage*. New York: Oxford University Press.

Scheler, Max. 1926. *Die Wissensformen und die Gesellschaft*. Leipzig: Der Neue-geist Verlag.

———. 1930. *Die Stellung des Menschen im Kosmos*. Darmstadt: Reichl.

Schubring, Walther. 1962. *The Doctrine of the Jainas*. Translated by Wolfgang Beurlen. Delhi: Motilal Banarsidass.

Śeṭh, Paṇḍit Hargovinddās Trikamcand. 1963. *Pāïa-sadda-mahaṇṇavo*. 2nd edition. Edited by Vāsudev Śaraṇ Agravāl and Pt. Dalsukhbhāī Mālvaṇiyā. Varanasi: Prakrit Text Society. Prakrit Text Series 7.

Shah, U. P. 1952. Age of Differentiation of Digambara and Śvetāmbara Images and the Earliest Known Śvetāmbara Bronzes. *Bulletin of the Prince of Wales Museum of Western India* 1, 30–40.

———. 1955a. A Forgotten Chapter in the History of Śvetāmbara Jaina Church *or* A Documentary Epigraph from the Mount Śatruñjaya. *Journal of the Asiatic Society of Bombay* 30, 100–13.

———. 1955b. *Studies in Jaina Art*. Banaras: Jaina Cultural Research Society.

———. 1955–1956a. Bronze Hoard from Vasantagaḍha. *Lalit Kalā* 1–2, 55–65.

———. 1955–1956b. Some Early Sculptures from Abu and Bhinmal. *Bulletin of the Museum and Picture Gallery* 12, 43–56.

———. 1959. *Akota Bronzes*. Bombay: Department of Archaeology, Government of Bombay.

———. 1961. An Old Jaina Image from Kheḍ-Brahmā (North Gujarat). *Journal of the Oriental Institute* 10, 61–3.

———. 1974. Monuments and Sculpture 300 B.C. to A.D. 300, West India. In A. Ghosh, ed., *Jaina Art and Architecture*, Vol. 1, 85–91. New Delhi: Bharatiya Jnanpith.

———. 1982. Minor Jaina Deities. *Journal of the Oriental Institute* 31, 274–90, 371–78.

———. 1987. *Jaina-Rūpa-Maṇḍana*, Vol. I. New Delhi: Abhinav.

Shântâ, N. 1985. *La voie jaina*. Paris: O.E.I.L.

Śīlcandravijay, Muni. 1973. *Śāsan Samrāṭ*. Ahmedabad: Tapāgacchīya Śeṭhśrī Jindās Dharmdās Dhārmik Ṭrasṭ—Kadambagiri Vāṭī.

Singh, Arvind Kumar. 1987. The Fresh Reading and Interpretation of Pañcāsara Pārśvanātha Temple Inscription. In M. A. Dhaky and Sagarmal Jain, eds., *Aspects of Jainology*. Vol. 2, *Pt. Bechardas Doshi Commemoration Volume*, 86–88. Varanasi: P. V. Research Institute.

Singh, Munshi Hardyal. 1895. *Riporṭ Mardumśumārī Rājmārvāṛ vābat San 1891 Īsvī Tīsrāhissā*, Vol. 1. Jodhpur: Vidyāsāl.

———. 1995. *The Castes of Marwar*. Jodhpur: Books Treasure. Originally published in Jodhpur: Marwar Darbar, 1894.

Śivprasād. 1992. Pūrṇimāgacch—Pradhānśākhā aparnām Ḍhaṇḍheriyāśākhā kā Saṅkṣipt Itihās. *Śramaṇ* 43.10–12, 49–66.

Smith, Charles W. 1989. *Auctions: The Cultural Construction of Value*. New York: Free Press.

Smith, Jonathan Z. 1978. *Map Is Not Territory: Studies in the History of Religions*. Leiden: E. J. Brill.

———. 1987. *To Take Place: Toward Theory in Ritual*. Chicago: University of Chicago Press.

Smith, Wilfred Cantwell. 1964. *The Meaning and End of Religion*. New York: Mentor.

Söderblom, Nathan. 1913. Holiness (General and Primitive). *Encyclopædia of Religion and Ethics*, Vol. 6, 731–41.

Sokal, Robert R., and Peter H. A. Sneath. 1963. *Principles of Numerical Taxonomy*. San Francisco: W. H. Freeman.

Sopher, David E. 1968. Pilgrim Circulation in Gujarat. *Geographical Review* 58, 392–425.

Srinivas, M. N. 1952. *Religion and Society among the Coorgs of South India*. Oxford: Clarendon Press.

Srivastava, A. L. 1991. *Nandyāvarta: An Auspicious Symbol in Indian Art*. Allahabad: Kitab Mahal.

Stevenson, Mrs. Sinclair [Margaret]. 1910. *Notes on Modern Jainism*. Oxford: Blackwell.

———. 1912. Festivals and Fasts (Jains). *Encyclopædia of Religion and Ethics*, Vol. 5, 875–79. Edinburgh: T. & T. Clark.

———. 1915. *The Heart of Jainism*. London: Oxford University Press. Reprint New Delhi: Munshiram Manoharlal, 1970.

Suśīlsūri, Ācārya Vijay. 1974. Attyutam Sāt Kṣetro. In *Suśīl Lekh Saṅgrah*, Vol. 1, 259–80. Bombay: Śrīmad Vijaylāvaṇyasūrīśvar Smārak Samiti.

Tambiah, S. J. 1976. *World Conqueror and World Renouncer: A Study of Buddhism and Polity in Thailand against a Historical Background*. Cambridge: Cambridge University Press.

Tarlo, Emma. 1996. *Clothing Matters: Dress and Identity in India*. Chicago: University of Chicago Press.

Tatia, Nathmal, and Muni Mahendra Kumar. 1981. *Aspects of Jaina Monasticism*. New Delhi: Today & Tomorrow's Publishers.

Thoothi, N. A. 1935. *The Vaishnavas of Gujarat*. London: Longmans, Green.

Tod, James. 1839. *Travels in Western India*. London: Wm. H. Allen.

Toffin, Gérard. 1990. Hiérarchie et idéologie du don dans le monde indien. *L'Homme* 30.2, 130–40.

Tracy, David. 1987. *Plurality and Ambiguity: Hermeneutics, Religion, Hope.* San Francisco: Harper & Row.

Tripāṭhī, Rudradev. 1970. *Epolo kī Candrayātrā?* Mehsana: Bhū Bhramaṇ Śodh Saṅsthān.

Tripuṭī Mahārāj (Munis Darśanvijay, Jñānvijay, and Nyāyvijay). 1952. *Jain Paramparāno Itihās*, Vol. 1. Ahmedabad: Śrī Cāritra Smārak Granthmālā.

Trivedi, R. K., ed., 1965. *Census of India 1961*. Vol. 5, *Gujarat*, Part 7–B, *Fairs and Festivals*. Delhi: Manager of Publications.

Turner, Victor, and Edith Turner. 1982. Religious Celebrations. In Victor Turner, ed., *Celebration*, 201–19. Washington, D.C.: Smithsonian Institution Press.

Underhill, M. M. 1921. *The Hindu Religious Year*. Calcutta: Association Press and London: Oxford University Press.

Upadhye, A. N. 1983. Bṛhat-kathākośa. In *Upadhye: Papers*, 1–108. Mysore: University of Mysore.

Vallabhsūri, Ācārya Vijay. 1957. *Navyug Nirmātā*. Edited by Pt. Haṅsrāj Śāstrī. Ambala: Śrī Ātmānand Jain Mahāsabhā Panjāb.

Vallely, Anne. 1999. Women and the Ascetic Ideal in Jainism. Ph.D. dissertation, University of Toronto.

van Buitenen, J. A. B. 1966. On the Archaism of the *Bhāgavata Purāṇa*. In Milton Singer, ed., *Krishna: Myths, Rites, and Attitudes*, 23–40. Chicago: University of Chicago Press.

van der Veer, Peter. 1989. *Gods on Earth: The Management of Religious Experience and Identity in a North Indian Pilgrimage Centre*. Delhi: Oxford University Press. Originally published in London: Athlone Press, 1988.

Varsani, N. R. 1991. *Census of India 1991*. Series 7, *Gujarat*, Supplement to Paper 1 of 1991, *Provisional Population Totals, Rural-Urban Distribution*. New Delhi: Government of India.

Vinaya Sāgar, Mahopādhyāya. 1984. See *Kalpa Sūtra*.

———. 1987. *Gautam Rās: Pariśīlan*. Jaipur: Prākṛt Bhāratī Akādamī.

Virji, Krishnakumari J. 1955. *Ancient History of Saurashtra*. Bombay: Konkan Institute of Arts and Sciences.

Vivekcandravijay, Muni. 1984. *Ārādhnā tathā Tapvidhi*. Palitana: Somcand Ḍī. Śāh.

von Hinüber, Oskar. 1974. Das Nandyāvarta-symbol. In Wolfgang Voigt, ed., *Zeitschrift der Deutschen Morgenländischen Gesellschaft*, Supplement II, 18. Deutscher Orientalistentag, 356–65. Wiesbaden: Franz Steiner.

von Stietencron, Heinrich. 1966. *Indische Sonnenpriester: Sāmba und die Śākadvīpīya-Brāhmaṇa*. Wiesbaden: Otto Harrassowitz. Schriftenreihe des Südasien-Instituts der Universität Heidelberg 3.

Wadley, Susan Snow. 1975. *Shakti: Power in the Conceptual Structure of Karimpur Religion*. Chicago: University of Chicago, Department of Anthropology.

———. 1983. Vrats: Transformers of Destiny. In Val Daniel and Charles Keyes, eds., *Karma: An Anthropoligical Inquiry*, 147–62. Berkeley and Los Angeles: University of California Press.

Wayman, Alex. 1989. The Mathurā Set of Aṣṭamangala (Eight Auspicious Symbols) in Early and Later Times. In Doris Meth Srinivasan, ed., *Mathurā: The Cultural Heritage*, 236–46. New Delhi: Manohar and American Institute of Indian Studies.

Weber, Max. 1922. *Religions-soziologie*. In Weber, *Wirtschaft und Gesellschaft*. Tübingen: J. C. B. Mohr (Paul Siebeck). English translation by Ephraim Fischoff as *The Sociology of Religion*. Boston: Beacon Press, 1963.

———. 1958. *The Religion of India*. Translated Hans H. Gerth and Don Martindale. New York: Free Press. German original 1916.

Williams, R. 1963. *Jaina Yoga*. London: Oxford University Press. Reprint Delhi: Motilal Banarsidass, 1983.

Williams, Raymond B. 1984. *A New Face of Hinduism: The Swaminarayan Religion*. Cambridge: Cambridge University Press.

———. 1985. The Holy Man as the Abode of God in the Swaminarayan Religion. In Joanne Punzo Waghorne and Norman Cutler, eds., *Gods of Flesh, Gods of Stone: The Embodiment of Divinity in India*, 143–57. Chambersburg, Pa.: Anima Books.

Wilson, H. H., tr. 1972. *The Vishnu Purana: A System of Hindu Mythology and Tradition*. 2nd edition. Calcutta: Punthi Pustak. Originally published in London, 1888.

Wittgenstein, Ludwig. 1958. *Philosophical Investigations*. Translated by G. E. M. Anscombe. New York: Macmillan.

Yatīndrasūri, Ācārya Vijay. 1983. *Śrī Jain Pratimā Lekh Saṅgrah*. Edited by Daulatsiṃh Loḍhā "Arvind." Bhilvada: Yatīndra Sāhitya Sadan. Originally published in 1949.

Yocum, Glenn. 1997. "On the Ground" Jainism in South India. *Religious Studies News* 12.3, 5.

Young, Katherine K. 1987. Hinduism. In Arvind Sharma, ed., *Women in World Religions*, 59–103. Albany: State University of New York Press.

Zwicker, Thomas. 1984–1985. Unpublished fieldwork notes, in the archives of the University of Pennsylvania Museum. References are to date of entry and that day's entry number.

Zydenbos, Robert J. 1993. *The Concept of Divinity in Jainism*. Toronto: University of Toronto Centre for South Asian Studies.

———. 1999. The Ritual Giving of Food to a Digambara Renunciant. In N. K. Wagle and Olle S. Qvarnström, eds., *Approaches to Jaina Studies: Philosophy, Logic, Rituals and Symbols*, 291–304. Toronto: University of Toronto Centre for South Asian Studies.

Index